THE PRACTICAL PLAYBOOK®

Public Health and Primary Care Together

THE PRACTICAL PLAYBOOK ®
Public Health and Primary Care Together

Edited by

J. LLOYD MICHENER

DENISE KOO

BRIAN C. CASTRUCCI

JAMES B. SPRAGUE

Oxford University Press is a department of the University of Oxford. It furthers the University's objective of excellence in research, scholarship, and education by publishing worldwide.

Oxford New York

Auckland Cape Town Dar es Salaam Hong Kong Karachi
Kuala Lumpur Madrid Melbourne Mexico City Nairobi
New Delhi Shanghai Taipei Toronto

With offices in

Argentina Austria Brazil Chile Czech Republic France Greece
Guatemala Hungary Italy Japan Poland Portugal Singapore
South Korea Switzerland Thailand Turkey Ukraine Vietnam

Oxford is a registered trademark of Oxford University Press in the UK and certain other countries.

Published in the United States of America by
Oxford University Press
198 Madison Avenue, New York, NY 10016

Library of Congress Cataloging-in-Publication Data
The practical playbook : public health and primary care together / edited by J. Lloyd Michener, Denise Koo,
Brian C. Castrucci, James B. Sprague.
p. ; cm.
Includes bibliographical references.
ISBN 978–0–19–022214–7
I. Michener, J. Lloyd, editor. II. Koo, Denise, editor. III. Castrucci, Brian C., editor. IV. Sprague,
James B. (James Baird), 1942– , editor.
[DNLM: 1. Primary Health Care. 2. Public Health Practice. 3. Cooperative Behavior. 4. Public-Private Sector
Partnerships. WA 100]
RA418
362.1—dc23
2015016480

1 3 5 7 9 8 6 4 2
Printed in the United States of America
on acid-free paper

Contents

SECTION I   Fundamentals of Partnerships Between Public Health and Primary Care

SECTION V   Success Stories

Foreword

The Value of Integration

The notion of a dichotomy between primary care and public health is a false dichotomy. As is the case in most human endeavor, positive change occurs when forces work synergistically to shape the dynamics in play at various points along the vector heading toward a desired state. Progress toward a polio-free world—or a diabetic retinopathy-free world—is made when those working in the community and in the clinic to reduce the burden of disease are both well-equipped and trained for the task. But for progress to reach its full potential, communication constancy and agenda consistency between and among those involved—including the affected individuals—is required for the precision, timing, and results needed.

There is a certain irony in the fact that at a time when public health and personal care have been driven further apart by technologic and economic factors, advances in health information technology and insights into the variation in susceptibility of groups and individuals hold the prospect for real gains in the ability for interventions that are deployed earlier and better targeted. Bridging the gap between the present and the possible is the promise of *The Practical Playbook: Public Health and Primary Care Together.*

Three things are clear. First, that the 2012 report of the Institute of Medicine, *Primary Care and Public Health: Exploring Integration to Improve Population Health,* sponsored by the federal Centers for Disease Control and Prevention (CDC) and Health Resources and Services Administration (HRSA), was not merely a statement of the facts, and it was not merely a description of the possible. It was a mandate. This *Practical Playbook* is therefore not optional.

Imagine that you are building a house, not a big mansion, but a simple, reliable, nurturing place to live your life. What if the plumbers and the electricians and the carpenters arrived at the scene and there was no foundation? Or what if the masons and the framers constructed the foundation and the superstructure, but the plumbers and the electricians and the carpenters were far away at another site and never even showed? The results would be chaotic inefficiency, ineffectiveness, and often damage to the end product.

Yet this is what we have with the parallel, often disconnected enterprises of public health and primary care, and with circumstances in which the foundational level of one is woefully unsupported in this nation. That's why we have in the nation today 30% of our $2.9 trillion national expenditures in health sector that registers virtually no impact on health outcomes. Progress is not optional. It is absolutely essential for the nation as a whole, and it cannot occur without the *Practical Playbook's* practical vision of the way forward.

Second, the time is right. The knowledge is in hand. We know that chronic diseases, our most prevalent health challenges in the nation, cannot be controlled without moving from inside the clinician's door into the community outside. We now know that there are essentially five determinants of the health of a population—medical care, genetic predispositions, social circumstances, physical environments, the behaviors we choose—and we also know that when it comes to the health of populations, or, for that matter, the lifelong prospects of each of us, medical care is among the least impactful of those determinants across the board.

The time is right for change because the technology is rapidly coming online, both literally and figuratively. We have the digital infrastructure developing to integrate what goes on within our clinic doors and our public health community to help shape our strategies.

The time is also right because the policies are aligning. In many ways, the 2,000+ pages of the Patient Protection and Affordable Care Act represent the most important public health piece of legislation in our history, since embedded in those words are the principles and the tools to drive payment for health care, which is driven by population health outcomes. The question is how we best develop the means and the blueprint for linking those two, and that's what this *Practical Playbook* is about.

Third, what is most needed moving forward is the leadership, the partnership, and the tools necessary to forge the links between primary care and public health. Leadership of the sort that has been provided by the de Beaumont Foundation as sponsor of and partner in the development of the *Practical Playbook* is key. The Foundation may not be the largest national foundation, but it is perhaps the only independent sector funder predominantly committed to ensuring that our public health infrastructure is a stable, reliable foundation on which we can build the nation's health, and to doing so by catalyzing and partnering for change nationally. The public–private partnership that included academic leadership (Duke University Department of Community and Family Medicine), federal-level leadership (the CDC), and philanthropic leadership along with the organizations represented on the National Advisory Committee should be a model for fostering effective, systematic change across multiple levels. Those involved in the planning and development of this important contribution have provided an important tool to forge the linkage of primary care and public health. The Institute of Medicine is proud to have been part of shaping that vision, and we look forward to collaborating in its execution.

J. Michael McGinnis, MD, MPP
Institute of Medicine, The National Academies
Washington, DC, USA

About the Editors

J. Lloyd Michener, MD, is Professor and Chair of the Department of Community and Family Medicine at the Duke University School of Medicine. He has spent his entire professional career at the interface between communities and academic centers, focusing on finding ways of making health care work better through teams, community engagement, and practice redesign. He has long been involved with the North Carolina Medicaid collaborative, and is actively engaged with multiple national groups about health care redesign that improves outcomes and controls costs. Dr. Michener now directs a national program for the *"Practical Playbook"* which facilitates the integration of Primary Care and Public Health, supported by the Centers for Disease Control and Prevention, the Health Resources and Services Administration, and the de Beaumont Foundation.

Denise Koo, MD, MPH, is Advisor to the Associate Director for Policy, Centers for Disease Control and Prevention (CDC), and Advisor to the (Acting) Assistant Secretary for Health, Department of Health and Human Services. Since medical school, where she combined a degree in epidemiology with her medical training at the University of California, San Francisco, she has had a passion for bringing together the worlds of public health and medicine. She has spent a majority of her career at the CDC focusing on building these linkages, first in public health surveillance and information systems and then in public health and health care professional workforce development. She currently leads development of CDC's Community Health Improvement Navigator (www.cdc.gov/CHInav). Dr. Koo holds appointments as Adjunct Professor of Global Health and of Epidemiology, Rollins School of Public Health, Emory University, and Consulting Professor, Department of Community and Family Medicine, Duke University Medical Center.

Brian C. Castrucci, MA, is Chief Program and Strategy Officer at the de Beaumont Foundation. Mr. Castrucci seeks to bring academic rigor to public health practice and a focus on actionable outcomes to public health research. He is responsible for identifying and fostering visionary public health projects and has ensured that public health research and practice go hand-in-hand through grants such as the *Practical Playbook*, the BUILD Health Challenge, and the Big Cities Health Coalition. His commitment to improving population health, furthering robust collaboration between public health and primary care, and strengthening public health infrastructure in the United States is informed by a decade of experience working in state and local health departments. Outside of his role at the de Beaumont Foundation, Mr. Castrucci blogs on public health topics at the Huffington Post, where he is committed to advancing an understanding and awareness of public health issues through new media.

James B. Sprague, **MD**, is Chairman of the Board of the de Beaumont Foundation and its founding Chief Executive Officer. Dr. Sprague worked closely with founder Pierre S. de Beaumont to define the Foundation's mission, which was shaped by Dr. Sprague's experiences as a CDC Epidemic Intelligence Officer in 1971. Under his leadership, the Foundation has built a unique portfolio of grants focused on investments in "boots on the ground" public health in the areas of workforce development, data and information, and public health infrastructure. A pediatric ophthalmologist, Dr. Sprague has been actively involved in public health ophthalmology studies, traveling extensively in developing countries with blindness prevention programs. Dr. Sprague was the Chief of Ophthalmology at Denver General Hospital and was an associate professor of ophthalmology at the University of Colorado. After entering private practice, he was a Clinical Associate Professor of Ophthalmology at Georgetown University. Dr. Sprague received his B.A. with honors from Harvard College and his M.D. from the University of Pennsylvania.

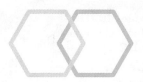

Contributors

Tanisa Foxworth Adimu, MPH
Georgia Health Policy Center, Georgia
State University, Atlanta, GA, USA

Philip Alberti, PhD
Association of American Medical
Colleges, Washington, DC, USA

Christina Arnold, MHA-I, RDN, LDN
Be Well-Lake County Diabetes, Lake
County Health Department and
Community Health Center, Waukegan,
IL, USA

Ivy Baer, JD, MPH
Association of American Medical
Colleges, Washington, DC, USA

Kevin Barnett, DrPH, MCP
Senior Investigator, Public Health
Institute, Oakland, CA, USA

Andrew Bazemore, MD, MPH
Robert Graham Center,
Washington, DC, USA

Seamus Bhatt-Mackin, MD
Duke University School of Medicine,
Durham, NC, USA

Michele Casper, PhD
Centers for Disease Control and
Prevention, Atlanta, GA, USA

Brian C. Castrucci, MA
Chief Program and Strategy Officer,
de Beaumont Foundation,
Bethesda, MD, USA

Joanne M. Conroy, MD
Association of American Medical
Colleges, Washington, DC, USA

Jeffrey Engel, MD
Council of State and Territorial
Epidemiologists, Atlanta, GA, USA

Clese Erikson, MPAff
Association of American Medical
Colleges, Washington, DC, USA

Susan Feinberg
Cambridge Public Health Department,
Cambridge Health Alliance,
Cambridge, MA, USA

Seth Foldy, MD, MPH
Medical College of Wisconsin,
Milwaukee, WI, USA

Scott D. Grosse, PhD
Centers for Disease Control and
Prevention, Atlanta, GA, USA

Sharon Hillidge, MA
Chula Vista Elementary School
District, Chula Vista, CA, USA

Claude-Alix Jacob, MPH
Cambridge Public Health Department,
Cambridge Health Alliance,
Cambridge, MA, USA

Paul E. Jarris, MD, MBA
Association of State and Territorial
Health Officials, Arlington, VA, USA

Frederick S. Johnson, MBA
Duke University School of Medicine,
Durham, NC, USA

Christina Khaokham, RN, MSN/MPH
Centers for Disease Control and
Prevention, Atlanta, GA, USA

Raymond J. King, PhD, MSc
Centers for Disease Control and
Prevention, Atlanta, GA, USA

Coleen Kivlahan, MD, MSPH
Association of American Medical
Colleges

Denise Koo, MD, MPH
Centers for Disease Control and
Prevention, Atlanta, GA, USA

Jonathon P. Leider, PhD
de Beaumont Foundation,
Bethesda, MD, USA

John W. Loonsk, MD, FACMI
The Johns Hopkins University,
Baltimore, MD, USA

Monica Valdes Lupi, JD, MPH
Association of State and Territorial
Health Officials, Washington, DC, USA

Michelle J. Lyn, MBA, MHA
Duke Medicine University School of
Medicine, Durham, NC, USA

Amanda Phillips Martinez, MPH
Georgia Health Policy Center, Georgia
State University, Atlanta, GA, USA

Pamela Maxson, PhD
University of Michigan,
Ann Arbor, MI, USA

J. Lloyd Michener, MD
Duke University School of Medicine,
Durham, NC, USA

Karen J. Minyard, PhD
Georgia Health Policy Center,
Georgia State University,
Atlanta, GA, USA

Marie Lynn Miranda, PhD
University of Michigan,
Ann Arbor, MI, USA

Sharon G. Moffatt, MS
Association of State and Territorial
Health Officials, Arlington, VA, USA

Kathleen Nolan, MPH
National Association of Medicaid
Directors, Washington, DC, USA

Robert M. Pestronk, MPH
National Association of County
and City Health Officials,
Washington, DC, USA

Robert L. Phillips, Jr, MD, MSPH
American Board of Family Medicine,
Lexington, KY, USA

Russell Phillips, MD
Harvard Medical School,
Boston, MA, USA

Karen Remley, MD, MBA, MPH, FAAP
Formerly Virginia Commissioner of
Health; currently American Academy of
Pediatrics, Elk Grove Village, IL, USA

Kate Reuterswärd
PR Collaborative, Washington,
DC, USA

Sara Rosenbaum, JD
George Washington University,
Washington, DC, USA

David A. Ross, ScD
Public Health Informatics Institute,
GA, USA

Eduardo Sanchez, MD, MPH
American Heart Association,
Dallas, TX, USA

Katie Sellers, DrPH, CPH
Association of State and Territorial
Health Officials, Arlington, VA, USA

Shaila Serpas, MD
Scripps Health, San Diego, CA, USA

Mina Silberberg, PhD
Duke University School of Medicine,
Durham, NC, USA

Lara Snyder
Duke University School of Medicine,
Durham, NC, USA

James B. Sprague, MD
de Beaumont Foundation,
Bethesda, MD, USA

Justine Strand de Oliveira, DrPH, PA-C
Duke University School of Nursing
Medicine, Durham, NC, USA

Steven M. Teutsch, MD, MPH
Los Angeles County Department of
Public Health, Los Angeles, CA, USA

Hugh H. Tilson, MD, DrPH
University of North Carolina at Chapel
Hill, NC, USA

Joshua L. Tootoo, MS
University of Michigan,
Ann Arbor, MI, USA

Virginia Watson, MA
Learning and Development Systems
Specialist, Atlanta, GA, USA

Julie K. Wood, MD, FAAP
American Academy of Family
Physicians, Leawood, KS, USA

Fundamentals of Partnerships Between Public Health and Primary Care

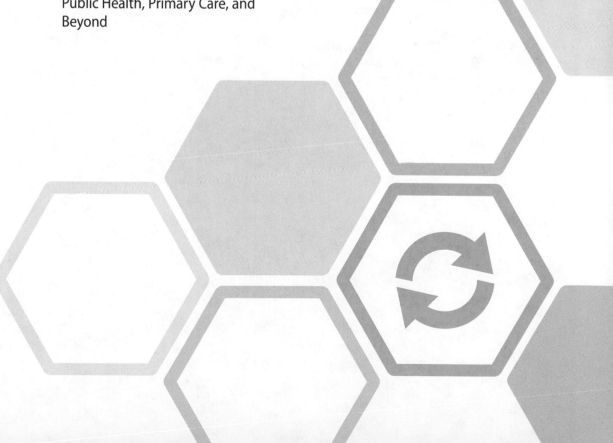

Why a *Practical Playbook* for Partnerships Between Public Health and Primary Care?

DENISE KOO, J. LLOYD MICHENER, JAMES B. SPRAGUE, AND BRIAN C. CASTRUCCI

INTRODUCTION: PURPOSE OF THE BOOK

This book is a response to the critical need and opportunity finally to heal the schism between public health and health care (White, 1991), and thus to improve the health of all who live in the United States. It is a guide—a playbook—to support public health and clinical practice in working together and in using new tools and technologies to improve the health and well-being of our communities, in short, to improve the health of the population. Throughout the *Practical Playbook* we have adopted the definition of population health proposed by Kindig and Stoddart (2003): "The health outcomes of a group of individuals, including the distribution of such outcomes within the group." This definition encompasses populations as geographic regions, ranging from nations to communities, as well as groupings such as patient populations, or by profession, ethnicity, disability, or other descriptive social parameters. Our goal is to support the *transformation* of our health care system from one focused on health care to one focused on health.

The overall concept of population health has long been familiar to the public health world. Additionally, the last decade has seen a continuously growing interest in population health among health care providers and health systems, particularly as the prevalence of chronic conditions such as obesity has increased dramatically. However, health care providers and health systems frequently define population health as health outcomes among those who seek clinical services, or the health of their enrolled patients. Public health agencies define populations and population health largely by jurisdiction and include those who do not seek or have access to care, or who use health care services irregularly. Thus, population health as defined and measured by public health extends outside the clinical office and can include complex social and environmental factors that are far beyond the reach of the biomedical model. We posit that public health and health care, which have traditionally been divided and worked in parallel, can work together along with other partners to reduce the burden of clinical illness and improve the health and well-being of our country.

BACKGROUND

The Current Problem

In recent years, to their surprise, Americans have learned that the United States falls short on many health metrics compared to other high-income countries. We live shorter lives; our infants and mothers die at higher rates; we have a higher prevalence of diabetes, obesity, and other chronic diseases; and we live with greater levels of disability (Davis et al., 2014; National Academy of Sciences, 2013; National Research Council, 2011; U.S. Burden of Disease Collaborators, 2013). Differences in life expectancy and disease incidence are also seen among advantaged Americans when compared to residents of comparable socioeconomic status from other countries. In other words, although we are the richest country in the world, with the most expensive health care system, we are not the healthiest as a nation.

Why might this be? The causes of sickness, disease, and death within the United States have gradually shifted over the last century from predominantly infectious to chronic ones. The contributing factors underlying chronic illnesses are rooted in complex social, behavioral, and environmental factors, making our health and well-being products not only of the health care we receive but also the places where we live, learn, work, and play. Our ZIP code can be more important than our genetic code. Yet, in our communities the public health and health care systems operate largely independently, without the kind of synergy with each other and with others, such as social services, that can address these root causes and improve our population's health. We need a transformation of the U.S. health care system from one focused on care of illness to one focused on health (Asch & Volpp, 2012; Fineberg, 2012; Halfon et al., 2014).

Why the Divide?

The divide between the public health and health care systems is multifactorial and dates to the turn of the 20th century. Until the late 1800s, medical professionals had a broad view of their responsibilities, recognizing the influence of social and environmental conditions on their patients' health. In fact, in the 19th century, the predominant miasma theory even postulated a primary role for the environment in causing illness. However, with Louis Pasteur and others came the rise of the germ theory, the identification of an increasing number of microbial causes of disease, and the subsequent discoveries of antibiotics and vaccinations. The health care system turned to a more biomedical model of disease, along with a more narrow emphasis on the treatment of individuals.

Concurrent major events in the educational systems of medicine and public health also played a role in the schism. In 1910 Abraham Flexner's study of American medical education acknowledged the duty of the physician "to promote social conditions that conduce to physical well-being." However, this message was lost amidst the well-received and widely highlighted emphasis on the need for stronger basic science in medical education (Maeshiro et al., 2010; White, 1991). The parallel development of the Welch-Rose report in 1915 emphasized the need for a similarly rigorous (although previously nonexistent) system of education in public health (Rosenstock et al., 2011; White, 1991). This report led to the establishment of separate schools of public health, with a stronger focus on social and environmental influences and approaches to preventing and controlling disease. Although primary care has always acknowledged the importance of the community (Institute of Medicine [IOM], 1966; National Commission on Community Health Services [NCCHS], 1967), in reality, these distinct academic endeavors led to increasingly siloed disciplines and separate operations. The resulting nonintegrated emphases on individual patient care and biologic determinants of health in medicine and in the health care system, and on populations, prevention, and nonbiologic determinants of health in the public health system have led to sub-optimal outcomes despite the most expensive health care system in the world (Asch & Volpp, 2012; Bradley et al., 2011; National Research Council 2011, White, 1991).

INTEGRATION: WHY NOW?
Critical Need for Change
Clinical care in the United States is famed for its excellence and its practitioners are well rewarded for providing medications and procedures. The U.S. public health system, itself a world leader, garners the most acclaim for its responses to outbreaks of acute disease. Yet, each year in U.S. communities increasing numbers of persons suffer and die from chronic disease. Chronic diseases comprised 7 of the top 10 causes of death in the United States in 2010 and two of these—heart disease and cancer—together accounted for nearly 48% of all deaths (Centers for Disease Control and Prevention [CDC], 2014). Traditional medical and public health approaches, which were originally developed to manage and care for those with acute disease, are inadequate for helping our communities and their members be healthy today.

The shift from acute to chronic illness has also affected health care spending; today, chronic diseases account for 75% of all health care expenditures (Agency for Healthcare Research and Quality [AHRQ], 2010). Many have argued that current disease, treatment, and cost trends are unsustainable

(Ahern et al., 2013; Berwick & Hackbarth, 2012; President's Council of Advisors on Science and Technology [PCAST], 2014). Given the greater impact on health outcomes of nonbiologic determinants compared to biologic determinants (Bunker et al., 1994), our own biomedically oriented health care system needs to expand its scope to encompass a greater emphasis on social, environmental, and behavioral determinants, and to include partners with expertise in these areas. In contrast to our current health care system, our future *health* system would be built upon multiple partnerships and would leverage contributions to health and well-being from public health as well as other sectors beyond health care (e.g., social services, urban planning), for greater population health.

… maintaining the status quo is not an option moving forward.

American Hospital Association, 2015, p. 14

Opportunities to Leverage

The urgent need "for dramatic change in U.S. healthcare" (Smith & Topol, 2013) has created a groundswell of recognition and support for a move to value-based payments and an emphasis on quality and outcomes, rather than the current volume-based, fee-for-service model (Asch & Volpp, 2012; Burwell, 2015; Fineberg, 2012; Halfon et al., 2014; Marvasti & Stafford, 2012; PCAST, 2014; Porter, 2010; Shaw et al., 2014; Sox, 2013). Even before the passage of the Patient Protection and Affordable Care Act (ACA), the Institute for Healthcare Improvement's triple aim of better care, lower cost, and improved population health underscored the critical need to focus on groups of patients (e.g., health plan enrollees, cardiac patients, patients in a given practice), as well as on individual patient care (Berwick et al., 2008). Health reform and the recent focus on value-based care and population health has renewed attention to and recognition of the role of social and other determinants on health and health outcomes (American Hospital Association, 2015; Bachrach et al. 2014; McGinnis et al., 2006; Stakeholder Health, 2013). The Innovation Center of the Centers for Medicare and Medicaid Services is testing several delivery models that link patients with social support and community services as well as State Innovation Models that require population health improvement plans to cover the entire state population (Kassler, 2015). The patient-centered medical home model is one notable effort to support primary care providers in moving to a more comprehensive approach (AHRQ, 2014; Larson & Reid, 2010). For maximum effect on total population health (Jacobson & Teutsch, 2012), public health needs to be a critical partner in these efforts.

With the explosion of ways to access and use information and tools as well as to share data, technology offers an enormous range of opportunities supportive of health system transformation. Patients can identify medical information and resources for themselves and their families and obtain guidance widely available online via various electronic devices. Providers use technology to improve care for patients by accessing just-in-time medical information or by using alerts and data from electronic medical records to remind them or their patients of treatment needs. With federal incentives and support, increasing numbers of health care providers are using electronic health records, which can facilitate identification of treatment options and embedding of other functions—such as clinical decision support—and can promote data sharing with public health. Clinicians can work with partners, including public health, to refer patients to community-based sources of healthy foods, transportation, or job support. Public health, with its traditional focus on denominators, can aggregate data and map patterns of disease using geographic information systems and can feed the information back to the health care system to inform care and improve population health. The two disciplines complement one another.

FOUNDATIONS OF A SOLUTION

Public Health and Primary Care

Public health: "fulfilling society's interest in assuring conditions in which people can be healthy."

Institute of Medicine [IOM], 1988, p. 140

Primary care: "the provision of integrated, accessible health care services by clinicians who are accountable for addressing a large majority of personal health care needs, developing a sustained partnership with patients, and practicing in the context of family and community."

IOM, 1996, p. 1

Public health and primary care are natural, foundational partners for addressing the challenges in today's health care system. Within the health care system, primary care providers have some of the broadest responsibility for addressing the various needs of the whole person/patient. Like public health professionals, they recognize the need to understand the social determinants impacting a patient's illness. Primary care providers are frequently frustrated by their inability to address these issues, whether due to lack of training or time (Robert Wood Johnson Foundation, 2011). Therefore, primary care providers are likely partners for public health, with public health's complementary experience and focus on the population and on addressing the determinants of health.

As the roles of each evolve in the context of health reform, primary care and public health have a strong opportunity and need to work together and with other partners. Primary care providers have both an interest and a need to address determinants of health, as they will increasingly be held accountable for population health improvement in a value-based health care system. In turn, public health is reassessing its core role and recognizing the critical need to partner more with the health care system (Auerbach, 2013; Teutsch

& Fielding, 2013). There are tremendous opportunities to improve the public's health through partnership between the public health and health care sectors. Working together, public health and primary care have the opportunity to lower the number of people who need care and the cost of that care, improve the quality of clinical care and other services that they receive, and improve the overall health of communities (IOM, 2012).

ONLINE *PRACTICAL PLAYBOOK* AND A BOOK?

'plā,book/
1. A notebook containing descriptions and diagrams of the plays that a team has practiced
2. A scheme or set of strategies for conducting a business or political campaign

Rationale

Readers familiar with the online *The Practical Playbook: Public Health and Primary Care Together* (https://practicalplaybook.org) will recognize that we use the playbook metaphor because improving collaboration between public health and primary care takes a thoughtful game plan. Like a sports playbook, the *Practical Playbook* defines the role of each team member as well as actions for different situations. As a playbook, it is neither a rulebook nor a set of peer-reviewed guidelines. It is something more practical—because we need real-life, flexible guidance to help apply the theoretical principles of integration to our work. Thus, the key target audiences for the playbook are public health practitioners and primary care providers as well as primary care networks. We have also learned that there is strong interest among educators of public health and health care professionals, health systems staff involved in transformation, and policymakers, as well as many others.

We chose to develop a written book as a complement to the online *Practical Playbook* for several reasons. First, the book provides hardcopy for those who wish to have the core *Practical Playbook* material in a single bound document. The hardcopy also facilitates navigation of the online version, for those users for whom seeing the whole framework increases the usefulness of the components. Second, expanding the online content into a printed book offered us an opportunity to engage additional authors with timely and relevant experience from public health and primary care. In addition, through the process of developing the book we revisited the online *Practical Playbook* content, revised original online material with updated content, and added new sections. Third, we hope that this book is used not just as a textbook but also as a "handbook," and that the power of the hardcopy, combined with references and links to continuously updated online resources, will enhance the utility of materials in either location.

Overview of the Book

The book is divided into five main sections: a foundational section, three guidance sections, and a section with concrete examples of specific initiatives in which primary care and public health were successfully integrated. This chapter and the next three chapters lay the foundation. This overview chapter provides the background information: brief historical perspective, why health systems transformation and the role of integration, why now, why this book, and how to use it. An appendix to this chapter lists the icons and symbols used throughout the book to underscore certain themes. The second chapter (value of integration) presents persuasive arguments for why public health and primary care should work together and provides examples of the impact on the public's health, with a roadmap to supporting guidance chapters that provide more details regarding how to do this kind of work. The third chapter (principles of integration) describes the principles of public health/primary care integration identified by the IOM, what they are and why they are important for effective partnership. The fourth chapter (stages of integration) includes checklists and concrete ideas for how to work through the stages of integration.

Guidance Sections II, III, and IV focus, respectively, on Working Together, Health and Health Care, and Working with Data. Working Together (Section II) contains chapters and essays on various steps and pitfalls encountered in bringing together public health and primary care. The chapters of Section III, Health and Health Care, outline the current context of the public health and health care systems in more detail, highlighting some specific opportunities for collaboration. Given the critical role of data—in identifying health problems, in aligning efforts and evaluating progress, and identifying success—Section IV, Working with Data, focuses on data and metrics, with special sections on using data in this digital era. All chapters include practical tips for navigating these domains. Essays are also distributed throughout these sections to provide additional reflections from differing perspectives.

The last section of the book (Section V) includes valuable supplemental materials. The three success stories of public health/primary care integration supply more detail than the short inspirational vignettes currently on the *Practical Playbook* website, with more information on how the partners got things done, and the stories behind the successes. The last section also contains a helpful list of acronyms and a glossary to help with communication between and among public health and primary care collaborators (cross-cultural communication).

Conclusion

We intend that the *Practical Playbook* serve as a stepping stone in the *transformation* of our health care system to one in which primary care and public health collaborate with other partners to improve population health and reduce health care costs. New generations of public health and clinical leaders are already finding ways to work together, for the health of their communities. The *Practical Playbook* provides helpful resources, such as lessons learned from some of these existing partnerships, further guidance from experienced public health and primary care leaders, and success stories from across the country. In addition, this unique book has a live site through which users/readers can provide feedback that will help us continue to evolve the *Practical Playbook* and adapt it to meet user needs. We hope the *Practical Playbook*, with its practical guidance and tips, will help others take the steps to meet and begin to work together to improve their community's health and well-being.

REFERENCES

Agency for Healthcare Research and Quality. Total Expenses and Percent Distribution for Selected Conditions by Type of Service: United States, 2010. Medical Expenditure Panel Survey Household Component Data. Rockville, MD: Agency for Healthcare Research and Quality. http://meps.ahrq.gov. Accessed October 21, 2014.

Agency for Healthcare Research and Quality. Patient Centered Medical Home Resource Center. http://pcmh.ahrq.gov/. Accessed Dec 2, 2014.

Ahern DK, Smith JM, Topol EJ, Mack JF, Fitzgerald M, eds. Addressing the cost crisis in health care: Stakeholder roles and responsibilities. Am J Prev Med 2013; 44: 1S1.

Asch DA, Volpp KG. What business are we in? The emergence of health as the business of healthcare. N Engl J Med 2012; 367: 888–889. doi:10.1056/NEJMp1206862

American Hospital Association. Leadership Toolkit for Redefining the H: Engaging Trustees and Communities. 2015. http://www.aha.org/research/cor/redefiningH/index.shtml Accessed Jan 30, 2015.

Auerbach J. Lessons from the front line: The Massachusetts experience of the role of public health in health care reform. J Public Health Manag Pract 2013; 19(5): 488–491. doi:10.1097/PHH.0b013e318299f5ef

Bachrach D, Pfister H, Wallis K, Lipson M. Addressing patients' social needs: An emerging business case for provider investment. Commonwealth Fund, May 2014. http://www.commonwealthfund.org/publications/fund-reports/2014/may/addressing-patients-social-needs Accessed Jan 24, 2015.

Berwick DM, Nolan TW, Whittington J. The triple aim: Care, health, and cost. Health Aff 2008; 27(3): 759–769. doi:10.1377/hlthaff.27.3.759

Berwick DM, Hackbarth AD. Eliminating waste in US health care. JAMA 2012; 307(14): 1513–1516. doi:10.1001/jama.2012.362.

Bradley EH, Elkins BR, Herrin J, Elbel B. Health and social services expenditures: Associations with health outcomes. BMJ Qual Saf 2011; 20(10): 826–831. doi:10.1136/bmjqs.2010.048363

Bunker JP, Frazier HS, Mosteller F. Improving health. Measuring effects of medical care. Milbank Q. 1994; 72: 225–258.

Burwell SM. Setting value-based payment goals—HHS efforts to improve U.S. health care. N Engl J Med 2015; 372(10): 897–899. doi:10.1056/NEJMp1500445

Centers for Disease Control and Prevention. Death and Mortality. NCHS FastStats Web site, last updated July 14, 2014. http://www.cdc.gov/nchs/fastats/deaths.htm. Accessed Dec 5, 2014.

Davis K, Stremikis K, Squires D, Schoen C. Mirror, Mirror on the Wall, 2014 Update: How the U.S. Health Care System Compares Internationally. June 16, 2014. http://www.commonwealthfund.org/publications/fund-reports/2014/jun/mirror-mirror Accessed Oct 22, 2014.

Fineberg HV. A successful and sustainable health system—how to get there from here. N Engl J Med 2012; 366: 1020–1027.

Halfon N, Long P, Chang DI, Hester J, Inkelas M, Rodgers A. Applying a 3.0 transformation framework to guide large-scale health system reform. Health Affairs 2014; 33(11): 2003–2011.

Institute of Medicine (IOM). The Future of Public Health. Washington, DC: National Academy Press, 2008.

Jacobson DM Teutsch S. An Environmental Scan of Integrated Approaches for Defining and Measuring Total Population Health by the Clinical Care System, the Government Public Health System and Stakeholder Organizations. Washington, D.C.: National Quality Forum, 2012. http://www.qualityforum.org/Publications/2012/06/An_Environmental_Scan_of_Integrated_Approaches_for_Defining_and_Measuring_Total_Population_Health.aspx Accessed Feb 4, 2015.

IOM. Primary Care: America's Health in a New Era. Washington, DC: National Academy Press, 1996.

IOM. Primary Care and Public Health: Exploring Integration to Improve Population Health. Washington, DC: The National Academies Press, 2012.

Kassler WJ, Tomoyasu N, Conway PH. Beyond a traditional payer—CMS's role in improving population health. N Engl J Med 2015; 372(2): 109–111.

Kindig D, Stoddart G. What is population health? Am J Public Health 2003; 93(3): 380–383.

Larson EB, Reid R. The patient-centered medical home movement: Why now? JAMA. 2010; 303(16): 1644–1645. doi:10.1001/jama.2010.524

Maeshiro R, Johnson I, Koo D, Parboosingh J, Carney JK, Gesundheit N, et al. Medical education for a healthier population: Reflections on the Flexner Report from a public health perspective. Acad Med. 2010; 85(2): 211–219. doi:10.1097/ACM.0b013e3181c885d8

Marvasti FF, Stafford R. From sick care to health care—reengineering prevention in the U.S. system. N Engl J Med 2012; 367: 889–891. doi:10.1056/NEJMp1206230

McGinnis JM, Williams-Russo P, Knickman JR. The case for more active policy attention to health promotion. Health Affairs 2002; 21(2): 78–93.

McGinnis JM. Can public health and medicine partner in the public interest? Health Affairs 2006; 25(4): 1044–1052. doi:10.1377/hlthaff.25.4.1044

National Academy of Sciences. U.S. Health in International Perspective: Shorter Lives, Poorer Health. Washington, DC: National Academy of Sciences, 2013.

National Research Council. Explaining divergent levels of longevity in high-income countries. In EM Crimmins, SH Preston, and B Cohen (Eds.), Panel on Understanding Divergent Trends in Longevity in High-Income Countries. Committee on Population, Division of Behavioral and Social Sciences and Education. Washington, DC: The National Academies Press, 2011.

NCCHS. Health is a Community Affair—Report of the National Commission on Community Health Services (NCCHS). Cambridge, MA: Harvard University Press, 1967.

Porter ME. What is value in health care? N Engl J Med 2010; 363:2477–2481. doi:10.1056/NEJMp1011024

President's Council of Advisors on Science and Technology (PCAST). Report to the President: Better Health Care and Lower Costs: Accelerating Improvement through Systems Engineering. 2014

Robert Wood Johnson Foundation. Health care's blind side: the overlooked connection between social needs and good health. December 2011. http://www.rwjf.org/en/research-publications/find-rwjf-research/2011/12/health-care-s-blind-side.html Accessed Jan 24, 2015.

Rosenstock L, Helsing K, Rimer BK. Public health education in the United States: Then and now. Public Health Rev 2011; 33: 39–65.

Shaw FE, Asomugha CN, Conway PH, Rein AS. The Patient Protection and Affordable Care Act: Opportunities for prevention and public health. Lancet 2014; 384(9937): 75–82. doi:10.1016/S0140-6736(14)60259-2

Smith JM, Topol E. A call to action: Lowering the cost of health care. Am J Prev Med 2013; 44(1S1): S54–S57.

Stakeholder Health. Health Systems Learning Group Monograph. Washington, DC: April 4, 2013. http://stakeholderhealth.org/wp-content/uploads/2013/09/HSLG-V11.pdf Accessed Oct 20, 2014.

Sox HC. Resolving the tension between population health and individual health care. JAMA 2013; 310(18): 1933–1934. doi:10.1001/jama.2013.281998

Teutsch SM, Fielding JE. Rediscovering the core of public health. Ann Rev Public Health 2013; 34: 287–299. doi:10.1146/annurev-publhealth-031912-114433

US Burden of Disease Collaborators. The State of US health, 1990–2010: Burden of diseases, injuries, and risk factors. JAMA 2013; 310(6): 591–606. doi:10.1001/jama.2013.13805.

White KL. Healing the Schism: Epidemiology, Medicine, and the Public's Health. New York: Springer-Verlag, 1991.

The Value of Public Health and Primary Care Partnerships

BRIAN C. CASTRUCCI, J. LLOYD MICHENER, DENISE KOO, AND JAMES B. SPRAGUE

SUMMARY

Chronic disease mortality increased fourfold between 1900 and 2000 (Linder, 1947; Mokdad et al., 2004). This epidemiologic shift has placed a greater priority on the influence of social and economic factors on health, factors that are not easily addressed through the current U.S. health care system. Despite this, nearly all of U.S. health care spending—nearly $3 trillion in 2013—goes to direct medical care (Centers for Medicare and Medicaid Services, 2014). With growing recognition that individual health is nearly inseparable from community health (Koh et al., 2011), to improve population health outcomes, health care must transform. This chapter will review how improved collaboration between primary care and public health, with breaking down of their silos, can address the challenges of improving population health through the improved use of data, policy, community change, and aligned health messaging.

> *"We've been talking about [improved collaboration between primary care and public health] for generations. The difference is that today there is an alignment of policy and economic forces and a recognition that focusing on quality of care is not sufficient. All of this is coalescing around a moment in time. This is the time."*
>
> *William J. Kassler, M.D., M.P.H., Chief Medical Officer, Region 1,*
> *Centers for Medicare and Medicaid Services (personal correspondence)*

HEALTH CARE COSTS IN THE UNITED STATES

The United States spends more on health care than any other country in the world (OECD, 2013), $2.9 trillion in 2013, double the spending in 2000 ($1.4 trillion) (Centers for Medicare and Medicaid Services, 2014). If the American health care system broke off from the rest of the country, it would constitute the world's fifth largest economy (The World Bank, 2014). Despite all that is spent, growth in life expectancy in the United States has slowed compared to that in other economically developed countries, which spend substantially less than the United States on health care (OECD, 2013). Worse, life expectancies in some parts of the United States are similar to those of Third World countries (Lewis & Burb-Sharps, 2013; The World Bank, 2014). Much of the spending on health care in the United States can be attributed to treating chronic disease (The Robert Wood Johnson Foundation, 2010; Triple Solution for a Healthier America, 2015).

THE RISE OF CHRONIC DISEASE

In the last century, mortality from infectious diseases, such as pneumonia, tuberculosis, and enteritis, has been largely replaced by that from heart disease, cancer, and stroke (Linder FE, 1947; Mokdad et al., 2004). Chronic disease accounted for four times as many U.S. deaths in 2000 as in 1900 (Linder, 1947; Mokdad et al., 2004). In 2012, 117 million American adults (about 1 in 2) lived with at least one of the ten most prevalent chronic illnesses, and one in four adults had multiple chronic conditions (Ward et al., 2014).

Part of the epidemiologic transition to chronic illness is related to social, physical, and economic influences on health, often generically referred to as the "social determinants of health" (Braveman et al., 2011; Whitehead & Popay, 2010; Williams et al., 2008) These include lifestyle choices—smoking, overuse of alcohol, poor diet, and lack of physical activity—as well as environmental exposures—air pollution; insect and rodent infestations; "food deserts" with no access to fresh meat, fruits, or vegetables; high concentrations of liquor outlets; high-crime areas; and no access to parks or playgrounds.

Nearly all of U.S. health care spending goes to direct medical care (Centers for Disease Control [CDC], 1992; McGinnis et al., 2002), while most of what makes people sick can be attributed to social, physical, and economic influences on health behaviors (County Health Rankings and Roadmaps, 2014). However, when it comes to spending on social services such as affordable housing, transportation, pensions, or accessible child care, which can directly impact these social determinants of health, the United States ranks last among industrialized countries (Bradley et al., 2011).

ECONOMIC IMPACTS OF CHRONIC DISEASE

Three of every four dollars spent on health care in the United States can be attributed to treating chronic conditions (Triple Solution for a Healthier America, 2015). Eighty-three percent of all Medicaid spending and more than 96% of all Medicare spending is on chronic disease (The Robert Wood Johnson Foundation, 2010). At the same time, workforce illness costs the U.S. economy $576 billion annually (Japsen, 2012). Forty percent of this is attributed to lost productivity (Japsen, 2012; Stewart et al., 2003). Obesity and related chronic diseases cost employers more than $90 billion annually in health insurance claims alone (Centers for Disease Control and Prevention, 2013). Tax breaks and a skilled, educated workforce may still be the primary focus when locating a business, but population health and rates of common chronic diseases are becoming increasingly critical (Whitney, 2013). Relocating to places with lower rates of common chronic diseases—for example, diabetes and heart disease—can lead to significant savings in health insurance claims and increased worker productivity (Whitney, 2013).

THE VALUE OF WORKING TOGETHER

The U.S. health care system focuses more on the consequences of disease rather than its actual causes. In doing so, it has created expensive treatments for those who are already sick and communities in which there is often better access to an MRI than to fresh fruits and vegetables. A major theme of U.S. health policy over the past decades has been the expansion of access to and quality of health care; in fact, most significant health legislation has focused on expanded insurance coverage, including multiple expansions of the Medicaid program, enactment of the State Child Health Insurance Program, and enactment of expanded coverage through the Affordable Care Act. This may lead to increased demand for primary care services, but does not address the community context that often influences how people manage their health, live their lives, determine their activity, or regulate their diets.

Today, there is greater recognition that an individual's health is indelibly linked to the community's health (Koh & Tavenner, 2012) and that the prevention and control of chronic diseases, such as diabetes, hypertension, and heart disease, cannot be achieved solely through a visit to the doctor. Yet, the clinical role of the primary care provider and the community-wide emphasis of public health traditionally function separately, not aligned to achieve the best health outcomes (Koh & Tavenner, 2012). Neither primary care nor public health can fix this problem alone.

Strengths of Primary Care and the Value of Working Together with Public Health

Primary care providers'—which includes physicians, nurse practitioners, and physician assistants—commitment to individual health offers a depth of understanding about patient needs from a clinical perspective. Primary care providers work with patients of all ages and conditions, and with this work comes an evolving relationship with patients over time. This provider–patient relationship can facilitate patient involvement in defining and addressing their community context, thus fostering patient engagement in population health efforts. Another offshoot of this provider–patient relationship is deep, timely clinical information on each patient. With the growing complexity of intertwined medical and socioeconomic factors, providers often voice concern about how difficult it is to do what they entered the profession to do—to advance the health of people in their communities and positively impact their lives. Although their medical bags are full of extraordinary tools and techniques, providers are able to do only so much in this world of growing medical complexities and chronic illnesses, particularly when these conditions are related to a patient's social and environmental circumstances. "Stabilizing a condition" is different from addressing its root causes, let alone preventing similar problems from occurring in the future.

Integration is a possible way to bring prevention back into that medical bag, because public health brings a mission to the table that powerfully complements that of primary care. Public health practitioners can help clinical care providers reach their goals by preventing disease before it occurs and creating healthy, supportive environments for those already sick.

> *"Primary care providers care for the whole person. We think about life's trade-offs to improve total outcome of care."*
>
> *Larry Greenblatt, M.D., Duke Health (personal correspondence)*

Strengths of Public Health and the Value of Working Together With Clinical Care

Public health's mission of understanding and treating the social determinants of health can reduce the incidence and complexity of disease. Public health practitioners are responsible for understanding, attending to, and impacting the community's health as a whole; both those with and without access to medical care. Public health practitioners have the knowledge and ability to respond when patient needs are grounded in conditions far outside of the reach of a clinician's toolset. Among these abilities are a deep understanding of data and the skill to analyze and deploy it to the benefit of communities, patients, and providers. When patient concerns are related to lifestyle choices or the environment in which the patient lives, works, and plays, public health practitioners can help shape the community to make health the default choice in working across sectors to elevate and address these issues.

While public health practitioners may have the knowledge and skills to address the social determinants of a disease, the timely understanding of the distribution of disease is limited. Primary care can provide access to real-time information that public health can use to more accurately target interventions meant to prevent disease and promote wellness. By joining forces to share and analyze data, public health and primary care can develop stronger strategies to improve neighborhoods and the lives of individuals who live there.

"Public health is so deeply satisfying because it allows us to look at the whole system of needs and address them through policy and environmental changes that impact individual lives. But, we need to complement primary care. That's where the greatest impact will come from."

Kate O'Leary, MPH, Recently Retired Public Health Administrator, Washington County, Oregon (personal correspondence)

Why We Are Better Together

Public health practitioners and primary care providers might see their work as components of an integrated health system if we are to improve population health, from clinic to community. When working together, primary care's commitment to individual health offers a depth of understanding about patient needs from a clinical perspective which, combined with public health's understanding about individual and population needs from an environmental or community context, can effect real and positive change. If we can recognize and react to the impact of the built environment and its impact on the disproportionate burden of disease in communities of color or where poverty is concentrated, we may improve health more effectively and less expensively than our current system is able to do.

"Stronger collaboration with public health will lead to better care for our patients. Most of us are coming to realize that we can't do everything. So, it behooves us to have a broader network."

Julie Wood, M.D., Vice President Health of the Public and Interprofessional Activities, American Academy of Family Physicians (personal correspondence)

PARTICULARS OF WORKING TOGETHER

An opportunity exists to test increased primary care and public health integration to improve population health aims at lower cost. The American Academy of Family Physicians 2014 policy statement, *Integration of Primary Care and Public Health,* identifies 14 activities in which public health and primary care can work together (American Academy of Family Physicians, 2014). These can be grouped into three broad collaborative activities—data and analytics; policy and environmental changes; and aligned health messaging.

Data and Analytics

Availability of Electronic Record Data
Federally funded incentives have contributed to a fivefold increase in at least basic electronic health record (EHR) adoption from 2008 to 2013 (Charles

et al., 2014). The increase in EHR adoption along with the proliferation of other electronically captured, digitized health information has increased the availability of clinical health care data. Primary care has individual patient data identifiable at the street address level and works with patients of all ages and conditions. If these data are collected in the EHR, there is an opportunity for real-time analysis at granular geographic levels such as neighborhoods or blocks. Such information can be used to improve decision making for the individual patient and, with appropriate protection of patient confidentiality, can inform decision making for the community. Moreover, these data are equally powerful for targeting disease-prevention and health-promotion efforts.

Using Data for Clinical Practice Improvement

Public health can help to improve provider adherence to evidence-based preventive services. The New York City Department of Health and Mental Hygiene's *Primary Care Information Project* has worked with clinical practices to analyze and improve provider adherence to clinical guidelines that reduce preventable death (New York Department of Health and Mental Hygiene, 2010). Improving clinical practice patterns relevant to population health resulted in a 33% increase in the management of high cholesterol and a 15% increase in blood pressure control. If the improvement in blood pressure control alone could be replicated nationally, an estimated 12,000 premature deaths could be prevented annually (New York Department of Health and Mental Hygiene, 2010).

Using Data for Public Health Practice Improvement

Data are the life blood of public health. However, data used by public health practitioners are typically old, incomplete, and lacking in geographic detail. Consequently, public health interventions for disease prevention or health promotion are often not efficiently targeted or tailored. Clinical care's commitment to individual health offers extensive data about patient needs with street address–level demographics, which could improve the use of public health data to benefit both disciplines. The ability to share important data beyond the clinic, while using well-established protocols for appropriate protection of the confidentiality of individual patients, can create early warning systems for epidemics and can also enable tracking of community vaccination efforts and monitor and ensure the safety of vulnerable populations. Health information technology will increasingly allow systematic collection and analysis of large-scale health care data, which could inform public health practice to develop strategies to improve population health (see chapter 20).

Data from a particular practice or provider only presents information on a limited group of people, who may or may not be from the same neighborhoods, share the same root causes of disease, or be governed by the same set of regulations and laws. In a competitive health care environment, public health can work as a neutral aggregator of data to achieve the most complete picture of the clinical experiences in a community.

The solution to an apparent clinical problem may not be clinical, but rather social or environmental. Public health practitioners can pair clinical information with their data regarding the availability of community assets and exposure to unhealthy environments. By aggregating clinical data, even within one practice, epidemiologists and other public health scientists can map cases of disease that can then be juxtaposed against social indicators such as distance to parks, arrest and crime data, location of toxic sites, local prevalence of foreclosed properties, and availability of fresh fruits and vegetables (see chapter 24).

Moving Toward Shared Data

If individual and community health are indelibly linked (Koh & Tavenner, 2012), could there not be a similar approach for consideration for individual and community health data? However, few examples of seamless data sharing between primary care (including hospitals and emergency rooms) and public health currently exist. Despite the perception that HIPAA acts as a barrier to this type of sharing data, the reverse is true—HIPAA explicitly permits disclosure of data to public health authorities without individual authorization, while carefully balancing the need to protect patients. HIPAA therefore empowers the use of clinical data for public health purposes, and points to the use of de-identified data and other approaches as appropriate to accomplish the goal of using patient data to improve community health (Goldin & Cardwell, 2014; U.S. Department of Health and Human Services, Not listed). However, other barriers to harnessing the power of health care and public health data include technical, motivational, and economic issues to which there are few structural solutions (van Panhuis et al., 2014). More models are needed to build a better data-sharing culture between health and health care in order to maximize the impact of information for improved population health (see chapter 20).

> *"There is an opportunity right now to push both primary care and public health out of their comfort zones. Together we can make fundamental shifts that will create historic and lasting change to how we view and provide for the health of our communities. Even small movement towards creating whole health practices has huge, observable ripples for patients and families."*
>
> *Mitch Anderson, MPH, Health Department Director,*
> *Benton County, Oregon (personal correspondence)*

Policy and Community Change

Public health practitioners bridge sectors and political agendas to elevate and advance evidence that can be used to support policy change that can contribute to a social environment that promotes population health. Policy and regulation can change the community context without requiring individually motivated changes to behavior. For example, California (2005), Rhode Island (2006), and Oregon (2007) enacted legislation to reduce access to sugar-sweetened beverages for public school students (Centers for Disease Control and Prevention, 2010; Oregon Public Health Institute, 2015). In another example, violent crime in Baltimore, Maryland was linked to areas with an overabundance of alcohol outlets. City and public health officials reviewed the city's zoning laws to reduce the number of alcohol outlets throughout the city, improving neighborhood health and safety (Kilar, 2013; Thornton et al., 2013).

On a larger scale, public health practitioners inform decision makers and elected officials on the health effects of a wide variety of government programs using health impact assessments (HIAs). HIAs look at the social determinants of health and try to integrate considerations of health, well-being, and equity in the development, implementation, and evaluation of policies and services (Corburn et al., 2014; Gakh, 2015; Wernham & Teutsch, 2015).

Public health practitioners can amplify the work that primary care providers do on an individual level by bringing it to the community through regulatory and legislative solutions that can directly impact the health of the population. Public policy is best changed through good data, real-world examples, and the involvement of people with credibility. Primary care brings access to all three. Localized data can be a powerful tool, especially with elected officials, as can stories of their own constituents' experiences and needs. Similarly, local primary care providers are often well known by decision makers and seen as community leaders by their neighbors and patients, especially in smaller towns. By partnering with primary care and helping providers to better understand major public health issues, public health can develop powerful citizen-allies with a stage from which to elevate the importance of these concerns; effectively leveraging the status granted medical providers would undoubtedly lead to healthier communities for all. Primary care providers also can be a positive force for community and policy change, and integration can further mutual goals of improving community health.

Aligned Health Messaging

> *"Although primary care providers are perceived as strong health voices, clinicians don't necessarily see themselves this way. Providers could play a pivotal role in advocating for the needs of a healthy life and powerfully help to realign how health is developed— moving us from a health care to a health focus."*
>
> *Steven M. Teutsch, MD, MPH, Former Chief Science Officer, Los Angeles County Department of Public Health (personal correspondence)*

The relationships that primary care providers develop with their patients allow them to influence their patients' behaviors—e.g., smoking or not exercising. Not only does the quality of the connection between primary care provider and patient lead to trust, but also to a deeply personal relationship that may enable primary care providers to discuss both personal and population health issues more effectively with patients, an asset to be leveraged in a partnership with public health. For example, the *Educating Physicians In their Communities (EPIC)* (http://www.gaepic.org/) program for immunization and breastfeeding is a partnership between the Georgia Chapter of the American Academy of Pediatrics and the Georgia Department of Health to provide free interactive, peer-to-peer education programs to Georgia's physician offices. Through education, this partnership hopes to promote increased immunization and breastfeeding rates.

Public health has the tools to continue health messaging at the community level. "Stop smoking," "be prepared for emergencies," "exercise," "use a condom," "get immunized," and "buckle up" are all familiar messages from public health mass media campaigns aimed at promoting health behaviors or discouraging unhealthy behaviors (Randolph & Viswanath, 2004). Public service announcements airing on television and radio are often augmented by community events, print materials, and press events and talks with public health leaders (see chapter 11).

In addition to mass media strategies, public health has leveraged existing relationships in the community to deliver health messaging. For example, barbers in African-American communities have been trained to provide health education messages related to HIV/AIDS and colorectal cancer screening (Project Brotherhood, 2015a, 2015b). Public health is also experimenting with communications technologies like the Internet, text messaging, and Twitter (Bennett & Glasgow, 2009; Choucair et al., 2015; Evans et al., 2012, 2014; Whittaker et al., 2012).

Primary care and public health could also reinforce each other's efforts to promote health by sharing observations of need, messaging jointly, and aligning responses. For example, every spring, as the weather begins to entice neighbors out onto their bikes, primary care could elevate bike safety in conversations around exercise with their patients. And, at the same time, public health could promote the need for safe streets with police departments, news media, and community-level messaging. By aligning health information messages received in the community with those received in the clinic, primary care providers and public health practitioners can deliver a formidable one-two punch.

WORKING TOGETHER: A PRACTICAL EXAMPLE

In his TED book, *The Upstream Doctors*, Rishi Manchanda, MD, argues for more "upstreamists"—physicians who see their work as including a "duty not only to prescribe a clinical remedy but to tackle sickness at its source" (Manchanda, 2013). As an example of upstream medicine in practice, he recounts the story of a former patient, Veronica, who suffered from severe chronic headaches. Her interaction with the health care system had resulted in inconclusive medical tests and an expensive visit to the emergency room, but no answers as to the cause of her headaches, let alone a solution.

Manchanda used a questionnaire to identify risk factors in her daily life and discovered that Veronica was exposed to mold and cockroach allergens that could be the cause of her health issues. Instead of subjecting her to more medical tests, she was referred to a tenants' rights group and received a follow-up visit from a community health worker. In 3 months, Veronica's headaches subsided.

Veronica's story illustrates how clinicians can effectively address the social determinants of health by using tools that assess a patient's community and environmental circumstances, as well as including non-medical providers as part of a health care team. If information about environmental hazards in the building were shared with public health authorities, they would be in a better position to look for other cases that signal the need for health or housing authorities to investigate conditions that may be posing a larger threat to public health. The public health department could then gather information about potential environmental triggers within the building, the frequency of tenant complaints filed with the local housing authority, and other variables that could help identify a common cause of this health issue.

If housing conditions were found to be a broader issue seen by multiple providers in a community, primary care providers and public health officials could work together to meet with community leaders and decision makers to highlight the issue and possible steps to intervene. Letters could also be sent to all rental property owners reminding them of their responsibilities as property owners and the consequences of failing to meet these responsibilities.

As a government agency, the local health department has regulatory and statutory options, which it can leverage to change health policies and promote regulations that directly address the root causes of disease. In Veronica's case, the local health department could have engaged the local housing authority to improve the oversight, monitoring, and enforcement of existing regulations or determine if new regulations were needed to improve housing conditions. In extreme cases, the local public health department could condemn buildings or revoke a property owner's ability to rent a property.

"The practice of medicine needs additional tools or we, as a profession, will fall short of achieving health outcomes that are within our reach. Public health employs many of these tools. It's time to come together and leverage each other's strengths."

J. Lloyd Michener, MD Chair, Department of Community and Family Medicine, Duke University School of Medicine (personal correspondence)

THE FUTURE TOGETHER

The simple truth is that our traditional model of health care delivery is no longer sufficient. It was designed to respond to acute illnesses like polio and typhoid, not to address causes of disease that occur far beyond the clinic walls. However, health care reform focused primarily on health care financing and organizational inefficiencies is not likely to address the root problem in our medical system. The nature of disease and illness in America has changed from acute conditions to chronic ones; our health care system has not changed with it. The solution, at least in part, may lie in bridging the gap between primary care and public health and enhancing their ability to address collectively the problem of chronic disease and social determinants of disease. Together, primary care and public health have a real opportunity to transform the nation's passion for health care to a passion for "health."

REFERENCES

American Academy of Family Physicians. Integration of primary care and public health (position paper). 2014. Retrieved from http://www.aafp.org/about/policies/all/integprimarycareandpublichealth.html

Bennett GG, Glasgow RE. The delivery of public health interventions via the internet: Actualizing their potential. Ann Rev Pub Health 2009; 30: 273–292. doi:10.1146/annurev.publhealth.031308.100235 [doi]

Bradley EH, Elkins BR, Herrin J, Elbel B. Health and social services expenditures: Associations with health outcomes. BMJ Quality & Safety 2011; 20(10): 826–831. doi:10.1136/bmjqs.2010.048363

Centers for Disease Control (CDC). Estimated national spending on prevention—United States, 1988. MMWR Morb Mortal Wkly Rep 1992; 41(29): 529–531.

Centers for Disease Control and Prevention. DNPAO state program highlights: Limiting access to sugar-sweetened beverages. 2010. http://www.cdc.gov/obesity/downloads/limitingaccesstossbs.pdf

Centers for Disease Control and Prevention. Worker productivity. 2013. Retrieved from http://www.cdc.gov/workplacehealthpromotion/businesscase/reasons/productivity.html

Centers for Medicare and Medicaid Services. National health expenditure data. 2014. Retrieved from http://www.cms.gov/Research-Statistics-Data-and-Systems/Statistics-Trends-and-Reports/NationalHealthExpendData/NationalHealthAccountsHistorical.html

Charles D, Gabriel M, Furukawa M. Adoption of electronic health record systems among US non-federal acure care hospitals: 2008–2013. 2014. (No. ONC Data Brief No. 16). http://www.healthit.gov/sites/default/files/oncdatabrief16.pdf: Office of the National Coordinator for Health Information Technology.

Choucair B, Bhatt J, Mansour R. (2015). A bright future: Innovation transforming public health in chicago. J Public Health Manag Pract 2015; 21(Suppl 1); S49–S55. doi:10.1097/PHH.0000000000000140

Corburn J, Curl S, Arredondo G. A health-in-all-policies approach addresses many of richmond, california's place-based hazards, stressors. Health Aff (Project Hope) 2014; 33(11): 1905–1913. doi:10.1377/hlthaff.2014.0652

County Health Rankings and Roadmaps. What works for health. 2014. Retrieved from http://www.countyhealthrankings.org/roadmaps/what-works-for-health

Evans WD, Wallace Bihm J, Szekely D, Nielsen P, Murray E, Abroms L, Snider J. Initial outcomes from a 4-week follow-up study of the Text4baby program in the military women's population: Randomized controlled trial. J Med Internet Res 2014; 16(5): e131. doi:10.2196/jmir.3297

Evans WD, Wallace JL, Snider J. Pilot evaluation of the text4baby mobile health program. BMC Public Health 2012; 12: 1031-2458-12-1031. doi:10.1186/1471-2458-12-1031

Gakh M. (2015). Law, the health in all policies approach, and cross-sector collaboration. Public Health Reps 2015; 130(1): 96–100.

Goldin S, Cardwell A. HIPAA and public health: Myths and facts. 2014. Retrieved from https://www.statereforum.org/weekly-insight/hipaa-and-public-health-myths-and-facts

Japsen B. US workforce illness costs $576B annually from sick days to workers compensation. 2012. Retrieved from http://www.forbes.com/sites/brucejapsen/2012/09/12/u-s-workforce-illness-costs-576b-annually-from-sick-days-to-workers-compensation/

Kilar S. Support grows for city zoning plan to reduce liquor stores. The Baltimore Sun Jan 10, 2013.

Koh HK, Piotrowski JJ, Kumanyika S, Fielding JE. Healthy people: a 2020 vision for the social determinants approach. Health Educ Behav 2011; 38(6): 551–557. doi:10.1177/1090198111428646

Koh HK, Tavenner M. Connecting care through the clinic and community for a healthier america. Am J Prev Med 2012; 42(6 Suppl 2): S92–94. doi:10.1016/j.amepre.2012.04.002

Lewis K, Burb-Sharps S. The measure of america 2013–2014. 2013. Retrieved from http://www.measureofamerica.org/wp-content/uploads/2013/06/MOA-III.pdf

Linder FE, G. R. Vital Statistics Rates in the United States, 1900–1940. Washington, DC: National Office of Vital Statistics, 1947.

Manchanda, R. The upstream doctors: Medical innovators track sickness to its source. 2013. TED Conferences.

McGinnis JM, Williams-Russo P, Knickman JR. The case for more active policy attention to health promotion. Health Affairs (Project Hope) 2002; 21(2): 78–93.

Mokdad AH, Marks JS, Stroup DF, Gerberding JL. Actual causes of death in the United States, 2000. JAMA 2004; 291(10), 1238–1245. doi:10.1001/jama.291.10.1238

New York Department of Health and Mental Hygiene. Health department findings show that electronic health records can improve health care by encouraging preventive services. 2010. Retrieved from http://www.nyc.gov/html/doh/html/pr2010/pr052-10.shtml

OECD. Health at a glance 2013: OECD indicators. 2013. Retrieved from http://dx.doi.org/10.1787/health_glance-2013-en

Oregon Public Health Institute. Nutrition standards in oregon schools. Retrieved from http://ophi.org/strategic-projects/healthy-eating/nutrition-standards-in-oregon-schools/. Accessed Feb 6, 2015.

Project Brotherhood. Project Brotherhood colorectal cancer prevention:Train the barbers. In partnership with the American Cancer Society and supported by a generous grant by Walmart. Retrieved from http://projectbrotherhood.net/colorectal-cancer/. Accessed Feb 6, 2015a.

Project Brotherhood. Project Brotherhood HIV/AIDS prevention: Train the barbers. Funded by the Illinois Department of PublicHealth. Retrieved from http://projectbrotherhood.net/hiv/. Accessed Feb 6, 2015b.

Randolph W, Viswanath K. Lessons learned from public health mass media campaigns: Marketing health in a crowded media world. Ann Rev Public Health 2004; 25: 419–437. doi:10.1146/annurev.publhealth.25.101802.123046

Stewart WF, Ricci, J. A., Chee, E., & Morganstein, D. Lost productive work time costs from health conditions in the united states: Results from the american productivity audit. J Occup Environ Med 2003; 45(12): 1234–1246. doi:10.1097/01.jom.0000099999.27348.78

The Robert Wood Johnson Foundation. Chronic care: Making the case for ongoing care. 2010. Retrieved from http://www.rwjf.org/en/research-publications/find-rwjf-research/2010/01/chronic-care.html

The World Bank. GDP ranking. 2014. Retrieved from http://data.worldbank.org/data-catalog/GDP-ranking-table

Thornton R, Greiner A, Jennings J. Will Limiting the Number of Beer/Wine/Liquor Outlets in Baltimore City Create Healthier Residential Neighborhoods? Research Strongly Suggests that it Will, vol 26, num 2-A. Baltimore: The Abell Foundation, 2013.

Triple Solution for a Healthier America. The impact of chronic diseases on healthcare. Retrieved from http://www.forahealthieramerica.com/ds/impact-of-chronic-disease.html. Accessed Feb 6, 2015.

US Department of Health and Human Services. Health information privacy: The privacy rule. Retrieved from http://www.hhs.gov/ocr/privacy/hipaa/administrative/privacyrule/index.html. Accessed Feb 6, 2015.

van Panhuis WG, Paul P, Emerson C, Grefenstette J, Wilder R, Herbst AJ, et al. A systematic review of barriers to data sharing in public health. BMC Public Health 2014; 14, 1144–2458-14-1144. doi:10.1186/1471-2458-14-1144 [doi]

Ward BW, Schiller JS, Goodman RA. Multiple chronic conditions among US adults: A 2012 update. Prev Chronic Dis 2014; 11: E62. doi:10.5888/pcd11.130389

Wernham A, Teutsch SM. (2015). Health in all policies for big cities. J Public Health Manag Pract 2015; 21(Suppl 1): S56–65. doi:10.1097/PHH.0000000000000130

Whitney E. Companies on the move look for healthy workers. 2013. Retrieved from http://www.npr.org/blogs/health/2013/04/09/176712349/companies-on-the-move-look-for-healthy-workers

Whittaker R, Matoff-Stepp S, Meehan J, Kendrick J, Jordan E, Stange P, et al. Text4baby: Development and implementation of a national text messaging health information service. American Journal of Public Health 2012; 102(12): 2207–2213. doi:10.2105/AJPH.2012.300736

Primary Care and Public Health: Partners for Population Health

JULIE K. WOOD

For years, public health and primary care professionals have worked diligently in parallel, rather than together, with similar goals but different approaches to promoting the health of individuals and communities. However, we are now at a pivotal and transformational time when those working in all health care disciplines are shifting toward collaborative approaches to improving population health across communities.

The idea that we should be working together is not new. Individuals and groups have made calls to action in the past, including the ardent advocacy for integrated approaches made in the 2012 Institute of Medicine report, *Primary Care and Public Health: Exploring Integration to Improve Population Health*. This appeal from the Institute of Medicine has stimulated robust, integrated efforts such as formation of the Association of State and Territorial Health Officials Primary Care and Public Health Collaborative. Groups such as the Collaborative and tools such as *The Practical Playbook: Public Health and Primary Care Together* answer those calls at a fundamental and foundational level.

Working with communities has long been a key facet of family medicine, as community medicine is included in the training of every family physician, and family physicians are working today to create a practical blueprint to improve the quality of health care in ways that will translate into a healthier population and lower costs. Our work includes developing the patient-centered medical home (PCMH) model, which puts forward the idea of a medical "home" that provides comprehensive care focused on the broad health needs of individuals in the complex context of their culture, values, and preferences. The PCMH model outlines a system in which high-quality care is always accessible and where all elements for care are coordinated and communicated. As the PCMH model evolves, primary care providers are now better positioned to integrate family medicine with public health as a crucial part of the "medical neighborhood." Both preventive care and chronic disease management are an important part of a successful PCMH, and partnerships with community groups will provide a variety of effective and powerful ways to improve the health of the individual as well as the full community.

That is what integration is all about: improving the care of our patients and our communities.

By working in tandem with our health care neighbors, we can change how health care is provided and hasten the speed at which integrated health projects are embraced on a national scale.

By using the strategies outlined in the *Practical Playbook,* we will all be able to better leverage the critical public health infrastructure, which has evolved over more than 200 years into a sophisticated, front-line service protecting those of us who live in the United States. Pair the public health organizational structure with the patient-centered medical home—wherein a team of health-care professionals provides preventive and medical care in the context of family and community—and an unstoppable health care force is created. Many factors will need to come to come together to make this model a reality, including a collective desire to provide health care to a population, new models of payment and funding, and tools such as the *Practical Playbook* that help us learn to improve care *together.*

A particular challenge in the climate of extreme changes in the health-care sector—affecting everyone from health care providers to administrators—is the development of new payment models that require primary care providers to demonstrate improved population health outcomes. Once short-term measures are taken to optimize treatment, primary care providers will need the support of public health officials to create structured, targeted, and ultimately integrative projects that have measurable impact that reaches from the local community to the nation at large.

Moreover, with ever-building time pressures and a growing emphasis on holistic wellness, doctors will be more effective if they leverage the competence of public health partners who can expand on their work beyond the walls of their clinics.

Family physicians train in community medicine and many now work in public health, although they do not necessarily recognize it as such. Those of us creating integrated programs are not asking doctors to take on more work, but rather to integrate what they are doing with similar efforts in public health, or at least to create an interface between primary care and public health efforts. Tools such as the *Practical Playbook* facilitate this integration and allow it to happen more seamlessly, in turn supporting family physicians in more easily accomplishing what they are trained and want to do.

Finally, there is the question of the enormous amount of data we are now capable of generating and analyzing. The average physician does not have the time, resources, or ability to make good use of the data available to improve health care, particularly data from the community that would help them with patient care. Successful efforts to integrate primary care and public health can address this gap by bringing together public health officials who have access to community data with primary care providers. As a team, these professionals can interpret and make use of the information to identify critical health problems and then create and execute successful public health interventions.

The interface of primary care and public health adds to the tools that family physicians have when working to meet the goal of improved population health. As family physicians work with our primary care colleagues to develop the PCMH model, we have come to understand the importance of team-based approaches to providing care and enhancing population health. Those reading this *Practical Playbook* and using the resources on the accompanying website (https://practicalplaybook.org) are well on their way to understanding and engaging in improving our nation's health care and our health care system through collaborations between public health and primary care professionals.

The Value of Integration: Public Health, Primary Care, and Beyond

Essay II

PAUL E. JARRIS AND KATIE SELLERS

Individuals and entities who contribute to population health can be found throughout society. Many are influencing population health deliberately (e.g., health care professionals, public health professionals, health-oriented non-governmental organizations), whereas others do not have health as part of their mission and may not even recognize the ways in which they influence health (e.g., pollution-producing industries, transportation, and agriculture). Policymakers influence health both intentionally and unintentionally—sometimes they purposefully develop policy to improve health, and sometimes they develop policy that favors other interests, such as businesses, economic development, and individual liberties without taking into account the likely impact on health.

None of these players has sole responsibility or control over population health, and none can improve population health alone. Each player brings a unique and important contribution, and all must work together to effectively improve population health. We must leverage the strength of each positive contribution to form a redesigned health ecosystem that will achieve optimal population health. Because the social determinants of health span the breadth of society, our efforts to improve health must include a similarly broad spectrum of partners.

Of all of these players, primary care and public health are the closest of kin. They share a focus on health, an appreciation for the influence of the physical and social environment on a person's health, and a dedication to meeting the needs of the underserved. Yet they are often trained and frequently work in isolation. They are sometimes separated by their difference in orientation (patient vs. population), methods (anticipatory guidance, clinical prevention and treatment vs. epidemiology, regulation, and policy development), and professional networks.

Primary care providers play a unique and critical role in the health of the population, by focusing on the health of the whole patient, in the context of the patient's environment, throughout the patient's life course. Infectious diseases still have a major impact on health, but chronic disease care is the fundamental driver of much of our ill health and skyrocketing health care costs.

Historically, primary care and public health have worked in silos, at times with mutual

awareness and even cooperation intersecting around critical functions, such as vaccinating the public. The public health system provides vaccines through the Vaccines for Children and 317 program (named for Section 317 of the Public Health Service Act). State health agencies handle the order management and distribution and primary care providers administer the vaccines.

Tobacco provides an example of a very successful partnership between primary care and public health. The public health system worked to motivate smokers to quit—through media campaigns, increased tobacco taxes, and clean air laws. Smokers then discussed quitting with their primary care providers, who counseled them and prescribed cessation aids. Public health worked to get tobacco cessation methods covered by insurance, and set up quitlines for smokers trying to quit, giving primary care providers effective tools to use with their patients who smoke. The resulting partnership between primary care and public health was a powerful force in reducing smoking rates.

We have seen some success with tobacco, but are still hoping for positive change with respect to many other determinants of health. Obesity, hypertension, maternal and child health, and asthma are just a few of the areas in which collaboration between public health and primary care shows great promise. Whatever the health issue, strong partnerships with primary care can increase public heath's effectiveness in critical ways:

- **Increasing public health access to individual level data.** Public health practitioners often think of themselves as the ones with the data, because they have population-level data. But health care providers have an abundance of individual-level data that can provide an in-depth complement to the often self-reported data public health collects.

- **Strengthening public health efforts to achieve health equity.** Studies have shown that although income inequality is associated with poorer health outcomes, a robust primary care system can counteract the impact of income inequality.

- **Maximizing funding opportunities.** When public health and primary care collaborate, they can pursue funding opportunities typically available to both public health and primary care, thus increasing the possibilities for each.

- **Co-locating services.** Public health and primary care often serve the same population. Whenever public health engages in work with individuals (e.g., providing WIC benefits, offering vaccinations and health screenings), services can be co-located with primary care to maximize benefits to clients.

- **Linking individuals to community resources.** Primary care has a strong orientation to the community in which patients live, as does public health. Public health and primary care can efficiently leverage the best resources available in the community if they build relationships with the providers of community resources together.

There are many other opportunities to collaborate, in which public health and primary care working together could be much more effective than either working alone. For example, primary care providers see a lot of children with asthma. Public health can use epidemiologic methods to identify specific environmental triggers (identifying lots of idling school buses or a chemical plant near a school where asthma rates are high) and influence policy to remove these triggers from school environments (e.g., school regulations prohibiting

Figure 2EII-1 ▼

Primary care and public health integration strategic map: 2014–2016.

(From Association of State and Territorial Health Officials. ASTHO: http://www.astho.org/PCPHCollaborative/revised-strategic-map/. Used with permission.)

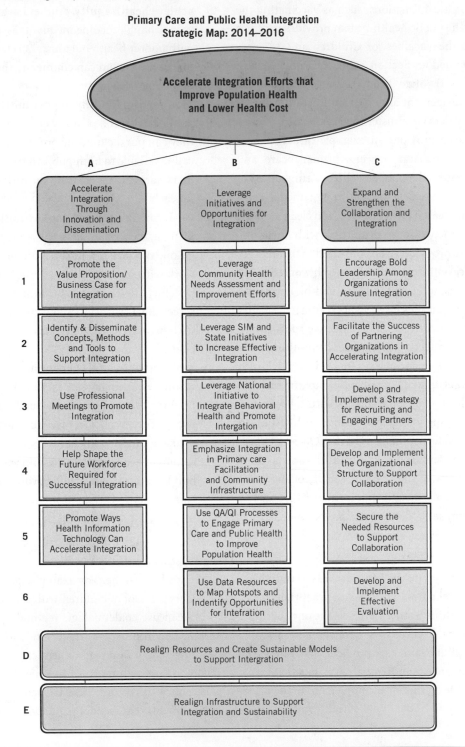

Primary Care and Public Health Integration
Strategic Map: 2014–2016

idling or moving a school location away from a chemical plant). Primary care providers can counsel individual families about possible in-home triggers, and public health can use larger scale dissemination methods (such as through mass media or through school communications with parents) to educate about in-home triggers. Public health can also work with the housing department to ensure public housing environments are free of triggers such as mold and tobacco smoke.

To facilitate the collaboration and integration of primary care and public health, the Association of State and Territorial Health Officials (ASTHO), the Institute of Medicine (IOM), and United Health Foundation partnered to develop a strategic map (Fig. 2EII-1) for primary care and public health integration in July 2012. The planning was held in response to IOM's March 2012 report *Primary Care and Public Health: Exploring Integration to Improve Population Health* and brought together key individuals from both sectors. The map outlined a strategic approach to integration created in response to the IOM report.

To support the implementation of the strategic map, ASTHO convened a Primary Care and Public Health Collaborative, which represents a partnership of more than 60 organizations and more than 100 individual partners seeking to inform, align, and support the implementation of integrated efforts that improve population health and lower health care costs. Organizations represent public health at the state, local, and federal level; primary care is represented by lead medical societies; health insurer partners include Medicare, Medicaid, and private insurers. Frequent communication and development of stories, tools, and connections between partners have been key to the ongoing success of this national collaborative.

This work goes far beyond community-based programs, such as walking clubs and nutrition education, and primary care providers and public health workers cannot do it alone. We must enlist policy makers in considering the health impact of all of their decisions in a health in all policies approach and factoring health as a critical component into decision-making. Health impact assessments performed by public health as a component of transportation planning have improved the viability of projects and promoted health. Collaborative decisions that create both economic opportunities and health have the greatest promise.

Successful examples of partnerships between primary care and public health are increasing. The de Beaumont Foundation, the Centers for Disease Control and Prevention, and Duke University are to be commended for compiling them and making them readily accessible to practitioners looking to replicate and build on these successes.

Primary care and public health will never reach their shared dream of a healthy nation unless we build robust primary care and public health systems that collaborate and leverage each other's unique contributions to the health of the population.

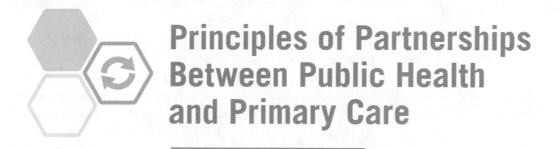

Chapter 3

Principles of Partnerships Between Public Health and Primary Care

J. LLOYD MICHENER, BRIAN C. CASTRUCCI, AND DENISE KOO

PRINCIPLES OF INTEGRATION

The 2012 Institute of Medicine (IOM) report entitled *Primary Care and Public Health: Exploring Integration to Improve Population Health* identified five principles or common elements of success that enable primary care and public health groups to work together (IOM, 2012). These principles were hallmarks of groups that had survived the test of time, unlike the vast majority of partnerships and programs that started, flourished for a while, and faded as time and early leaders moved on. These "survivors" had several elements in common, including:

- A shared goal of population health
- Community engagement
- Aligned leadership
- Sustainable systems
- Shared and collaborative use of data and analysis

These principles might not be equally apparent when work begins, because they become increasingly visible and important as work progresses. They also require nurturing, and, similar to the five stages of integration discussed in chapter 4, they are interconnected and fluid. Two are particularly important when groups begin working together: 1) a shared goal of health of the population, beyond improved health care or public health alone and 2) leaders who have realized that population health requires more than they or their organization can provide alone, and who are therefore willing to align with partners to achieve this goal. These two principles help create a common vision against which efforts can continually be measured.

Principle 1: A Shared Goal of Population Health

What Is Population Health, and Why Is a Shared Goal of Population Health Important?

Population health, meaning the "health outcomes of a group of individuals, including the distribution of such outcomes within the group" (Kindig & Stoddart, 2003) is an aspiration of both primary care and public health groups, but is often approached from different, complementary perspectives. To primary care providers, population health begins with preventing illness and improving the care of patients, individually or collectively, especially those seen in clinical settings. For public health providers, population health is achieved by efforts to address social and environmental factors that influence health of broad and often geographic areas, especially preventive efforts to affect health behaviors and exposures (IOM, 2012, p 19). Keeping a focus on the shared goal can support discussion and decision making about how different approaches can be most effectively sequenced and combined.

How Is a Shared Goal of Population Health Achieved?

In working toward a healthy population, diverse members of a community develop a shared view of health for their community. This process is iterative and takes time, as the mental framing of "health" and the top priorities for improving health can be both strikingly and subtly different across partners. Building consensus begins with discussions with potential partners to understand their perspectives on and motivations for wanting to improve the health of their community.

For example, the head of a health center may be focused on improving access to care, the head of the health department may prioritize reducing smoking rates, whereas local community agencies may be concerned about rising obesity rates, and employers may be concerned about the cost of care. All are legitimate concerns, but each requires different strategies and resources. Discussions may uncover common root causes to all these problems, such as limited access to healthy foods or transportation and lack of safe places to exercise. By focusing on a common goal of health, the different perspectives can be seen as complementary views that require a coordinated set of activities to achieve. Finding an area for common action that tackles these priorities requires listening, data, and negotiation.

How Do You Know that You Have Developed a Shared Goal of Population Health?

1. Have you been able to agree on health-related goals?
    a. If no, what has brought you together? What are the "ties that bind," and how can you create a shared goal of population health from that commonality?
2. Is there a willingness and ability to contribute to the shared goal and a commitment to an ongoing process and continual dialogue?

a. If no, take heart, this process takes time. Make space for authentic conversations to take place. Read more in chapters 5 and 6.

Principle 2: Community Engagement

Within the context of integration, community engagement is "the process of working collaboratively with groups of people who are affiliated by geographic proximity, special interests, or similar situations with respect to issues affecting their well-being"

Centers for Disease Control and Prevention [CDC], 1997.

Why Is Community Engagement Important?

Community engagement is essential in projects aimed at integrating population health activities because health problems—and solutions—are rooted in everyday life (CDC, 2011). Although primary care and, even more, public health groups may view themselves as being deeply rooted in their communities, successful integration to improve health requires working with and understanding the perspectives of more than health care and public health professionals. It is vital to engage the members of the community early and throughout the planning process, as they will offer insights and support in choosing problems, and in selecting effective interventions. Moreover, you want community members to "own" some or all of the project. Conversely, they can derail projects undertaken without full recognition of their priorities and constraints.

How Is Community Engagement Achieved?

Public health professionals and care providers must reach outside of their traditional domains to work with diverse stakeholders in the community. Local stakeholders provide perspectives that reflect site-specific values and priorities, and incorporating those points of view is a central ingredient in designing projects that are realistic, achievable, and sustainable at ground level.

Communities include a range of formal and informal leaders and organizations, and key stakeholders may differ by subject and geographic area, so it takes time to identify the appropriate community leaders to help tackle specific population health challenges (CDC, 1997, p 49). For example, community leaders who are effective in helping to address drug abuse problems in a dense, ethnically diverse urban community may be different than those leaders who would be helpful in rural, more homogeneous regions. Similarly, the leaders who can be effective in addressing drug abuse problems may be different than the community leaders who will be most helpful in addressing issues related to diabetes or asthma.

Ways to Engage the Community

The community must be engaged throughout all phases of an integration project (CDC, 1997). As projects develop, community stakeholders should continue to be actively involved and invited to participate, and their perspectives, ideas, and insights considered with input from public health and primary care professionals. Meetings should be held at times and places when diverse attendance is possible, and attention given to ensure that those speaking represent the breadth of the community. Translation services for non-English speakers, or meetings held in the language of the community members can be helpful, as can sensitivity to community norms about demonstration of respect for community values and leaders. Community members who are fully engaged throughout integration projects will often become ardent advocates in the community and will foster local buy-in and participation. In the best-case scenarios, communities will function as core partners, although in other situations they may function as key consultants.

Community Engagement During Evaluation of Processes and Outcomes

When evaluating your program, identify the interests and expectations of potential and current stakeholders and funders. What will they want to know? What types of data will be most convincing to them? Evaluations should answer partner and funder questions in a timely and convincing fashion. Designing and implementing a useful assessment requires ongoing collaboration among assessors and stakeholders. When done right, the assessment can be used to answer a wide variety of questions that help partnerships carry out their work more effectively and efficiently.

A local community health assessment, conducted by the health department, perhaps with a local not-for-profit hospital, can be an excellent starting point for identifying community needs as well as the local groups interested in health issues. Community health centers, as well as nonprofit health systems, will have community boards made up of concerned members of the local community who can provide additional perspectives. Building on work that has already been done, and with community groups that already exist, demonstrates genuine community engagement.

How Do You Know When You Have Engaged Your Community?

1. Are diverse community stakeholders engaged as ongoing partners?
2. Are accountability and ownership shared among stakeholders and community members in each stage of the project?
3. Does the project maintain involvement by people who represent the broad interests of the communities?
4. Are both organizational and institutional leadership publicly embracing the project?

Principle 3: Aligned Leadership

Aligned leadership occurs when institutional and community leaders agree to a shared goal, and then begin to develop a set of values and the key competencies required to achieve that goal. The process of aligned leadership assures that partners are consistently mindful of the key areas of alignment, know where they stand at any given point in time, and adjust their behavior as needed to achieve their shared goal.

Why Is Aligned Leadership Important?

Aligned leadership is important because it is a critical element in creating a shared vision of health that is larger than the work of any one organization; in addition, it is central to creating shared goals and outcomes and to linking and sharing resources to achieve that vision. Aligned leadership is also important because if it is not there, or if misalignment occurs, the divide can split the energy, focus, trust, and power of the group. As you think about aligning leadership, begin to think about ways in which you already are or can be aligned with your partners. Alignment doesn't have to occur on every issue, but it is important that leaders agree about the core aspects of their shared work and about the larger goal of population health.

How Is Aligned Leadership Achieved?

Although aligned leadership may start at the top, for a project to be truly aligned, it doesn't just stay at the top. Leaders come from those who have a stake in the work at hand and have responsibility for ensuring the project is successful. Public health and primary care integration is based on a team model, and leaders of teams, such as program officers at a public health department or the head nurse at a primary care clinic, will need to be linked and supported by their own leaders. In turn, the project staff will be looking to leaders within their own entities to see how they model working with their partners, which will require an alignment of themselves as well. Sensitivity to issues of power, and attention of leaders to hearing the voices of those closest to the work and need, are common elements of successful teams.

According to the Institute of Medicine Committee (IOM) on Integrating Primary Care and Public Health, aligned leadership (see chapter 2, IOM, 2012, p 60) has the following characteristics:

- It has a broader scope than program direction.
- It entails the ability to clarify roles and ensure accountability.
- It has the capacity to initiate and manage change across organizations.

Broader Than a Program

A specific project or program is a great place to start a collaborative project, but leaders need to see individual programs as steps toward the goal of population health, not as independent projects alone. Aligned leadership should transcend individual initiatives and be a part of a larger framework for working together.

Ability to Clarify Roles and Ensure Accountability

To sustain aligned leadership, partners must maintain mutual accountability. Mutual accountability is in contrast to direct accountability, which occurs with contract relationships or clinical care, for example. To accomplish tasks that are complex, roles need to be clarified and re-clarified, and contributors must fulfill their responsibilities. The way to ensure they do that is for the group to hold each other accountable through mutual or compact accountability.

Beyond accountability, team members will need to be alert to misalignment, which can be caused by individual egos, miscommunication, or just lack of communication. Leaders are often strong-willed and fiercely independent personalities. Although this can create a constructive tension, it is not uncommon for the tensions to produce dysfunctional and disruptive influences as well. See chapter 9 for common challenges in integrative projects and guidance in how to overcome them.

Capacity to Initiate and Manage Change

Integrating primary care and public health is hard, requiring rethinking of roles and relationships and new practices and partners. It is important that each partner assess how these changes will impact their individual organizations, what will be gained and what lost or diminished, and that these changes be incorporated into the wider organizational values and operations. "Organizational alignment occurs when strategic goals and cultural values are mutually supportive, and when key components of an organization are linked and compatible with each other" (Tosti & Jackson, 2001).

Leadership also plays an important role in modeling the expected collaboration in integrative efforts. By demonstrating the respect and flexibility required for managing collaborative work, both inside their organizations and with partners outside, leaders model the behaviors required of other members of their teams.

Danger of "Surface Alignment"

Leadership alignment is about genuinely sharing and crafting common goals and aspirations that will build the project. This means that alignment is based on authentic, open, and honest relationships. Teams like to believe that they are behaving in this way, but too often they are not. Members sit in meetings, nod their heads at appropriate moments, say what they believe others want to hear and what will keep them safe in their positions, and then go out and speak and behave according to their own goals and personal agendas. This is referred to as "surface alignment," which can be catastrophic to your project. The antidote to having surface alignment lies in ensuring that the individuals around the table are demonstrating mutual respect, sharing their personal agendas and insights, working honestly toward integrating their personal agendas with the corporate goals, and releasing those personal agendas that do not fit with their leadership role and the goals of the project.

How Do You Know When You Have Aligned Leadership?

1. Are leadership discussions broader than the day-to-day operations of the program?
2. Do partners clarify roles and accountability as the project progresses?

3. Do partners realign their internal functions to support the broader collaborative, including funding, staffing, visibility, and business culture?

Principle 4: Create Sustainable Systems

Why Are Sustainable Systems Important?

The history of primary care and public health is full of attempts at integration and of early successes, but contains very few examples of sustained individual programs or systems over time. Those leading integration efforts must consider sustainability during the earliest stages of planning and must evaluate and adjust methods of sustainability as circumstances and context evolve. Development of shared infrastructure and a foundation for demonstration of enduring value and impact are the key elements of sustainability (IOM, 2012).

The Guide for Assessing Primary Care and Public Health Resources (ASTHO, 2013; http://www.astho.org/pcphcollaborative/resources/guidance-document/) proposes that integrative projects conduct a four-phased approach toward long-term sustainability:

1. Conduct current-state analysis of available resources—Categorize all resources in order to understand what resources are currently utilized and/or available to the program.
2. Analyze resource gaps—Assess the current state of resources and funding channels in order to identify where gaps exist in the allocation of resources and funds.
3. Develop a resource improvement plan—Use information collected to develop a plan that will better utilize resources and identify strategies to receive new resources through new funding mechanisms. Developing shared infrastructure can be a critical element of the plan.
4. Outline monitoring and evaluation efforts—Ensure that the resource improvement plan is regularly reviewed and updated using data which demonstrates value and impact for the partners, and analysis of program resources.

Resources are more than funds, and can be broken down into five categories:

1. Human: Community health workers, information technology (IT) staff, case managers, public health workers, doctors, nurses, physicians' assistants.
2. Financial: Grants, annual budgets for health departments, community health benefit funding from nonprofit hospitals
3. Data: Surveillance, health IT, evaluations, IT infrastructure
4. Goods: Medication, training and/or promotional material
5. Physical space: Buildings, community centers, offices, clinics

When building your work plan, identify what each organization needs to do to successfully sustain your efforts. Possible capacity-building activities include training or mentoring, coaching, supporting continued education or skill development, and creating the opportunity to try new things. Build a case for any necessary systems or policy changes. Ask yourself questions such as: What are the barriers to sustainability? What changes would reduce those barriers? Who are the audiences we need to convince to make those changes, and what will influence them?

Finally, as your work proceeds, invite others to the table. When conversing with community leaders ask for the names of other stakeholders who might have expressed an interest in the same areas of concern. At each step of the process, be open to unlikely voices that could benefit the project in the long term as well as the short term. Celebrate and share your success to build public support for sustaining your project. If you achieve a goal, make sure you publicize it! Sustainability requires ongoing partnerships, shared infrastructure, and the ongoing demonstration that the project is providing value and impact beyond what the partners could have done alone. (For more information, see chapter 8.)

How Do You Know When You Have Created a Sustainable System?

1. Are integration activities embedded in existing infrastructure when possible, including personnel, policy, and physical structure?
2. Are new, shared resources developed when needed?
3. Is the plan regularly evaluated and updated to demonstrate effective use of resources and achievement of value and impact?
4. Are project partners, their leaders, and public officials publicly committed to continuation of the system?

Principle 5: Share Data and Analysis

Why Is Sharing and Analyzing Data Important?

For the goal of improving population health to be achieved, primary care and public health professionals and the organizations they represent must commit to sharing data and analyses. Integrated population health projects should include open communication—between people and between technologies—for sharing and cooperatively analyzing health-related data. By working together to analyze and interpret primary care and public health data, professionals can improve understanding of the interconnections between individuals and their environments, identify groups within the community in which the need and opportunity for health improvement is greatest, and develop and test models for improving community health.

How Is Shared and Collaborative Use of Data and Analysis Achieved?

Sharing and collaboratively analyzing data is a daunting task. First, there is the question of which data and how much data to share. Sharing everything for the sake of sharing is impractical and can be unethical or even illegal. Rather, leaders of integrated projects need to decide which data will help them understand the health issues in a community, which data will help create projects to

Figure 3-1 ▼

Schematic diagram of steps in sharing data.

(Courtesy of Fred Johnson.)

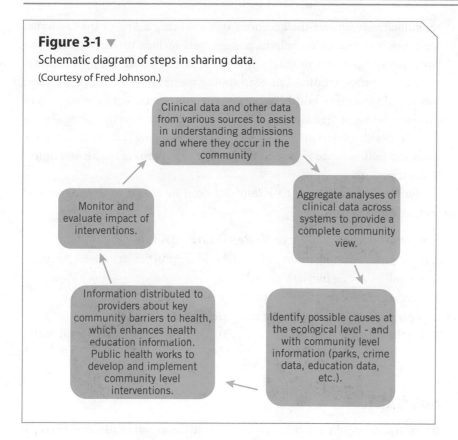

address those issues, and then which data will help them assess the effectiveness of the interventions they have put in place (Fig. 3-1).

It is usually not sufficient to share already-collected data. Integrative project planners also need to assess whether their current data are sufficient to address the project needs. Will ongoing surveillance provide timely information needed for a particular project, and will those data be sufficient to monitor the impact of interventions? Should the participants look for additional sources of data, bearing in mind the quality of those data and the effort they will require for retrieval and use? The increasing availability of large electronic datasets, particularly in clinical medicine, opens new possibilities for measuring population health. The growing availability of data in electronic formats supports expanded joint analysis and long-term cooperation and partnership between public health and primary care.

Project leaders also need to assess internal capacity for data sharing and analysis. Data collection, management, and analysis require specialized skills, and not every organization or team will have members with appropriate expertise. Skilled data analysts will be able to communicate with others about what data will be used and how, and in so doing will help to build trust among group members. Analysts will also be able to gauge the complexity of the data needs of a project and predict if the quality and quantity of data are sufficient to answer the questions that are being asked or the tasks that are being planned. Other helpful professionals include privacy officers who know the complexities of sharing protected health information data across private and public entities, and geomapping specialists who can create maps that reveal patterns of health and community resources. With the support of these specialists, skilled analysts will be able develop reports that bring out the value in health-related information that is already being collected, and allow users and leaders to see a more complete view of patterns of health and illness in the community.

Further discussion of the role of data can be found in the chapters of Section IV.

How Do You Know You Have Shared Data and Analysis?

1. Is the project linking information gathered from different systems for analysis and assessing impact?
2. Have agreements been forged to ensure protection and security of data and to permit routine data-sharing and analysis?
3. Are the data reviewed to ensure they are useful in demonstrating value and impact?

SUMMARY

By incorporating the five principles of integration, communities and primary care and public health groups can come together to do what none can do alone: sustainably improve the health of the populations they serve.

REFERENCES

Centers for Disease Control and Prevention. Principles of community engagement, 1st ed.). Atlanta: CDC/ATSDR Committee on Community Engagement, 1997.

Clinical and Translational Science Awards Consortium, Community Engagement Key Function Committee Task Force on the Principles of Community Engagement. Principles of Community Engagement, 2nd ed. Bethesda, MD: National Institutes of Health, 2011. http://www.atsdr.cdc.gov/

Institute of Medicine. Defining Primary Care: An Interim Report. The National Academies Press. Washington, DC, 1994. www.nap.edu/openbook. php?record_id=9153&page=1

Institute of Medicine. Primary Care and Public Health: Exploring Integration to Improve Population Health. Washington, DC. Institute of Medicine of the National Academies. http://www.iom.edu/Reports/2012/ Primary-Care-and-Public-Health.aspx. Accessed March 28, 2012.

Kindig D, Stoddart G. What is Population Health? Am J Public Health 2003; 93 (3): 380–383.

Tosti DT, Jackson SF: Organizational Alignment. Novato, CA: iChangeWorld Consulting, 2001. http://www.ichangeworld.com/docs/icwOA0303.pdf

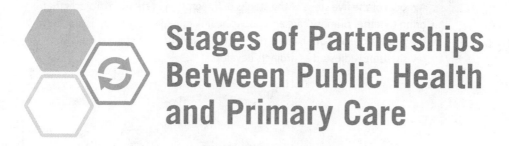

Chapter 4

Stages of Partnerships Between Public Health and Primary Care

J. LLOYD MICHENER AND BRIAN C. CASTRUCCI

Integrating primary care and public health is a powerful tool for improving the health of communities. However, understanding the values and principles behind integration is not enough: You must put that knowledge into action. This chapter discusses the stages that health care and public health teams commonly experience as they move from initial meetings to fully engaged partnerships. These stages are based on the experience and comments of hundreds of teams of clinicians, public health officers, and community members from across the country. However, much as these stages appear to be common experiences, it is also clear that communities differ, and can journey through the stages at different speeds. The guidance provided here is intended to provide practical information on working together and on helping to avoid common misunderstandings.

The process of integrating primary care and public health efforts involves five stages (Fig. 4-1):

1. Organize and prepare
2. Plan and prioritize
3. Implement
4. Monitor and evaluate
5. Celebrate and share

The complex processes of change can be made more manageable by working through these five stages of integration in sequence. Evaluating and improving efforts can be made easier by having an understanding of the process of change.

A few key points are critical to remember: The stages discussed here are discrete and unique; each one must be considered during the process of integration work. Each step is important and should be given sufficient attention. Rushing through preparations or evaluations will end up doing more harm than good. Each stage also needs to be done in a way that is mindful of the

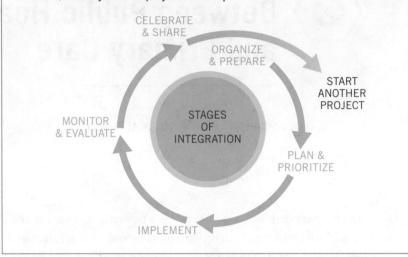

Figure 4-1 ▼

A model of the five steps of the stages of integration in creating projects that bring together primary care and public health activities. Each step is linked to the step before and after, indicating that the work of each stage is built upon, revisited, and adjusted as projects develop.

previous stage—its foundation—and of how the current work will serve as a stepping stone for the stage to come.

However, the five stages are interconnected and iterative. By their nature, integration projects are recursive, and work done at each stage will need to be adjusted in response to how plans and resources are actually coming together.

STAGE 1: ORGANIZE AND PREPARE

Overview

The first stage—organizing and preparing—is the one in which you do an internal examination of why you are interested in working with your partners.

Know the Data

The first step is to identify the population health concerns that will be addressed. In the data you have access to, are trends present that raise concerns? Has there been an increase in a specific chronic disease over the past few years, or the number of preterm deliveries among minority women in your constituency, or are you preparing for flu season and are concerned over the number of influenza cases during the past years in older adults? Before approaching a partner about a project, identify three to four health issues that you want to address. Individual entities need to identify the health issues that they are interested in addressing before they come to a partnership table. It is important that each partner has an idea of what his or her own data means, and which health issues each partner is passionate about addressing.

Identify Potential Partners

Once you have identified a few health issues that you are willing to put time and effort toward, it is time to think about which partners you could engage with. Building collaborative teams that bring together different disciplines can be a challenge. What makes building integration teams possible is that the end result—improved community health—is both a shared value and shared goal for diverse groups. When working on identifying partners for a project to integrate primary care and public health, a few guidelines and processes are good to keep in mind.

First, reach out to those you know. Convincing people to make time for a new project will be easier if you are known and respected. Coming armed with clear information about your goals and evidence will persuade people that the goals are realistic and achievable. In turn, your colleagues will have their own networks and affiliations and, once on board, will be able to help in finding additional partners who can solidify and amplify the integration effort.

Many teams in public health and primary care will already be overcommitted, so when you reach out to them, you need to describe how collaborating on an integration project will be worth the time and effort and will yield truly meaningful rewards, both for them and for the community as a whole. Once you reach out, if you don't get a response as immediately as you would like, don't take offense. Remember, your partners are as busy as you are.

Finding the right public health and primary care partners can be a critical factor, sometimes requiring reaching out to groups and individuals previously unknown. Working with national and then state associations can help identify the right local contacts (Box 4-1).

Be open about engaging partners and stakeholders who might not be included on your initial list of potential partners, but who might end up being powerful players in your efforts, including nonprofit organizations such as the following:

- Agriculture, food, and nutrition organizations
- Addiction and substance abuse organizations
- Chambers of commerce
- Community improvement organizations
- Faith-based organizations
- Housing organizations
- Mental health and crisis services
- Public safety organizations

See chapter 3 for ideas on how to engage your community.

Tip

Refer to Guidestar, a comprehensive database to charities and not-for-profit organizations in the United States, to find possible partners (http://www.guidestar.org).

Box 4-1 | Resources for Finding Public Health and Primary Care Partners

Resources for identifying local clinicians or public health officials as potential partners to integration projects. National organizations are listed herein, but many will have state chapters that can be very helpful.

Primary care

- American Academy of Family Physicians (http://www.aafp.org/)
- American Academy of Pediatrics (www.aap.org/)
- Academic Pediatric Association (https://www.academicpeds.org/)
- American College of Physicians (https://www.acponline.org/)
- American Medical Association (http://www.ama-assn.org/ama)
- National Association of Rural Health Clinics (http://narhc.org/)
- National Association of Community Health Centers (http://www.nachc.com/)

Public health

- Association of State and Territorial Health Officials (http://www.astho.org/)
- American Public Health Association (http://apha.org/)
- National Association of City and County Health Officials (http://www.naccho.org)

How Do You Know You Have Completed the First Stage of an Integrative Project?

1. Have you identified three to four health issues in which you are willing to invest time and energy?
   a. If not, then spend some time looking at the data and talking to colleagues, and the members of the population you serve.
2. Are your partners inclusive of leaders in:
   a. Public health? If not, contact your local health department. Not sure who that is? Visit NACCHO.org or ASTHO.org for help.
   b. Primary care? For medical groups, there isn't a standard answer. It is important to know your community landscape. As a start, is there a group of physicians with whom you could start a conversation? Not sure who that might be? Visit the practicalplaybook.org for help in identifying your primary care partner through national associations.
   c. The wider community? See chapter 3 for advice about how to engage the community.

STAGE 2: PLAN AND PRIORITIZE

Overview

This stage is your call to action. You have identified a few health issues that are important to you, have identified potential partners, and are ready to meet your partners. During this stage you will identify the health issue that you want to address as partners and develop tools to help your project succeed.

First Contact

Your first meeting should be simple. To some extent, the greater the variety of people involved in an integration project, the stronger it will ultimately be. However, it is generally wise to start with a number of people that can fit around a coffee table. Meet in a place that is easy to find, and use the time to get to know your partners. Communities have places where groups can come together to work on issues of common concern. Whether that is a restaurant or social setting, take advantage of the community history—this could become a historic moment! Share common frustrations and motivations, but do not expect to walk away from an initial meeting with a solid agreement or plan. The goal of the first meeting should be to demonstrate respect, gain an appreciation for your new partners, and arrange a follow-up meeting.

Add More Chairs

At subsequent meetings, think about who else needs to be at the table to bring new points of view to the process; in this way you will often be able to predict—and sometimes prevent—potential roadblocks and challenges to integration efforts. Bringing in people who are not *directly* involved in health care will present its own challenge in convincing such people that the effort will be worthwhile. In the end, laying broader foundational groundwork for the project will yield a stronger outcome. When meeting potential partners, particularly those who don't know you or those who are not familiar with working on health issues, remember to listen as much as you talk. By actively asking about *their* concerns, constraints, and questions, you'll set up the project as an effort focused on others and on working in a truly collaborative manner.

As you meet, ensure that everyone on the team understands why the project is important. The process of working together should serve as a reminder of what matters to you and your partners. Clearly defining a shared goal of population health will help keep you on track and is discussed later in this chapter. Bring stakeholders for your issue to the table and get their guidance on high-risk and high-need populations. Review location-based data, including, if available, a spatial analysis to see what specific geographic areas are in need, and population stratification by race/ethnicity and other relevant subgroups. In addition, consider funding sources related to your health outcome to determine the reach that is feasible for your project.

Create a Vision Statement

Ask yourself what you are trying to achieve both personally, and as part of a coalition. This step is linked with the next: identifying a shared goal. In fact, it is common to formulate a goal and then to create a brief vision statement, which will be a touchstone during the process, to ensure that the refined goal and the vision statement are still closely aligned. Also, establishing a short vision statement can assist in fostering and maintaining aligned leadership around your health issue. That said, there is a risk in spending so much time writing statements that harder work is avoided; strive for a concise statement of your common vision. "Thriving people living healthy lifestyles in a vibrant community" is the vision statement that emerged from the planning process led by the Northern Kentucky Health Department (Northern Kentucky Health Department and the MAPP Leadership Team, 2009).

Identify a Shared Goal

As the first step in identifying an issue together, teams have found that it is useful to begin by gathering, sharing, and studying available data on health issues that are affecting patients and their communities. In stage 1, you identified several health issues based on the available data; now is a good time to bring in that information. Primary care clinicians will often know which issues are most critical to the patients in their practices, whereas public health officials will be familiar with the health problems that are most important in their communities. Those perspectives may align, but they may also be widely divergent. Be open; make sure that your personal preferences don't trump the true needs of the community. Rather than choose an initial area of focus quickly, or assume agreement on priorities, successful teams have thought about the following:

- Which problems appear to be most urgent in the community?
- Which problems are recognized within the community?
- Which problems have advocates who can become partners in an integration effort?

Picking an issue that meets these three criteria, and is jointly agreed upon, is a key to success. This first step, of selecting a health issue, requires gathering data and perspectives and is discussed in greater depth in the chapters of Section IV.

Plans to address health problems in a community should be based on specific data that maps out the dimensions of the problem. In other words, begin working on integration projects by compiling and analyzing data about the health problem, and let those data help determine the pathway to a solution. Being able to and taking the time to drill into the data can help identify groups particularly affected, and whose counsel can be sought, thereby avoiding interventions that target the wrong audience. Rates of obesity and diabetes, for instance, are not evenly distributed across states, communities, or neighborhoods, nor by age, gender, race, or ethnic group. Knowing who you are trying to help allows interventions to be done with greater engagement and precision.

Clinicians can draw data from their own practices and often can pool data from other practices, a process made easier when practices are organized into networks. Public health officials can draw from a wide set of sources to assess the most pressing health issues in the community, from community health needs assessments to conversations with key stakeholders. The data used to fill out the picture of the community can be both quantitative and qualitative, and it can come from a huge variety of local, state, regional, or national sources. Think beyond traditional data sources. Rich, diverse data will not only help paint a more detailed and accurate picture of the characteristics of a health problem, but can also be key elements in creating an effective strategy.

There will likely be many different issues that could be effectively addressed through an integrative project. However, once the data are compiled, shared, and analyzed, the problem—or health outcome—will need to be identified to focus the project. You may have a health outcome that you want to address, but try to remain open to other ideas. By working with partners, you may uncover issues that everyone in the partnership would benefit from working on.

Identify Potential Strategies

As you meet with your partners, think about where you want the project to be in 2 or 3 years, and what impact you want to make in your community. The nature of your issue will define the overarching strategy of your project. For example, if you are addressing a health system issue, you may need to focus on changing something within the health system, such as the addition of case managers or care coordinators to ensure continuity and improved quality of care. However, if you are focusing on a community issue, your solution may need to focus on adding resources, such as parks and sidewalks for safe recreation. As you identify your issue, consider the following questions:

- Is this a health care matter, a regulatory concern, a public policy initiative, a legal conundrum, and/or a resource gap problem?
- Who does this health issue impact? Is it a community-wide issue, or does it only affect certain groups?
- What defines the community or location facing the issue?
- What has worked in the past? What has failed?
- Are there local projects in the works that address the same issue?
- Are there other community partners who should be involved?
- What resources are available to help to achieve these goals?
- Does this initiative require a solution from a large organization?
- Can we achieve early wins?
- What funding sources are available?

Identify Resources

- Identify a "champion" who can increase your value and help you accomplish goals.
- Identify the best resources to fill gaps and prepare a request for support. Include any evidence you possess to demonstrate that the need you have identified is real.

- Make your requests for resources as specific as possible but also reasonable enough to be achieved.
- Do your homework. Assure that stated facts are substantiated.

Do you need support in the form of advocacy, cooperation, or funding? If so, you'll have to pitch your project. Although having to approach someone in your community with an "ask" can be daunting, it is possible! See chapter 7 for tips on making the "ask."

Develop a Logic Model

A logic model will provide a visual framework for your project, including the intended outcomes of your initiative (WK Kellogg Foundation, 2006).

A logic model paints a picture of how your effort will achieve your shared goal of population health. It explains the issue, discusses applicable strategies and potential solutions, and shows the intended results. A logic model will help keep the project focused (Fig. 4-2).

Create a Work Plan

Out of a logic model you can develop a more detailed work plan to help guide your team. A well-informed work plan should include the following:

- Budget and resource allocations
- Outcomes and measures of achievement
- Communication activities
- Roles and responsibilities

Although identifying resources is important, it is equally important to identify sections of your project that do not need funding. Policy development and advocacy generally require fewer resources, but can have considerable impact. Remember to include costs for media dissemination, including travel expenses, seminar and webinar bridge lines, printing and mailing of newsletters, reports, books, manuals, and any other printed documents. This will help ensure that your project is recognized and is sustainable (Fig. 4-3; Box 4-2).

Monitoring and Evaluating Success

It's essential to develop an evaluation plan at the beginning of your project. This will help you to assess your project's success or failure. While drafting your evaluation plan, be sure to clearly define each element to be assessed. Your short-term objectives might include an evaluation of the process of implementing your strategies. For example, if you are running an education project, you might ask whether patients are being referred to classes and whether patients are acting on these referrals. At the same time, your long-term objectives might include evaluation of the impact on health outcomes. It will be important to determine your methods, how you'll measure the results, and how you will interpret success (for a more detailed discussion, see chapter 22).

How Do You Know You Have Completed the Second Stage of an Integrative Project?

1. Do you have data that:
   a. Demonstrate the current state of the problem?
   b. Can be used to track change over time?
      (1). If yes, how do you know? If unsure, see Section IV.
2. Are your meetings in places and at times convenient to the partners?
   a. If not, consider taking turns hosting the meeting.
3. While working with your partner, have you identified a health issue that:
   a. Is urgent and recognized within in the community?
   b. Is something that all partners are concerned about?

Figure 4-2 ▼

Draft of logic model developed by the Durham Familiar Faces Collaborative, a group of about 50 local medical, social service, and law enforcement agencies who have collaborated to address solutions to the problem of "familiar faces," or people who are seen repeatedly in ERs and jails and are disproportionately driving up costs without a solution to their core problems.

CONTEXT	ORGANIZATION	STRATEGIES	TACTICS	RESULTS
System Characteristics Separate BH and PH systems w/some local integration (shared staff, dual HIT access) One hospital system w/2 hospitals, X# of Medicaid enrollees, rapidly shifting regulatory, economic, and political environment New payer incentives to increase quality of care, improve outcomes, contain cost **Client Characteristics** High-need, high-cost adult Medicaid population with SMI and PH chronic diseases, unable to meet basic needs, engaged with multiple safety-net services **Partners*** Medical, behavioral health, social services, and EMS service providers, law enforcement, public health, hospital system, BH Medicaid MCO, NPCC, Medicaid network **Resources** Support from leadership of key stakeholders, infrastructure of partner agencies, CIT, existing business relationships, clinical expertise, existing programs for complex patients, new ACA patient navigators	**Clarify Needs and Stakeholders** **Convene** partners **Identify** pilot target population Establish safeguards to **protest PHI** Develop **process to improve coordination** **Inventory exiting resources and gaps** Establish **work groups** Develop **evaluation plan** **Refine** patient stratification and identification **strategies** --- **Inclusion Criteria** Cross-over among *at least 3* partner agencies FF list ***AND*** Medicaid **OR** no insurance	**Patient/Provider Level** • Patient outreach and engagement • Referral to services and supports • Consistent reinforcement of goals across providers • Increase identification of medical utilization driven by BH conditions • Improve clinical decisions in Emergency Depts. • Standardize data collection across agencies • Increase accountability **Systems Level** • Expand HIT capacity across system • Develop hospital ED diversion for BH crisis • Increase coordination across partner agencies • Align incentives • Impact social determinations of disease • Strength safety-net providers • Remove unnecessary barriers to exchange of PHI • Review and re-align institutional policies that impede attainment of objectives	**Patient/Provider Level** Embed Behavioral Health CM in ED • Establish new Care Review process • Establish process for creating and sharing care plans • Use care plans and case conferencing to highlight BH driving utilization • Increase utilization of Prescription Monitoring Program (CSRS) and plans • Develop template for data reporting • Develop clear roles for "action teams" **Systems Level** • Use new EHR (EPIC) in hospitals to deliver care plans • Enable EMS ED diversion to DCA w/ new protocols and payment model • Expand access to HIT through COACH and EPIC • Support efforts to address social determinates • Develop patient registry clearinghouse • Review/revise patient satisfaction survey process	**Outcomes** Decreased hospital utilization Increased PCP utilization Reduced harmful narcotic prescribing Reduced unnecessary imaging Increased patient and provider satisfaction Evidence to inform practice improvement --- **AIMS** Improved care quality Improved health outcomes Improved patient experience Reduced costs

c. Has advocates who can become partners in an integration effort?
      (1). If yes, how do you know? If unsure, see Section IV.
4. Is there agreement on an overarching vision for your work together?
5. Do project members know who may be working on the issue already, and/or whose resources may be brought to bear?
6. Has a range of strategies been considered, from which one or a few have been selected that have a champion and can provide early wins?
7. Do you have a project logic model and work plan?

STAGE 3: IMPLEMENT

Overview

Throughout this stage of integration, you will launch and sustain methods for effective project management, including ongoing communication strategies with your partners. Having drafted your work plan, which includes an evaluation plan, you can begin monitoring your progress. Depending upon the scope of your project, this stage could take months, or years. This stage is where you "stay the course," keeping as the end goal your initial shared goal of population health. There will be challenges to your work, but with sustained energy and commitment these challenges may become detours, but they will not become roadblocks.

Don't Be Afraid to Start, and Be Prepared to Shift

You have developed several helpful project management tools—project strategies, logic model, and a project work plan. Now it is time to put those tools to use. Many collaborations are so concerned with getting the planning right that they fail to act. Don't be afraid to begin your work, and be open to learning

Figure 4-3 ▶
Sample work plan.

November 1st 2013 – October 31st 2014

Activity	Specifics	Key Personnel	Indicators of Completion	Results (as at 11/31/14)	Comments	Budget	Year											
							Q1			Q2			Q3			Q4		
							Nov.	Dec.	Jan.	Feb.	Mar.	Apr.	May	Jun	Jul	Aug	Sep	Oct
Project Development																		
Project Implementation																		
Project Media & Communications																		
Partner Coordination																		
Project Management																		

as you go. As you work together your understanding of the needs of the community will deepen, and you will be able to refine your strategy. As the needs of your population change, so will your project strategies, and your plan will need to be nimble enough for those shifts.

Identify Champions

Each organization should identify a project champion to help ensure that the project stays the course. Staffing the project is a critical resource to sustaining the project. These champions are beyond the "front-line implementers" of your project; like the providers who are serving the population, they are individuals who are able to staff the project and monitor progress. They do not have to be individuals in high-level management, but they do need to be able to speak on behalf of management.

Generating Data

You will need to generate data on an ongoing basis to see if your project is being implemented as expected, what's getting in the way if not, and whether the results of implementation are what you expected. A mix of qualitative and quantitative data is usually going to be your best bet for measuring what's happening and understanding why it's happening.

Speaking the Same Language

Every organization has a unique set of labels, terms, and acronyms. If possible, avoid describing your program with an acronym. Differences in language or terminology may be seemingly insignificant, but they can become increasingly problematic over time. Take time to define labels and programs in ways and terms that are mutually acceptable, and be comfortable creating and promoting new terms. See chapter 6 for additional suggestions on the use of language within integrative projects.

Staying Connected

You should hold physical meetings as often as practical and necessary. Face-to-face meetings can help foster a sense of trust and respect. When meeting face-to-face, there are a few suggested guidelines, which are sometimes most notable for being forgotten.

- Keep meetings short. If longer than 90 minutes, offer a short break in the middle.
- Prepare an agenda (Fig. 4-4). Send an agenda several days in advance and ask for any additions or edits.
- Define the group's purpose, which should focus on a single issue.
- Define expectations and ground rules.
- Consider creating a rotating host or leader position.
- Don't allow anyone to stay in the hot seat for more than 15 minutes, unless group conscience dictates otherwise.

Figure 4-4 ▶
Sample telecon agenda and meeting notes template.

The 1234 Working Group Meeting

10:00am – 12:00noon

Monday, December 9, 2013

The Pleasantville County Chamber of Commerce

Participants:

1. Joe Baker, Pleasantville County Health Department Director
2. Kimberly Stonebraker, Pleasantville County Health Department, Health Educator
3. Tammy Sneed, Pleasantville Hospital, Communications Officer
4. Brian McKensie, Pleasantville Hospital, Quality Improvement Officer
5. Mark Jacobs, Social Services Department, Case Manager
6. Lana Smith, Pleasantville University, Research Assistant

Agenda

Item	Agreement/Outcome/Steps	Person Responsible	Deadline

Next Meeting Date, Time, and Location:

- Maintain records of your meetings and decisions. Take notes. This should not be an exhaustive process. Capture the main action items. If detailed project memory is important, consider recording your meetings.
- Share notes. Aim to send notes to the group within a few business days. This will help keep next steps top of mind.

When meeting is not practical, there are innovative forums you can use to stay connected. Virtual applications such as Dropbox, Google Docs, and SharePoint are innovative methods of convening and interacting that can provide freedom to see issues from new perspectives, to respond online when a face-to-face meeting is not possible, and to find new solutions.

The *Practical Playbook* website (https://practicalplaybook.org) is developing a portal for your group to use when collaborating on community health issues. You can find people in other communities who are working on the same problems and share the same interests, lessons learned, data, and resources.

Use email as a tool to keep conversation flowing outside of meetings. Follow these guidelines to ensure success:

- Preface each subject line with [Group Name] in brackets to help members easily scan their in-boxes.
- Make sure the subject clearly relates to the message.
- If an email discussion leads to a change in topics, change the subject line to prevent confusion and idea loss.
- Keep emails concise—even telegraphic.

How Do You Know That You Have Completed the Third Stage of an Integrative Project?

1. Are regular meetings being held to discuss how the project is progressing?
2. Has each partner identified a champion who acts as the point person on the project?
3. Are communication channels an embedded part of the project?

STAGE 4: MONITOR AND EVALUATE

Overview

You monitor and evaluate a project to understand if things are going as planned. It is not meant to find fault or assess blame. You may have to remind partners of this who feel threatened by this stage of integration. Evaluations should answer questions of interest to partners, political and community leaders, and funders in a timely and convincing fashion. Designing and implementing a useful assessment requires ongoing collaboration among assessors and stakeholders. When done right, it can be used to answer a wide variety of questions that help partnerships carry out their work more effectively and efficiently. Use the following guidance to drive your evaluation plan.

Defining Evaluation

Program evaluation has been defined as, "the systematic collection of information about the activities, characteristics, and outcomes of programs for use by people to reduce uncertainties, improve effectiveness, and make decisions" (Patton, 1986). When people think of program assessment, they generally think about whether or not a program has achieved its goals. However, evaluation can be used to answer a wide variety of questions, such as how the program achieved its desired outcomes, the pros and cons of the way you implemented the program, and why things went awry or might be done better. Evaluation is commonly thought to encompass five different types of assessment:

1. *Process evaluation* tells you whether or not a program was implemented as envisioned.
2. *Formative evaluation* provides a wide variety of information to help you design and modify a program.
3. *Outcome evaluation* assesses the extent to which a program achieved its desired outcomes.
4. *Impact evaluation* asks whether or not the program had an ultimate long-term impact.
5. *Summative evaluation* assesses the overall value of a program and highlights lessons learned.

Understanding the Need for Evaluation

Program evaluation is a learning tool to be used when you want to understand what's happening and why. However, there can be a number of different reasons for undertaking this activity, including the desire to do the following:

- Track how well you are implementing the program.
- Learn whether or not your program is successful.
- Understand what went well, what didn't, and why.
- Make changes to the program along the way.
- Determine the strength of your partnership.
- Decide what to do once the grant period is over.
- Seek additional funding.
- Provide support for individual partners to seek funding for their own.
- Document what you have done for the community as an aid to strengthening their support.
- Present and/or publish in professional, practice, or other settings.

Evaluation can clarify partner goals and areas of alignment and disagreement. It can also provide information necessary to create program sustainability, identify barriers to sharing data and resources, and highlight failures and successes in community engagement. The integration principles, then, are some of the "whys" of evaluation.

Implementing an Evaluation Plan

How and when will you evaluate your project? Who will conduct the evaluation? The answers to these questions should be based on what you want to know, and why you want to know it. Create your evaluation plan early to ensure that you have the data you need, when you need it.

As noted, evaluation often takes the form of listing what was done, rather than answering the questions you really need answered. It's often easier to list activities completed than it is to figure out whether you achieved an outcome. However, trying to answer the hard questions—even if definitions and data are a little "squishier" than when counting "beans"—will ultimately yield more useful evaluation. If your staff can't take on a true evaluation, and you don't have resources to hire someone new, see if your partners can help.

When developing an evaluation plan, ask yourself the following questions:

- What resources can you, your partners, or your community provide to help carry out the evaluation?
- What type of data are required to answer your inquiries? Will these data be convincing to the partners?
- How can you collect stories that illustrate the impact of the project, and provide a human dimension to the data?
- How can you conduct the evaluation in a way that is feasible and not excessively burdensome for the program?
- When do you need your answers? Is there a deadline you must meet?
- Does your evaluator or evaluation team have the necessary skills to collect and analyze the data involved in your project?
- Will your evaluator work collaboratively and iteratively to make sure that the evaluation answers the important questions?
- Can you present the evaluation in a way that will be convincing to your intended audience, but not overly onerous for your program?

Different datasets provide different information about the health of the public. When used together, these data provide exceptional insight to opportunities for making an impact on population health. The growing availability of data in electronic formats has expanded cooperation and partnership between public health and primary care. Available data range from encounter data to publicly available datasets that address issues of health behavior, clinical status, and health expenditures. Analysis of these data can support partnerships at each stage of integration; however, it can also present a number of challenges. Remember: Improving community health begins with better utilization and understanding of this data. See chapters 23 and 24 for more detailed information.

Defining the Role of Data

Data are pieces of information that must be transformed in order to become useful. As such, they come in multiple shapes and forms. Common data used in integration projects include: community health status data collected through public health surveillance, health care quality data extracted from medical records, data from opinion polling carried out using validated survey methods, and qualitative data collected from meetings and interviews. Do you know the data that your community is concerned about and interested in? It is important that you continue to provide avenues of community input. For more guidance on how to engage your community, see chapter 3. For additional guidance on the role of data, see Section IV and chapter 22.

Modifying Evaluation Plans

If you discover that things are not going according to your plan (an almost universal experience), don't take an attitude of blame. It may be that the project goals are unrealistic and need to be adjusted. Sometimes, even a simple fix can get you back on track. Get together as a team and try to understand why things aren't going as expected. Your partners may have no problem refining their work based on evaluation results. However, they may be resistant to change. Pick your battles.

If you think changes are needed, engage partners in a concrete, grounded discussion about the action implications of the evaluation findings. If things don't improve, analyze where the resistance to change might be coming from. Once you discover the root of your partner's resistance, you'll be better equipped to address it. Sometimes working together may require having a difficult conversation with your partners For more information about such conversations, see chapter 5.

How Do You Know You Have Completed the Fourth Stage of an Integrative Project?

This is a bit of a trick question. Monitoring and evaluation really shouldn't have an end point. From the onset of your project, you should be looking at data and thinking about what you want to change, how you want to change it, and what you will do to measure your impact. Here is a checklist to ensure you are on the right track with your monitoring and evaluation efforts.

1. As the project proceeds, are you capturing the data and stories that identify what is working and for whom, and where the project may be falling short of expectations?
2. Are you adjusting the plans to build on successes, and to modify the plan as needed?
3. Are the data helping identify the benefits of the program, so that a strong case for sustainability can be made?

STAGE 5: CELEBRATE AND SHARE

Overview

Do not wait until the end of the project to share your success and lessons learned. As your project develops, identify your early wins and share them!

It's common during the course of work on one issue for a stakeholder to raise a different concern that has been intractable, due mainly to a lack of community awareness. Once a successful strategy has concluded, take advantage of the success and begin conversations about a more complex problem.

Sharing Stories and Outcomes

Sometimes people forget to share project outcomes with those involved. Don't make that mistake. Even if things didn't go exactly as you planned, there will be things to celebrate in your data and stories, including the lessons you learned from what went wrong. Integrate data into your celebration.

The data that are going to fascinate the audience for a peer-reviewed journal are likely not the same data that are going to fascinate medical providers, which are likely not the same as those that are going to fascinate community leaders. Even if these groups are interested in the same data, they may respond to different ways of presenting the data (e.g., figures vs. maps vs. tables) and to different language (watch for scientific jargon when you're not writing for a scientific population). The best way to find out what data your audience wants and in what format is to ask them.

Work With the Media

There are a variety of ways to celebrate and share your success. If you aren't sure where to start, view these tips:

- Ask local personalities or political figures to speak about your project.
- Contribute articles to a professional journal or newsletter in your field.
- Present at community events.
- Share your project at a professional conference.
- Report your success at a meeting or event.
- Distribute news releases.
- Produce promotional videos.
- Start a blog.
- Publish articles online using key words that help search engines share your information.
- Offer webinars for potential adapters/adopters.
- Write and publish a final report.
- Host a media gallery on your webpage.

For more ideas on how to make the media work for you, see chapter 11.

How Do You Know When You Have Completed the Fifth Stage of an Integrative Project?

1. Do you regularly celebrate successes with partners and the wider community?
   a. If not, see chapter 11 for tips on how to leverage media.
2. Are the results of the program shared with others in the community in a way they can be understood and valued, especially by all who may benefit from it?

a. If you aren't sure, see chapter 3 for how to engage your community.

3. Does the project prepare the group to take on another, more complex project?

a. If yes, then go back to stage 1 to start organizing your next project!

b. If you are not sure, it's probably time to continue with this project a while longer.

NOW WHAT?

Remember that the stages of integration are iterative, a cyclical and intersecting process. In essence, the project cycle never finishes, but as you go through the process, your partnerships and projects evolve. In the lifespan of your project you may go through the project stages more than once, or, after one cycle you may have identified your next project. There is *always* more to do.

REFERENCES

Institute of Medicine. Primary Care and Public Health: Exploring Integration to Improve Population Health. Institute of Medicine of the National Academies. http://www.iom.edu/Reports/2012/Primary-Care-and-Public-Health.aspx. Accessed Nov 25, 2013.

Northern Kentucky Health Department and the MAPP Leadership Team. Vision for a Healthy and Vibrant Community. Northern Kentucky Health Department. 2009. http://www.nkyhealth.org/docs/DDH/MAPPReport_final.pdf

Patton MQ. Utilization-Focused Evaluation. Sage: Newbury Park, CA, 1986.

W.K. Kellogg Foundation: Logic Model Development Guide. Feb 2, 2006. http://www.wkkf.org/resource-directory/resource/2006/02/wk-kellogg-foundation-logic-model-development-guide. Accessed Nov 4, 2014.

Working Together

Chapter 5

How to Have Difficult Conversations

JUSTINE STRAND DE OLIVEIRA

Across all types of business and industry, work is accomplished and goals are reached through the use of working groups and teams. High-tech startups, food services, and design and marketing firms all organize work in groups: Even health care, long the province of the lone physician, is now a team sport. The value of group work lies in the synergy of different viewpoints and perspectives being brought to bear on complex challenges. Yet those same valuable perspectives can lead to maddening disagreements when differences of opinion lead to impasse.

We've all been there. Working with a team of people from diverse backgrounds, on an exciting project that you feel passionately about. Things are going well . . . until:

- A team member just isn't pulling her weight. Everyone else is working hard and meeting deadlines, but she always has an excuse—she was busy (aren't we all?), she had a competing priority, and, and, and . . .
- A team member increasingly acts like he "owns" the project. No one else has any useful ideas—it's his way or the highway. And to make things worse, he takes credit for everything.
- A small group within the team, who share a discipline, don't believe in a fundamental concept that underpins the project. It just has never been on their radar screen, and they can't seem to "see" it.
- A small group from a shared background wants to take the project in an entirely different direction than the rest of the group, and digs their collective heels in to resist the rest of the group.

In spite of this, we can all recount the value of working with people from different backgrounds and experience, gaining ground through inviting a diversity of viewpoints, seeing new pathways by having many sets of eyes on a problem, and engaging productive brainstorming to find solutions. We don't tend to identify as many fresh, new ideas when we only talk with people who think like us. It's wonderful to be part of a high-performing team doing meaningful work that makes a difference in people's lives. It's easy to resolve disagreements when the outcomes aren't that important to us. But when we are passionate about the work, and feel strongly about an approach or decision, it's not so easy to accede to others who we believe are moving in the wrong direction.

When our initial attempts to resolve a disagreement fail, we often turn to understandable, but unproductive, approaches. Often the first step we take is to patiently explain why the other person is wrong—which can be a toxic approach when they feel as passionately as we do, but are diametrically opposed to our approach. We try to distill things down to "just the facts" and make logical arguments for our position. When that fails, the next step may be to dig in our heels and prepare for combat. Or we may withdraw from contributing to the project. It's easy to forget that we can never see the world through the other person's eyes, and our assumptions about their motivation and intentions may not be accurate. Worst of all, we lose sight of what we were trying to accomplish in the first place (Weeks, 2008).

It's true that everyone brings a variety of motivations to the table. Although all may share the lofty goals identified by the group, other motivations may be at play to varying degrees. People are motivated by power, prestige and control, by the need for acceptance and belonging, by financial pressure, or by expectations of family, friends, and colleagues. There may be troubled relationships with others due to prior events we're unaware of, visceral reactions to seemingly innocuous things because of past experiences and beliefs that are opaque to us. The biggest black box? Our own deep-seated beliefs and motives, which may be outside our conscious awareness.

Nowhere are the potential challenges of group work more evident than in extremely diverse groups working together on community problems. When public health and primary care come together, they each bring their own set of language, goals, and values. These differences are what supports dynamic partnerships, but also can create challenges in working together.

How can we approach these challenges without derailing work when passionate disagreements arise? When groups have cooperative goals, it's important to air disagreements in order to achieve the best outcomes. "Constructive controversy" is a characteristic of well-functioning teams (Alper et al., 1998). How can we disagree without being disagreeable, building and sustaining positive relationships with our partners? First, take a learning perspective and try to understand the viewpoint you see as problematic. Ask for clarification and listen deeply without leaping to assumptions. Maintain equanimity and avoid going into combat mode.

What follows are some proven approaches and tips from the business literature and beyond. Keep in mind it is a journey of self-awareness and discovery, and none of us ever arrives at perfection in our human interactions. We can improve or enhance our ability to manage difficult conversations, and most importantly, build social capital with our partners that will make our work together more effective and enjoyable going forward. When groups work well, they identify innovative solutions to intractable problems. Through dynamic interplay, balancing passion with open-mindedness, teams often identify solutions that none of them individually could have imagined.

The familiar situations mentioned above aren't just annoying, they're exasperating! Some examples are: Free riding, letting others do the work while contributing nothing. Free riding's evil twin, micromanagement and over-control. Responsibility bias: the person who takes credit for the group's accomplishments, perhaps even believing they were the only one doing any real work. Inability to recognize problems that are important to others—a common example is a member of the majority culture who believes discrimination and bias don't exist. The person who has a dogmatic belief in his own approach and tries to derail the group's work in a dogged effort to do things his way. All of these situations can arise in primary care-public health teams.

It's so hard to take a deep breath (or ten) and take a cool, calm approach to situations like these. What to do? Here are some common themes and tips:

Tips

1. Take a deep breath and a step back—and ask yourself some questions:
   - ✔ Who is the person you need to talk with? How can you better understand their perspective?
   - ✔ Think about assumptions you may have about their intentions.
   - ✔ What would be the ideal outcome of the conversation?
   - ✔ How might you have contributed to the problem? How have they?
2. Come to the conversation with a desire to learn, and open the dialogue with that approach.
   - ✔ Adopt a neutral tone: "I wonder if we could talk about our shared goals for the project."
   - ✔ Begin with the positive: "The project has been going really well, and I'm excited about the changes we'll be able to achieve for our community."
3. Maintain positive regard for the person or group, and hold that in your mind separately from the problem you want to address.
   - ✔ Keep it respectful.
   - ✔ Keep in mind the unique ideas and contributions of the person to the team's work.
4. After you lay out the problem or concern, be quiet.
   - ✔ Resist the urge to respond to points being made, even though you may find them to be inaccurate.
   - ✔ Really listen, rather than planning what to say next.
   - ✔ If the person offers a very abbreviated response, ask them to say more.
5. Be attentive to what's below the surface.
   - ✔ The sticking point for the other person may be different than the conceptual or logistical issue that prompted the conversation.
   - ✔ A seemingly minor issue may be about something deeper for the other person—it may go to the core of their personal or professional identity.
6. Work together to find a new approach neither of you had thought of before, that may be better than the solution either one of you had in mind.
   - ✔ The best solutions are usually the most creative ones.
   - ✔ What started as a disagreement may turn out to improve the project process or outcome.

7. Use the language "Yes, if ... "
   - ✔ Beginning with "no" sets a negative tone, as in "No, but ... "
   - ✔ "Yes, if ..." is usually well received, even though it is a qualified response.
8. When you come to agreement, summarize and memorialize.
   - ✔ Verbally state your understanding of the solution, and ask the other person to voice agreement.
   - ✔ Thank the person for the positive conversation and their openness within the dialogue.
   - ✔ Express a positive view of the future.
   - ✔ If appropriate, send a thank you and summary of the solution arrived at, through email or other means.
   - ✔ Failure to elicit and document the agreement reached is a common failing, undoing all the work that went into the difficult conversation.

Working together to achieve improved health in our communities is vitally important work. There is tremendous potential for devising innovative solutions through partnership and collaboration, harnessing the rich diversity of perspectives, knowledge, and experience. The promise of synergy is great. Disagreements and differences are to be celebrated, as they are a characteristic of high-functioning teams. The work of learning together through difficult conversations is worth the energy and commitment.

REFERENCES

Alper S, Tjosvold D, Law KS. Interdependence and controversy in group decision making: Antecedents to effective self-managing teams. Organ Behav Hum Decis Process 1998; 74(1): 33–52.

Weeks H. Failure to Communicate: How Conversations Go Wrong and What You Can Do to Right Them. Boston: Harvard Business Press, 2008.

Additional Resources

Appreciative inquiry. "Rather than focusing on problems, Appreciative Inquiry elicits solutions." http://centerforappreciativeinquiry.net/

Stone D, Patton B. Difficult Conversations. New York: Viking Penguin, 1999.

Weeks H: Difficult conversations: Nine common mistakes. http://hbr.org/web/slideshows/difficult-conversations-nine-common-mistakes/10-slide

Chapter 6

Group Dynamics

MINA SILBERBERG AND SEAMUS BHATT-MACKIN

Groups can accomplish things that individuals could never do alone. However, group dynamics can be extremely challenging. Although groups do not need to agree on every point in order to work together, groups do need to establish agreement about basic goals and procedural issues, both big and (seemingly) small. When public health, primary care, and other sectors come together to address population health, issues of race, class, and power can be particularly salient for group dynamics. Partners will also face the discomfort of dealing with uncertainty and ambiguity, and the pitfalls of collaborators using language in different ways.

THE CHALLENGES OF WORKING AS A GROUP

Groups can develop innovations and solutions to problems that their members could never have dreamt of or tackled on their own. However, disagreements and misunderstandings can easily derail the group process. How can you reduce the challenges of working as a group—or even embrace them as part of the process by which you will create something completely new?

In the formation of a working group, establishing agreement about basic issues can create a greater sense of safety and increase the likelihood of success. In this way, agreements are often described as the "foundation of relationships." Start with the most basic issues:

- Meeting location
- Meeting time
- Meeting frequency
- Group size
- Leadership selection

These are not trivial issues. Consider groups that have met in a space or at a time that is very convenient for some members and inconvenient for others. This is not a great way to start, especially if there are power dynamics involved related to profession, gender, socioeconomic class, or other factors. For example, health-care providers are generally scheduled to see patients most of the day, and, as a result, will often hold meetings early in the morning before clinic starts or late in the day, after work ends. They are also accustomed to having people (patients, pharmaceutical company representatives, other vendors) come to them. They may not realize that 7:00 a.m. or 5:30 p.m. at their clinic site won't be convenient for some public health partners or that these partners are themselves extremely busy. Similarly, individuals who participate in population health efforts as part of their professional roles may not realize that community volunteers working paid jobs are often unavailable during the day. Remember: Group norms are established early, and they are often durable. For this reason, it is important to attend carefully to the beginning of any new working group and get true agreement on these issues ahead of the first meeting, if possible.

The optimal size of a working group is a topic of debate for theorists and researchers of group dynamics, although in the business world, estimates seem to fall somewhere in the 5- to 12-member range. What is clear is the requirement that the size and composition of the working group match the task at hand. Small-group dynamics occur when members can easily track what each person is saying. As anyone who has attended a large forum-style discussion knows, the dynamics of large groups do not allow for the same kind of collaboration.

Whereas groups with members who obviously are alike in some way (e.g., all men or all women) often go on to learn the ways in which the members are different, groups with members who are obviously different in some way (e.g., various types of professional training and practice) often go on to learn the ways in which the members are similar (e.g., helping others for people involved in population health across professional disciplines). Keeping this in mind can move the group forward in its development, especially if it is possible to facilitate the discovery of these similarities by the group members themselves. For example, collaborators on population health improvement projects often "get down to work" without first getting to know one another. A discussion of what brought group members to their interest in health or the particular focus of the group's activity will often reveal similarities in internal motivation, values, or even experience that might be obscured by differences in profession, race, age, and other more visible personal characteristics.

Over time, groups can establish more cohesion and tolerate more disagreement and conflict. There is a sweet spot for different kinds of conflict at different developmental stages of group formation. In most situations, explicit conflict is preferred to hidden conflict. A strong working group has members with a willingness to openly address disagreement when it inevitably occurs. Respectfully expressing disagreement and exploring the reasons and rationale behind it can allow teams to air important issues and to arrive at approaches that meet everybody's needs (see chapter 5). Following are two examples of groups' experiences and solutions to problems in the process of collaboration.

Michigan's Healthy Futures

Since 2009, Munson Medical Center, local health departments, and local health care providers in one region of Michigan have partnered in the Michigan Healthy Futures program to provide pregnant women with the clinical and nonclinical resources needed for a healthy pregnancy and a healthy birth. Collaboration was initially complicated. A participant notes that trust and understanding have grown among partners over time. Partners are now willing to share views, even when they disagree, and collaboration seems simpler now than it did when they began.

The New York City Office of Minority Health

The New York City Office of Minority Health originally found religious congregations to be wary about introducing new technology for blood pressure monitoring into their congregations. Use of the new technology only became possible when the state office engaged the congregations in dialogue about their existing blood pressure monitoring systems, the challenges they faced with their systems, and how new technology might address those challenges. It was also necessary for the Office of Minority Health to provide significant support to the congregations and recognize the need for each to go at its own pace.

RACE, CLASS, AND POWER IN GROUP DYNAMICS

Even when we are united by a common goal, we are often divided by history, culture, power, or our own (sometimes unconscious) biases and assumptions. Being effective in our work means learning to recognize and address this uncomfortable reality. Yet, the dominant group in a society is often unaware of its role in suppressing or neglecting minority views. We can mitigate our lack of awareness of these dynamics by educating ourselves about the history and realities of the communities with which we are working, listening without leaping to judgment (of self or others) when a team member or collaborator offers us their perspective, observing ourselves, observing what works and what doesn't in the interactions of others, and asking for clarification and feedback.

If you understand social determinants of health, then you know that the distribution of health is largely based on who has power and resources. Working to address population health means working in diverse groups to address an issue that is intrinsically political. Historical conflicts and power imbalances make the situation that much more complex. Frequently, for example, the larger community may have experienced its local medical institutions as exploitative employers or research sites. This history not only affects engagement within the larger community, but affects dynamics among individuals within and across primary care sites and public health institutions.

Moreover, beyond race, class, and the other salient differences in society in general, public health officials are likely to see the medical community as having relatively more power, prestige, and resources than they do. In such cases, groups will benefit from an agreement that differences will be addressed with respect, honesty, receptivity, and self-reflection.

"Even in the face of powerful structures of domination, it remains possible for each of us . . . to define and determine alternative standards."

bell hooks

Talking Back

DIFFERENCES IN LANGUAGE

A common speed bump on the road to effective collaboration is differences in vernacular across sectors; words that may be thought of as straightforward often aren't. This is certainly true for public health and primary care. Take the term "population health," which is so central to this book. In public health, "population health" refers to the health of a defined community—generally a geographic community, (e.g., residents of a county or state) for whom they are responsible. For many primary care practitioners, "population health" refers to the health of their specific patient population. Kindig and Stoddart (2003) use the term "population health" in two ways. Its definition, they state, is "the health outcomes of a group of individuals, including the distribution of such outcomes within the group." This generic definition encompasses both the stereotypical primary care and public health perspectives, since the "group of individuals" to which Kindig and Stoddart refer can be defined differently in different circumstances. In addition to thinking of population health as a definition, they think of it as a field of inquiry that encompasses population health outcomes, "patterns of determinants, and the policies and interventions that link the two" (Kindig & Stoddardt, 2003).

In another example, public health professionals will most often think of prevention as primary prevention delivered on a mass basis (e.g., through fluoridation of water or social media campaigns) or individually (e.g., through vaccination). In contrast, in the normal course of primary care practice as it currently exists, primary care practitioners deliver preventive care individually and may be more likely to address secondary and tertiary prevention than primary.

These differences can be singularly frustrating, as time and energy are often invested in one direction before partners realize they have been speaking at cross-purposes. Partners can prevent some of this waste and frustration by informally checking in periodically to see what others mean when they use a term or by making explicit their own understanding.

Differences in language are not necessarily only about language. They also can reflect differences in world views and experiences—and/or are taken by listeners as symbolic of such differences. Frustrations over language are exacerbated when parties take a positional stance over which meaning of a shared word is the right one.

Deborah Tannen, a professor of linguistics, has written a number of books about how differences in language and conversational style affect personal and work relationships. (See, for example, Tannen, 1986 and Tannen, 1990.) A key insight from Tannen's work is that differences in language often lead to misunderstanding and conflict. Understanding these differences, Tannen proposes, is a crucial tool for relationship building, particularly when conflicts arise. Just as collaborators must forge agreements about where and when to meet, they will also need to forge agreements around common language. Having a common language will foster communication, clarity of purpose, and unity. Moreover, the process of coming to agreement around language will allow for important discussions around differing points of view and common goals. The story of the San Diego Healthy Weight Collaborative (see chapter 26) illustrates the challenges of language differences and the benefits of addressing them.

BECOMING COMFORTABLE WITH AMBIGUITY AND UNCERTAINTY

Working to improve population health involves ambiguity and uncertainty. Deciding how to choose one of the many health problems your community faces—differing in, say, prevalence, severity of sequelae, ease of resolution—is complicated. So are interpreting data, choosing among alternative interventions, designing evaluation plans, and all the other work of population health improvement. Moreover, the path of implementation is never straightforward. Expected resources do not materialize, posited changes do not occur, and new obstacles arise.

Partnering with outside agencies brings even greater ambiguity and uncertainty to this work, multiplying competing views, communication problems, and dependence on others over whom you have little to no control. We can reduce ambiguity and uncertainty to some extent by establishing agreements, but we can never eliminate them. Rather, we must plan for that which we haven't planned (e.g., by building slack into our schedules and budgets) and learn to feel comfortable with uncertainty and ambiguity, recognizing them as part of a creative collaborative process and as transient states.

Three general approaches to collaboration can help us feel more comfortable with ambiguity and uncertainty and with the differences in perceptions, language, and concerns described throughout this chapter.

Value Your Partner's Input

You may have a specific idea about how to address a certain problem. However, integration means considering ideas other than your own. Primary care providers often believe that health problems require clinic-based solutions or expanded access to clinical care. At the same time, public health officials tend to focus on community outreach and health education or changes to the built environment. Try to remember that the synthesis of different perspectives and experiences is one of the great strengths of integration. You may not always agree with the views of others, and managing difficult conversations (see chapter 5) is part of the process of working together.

Recognize Other Decision Makers

Decision making belongs to the group, not to one person, agency, or sector. The collective process makes the outcomes of decisions uncertain. If you can feel assured that your partners share your goals, the discomfort associated with the uncertainty of collective decision making will be easier. It is also helpful to recognize that, if all goes well, this working relationship will be one that is long-term, with different actors having their say in different moments.

Evolve and Grow

You will try things that won't work, but formative evaluation (discussed in chapter 10) will strengthen your work. Working through differing ideas and coming upon unexpected roadblocks and unanticipated consequences is uncomfortable. However, learning to live with ambiguity and uncertainty is essential to population health and to integrated work, as is understanding that mistakes are part of the process. We are still headed in the right direction if we learn from experience.

Tips

1. Be prepared to have disagreements, conflicts and misunderstandings.
2. Be prepared to establish agreements.
3. Even seemingly small issues—meeting location, meanings of words—can be of great importance to group dynamics.
4. Demonstrate the respect you feel for others by soliciting their input, listening to them purposefully, acknowledging areas of agreement, and agreeing sometimes to disagree.
5. Remember that the synthesis of different perspectives and experiences is one of the great strengths of integration.
6. Understand that mistakes are part of the process. You are still headed in the right direction if you are learning from your experience.
7. Learn the words and terms whose different meanings impede effective communication and collaboration.
8. Keep in mind that redefining a word is redefining a paradigm. Done effectively, it will advance your thinking and your work.

The challenges of group work can be lessened when we see value in group decision-making and partner input. More importantly, the ideas arrived at by considering the value of different and even opposing points of view can sometimes lead to superior understanding of a topic. This chapter suggests the need to refine our attitudes and our collaborative skills so as to make group dynamics fruitful rather than destructive.

REFERENCES

Kindig D, Stoddart G. What is population health? AJPH 93(3); 380–383: 2003.

Tannen D. That's Not What I Meant: How Conversational Style Makes or Breaks Relationships. New York: Ballantine Publishing Group, 1986.

Tannen D. You Just Don't Understand: Women and Men in Conversation. New York: Morrow, 1990.

Additional Resources

CTSA Community Engagement Key Function Committee Task Force on the Principles of Community Engagement. Principles of Community Engagement, 2nd edition. Bethesda, MD: National Institutes of Health, 2011 (#11-7782). *Provides guidance and case studies on collaborative efforts to improve health.*

Knowledge@Wharton. Is Your Team Too Big? Too Small? What's the Right Number? http://knowledge.wharton.upenn.edu/article/is-your-team-too-big-too-small-whats-the-right-number/

Harvard School of Public Health. http://www.hsph.harvard.edu/hcncr/publications/ *Lists evidence-based books and articles from the faculty of the school's Program on Health Care Negotiation and Conflict Resolution.*

Patterson K et al. Crucial Conversations tools for Talking When Stakes Are High, 2nd edition. New York: McGraw-Hill, 2011. *Provides ways to make high-stake conversations safe and productive.*

Ward D, Ward C. How to Help Leaders and Members Learn From Their Group Experience. London: Sage Publications, 2014.

Chapter 7

Pitching Your Project

JUSTINE STRAND DE OLIVEIRA

Tirelessly working to craft a proposed project or policy that would have a major impact on community health can quickly lead to the need for support in the form of advocacy, cooperation, funding, or other resources. There will come a time to make a pitch to key decision makers. The target audience may be elected officials, philanthropic organization leaders, or captains of industry. Having to approach a powerful leader in your community with an "ask" can be daunting. Here are some things to consider as while planning your visit.

THE APPROACH

First, think about the approach to presenting your proposal. Work with members of your team or working group to come up with answers to the following considerations:

1. What is the problem? Boil it down to a brief and pithy statement.
2. What is the solution? How will your proposal make a difference?
3. What will it cost? Be sure to consider opportunity costs, people's time, and good will, not just money.
4. What are the barriers? Be brutally honest with yourself, and disclose all the major barriers identified.
5. What would a successful outcome look like? Paint a vivid picture of a changed community in your envisioned future.
6. Who will be opposed? Disclose your analysis of forces against your idea. Come up with these in advance, as most decision makers will want to know who might be unhappy if the idea goes forward. Know that even the best ideas have naysayers.
7. Who is in support? Identify allies and get their agreement before claiming their support. There is nothing more deadly to an idea than having supposed supporters derail it when they discover they've been touted as advocates.

PRESENTING YOUR IDEA

After considering the pros and cons, obstacles and facilitators, opponents and supporters for your idea, focus on how to present it. It's unlikely you will have much time, and decision makers are often interrupted due to the press of events related to their many responsibilities. And in the age of YouTube and TED Talks, none of us has a long attention span anymore.

In addition to keeping the presentation brief, clear, and focused on the key ideas you need to get across, it's important to maintain a positive tone, even when faced with hard questions or opposition to your idea. And make sure disagreements among group members are ironed out before your important meeting (see chapters 5 and 10).

1. Be concise. Decision makers are busy people, and you will lose them if you go on and on. After making a brief pitch, you can provide more detail in response to questions.
2. Be polite to opposing viewpoints. Cast aspersions on no one. Think about those who are not friendly to your proposal, and come up with neutral, "canned" statements before the meeting, so you aren't caught off guard. If you haven't thought about naysayers beforehand, it can be hard to respond with equanimity.
3. Be persuasive. Synthesize your issue in one page, organizing a few background materials, and practice the pitch with people you trust to give honest feedback.
4. Be united. Nothing is deadlier than team squabbles in front of your target decision maker. When preparing for the presentation to the decision maker, don't sweep group disagreements under the rug. Be honest with each other, present what is agreed upon, and avoid internecine warfare when working to garner support.

CONNECT WITH THE DECISION MAKER

At this point, your presentation is developed and is brief and to the point. You have identified every issue or question that might be asked, and are ready to respond in a neutral fashion. The team that will visit the decision maker feels confident and ready to make the case for your project. Now you need to get on the decision maker's calendar. Some things to think about when scheduling the visit are:

1. Get in the door. Contact the individual's office and request an appointment (there is usually an assistant who handles the person's calendar) and briefly describe who you represent and the issue you wish to discuss. Some assistants are very protective of their boss's time and seem to have developed a science of blocking the door to the person they report to. If you aren't successful despite polite requests, it may be necessary to find someone who is a "bridging person," who knows your group and the decision maker, and can intercede for you.

2. Ask for an appropriate amount of time. Decision makers are very busy, so an hour is probably not going to work. But don't say you need "just a few minutes" when you need 30.

3. Be prepared by learning about the decision maker. Read the local paper, listen to local talk radio when she is featured, and talk to people in the know. Research the decision maker's background. Ask for advice if you know people who have presented to her before. You can learn a lot on Google, but insight about what she likes or dislikes is invaluable.

4. Keep it measured and professional. When we feel passionately about an issue, it can be hard to keep emotions in check. You may not win over support every time, but you want there to be a next time.

5. Accept that you may be delivering information the decision maker doesn't want to hear. He may have a differing viewpoint, even different values. Or, the issue may require money or time he can ill afford.

6. Don't personalize it. You are arguing on behalf of the community's health, it's not about you. Keeping this top of mind can help in getting over the reluctance to make an "ask," and remain calm if the conversation isn't going the way you'd hoped.

7. Offer a solution—don't just present the problem. Provide an action step the decision maker can embrace.

8. Summarize and agree on next steps. Apparent success can turn into failure when the outcome is not clear to everyone in the conversation. People see (and hear) things through different lenses.

9. Keep to the established time. If the meeting was scheduled for 30 minutes, finalize the conversation and leave well within that time frame.

10. Express appreciation. Even if the conversation doesn't result in the desired outcome, the decision maker has given you the gift of time in her busy schedule. If you leave on good terms, something could come of this connection in the future.

11. Follow up and memorialize the conversation and any agreement. It's important to put things in writing, and if an agreement didn't result, think of the follow-up thank you communication as another opportunity to advance your cause.

BUILDING A RELATIONSHIP

Above all, think of your first visit as the beginning of a relationship you will build over time. Dealing with policy and funding proposals can be frustrating, as success is never guaranteed. When we feel passionately about improving the health of our community, refusals can be a bitter pill to swallow. But neutrality and a balanced approach are critical to long-term success. We learn to engage in "Janusian thinking," the ability to see both sides of an issue at the same time (Rothenberg, 1971). To see the pros and cons, the positive effects and potential unintended effects, to embrace opposition and learn from it, and most importantly, to keep a sense of humor and the energy to keep striving for change requires this approach. Some considerations:

1. *Never assume support.* Allies can change their minds due to shifting political winds. There are so many interwoven issues in any community, it can be difficult to know when unrelated events may cause someone who has been a supporter to surprise you with a different point of view.

2. *Never assume opposition.* Those who have been opposed can shift their viewpoints. Don't make assumptions about political affiliations and resulting attitudes, even in our polarized environment. Especially when it comes to the community's health, you may be surprised at whose support you can garner. Remember that health is about quality of life, but it's also necessary for a community to be vibrant economically.

3. *Maintain relationships.* Even if a leader isn't a target for the current proposal, you may need his help on another proposal, or he may seek you out to collaborate in areas of common interest. And if he has your group and its work on community health in mind, he may help link you to new opportunities you would otherwise be unaware of.

4. *Live to fight another day.* If a leader can't help you this time, don't burn bridges. There are always considerations behind the scenes that you aren't aware of. Next time may be different.

5. *Money and power don't guarantee success.* So don't be daunted by the fact that you don't have any. Being motivated by improving the health of the community is powerfully persuasive.

6. *Keep it a team effort.* One member of the group may have powerful connections, but all of your team members have valuable perspectives.

7. *Express appreciation.* Always send a thank you—the old-timey written thank you note is always in style.

8. *Keep in touch.* Don't just communicate when you want something—keep your key contacts informed of your activities. Make them feel they are part of your team!

What is difficult about speaking truth to power and making a persuasive pitch? If the truth you need to convey were already accepted by the target audience, there would be no need for persuasion—in fact, you wouldn't need to meet with them. The challenge lies in presenting ideas that may be unwelcome or uncomfortable, despite potential personal or professional risk. Speaking truth means giving voice to the unsaid or unrecognized, creating a tension in the listener by laying bare the need for action. In these delicate moments, passion for the cause can be perceived as arrogant and self-righteous. Maintain an inner calm while putting a human face on the suffering or injustice you seek to alleviate. Share stories about real people to illuminate the need for change and the social cost of inaction.

Like all skills, making a pitch gets a bit easier with practice. Begin now to prepare for future conversations by being voracious about learning what's happening in your community—and what the decision makers in the community are up to. Your natural curiosity and awareness of what's happening around you will be infectious and engaging.

REFERENCE

Rothenberg A. The process of Janusian thinking in creativity. Archives of general psychiatry 1971; 24(3): 195–205. doi:10.1001/archpsyc.1971.01750090001001

Chapter 8

Positioned for Sustainability

KAREN J. MINYARD, AMANDA PHILLIPS MARTINEZ,
AND TANISA FOXWORTH ADIMU

INTEGRATION OF PUBLIC HEALTH
AND PRIMARY CARE

Public health and primary care are distinctively different and historically separate disciplines. Beliefs, values, norms, and culture have developed in relation to these disciplines. Integrating public health and primary care will require changes in mindsets, systems, and patterns of behavior for public health, primary care, communities, and individuals who seek medical and preventive services.

New partnerships and collaboration will be needed to accomplish this change. This approach will require shared stewardship of the health and health care system of communities. Primary care providers will need to consider the broader health of the community; public health professionals will need to understand primary care systems and financing. This bridging will require that individuals who seek medical and preventive services be able to navigate between clinicians, public health entities, and community services in a straightforward manner. In addition, the partnerships must help to support the communication and the flow of clinical information between public health professionals and clinicians, serve as a shared resource for all partners, and provide information and data to inform and guide collective actions. Resources will need to be aligned to support the new system effectively and efficiently. Building and sustaining such partnerships over time requires careful planning, constant attention, and the dedication of resources to ensure that communication, coordination, the provision of integrated services, and collaborative stewardship of health will endure for the long term.

This chapter focuses on planning for long-term sustainability and illustrates the correlation between the components of successful integration and the factors that influence sustainability. We present an expanded view of sustainability that moves beyond the identification of funding and includes the consideration of the factors that influence sustainability.

Five Principles for Integration of Primary Care and Public Health

In its report *Primary Care and Public Health: Exploring Integration to Improve Population Health*, the Institute of Medicine (IOM) (2012) sets forth five principles for the successful integration of primary care and public health:

- A shared goal of population health improvement
- Community engagement in defining and addressing population health needs
- Aligned leadership that reduces fragmentation, clarifies roles, supports appropriate incentives, and effectively manages change
- Sustainability, key to the establishment of a shared infrastructure and building a foundation for enduring value and impact
- The sharing and collaborative use of data and analysis

With language like "shared goal," "community," "aligned leadership," "shared infrastructure," and "collaborative," these five principles independently and collectively accentuate the importance partnership and collaboration. The principles are interconnected; none stands alone. The presence of a shared vision among partners; dedicated leadership with the authority and will to bridge silos and ensure accountability; and partners engaged in meaningful collaboration are all key to the sustainability of primary care and public health integration.

WHAT IS SUSTAINABILITY?

The Constitution of the Iroquois Nations espouses seven-generation sustainability. Leaders must think seven generations ahead (about 140 years into the future) and decide whether the decisions they make today would benefit their children seven generations into the future. The Centers for Disease Control and Prevention Healthy Communities Program Sustainability Guide defines sustainability as "A community's ongoing capacity and resolve to work together to establish, advance, and maintain effective strategies that continuously improve health and quality of life for all." The Georgia Health Policy Center (GHPC) considers partnerships, innovations, or programs to be sustainable if they are valued and draw support and resources. Each of these definitions of sustainability recognizes the complexity and need for broad collaboration inherent in the integration of primary care and public health. These three definitions together consider the importance of planning for the future, a broad view of health, and creating value, which are all fundamental to sustainability.

Sustainability does not necessarily mean that an innovation continues in the same form as originally conceived, funded, or implemented. In fact, innovations often evolve over time to adjust to the changing levels of support and the needs of the community (Wiltsey Stirman et al., 2012). For instance:

- Partnerships may start with one approach, but end up sustaining a different model after testing it in the community.

- An initial investment may fund a model or pilot that evolves and is integrated into an organization's standard operating procedures.
- Some grant-funded innovations may be sustained, but the services provided or the coverage area is scaled back to reflect a reduction in resources to support the program.

While most definitions of sustainability focus on the continuation of a service or program, this perspective may understate the full range of program impacts, as it does not explicitly describe the potential for lasting effects on a system or in the community that are distinct from the service itself. There are multiple ways that an initiative can have impact on the health of the population. This sustained impact could include the maintenance of health or other benefits achieved through the initial program; changes in knowledge, attitudes, and practices of community members and providers; development of new capacity in the recipient community (i.e., changes in the way that agencies work together to serve community members, cultural shifts and practice changes at the individual, organizational, and community levels); and policy changes (Fig. 8-1) (Georgia Health Policy Center, 2010; Scheirer & Dearing, 2011; Shediac-Rizkallah & Bone, 1998).

Figure 8-1 ▼

The range of potential sustained impacts. Sustained impacts are those long-term effects that may, or may not, be dependent on the continuation of a program. These long-term effects may go beyond services that are put into place and may include changes in the way agencies work together to serve community members, cultural shifts, practice changes, policy changes, and changes in the knowledge, attitudes and behaviors of community members and providers.

(From Georgia Health Policy Center. Bringing the Future Into Focus: A Step-by-Step Sustainability Planning Workbook. The Board of Regents of the University System of Georgia by and on behalf Georgia State University. 2010. http://www.raconline.org/sustainability/pdf/bringing-the-future-into-focus-sustainability-planning-workbook.pdf)

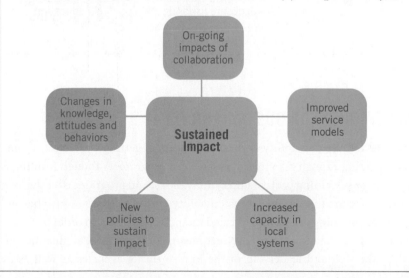

Examples of Impacts

Ongoing Impacts of Collaboration. Through the implementation of a new service, provider agencies and public health departments can develop a new way of working together to serve patients and the community; new lines of communication are established, interagency referral mechanisms are built, and the culture of collaboration in systems and throughout communities may be changed.

Improved Service Models. Agencies may develop and implement new practice standards that are institutionalized for the long term. For example, new programs may result in a new model for coordinating care across entities, co-location of services, or shared staffing models between public health and primary care.

Increased Capacity in Local Systems. Funding can be used to build the capacity of the local health and human service infrastructure (e.g., establishing an HIT infrastructure for data exchange among public health and health care partners), develop curricula (e.g., a diabetes self-management training program that can be used by nurses or community health workers, or a physical activity program that can be used by math and science teachers in the classroom), or develop the capacity of providers and systems to provide quality care (e.g., form partnerships between local providers and public health to implement quality improvement processes and ensure that providers meet recommended standards of care).

New Policies to Sustain Impact. An organization or collaboration may engage in local or state-level advocacy to effect change in a policy that supports the services provided through their programs. Those policy changes (e.g., a change in Medicaid reimbursement, or the establishment of a hospital taxing district) have an enduring impact on the way services are delivered and financed. Government agencies may focus funding in such a way that encourages new service provision models or supports collaboration across provider agencies For example, a state department of public health may leverage federal or other sources of funding to partner with primary care organizations and community organizations to address obesity or other health concerns among targeted populations.

Changes in Knowledge, Attitudes, and Behaviors. A community may see impacts that are beyond services and infrastructure. As a result of outreach efforts, public awareness of a health issue may increase, and cultural attitudes about certain health behaviors or illnesses may shift. For example, a program to integrate mental health services into the primary care setting may help reduce the stigma associated with accessing mental health-related service. Public health campaigns that educate providers and families alike on the dangers of lead exposures can ensure that pediatricians are effectively screening patients for exposure risk and providing direct education and resources for families at risk.

POSITIONING FOR SUSTAINABILITY

Often the term sustainability evokes the concept of getting a grant or in some way garnering enough resources to continue a program. Although funding is essential for sustaining partnerships, innovations, and programs over the long term, the factors that influence sustainability are complex and move beyond success at obtaining grants or dedicated financial resources. In order to attract support, either financial or by indirect means, program efforts must be valued by the staff and leadership of the implementing agencies as well as by partners, patients, and other community stakeholders. This can be thought of as upstream sustainability.

Innovations, partnerships, and programs that are maintained over time are usually successful because they are *positioned for sustainability*. Being positioned for sustainability means garnering support because a function that is valued and viewed as worthy of the commitment of time, resources, and continued attention is served. "Positioning" is understanding why, or why not, an innovation, partnership, or service is likely to be maintained over the long term, and it requires a consideration of the multiple factors that influence long-term sustainability.

Factors That Drive Sustainability

Experience has elucidated eight key factors that underlie sustainability (described below). A broad range of contextual, programmatic, and interpersonal dynamics combine in numerous ways to drive sustainability outcomes at the programmatic, organizational, and community levels. A number of published studies provide insights and categorization of these sustainability factors, with a high level of agreement on the most important factors (GHPC, 2010; Sheirer & Dearing, 2011; Wiltsey Stirman et al., 2012). The factors described below are key to positioning a service, program, or partnership for sustainability, and they should be considered both early and throughout an initiative's development and implementation.

1. Strategic Vision. Directly corresponding to the IOM's principle of a shared goal of population health improvement (2012), the strategic vision dynamic begins with determining a clear vision of the desired future. The vision defines what should be different as a result of program implementation, either within the wider community or a specific group. A vision that is shared by individual primary care and public health agencies, as well as the collective partnership, provides inspiration and direction for everyone involved in the initiative (Scheirer & Dearing, 2011).

2. Leadership. As with the IOM's principle related to leadership (2012), sustainable programs require leadership that can "de-silo" the individual efforts of primary care, public health agencies, and other community partners to align their interests toward a shared strategic vision. Leadership does not have to lie in a single individual, but should include those who can inspire others to work together, resolve conflict, and manage change. A primary function of leadership is bringing influence and authority to make commitments on behalf of the organizations and to leverage support and resources for the program.

3. Collaboration. In meaningful collaborations, all partners have a role in the planning and implementation of program activities that is matched to their strengths. Incorporating partners from throughout the health care system and community broadens the program's ability not only to meet individual patient needs, but also to focus on broader improvements in population health. Additionally, collaborations contribute to long-term sustainability by the adoption of program activities by collaborative partners (GHPC, 2010).

4. Organizational Capacity. Long-term sustainability is facilitated by an organization that has the capacity to deliver high-quality services in a timely manner through a wide range of capabilities, knowledge, experience, and resources. For example, having influential leadership, personnel with the necessary skills and knowledge, agency experience in delivering programs with a similar focus and scope, an appropriate management structure, and meaningful engagement of partners increases the likelihood of viability and long-term success (David, 2002; Edwards et al., 2007).

5. Program Relevance (Adaptation). Aligned with the IOM's principle of community engagement (2010), the dynamic of *program relevance* reflects a program that meets a documented need that has considered and incorporated community input, and is tailored to the cultural, political, and economic environment (GHPC, 2010; Scheirer & Dearing, 2011).

6. Effective and Efficient Program Approach. This sustainability dynamic refers to a program that is integrated into the system within which it operates by drawing from and contributing to existing community resources. Duplication of effort is minimized and opportunities to achieve economies of scale and increased integration are identified and utilized (GHPC, 2011).

7. Program Evaluation. A well-defined and executed evaluation is essential for monitoring and documenting the impacts of programs. Regular review of evaluation data allows those persons implementing programs to track progress toward goals and to make any necessary adjustments to the program to ensure program integrity and quality. In addition, evaluation data can be used to generate additional funding, engage new partners, and demonstrate the health, social, economic, and other benefits of the program to the community, partners, and other stakeholders (Center for Public Health Systems Science, 2012). The dynamic of *program evaluation* corresponds to the IOM's principle of sharing and collaborative use of data and analysis (2012).

8. Communications. Effective communication, both internally and externally, is a cornerstone of positioning for sustainability. Internal communication keeps collaborating partners aware of successes and challenges in program implementation; external communication alerts the community, potential funders, and supporters of the impact and importance of the collaborative work being done by the implementing agencies. (Alexander, 2003; GHPC, 2010).

By understanding their strengths and weaknesses related to the dynamics enumerated above, organizations can build capacity to better position themselves and their programs for long-term sustainability. Both the GHPC and Washington University have developed tools that allow organizations to conduct such self-assessments (see Additional Resources).

DIVERSIFIED FUNDING

Although being positioned for sustainability is important, the need for adequate financial resources is still a reality. Organizations that are most successful at sustaining their programs over time utilize a combination of funding strategies that include earned income, grants and contributions, and fund-raising events, among others (Fig. 8-2). Sources of support are not solely financial, as in-kind contributions and volunteerism are often methods that contribute to sustaining efforts over the long term (Emekalam, 2012; GHPC, 2010). Sustainability should be viewed as a rope woven from multiple threads that holds a program together. Each thread is a source of support (e.g., earned income, indirect funding sources, grants, government budgets, contributions/sponsorships, events, volunteerism). If one "thread" breaks, the other threads, or resources, can continue to support the program. A common method of sustainability that is particularly relevant to service reorganization and primary care/public health integration is the absorption of new practices by an organization and/or its collaborative partners.

Figure 8-2 ▼

Breakdown of funding strategies to promote sustainability. This figure shows a range of potential sources of support to sustain programs and partnerships over the long term.

(From Georgia Health Policy Center. Bringing the Future Into Focus: A Step-by-Step Sustainability Planning Workbook. The Board of Regents of the University System of Georgia by and on behalf Georgia State University. 2010. http://www.raconline.org/sustainability/pdf/bringing-the-future-into-focus-sustainability-planning-workbook.pdf)

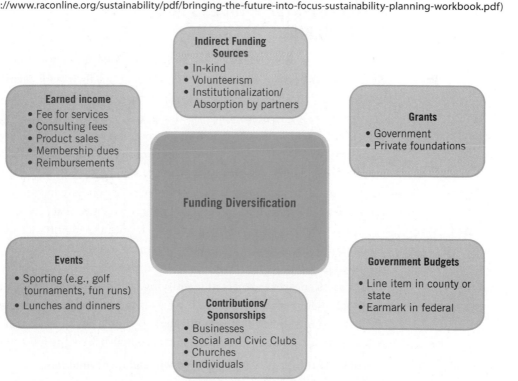

In these instances, the services become part of the day-to-day operations of the organization and partner agencies (GHPC, 2010; IOM, 2012). A thoughtful process of planning for sustainability will lead to the consideration of multiple means of sustaining program activities. Although not every source of funding is needed by every initiative, each initiative should have several sources in place to stabilize sustainability, as in the rope/threads metaphor used earlier. A way to gauge how many resource should come from each source as well as how many sources of funding to seek is to consider the question, "could the effort continue if this one source were discontinued?" It is important to structure resources so that the loss of any one source of funding does not threaten the entire effort.

Innovations in funding for population health are emerging. Recently, ReThink Health (2014) surveyed 200 regional collaboratives across the United State and identified 35 different funding strategies that were being used. The Prevention Institute issued a report on prevention and wellness funds (Mikkelsen et al., 2015). A prevention and wellness fund is a pool of funds raised to finance community prevention interventions as part of health improvement and cost-containment strategies. The Robert Wood Johnson Foundation just identified a National Coordinating Center at the Georgia Health Policy Center to guide states, regions, and communities that are working to advance a Culture of Health through innovations in financing.

A STEP-BY-STEP PROCESS FOR SUSTAINABILITY PLANNING

Sustainability is sometimes an afterthought. As grant funding is coming to a close, grantees begin to wonder how they will continue their work. Steps can be taken in the planning and early stages of a partnership, innovation, or program to prepare for long-term sustainability. Long-term sustainability is neither accidental nor a last-minute consideration. A common view in the sustainability literature is that sustainability is much more of a process than a clearly defined outcome or endpoint. As such, sustainability should be built into the earliest stages of program planning, as decisions made early on have long-term implications for the sustainability potential of programs (Pluye et al., 2005).

The process of sustainability planning clarifies the importance of a program in the community and allows partners and stakeholders to make informed decisions about the future of the program. The sustainability planning process engages partners in identifying funding strategies to sustaining the program long term. This planning may help partners see the importance of the work and decide that they themselves should invest in continuation. A sustainability planning process should accomplish all of the following:

- Identify the long-term impact that will endure beyond the funding period

- Determine which program activities should continue and connect the operating costs of those activities to funding and other support strategies
- Clarify the roles and commitments of the implementing agencies and other stakeholders in ensuring the long-term sustainability and impact of the program

Sustainability Planning Steps

Below we offer a step-wise process to lead you through thoughtful sustainability planning. These steps can be included in the planning stages of an initiative or considered after initial implementation and then revisited over time. Included are questions to help focus and guide your sustainability planning discussions.

Assess the Need

The first step in sustainability planning is to assess the current need in your community or among your patient population. The program approach was originally developed to address an unmet need. Over the course of initial implementation, circumstances may have changed. The following questions can help to establish a clear picture of the current context and help ensure that your approach is relevant:

- What led us to develop our program? What factors indicated a need for our work?
- Has that need changed? Are the circumstances in the community different now than when we began? Is the need less or more intense?
- Are there new programs/organizations—other than ours—that are trying to address the need?
- Based on our current understanding of the need, is there a reason for us to continue our current program as is, or should we make changes in the way we are implementing these activities?

Program Outcomes

Once you are clear on the current need in your community, you can reflect on how your current initiative is (or may not be) meeting that need. Gathering program evaluation data will help provide a true picture of what has been accomplished and allow you to take stock of the effect the program is having on the people you are serving and the system as a whole. The following questions will help to clarify what, if any, your impact efforts have had to date and how effective and efficient your approach has been:

- Were we able to accomplish what we planned to do?
- Were we able to implement the work plan as we envisioned? If yes, what has contributed to our success? If not, why not?
- Are we having positive outcomes? If yes, what has contributed to our success? If not, why not?

Sustained Impact

Next, take some time to envision what long-term impact you want to sustain beyond the funding period. Almost all initiatives and collaborations leave some type of legacy or impact on a system or in the wider community even when the direct services are not sustained. To discover the sustained impact of your efforts, partnering agencies should contemplate the potential for impact in the following areas:

- Changes in knowledge, attitudes, and behaviors
- Ongoing impacts of collaboration
- Improved service models
- Increased capacity in local systems
- New policies

Prioritize Components

After all of the necessary program data are gathered, organized, and considered, you should establish the criteria that will be used to determine which components of the program should continue. By establishing criteria for making decisions about which program activities to continue, you can make an often-subjective process more objective. Developing criteria that match the values and priorities of program partners will help to ensure their commitment to the decision-making process and the eventual outcome of the priority setting. Some potential criteria to consider include:

- Having a positive impact on individuals
- Having a positive impact on the community
- Being cost effective
- Showing a positive return on investment
- Having sufficient community support
- Having resources available for continuation

Confirm Role and Structure

The staff responsible for program implementation and the partners who provide program guidance and support are key factors in the ultimate success or failure of a program. In order to determine the most effective structure for program continuation, it is important to assess aspects of the program structure and determine what changes may be needed to achieve maximum efficiency. The following questions can help guide that discussion:

- How efficiently has the program been staffed?
- How well have partners collaborated in implementing the program?
- What partners and staff will we need to continue our program activities?

Match Sources of Support to Program Components

The last step in this planning process is to identify sources of support for the activities you hope to sustain beyond the funding period. Having a clear idea of the cost of sustaining prioritized activities is an essential part of the sustainability planning process. It may be helpful to project costs for a minimum of 3 years in order to have a complete picture of the total cost of the activity, including one-time cash expenditures and ongoing operational expenses. From there, partners should identify potential sources of support for each component of the budget. Because sustainability often depends heavily on in-kind support by the implementing agency and partners, it is important to discuss the role that each partner can realistically play in the long-term support of ongoing activities.

It is important to remember that the work of sustainability is never done. You and your partners will continue to develop new activities and seek new support and resources, as well as identify more efficient ways of achieving impact in your community. A sustainability plan serves as an initial roadmap to help guide your next efforts.

REFERENCES

David T. Reflections on Sustainability. The California Wellness Foundation; Reflections 3.1. 2002. http://www.tcwf.org/pdf_docs/reflections/feb2002.pdf Accessed Oct 10, 2014.

Edwards JC, Feldman PP, et al. Sustainability of partnerships projects: A conceptual framework and checklist. J Comm J QualPatient Saf 2007; 33(12): 37–47.

Emekalam AU. A conceptual sustainability strategy for a rurally-based community health promotion initiative. J Health Med Informatics 2012; 3.1: 1–6.

Georgia Health Policy Center (GHPC). Bringing the Future Into Focus: A Step-by-Step Sustainability Planning Workbook. The Board of Regents of the University System of Georgia by and on behalf Georgia State University. 2010. http://www.raconline.org/sustainability/pdf/bringing-the-future-into-focus-sustainability-planning-workbook.pdf

GHPC. Dynamics of Sustainability: A Primer for Rural Health Organizations, The Board of Regents of the University System of Georgia by and on behalf Georgia State University. 2011. http://www.raconline.org/pdf/sustain_primer508.pdf

Institute of Medicine. Primary Care and Public Health: Exploring Integration to Improve Population Health. Washington, DC: Institute of Medicine of the National Academies Press, 2012. http://books.nap.edu/openbook.php?record_id=13381. Accessed Oct 7, 2014.

Mikkelsen L, Haar WL, Cohen L, Cantor J, Bennett R, Aboelata M: Sustainable Investments in Health: Prevention and Wellness Funds. Oakland, CA; Prevention Institute, 2015.

Pluye L, Potvin L, Denis JL, Pelletier J, Mannoni C. Program sustainability begins with the first events. Eval Prog Plan 2005; 28(2): 123–137.

ReThink Health. Preliminary Findings from Profiles of Multi-Sector Partnerships. Roundtable on Leveraging Investments in Health and Resilience. Chicago, IL. Sept 8–9, 2014.

Shediac-Rizkallah MC, Bone LR. Planning for the sustainability of community-based health programs: Conceptual frameworks and future directions for research, practice and policy. Health Ed Res 1998; 13: 87–108.

Scheirer MA, Dearing JW. An Agenda for Research on the Sustainability of Public Health Programs. Am J Pub Health 2011; 101(11): 2059–2067.

Wiltsey Stirman S, Kimberly J, Cook N, Calloway A, Castro F, Charns M. The sustainability of new programs and innovations: A review of the empirical literature and recommendations for future research. Implement Sci 2012; 7: 17–35.

Additional Resources

Center for Public Health Systems Science. The Program Sustainability Assessment Tool. Washington University in St Louis. 2012. https://sustaintool.org/. Accessed October 7, 2014. *The Program Sustainability Assessment Tool is a 40-item self-assessment that program staff and stakeholders can take to evaluate the sustainability capacity of a program. Each staff person or stakeholder can take the assessment online and receives an automated summary report of their overall sustainability. Multiple staff and stakeholders can take the assessment individually for a more complete picture of the target program. The results can be used to engage in sustainability planning.*

Georgia Health Policy Center. Sustainability Formative Assessment Tool. The Board of Regents of the University System of Georgia by and on behalf Georgia State University. 2011. http://www.raconline.org/sustainability/pdf/sustainability-s elf-assessment-tool.pdf *The Sustainability Self-Assessment Tool may assist agencies, collaboratives and program staff to capture their general level of functioning related to the components of the GHPC Sustainability Framework©; provide guidance as to what activities or capacities indicate improvement or movement along the developmental spectrum; isolate or highlight areas where continued work or development related to sustainability might be needed; and provide a baseline against which change (positive or negative) can be viewed over time.*

The Role of Early Wins in Long-Term Success

FREDERICK S. JOHNSON

Remember the classic cliché, "winning breeds success"? Early wins are vital to successful collaboration, particularly the first cooperative undertaking. If the first collaborative project produces an organizational victory, then the joint venture has established an immediate track record that accelerates confidence, momentum, hope, resiliency, trust, and leadership development—foundations for an even greater future. Without a clear-cut early win, bringing together institutional stakeholders for a second attempt at collaboration will be problematic. Choosing the first project to turn into an early win isn't difficult; it just takes patience and simple task analysis. Following a few key steps outlined here will help ensure an early victory, establishing a blueprint for long-term success (Foster-Fishman, 2014).

WHY EARLY WINS ARE CRITICAL

Whether your views follow those of American agitator/organizer Saul Alinsky—who advised community activists to start with little battles that can be won first, in order to build up people's confidence—or your outlook is that of a new college graduate or new program manager, one of the keys to success in a new role is to secure early wins: "Early wins excite and energize people, build your credibility, and quickly create value for your organization" (Watkins, 2003).

Long-term goals are essential, but so are early wins. Early wins are like yeast—they produce a response that raises the likelihood of future success and sustainability of any initiative. This is true for projects led by a team of one, but is even more important for projects involving multi-stakeholder teams in which differing cultures and expectations are being brought together. Early wins can foster progress toward goals while at the same time building optimism, momentum, and—in the case of multi-stakeholder efforts—relationship and initial agreement around how to work together effectively. If early wins are the leavening of success, these interpersonal objectives are the structure upon which the rest of the vision can be built.

Please bear in mind that the goal of primary care and public health integration is improved health of the community; the issues you choose to address and solve are the means to that end. Therefore, choosing the first issue wisely establishes a framework to build upon. What is essential to the collaboration is the development of relationships to accept more difficult challenges and issues facing the community and your respective organizations, from poverty to chronic disease epidemics such as diabetes, to redesigning preventive care across a community. Because the goal is to build long-term organizational collaboration, then the means to that end begins with an early win.

PRIMARY CARE AND PUBLIC HEALTH PARTNERSHIP

When public health and primary care leadership within the community begin to discuss and meet, their nascent affiliation will be undefined and tenuous until the first issue to address is agreed upon. In the first set of meetings, questions and concerns around process, such as "who will lead, who will do the work, who gets to decide" will be present in the room, even if not yet on the table. These questions are normal as are the group dynamics that will naturally arise out of them. Leadership should try to avoid getting bogged down in process questions; try to have everyone focus on a common problem or idea, and after the first victory, sit down and lay out the framework for institutionalizing group process and decision making.

WHAT TO DO: PRACTICAL GUIDELINES

In determining the first collaborative issue, key leadership should try to follow the specific criteria. The individual or individuals who bring stakeholders together should use the guidelines below. On the other hand, if you are invited to a first meeting and the conversation begins to sound like the convener wants to solve world hunger, ask the person to consider some practical steps (see following list). If the institutional convener cannot appreciate the value of small steps or if the person's definition of the community problem is beyond the reach or the resources of your community, go home. Practical guidelines include the following:

- Pick low-hanging fruit—something that the group has the ability to achieve in a matter of months (Bandura, 1982; Foster-Fishman, 2014; Institute for Healthcare Improvement, 2014; Weick, 1984). Among other things, this could be an event, an application, a proposal that requires coordination, or a project that one group has already initiated and the other could help strengthen. It could be as simple as working together on community health assessment or a grant proposal. If the first issue chosen is perceived by some in the group to be a controversial problem, such as a smoking ban or living wage clauses in public contracts, make sure the group represents a diverse set of interests. If the group clearly represents multiple interests, you will quickly learn that the controversial perception of the issue was unfounded, and the issue campaign can achieve success within months.

- Follow the "Goldilocks principle": Choose a project that is not too big but not too small, not too difficult but not too simple. For example, instead of geo-mapping every food desert in your community, pick one neighborhood and then develop a strategy to address the problem. Or if you have the food deserts mapped, pick one neighborhood at a time to solve the problem, as each neighborhood will have its own unique attributes to take into account. In this example you want to be sensitive to each neighborhood's characteristics, but you do not want your first campaign getting lost or misdirected by learning everything everyone wants to tell you about their neighborhood.

- Choose something tangible that you and your community care about, something fun that will actually affect change (see chapter 3). For the earlier example of a food desert, you may choose to set up a fresh market or to create something in the built environment, such as sidewalks in a particular area. After a few victories with getting sidewalks in particular areas, then you may have a large enough coalition and a sufficient number of victories to approach your town or county to adopt new ordinances that require sidewalks for all new housing construction sites.

- Avoid agreement on a solution until everyone has agreed on the problem, and continuously validate original assumptions about the problem. If you cannot agree on the existence of the problem, then you will have difficulty agreeing to an achievable solution.

- Involve everyone, but not to the point where you spend more time managing invitations than working on the project. Especially at the beginning, it helps if everyone can fit around a table. Research indicates that important decisions are hard to make in large groups (see chapter 6); the "rule of seven" teaches that for every individual beyond seven that you add to a group, decision effectiveness declines by 10% (Blenko et al., 2010; Mankis, 2013).

- Pick a neutral meeting spot at a mutually convenient time and bring food. "Breaking bread" together changes the dynamics of groups. Another option that many institutional and community leaders adopt is to rotate the location of the meeting so everyone has an opportunity to use the meeting to also tell their story (organization mission and services).

- Pick a problem that is immediate, specific, and winnable:
  - Immediate—Everyone perceives the problem to be "in their face," and the solution can resolve the problem quickly (e.g., getting the neighborhood gassed and baited for cat-sized rats).

- Specific—The solution has to be something very concrete, and not a global idea (see chapter 22). What specifically does the group want to achieve? Quantify the problem, volume, costs, or impact on quality of life of the population. Put a face and a name to the solution. People believe they cannot beat city hall and they are correct: Talking to a building is silly, but talking to the city manager or county commissioner can produce results.
- Winnable—Shared confidence occurs with the first win, so an issue must be winnable. Make sure the leadership believes the solution is realizable and achievable. If you are not sure of winning, do not start the campaign.
- Finally, always celebrate the win; do not be a stoic. Savor the win among the group and use the celebration to build personal relationship and begin the conversation. Many new organizations become remiss in accepting and celebrating their hard-fought victory. Some will even begin to believe the victory was the result of some other action or activity by a different set of community or political stakeholders. Own the victory, and with today's digital media, get it out quickly through websites, Facebook, or Twitter, for example (see chapter 11).

WHAT NOT TO DO: FURTHER GUIDELINES

Achieving an early win also depends on avoiding certain activities. I suspect that once you've gone through your first collaborative campaign, you will want to add to the following list. Please go to our website (https://practicalplaybook. org/) and add your commentary on what not to do.

- Don't just throw a party or a meeting unless it is a tangible step toward a larger community goal. For example, a meeting to acquire community support to construct walking-trails can be a very effective short-term campaign with a win, so long as the county or city has capability to fund the trails (capital budget), and the campaign leads to a budgetary victory.
- Don't choose to "develop a plan" as the first venture. This will bore half your group.
- Don't pick something that takes years to change, such as building a new community wellness center. The coalition may not be able to sustain itself through such a project without earlier successes.
- Don't expend energy searching for "the silver bullet."
- Don't "wing" meetings and agendas; respect your partners. Always have a preplanning meeting before the meeting with two or three key people, share the agenda with them, and always collect sign-in sheets with a timely follow-up response to any issues or concerns raised during the meeting.

CONCLUSION

Getting the collaboration off to a positive birth begins with picking a problem to solve that is perceived to be achievable, facilitates mutual support as well as acceptance of each other's roles and functions within the coalition, and allows leadership to quickly plow through meeting structures. Early wins enable leadership to establish meeting formats and decision-making processes while also building trust, capacity, confidence, and resiliency for addressing more complex and potentially divisive issues affecting each other's organizations and the community.

REFERENCES

Bandura. Self-efficacy mechanism in human agency. Am Psychol 1982; 37(2): 122–147.

Blenko MW, Rogers P, Mankins MC: Decide and deliver: Five steps to breakthrough performance in your organization. Cambridge, MA: Harvard Business Review Press, 2010.

Fitzgerald K, Brandell C, et al. Mobilizing residents for action: The role of small wins and strategic supports. Am J Community Psychol 2006; 38(3–4): 143–152.

Foster-Fishman PG et al. National Center for Biotechnology Information. http://www.ncbi.nlm.nih.gov/pubmed/17006773. Accessed Feb 2, 2014.

Institute for Healthcare Improvement. How to Improve. http://www.ihi.org/resources/Pages/HowtoImprove/default.aspx. Accessed Feb 2, 2014.

Mankis M. The Five Traps of High Stake Decision Making. Harvard Business Review On-Line. http://blogs.hbr.org/2013/11/the-five-traps-of-high-stakes-decision-making/. Accessed Feb 2, 2014.

Watkins M: The First 90 Days: Critical Success Strategies for New Leaders at All Levels. Boston: Harvard Business School Press, 2003.

Weick KE. Small wins: Redefining the scale of social problem. Am Psychol 1984; 39(1): 40–49.

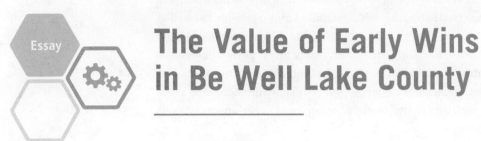

The Value of Early Wins in Be Well Lake County

CHRISTINA ARNOLD

BE WELL LAKE COUNTY PROGRAM HISTORY

Early wins, such as building trust between organizations, increasing stakeholder involvement, and establishing a data collection and evaluation plan were critical to the success of the Be Well Lake County (BWLC) program because it established the critical building blocks for the program. Building program design, establishing community relationships, and producing summary reports to demonstrate the program's impact were all early wins in this program. BWLC is a program that helps patients to manage their diabetes so that they can remain healthy and active and prevent complications associated with the disease. The program's goal is to build greater access to health care and support resources targeting the underserved diabetes population in Lake County, Illinois.

BWLC is a partnership between NorthShore University Health System (NorthShore) and the Lake County Health Department and Community Health Center (LCHD/CHC), funded by an initial commitment from the NorthShore University

Foundation and in-kind support through the NorthShore University Health System. LCHD/CHC functions as the local public health department for Lake County and has six federally qualified health center sites. NorthShore operates four hospitals within its system in the northern suburbs of Chicago. Diabetes services are offered to patients of BWLC in three ways: 1) primary care, 2) specialized diabetes support, and 3) specialty care at NorthShore. Within the LCHD/CHC model of care, a patient's medical visit is done through an interdisciplinary team (Fig. 9E-1). The patient sees the primary care provider, dietitian, nurse/certified medical assistant, and case manager all in one visit. Through this collaboration, the patient receives specialized diabetes support. The program offers a variety of programs to fit each patient's specialized needs. This includes support groups, diabetes self-management education classes, fitness programs and gym memberships, transportation, and a community garden. The core specialty care services needed for optimal diabetes management are provided through referrals to NorthShore specialty physicians (cardiology, ophthalmology, nephrology, podiatry, and

Figure 9E-1 ▼

Schematic diagram of roles of various stakeholders in the Be Well Lake County diabetes program, from patients to caregivers.

(©Christina Arnold, 2014).

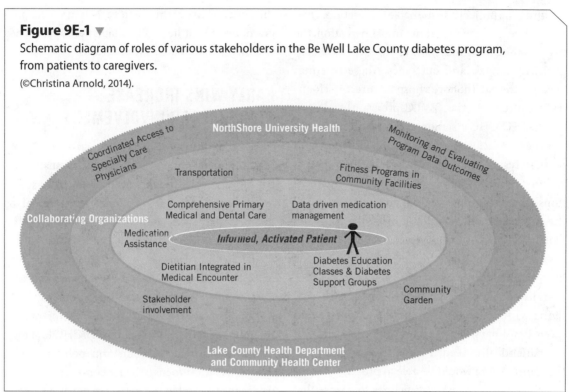

endocrinology). Without the collaboration from NorthShore, LCHD/CHC patients would not have access to these critically needed specialty care services to manage their diabetes.

Members of the LCHD/CHC clinical staff provide a consistent standard of care to each patient, including assistance with medication and testing supplies, on-site hemoglobin A1C testing, and education to promote a healthy lifestyle for the entire family. The program advances NorthShore's mission by empowering and preparing patients and families to manage their own health care. BWLC is also aligned with the LCHD/CHC mission of providing access to high-quality, comprehensive primary care. The program contributes to comprehensive disease management. It provides a message of prevention to decrease the trend of

hereditary diabetes, through a family approach to care and education about healthy living through nutrition and physical fitness. NorthShore's initial commitment launched BWLC at LCHD/CHC North Chicago Health Center, and the program expanded to the LCHD/CHC Belvidere Medical Building location in 2013. Since its inception in 2009, BWLC has enrolled over 850 individuals into the program.

EARLY WINS FOSTER TRUST, COLLABORATION, AND MUTUAL RESPECT

The first early win of the BWLC program was building trust between NorthShore and the LCHD/CHC. Trust among partners was instrumental in

building the project's sustainable foundation. Over the first year of the program's implementation, the two organizations met monthly to identify shared goals, objectives, and outcomes. These meetings between the NorthShore's hospital directors, foundation directors, the BWLC program evaluator, and LCHD/CHC's senior administrators started to foster a relationship of trust, collaboration, and mutual respect between the partnering organizations. During the first year, the two organizations together built the initial program design. As the primary financial supporter of the program, NorthShore had a strong vested interest in its success. As the program goals and objectives became more defined by the two organizations, it was clear that the patients of LCHD/CHC in North Chicago living with diabetes would be at the center of an interdisciplinary approach to patient care and that the patients also needed supportive care services that NorthShore would be able to provide.

The team established timelines to ensure that the defined project goals and objectives stayed on track. During meetings, the two partner organizations discussed data collection, staffing, standards of care, and reporting between organizations. NorthShore wanted to ensure that the program could clearly demonstrate outcomes and LCHD/CHC wanted to ensure that patients could receive optimal care for their diabetes. The organizational collaboration also fostered a method to highlight other social and community factors that BWLC patients are facing that directly impact their health. Patients in the program often experience food insecurity or transportation barriers. During the patient medical visit, the patient is asked to complete a food security questionnaire, and this information is entered into the BWLC patient database. Through collaboration with NorthShore, the program evaluator was able to use this data to identify food insecurity as a significant issue affecting the patients' lives. This is an early win of the program, because it helped to shape new approaches to assisting patients in the program.

EARLY WINS INCREASE STAKEHOLDER INVOLVEMENT

Considering differences in perspectives is important to understand when initiating and sustaining collaborations with stakeholders. "Whether stakeholders are working at systemic, organizational, or interactional levels, their perspectives need to be considered to effectively move collaborations forward" (Akhtar-Danesh et al., 2013). Community engagement helped to increase awareness and support for the program. This was a key early win. At the onset of the program, when the NorthShore Foundation and members of LCHD/CHC first met, a forum was held to brainstorm potential ideas for the program focus. Then a community forum was held to see what the patient needs were. "Each stakeholder is influenced by a set of values and information that are formed by education, background, heredity, and environment" (Farquhar et al., 2005). The values, beliefs, and knowledge that stakeholders and community members brought to the forums helped to shape the BWLC program. Staff members from both organizations and patients have all remained key stakeholders.

NorthShore specialty care physicians are an integral part of stakeholder involvement into the program. This component of the program is vital for patients who need to have medical consultation and treatment above what BWLC primary care providers can offer. NorthShore specialists agreed to accept reduced rates for their services for BWLC patients. This integration of NorthShore specialists as part of the care team allowed the program to maximize the dollars raised by the foundation and to optimize patient care. Meanwhile, through

the NorthShore Foundation and Highland Park Auxiliary (another stakeholder in the program), the word began to spread about how patients within the BWLC program did not have access to healthy food sources. This garnered new stakeholder involvement in the program; food banks donated food, and through a generous funder, a community garden was started for the BWLC patients, which is in its fourth growing season. Another stakeholder committed to providing a physical fitness component to the program. The fitness program engages previously inactive patients in physical activities, and improved glycemic control is being demonstrated in these participants.

EARLY WINS IMPROVE DESIRED OUTCOMES

Another early win to the BWLC program and one of the most vital to the program is the early establishment of a data collection and evaluation plan. NorthShore and LCHD/CHC, in the early collaborative period, knew that this was essential to the design in order to demonstrate program impact. The team chose 16 measures related to diabetes care that would be entered weekly into an MS Access database. Data abstraction is completed quarterly, and a summary report is compiled and analyzed by the evaluator. This report is provided to LCHD/CHC administration, the BWLC program coordinator and staff, NorthShore administration, and the primary care physicians caring for the patients. This information is also used to measure progress toward program objectives, and providers use this data to make changes with patient care management.

The comparison that NorthShore and LCHD/CHC wanted to make was between privately insured patients with diabetes receiving care through the NorthShore medical group and the cohort of patients in the LCHD/CHC BWLC program. The object of the comparison was to see if there were any differences in outcomes between the groups. Through the program data, the BWLC program was able to show that poor diabetes outcomes are related to food insecurity, especially for those with high hunger. It also showed that a multidisciplinary approach to care helped to reduce HbA1c and LDL levels. Having the ability to track data outcomes helps the providers to do more population-based care management. For example, patients can be grouped according to HbA1c level into three groups: 1) those with a value <7%, 2) those with a value between 7% and 9%, and those with a value >9% at baseline. Then we can let the providers know what percentage of those patients are on insulin at baseline. From there, the provider team can make decisions on how to treat specific patients to improve quality outcomes. Without this data availability, this care management approach is not possible.

Data on food insecurity have also proved invaluable. The BWLC program used the food insecurity information obtained at the onset of the program for community garden collaboration and to identify food resources for the community. The information is used to spread awareness to patients and the community about food deserts. The food insecurity data allow the collaborating partners to analyze relationships between food insecurity and patient outcomes. Recent BWLC food insecurity data demonstrate that food-secure patients have significantly lower HbA1c levels at enrollment when compared to food-insecure patients (8.46±2.24 vs. 9.04±2.38, $p = 0.03$). Data collection also helped to show the collaborating partners if they were meeting targeted patient numbers and program goals via dashboards. This information is reported monthly from LCHD/CHC

to NorthShore. The data outcomes were able to show early successes in the program, which was vital to the program continuation and also to long-term sustainability.

The early wins of BWLC made it possible for the underserved diabetes population of Lake County to access health care and supportive resources. In establishing a strong partnership between LCHD/CHC and NorthShore, the BWLC had early wins in building trust, securing stakeholder involvement, and implementing data collection, all of which continue to make this a successful program and partnership.

REFERENCES

Akhtar-Danesh N, Ruta V, O'Mara L, Austin P, and Munroe V. Viewpoints about collaboration between primary care and public health in Canada. BMC Health Serv Rese 2013; 13: 311.

Farquhar SA, Michael YL, Wiggins N. Building on leadership and social capital to create change in 2 urban communities. Am J Public Health 2005; 95(4): 596–601. doi:10.2105/AJPH.2004.048280

Challenges of Working Together

LARA SNYDER

CHALLENGES ARE INEVITABLE

Relationships, of any nature, will have their challenges. When individuals and groups come together, they bring their own expectations and assumptions of how the relationship should work and be structured. Like families, cross-sectoral teams can work brilliantly together—or be totally dysfunctional. It is hardly surprising that when you assemble a diverse group of people with varied skills into a team, things don't always go smoothly. Nevertheless, multi-professional teams are central to improving population health. So, how can teams work together efficiently? One important key is to acknowledge that there will be challenges and to try to mitigate them before they cause harm to your relationship. Whether this is your first collaborative project or you have a long-standing history with your partner, challenges are inevitable. It is how you address these issues that will determine the success and sustainability of your relationship. This section highlights a variety of trials that integrative partnerships may face. The guidance provided will teach you how to handle these trials in a manner that will build your relationship—not destroy it.

POTENTIAL CHALLENGES (AND HOW TO OVERCOME THEM)

Starting Off on the Wrong Foot

First impressions set the tone for every meeting that follows. Remember, you are building what will hopefully be a lasting and mutually beneficial relationship. How you enter that relationship will shape how it progresses. Communities often have meeting places where power brokers meet and deals are cut. If appropriate, use local culturally appropriate meeting locations instead of summoning your partner to your office.

Assuming Everyone Speaks the Same Language

The similarities between primary care and public health are strong enough that it is easy to miss the differences in culture and language, and discover them only later, when there are misunderstandings. Use active listening techniques such as repeating back what you think you heard to make sure you are capturing and understanding what the other is saying.

Blurred Roles and Responsibilities

Primary care and public health practitioners have different training, ways of working, and cultures. They are also going through huge changes, restructuring, and reorganization. Evolving roles and boundaries consequently affect how professionals work together and can cause confusion. Everyone needs clarity on his or her own role as well as on what other team members do. Developing and documenting agreed-on operational procedures can help clarify the business of the team and the roles of the individuals that comprise it.

Issues of Territory and Ownership

The essence of an integrative project is that no one has sole proprietorship. Be careful that your actions don't suggest otherwise. For example, when sending out correspondence on the project, think through small items such as whose logo is on the material and where the different logos are placed. You should aim to make the message as neutral as possible to avoid conflict. When scheduling a meeting with your partner, did you "summon" that person to your office for a meeting? You may have a beautiful board room to meet in, but it could be intimidating to your partner. Pick a location that will encourage interactivity and put individuals at ease. If there are more than two or three people, seek out a community building, such as a chamber of commerce or local library. If there will be just a couple of people, maybe your local coffee shop would be appropriate.

Choosing a Single-Sided Goal

You and your partners may have your own ideas about the goals you want to achieve, but confirm that it is something that your community also wants to see happen. Put yourself in the shoes of someone who has a whole team of professionals discussing their welfare. Wouldn't you like the chance to contribute? Don't underestimate the value of listening to service users. Your team needs to be very clear on the needs of the population it is serving and on meeting those needs. This focus should inform the roles and responsibilities of team members and should also determine the competencies required by the team. Refer to the principle of community engagement for more ideas on how to involve your community.

Picking a Project That Won't Show Results for 10 Years

If this is your first integrated project, pick low-hanging fruit that can demonstrate a difference within a year. After a year you should be able to look back and clearly recognize the accomplishments you made in working to accomplish your goal. These goals don't necessarily have to show an improvement in health outcomes or a decrease in health costs, but can speak to accomplishments in your project's process. Maybe you have established a new protocol or have started to gather additional data that will help you make informed decisions in the future.

Attempting to Use a One-Size-Fits-All Model

Remember that what has worked in one setting may not work in another. There is no need to recreate the wheel, but there may be a need to tailor a strategy to your context.

Not Thinking for the Future

Bring in partners who can help sustain your initiative. Sustainability is the ability of a project to be maintained and supported beyond a short grant or award. Start thinking about it from day one. Consider the resources it will take to sustain your project. Is it realistic to think that you can obtain these resources within the given time frame? You don't need to be certain that you can get the resources, but you have to know that it is within the realm of possibility. In the long run, what is the value, even beyond cost savings/avoidance that you are trying to produce? Value will emerge out of collaborative efforts. Examples like the Citizens Health Initiative in New Hampshire prove it's possible. Early evaluation from the New Hampshire Multi-Payer Medical Home Pilot, a Pillar Project of the Initiative is showing that a Patient-Centered Medical Home practice can indeed "bend the cost trend." However, it will take initial investment and time before these outcomes are realized. Remember: alignment and integration is a journey (see chapter 8).

Having Tunnel Vision

Develop metrics that matter to all of your partners. Designing and implementing a useful assessment requires ongoing collaboration among assessors and stakeholders. When done right, it can be used to answer a wide variety of questions that help partnerships carry out their work more effectively and efficiently. Take a look at chapter 21 to gain a deeper understanding of how to develop metrics that matter.

Not Taking Time to Reflect

Make time to reflect on your progress. So often when we are implementing a project we do not take the time to celebrate the accomplishments, however small, that have been made. At one of your regularly scheduled meetings, take 10 minutes to do a review of accomplishments, highlighting key personnel and effective strategies. Then, make sure you are sharing those successes intermediately to individuals and groups who may not be as close to the project as you are. Make time to celebrate your successes and appreciate the effort invested to get there. This step is critical to sustaining partnerships. See Leveraging Media (chapter 11) for tips on sharing your story.

Not Putting Yourself in the Other's Shoes

To realize the potential of a new partnership, you must be willing to understand where the other group is coming from. Create a bridge from "my way" to "our way." Time, resources, and sustaining momentum have to make sense for both parties. Get into your partner's shoes. Take the time to get to know your partner, his or her daily world, and some of the obstacles that he or she faces. If our partner doesn't respond to your email as quickly as you think should be the norm, be patient and understanding. Some people don't use email at all (to this day). Some team members feel that if an issue is important enough to discuss, they expect a phone call or, better, a face-to-face meeting. Appreciate that everyone is wearing multiple hats and juggling priorities. Team members bring different ideas, goals, values, beliefs and needs to their teams, and these differences are a primary strength of teams. These same differences inevitably lead to some conflict. One of the ways in which team members can help each other improve their abilities to function in multidisciplinary teams is to work with each other to develop their understanding of conflict and their capabilities to manage and resolve conflict. It is important to have an appreciation for the complexity that relationships can bring.

Lack of Planning

Without a comprehensive project plan with goals, task descriptions, and milestones, team members lack direction. Work to establish specific, measurable, attainable, realistic, and time-constrained goals for the project, so that all team members know what they need to do. When expectations are clearly set in a project plan document, teams tend to function more effectively. You can work to establish a process for making decisions about changes to the plan that include team members, including the community, in the process. When team members feel empowered to contribute their opinions, overall communication tends to remain open and productive. Although planning is important, don't wait for things to be perfect before you begin. Get started and learn together as you go. What can keep you from moving forward is the desire for your planning tools to be perfected before you proceed. Planning exercises should be used to aid your implementation, not hinder it.

Waiting for Leaders to Take Initiative

A shared goal of population health and aligned leadership are two of the most important principles of integration—and important to establish from the beginning of your project and continue to nurture. However, people in formal leadership positions may not be ready to enter a new partnership. Fortunately, although commitment of leadership is necessary for large-scale reform, it is not always necessary to achieve smaller successes. In fact, leadership can be demonstrated at a variety of levels. For example, a waiting room reception-ist can take the initiative to speak to a Latina mother about the new soccer team for Latino children at a nearby park. She or he could also hand out extra brochures for the mother to take to friends and neighbors. Although a seem-ingly small example of integration, the receptionist's actions can have a large impact. In some instances, clinics are bringing receptionists into medical home teams, because patients often find it easier to relate to a receptionist from their local community. Rather than waiting for top leadership to iden-tify a health issue and then provide solutions, program and/or clinical staff have a front-row seat in understanding some of the most pressing community health needs and can be strong assets in defining the need and the appropri-ate strategies. If you are in a leadership position, encourage your staff to share their ideas with your team, maybe at a monthly staff meeting. If you are a staff member, be encouraged that small ideas can make a huge difference (see chapters 3 and 7, and Section V).

Allowing Concerns of Loss to Trump Action

Concern that one partner may overshadow the other can lead to inertia. Remember that everyone is experiencing change and potential loss in our shifting world of health, and that everyone has much to offer. Bear in mind that there is more to be done than can be accomplished by one group of pro-fessionals alone, and try to let go of where you practice and embrace the ser-vice and outcome. Consider that collaboration could lead to more gain than loss—to both individual professionals and patients.

Waiting to Be Paid

Global payments and alternative payment methodologies that incentivize cost containment and improved health outcomes are emerging quickly. However, it may be awhile before there are direct incentives to work together across primary care and public health. While payment is a reality, so are the benefits to partnering—for clients/patients, communities, and public health and primary care professionals. The following tips will help you and your team move forward in the absence of cash incentives.

> "Begin with the people and the problems, not the money. Otherwise, you get hung up on turf and power, before you have experience doing the work. Then manage the money to support those who are actually doing the work needed."
>
> *J. Lloyd Michener, MD*
> *Chair, Duke Department of Community and Family Medicine*

Tips

1. Know that others are taking steps to collaborate in the same fee-for-service environment.
2. Take small steps that don't cost money.
3. Jointly apply for grants to fund your collaborative efforts.
4. Look for ways to leverage existing funding.
5. Primary care must remember that public health has, generally, been funded to a lesser degree and will need to work to create equal partnerships.

DON'T LOSE SIGHT OF THE OPPORTUNITY

Collaborations across public health and primary care create great momentum and accelerate attainment of our goals for quality of life, equity, and community health. Partnerships can be rewarding professionally, personally, and with regard to outcomes. However, they aren't always easy. Collaboration is a journey. Some days it will be two steps forward, one step back, whereas other days it may be two steps back and one forward. Remember that partnering is a human process composed of relationships, trust, and failures. It's about learning to work together. It's easier if everyone is allowed to be different. Find differences that can be leveraged rather than trying to make everyone the same. Good intentions are, unfortunately, not enough. There will be misunderstandings and setbacks. Don't give up!

Starting Off on the Right Foot: A Communication Strategy Is Essential

Essay

KAREN REMLEY

D r. Harvey Fineberg, President of the Institute of Medicine, past Provost of Harvard University and past Dean of the Harvard School of Public Health, says it well, "Public Health and Medicine approach the challenge of health and health care from distinct, complementary perspectives" (Fineberg, 2011). This insightful comment is a great stepping-off point in any discussion about the challenge of communicating and collaborating between these two health professions, as the majority of their activities are complementary, rather than overlapping. There are other simple ways to think about how these two disciplines differ. The first is the issue of scale. Public health professionals routinely think in terms of populations with sample sizes of greater than 30, who represent data points to be anonymously combined and analyzed, and public health professionals feel responsible for impacting the community's health. Physicians see each patient as a separate unique data point to be highlighted and pulled out of a sea of patients and have a sense of ownership for that individual's health needs. Then there is time. Whereas physicians think in 15-minute patient visit increments, public health

professionals think in terms of 15-month projects. Finally, physicians document as they go, whereas public health officials provide reports along scheduled time intervals.

How do we start to bring these two groups together? Aretha Franklin's song, R.E.S.P.E.C.T. (Redding, 1967), immediately comes to mind. Through respectful, valuable, and collegial interactions between these two groups, we can begin to move from complementary work to inclusive efforts, impacting both the health of individuals and populations. And where to start? I suggest we become pen-pals. You may think I am joking, but by sharing communications, important information, and a mutual responsiveness to questions, we can quickly become each other's valued colleagues. Let's walk through a time when this approach not only worked but also established a new relationship between the clinical community and public health.

EXAMPLE OF SUCCESSFUL COLLABORATION: H1N1 PANDEMIC

Let's return to the early days of the H1N1 pandemic in 2009. In those first weeks, information

was rapid-fire, confusing, frequently changing, and, at times, frankly scary. We were not sure if we were facing "the BIG pandemic," one that would significantly disrupt society and its infrastructure, or whether this would end up being just a "bad flu" year. Add into this atmosphere the hype of media attention, particularly in the face of many young people and children being disproportionately affected by illness and death. Public health was struggling to define what we were seeing epidemiologically; adjusting avian flu plans to meet this seemingly different presentation; developing vaccine strains and strategy; advising on prevention, quarantine, and isolation; and determining allocation strategies for potentially scarce health care resources such as antiviral drugs. The physician community was struggling with similar challenges, but with even less access to timely, accurate, and actionable information to assist them in making important bedside clinical decisions about treatment and expected clinical courses. Patients were confused, worried, and distrustful.

First Communication Strategy: Email Blasts

In our state of Virginia, we already had a tool to send email blasts and faxes to all licensed physicians during an emergency, but had never used this capability beyond a test case. We decided to use this existing authorized communication avenue as the center of our information exchange strategy with the clinical community. Starting with the very first email, we developed a format that stressed a direct relationship with the state health official, purposefully structuring the email more like a colleague-to-colleague consultation, as opposed to a press release or summary from a large entity to an individual. Using pronouns such as "I" rather than "we" or "the Department of Health," physicians were first sincerely recognized

and thanked for the important role they were playing in this evolving situation. Knowing that clinicians would want timely and concise information, the email itself was by design a maximum limit two-page document, inclusive of important graphs, tables, and recommendations. The format followed the four pillars being used by national and state authorities to categorize activities: 1) surveillance, 2) mitigation, 3) immunization, and 4) communication. Epidemiologic tracking of disease in the state was presented district by district in a color-coded map, followed with brief explanatory language. The mitigation section included information about antiviral therapy, availability, and key phone numbers to call if access was an issue. Types of patient isolation and health care worker protection, including use of N95 respirator masks, were highlighted. The vaccine section provided regular updates on vaccine production, availability, and, eventually, administration rates. Last, concise, printable one-page documents for use in the office and hospital setting to inform patients and coworkers were attached. Links to original documents, Centers for Disease Control and Prevention (CDC) websites, and contact information were provided. The letter concluded with another personal thank you and a request to contact the Commissioner directly with any concerns or questions. Our goal was to establish a communication strategy that would not only work well with the H1N1 pandemic, but also could be used for other urgent and emergent communications.

The Response

The first day, we received countless emails from physicians offering their thanks for the information. As I traveled around the state, I saw my letters printed and hanging in doctors' offices. They were so well received that we began to send them to all health care providers licensed through the

Department of Health Professions with the goal of even wider dissemination of important information. We encouraged the forwarding of the emails to any and all. At the peak of the early days of the pandemic, we estimated over 50,000 people were communicating with us through this approach. Each email was "tested" with a small group of clinicians before it was sent out, frequently resulting in modifications based on their unique perspective.

Does it have staying power? Even today, as I travel around the state in a new role, clinicians will talk about how I was their pen-pal, how they counted on my emails to inform them, and how happy they are that the current state health official continues the strategy. What are potential pitfalls? Overuse of the email list: It cannot be distributed or used beyond the Commissioner's office; becoming too wordy, using "public health speak," and thus diluting the message or, even worse, having clinicians quit reading halfway through; or not providing information for an important health issue when expectations have been developed. This communication model was again a very important component of the collaboration between public health and primary care in identifying and caring for patients during the fungal meningitis outbreak in the Southwest region of Virginia. Although we hope we never have another bioterrorism or dirty bomb event, it is our expectation that physicians around the state would reach for their smart phones, expecting to get an email from the state health official with timely, concise, and actionable information.

Second Communication Strategy: Virtual Committees

A second strategy used to engage the clinical community during this prolonged event was to set up three "virtual committees" comprising clinicians who were experts, well respected in their field, and well known in their communities. Knowing that we were not going to be able to arrange face-to-face meetings quickly enough, and that we were in an environment of increased demands on the health care delivery system as a result of mushrooming patient volumes in health care facilities and doctor's offices, I sent personal emails asking the expert clinicians to join one of three Commissioners' advisory committees. I purposely selected individuals from all areas of the state and encompassing all major health centers. The three committees were composed of clinician with expertise in 1) infectious disease and infection control; 2) pediatric care, pediatric ICU care, and pediatric surge issues; and 3) obstetrics, as the pandemic was particularly brutal to pregnant women. Physicians on these committees came from general outpatient practices, academic medical centers, and busy hospitals. I had a previous relationship with all, albeit it many times based on a single meeting.

The Response

The tone of the committee meetings was of my gratitude for their willingness to help me navigate important decisions for the Virginia response, information seeking and validation of "ground truth," and solicitation of their insights and views about how to best treat our population in a rapidly evolving situation. Each call was scheduled around the clinicians' schedules, not mine, and an agenda was always sent out the day before, which consisted of a brief update by us and then a series of questions that we needed their help in addressing. Rarely did any member miss a call, and when the pandemic stabilized, we were able to suggest that we would no longer meet but also would like to "activate" the groups again for any future events. I sent personal letters to both the committee members and their supervisors, which were signed by the Governor

of Virginia and me. Our success story included being able to discuss and understand how infection prevention control was being undertaken in a time when resources were rapidly diminishing, setting up a pediatric ICU bed tracking system that continues to be used today, obtaining buy-in and support of difficult decisions regarding vaccine allocation, and, most important, having ambassadors throughout the state who could share a common message and decrease rumors.

SUMMARY

In summary, during crises, events, and outbreaks that impact the health and health care delivery to members of the community, public health is uniquely situated to become a "bedside" consultant to the primary care provider. By presenting information in formats that are most conducive to physicians being able to synthesize and use the information in their practice, and by "bringing them under the tent" when we are faced with unusual public health events, we can establish a trusted two-way relationship which can then morph into a true partnership, with the ultimate goal of improving the health of our shared population.

REFERENCES

Fineberg H. Public Health and Medicine. Am J Prev Med 2011; 41(4S3): S149–S151.

Redding O. Respect. 1967, Volt Records.

Chapter 11

Leveraging Media

KATE REUTERSWÄRD

As a public health or primary care practitioner, working with the media represents a tremendous opportunity to amplify the impact of your work in your community. Whether you're seeking to raise awareness of the services you provide, document your achievements in order to appeal to grant-making organizations, or simply celebrate your organization's successes, both traditional and social media can expand your reach beyond your personal and professional networks to a bigger, broader audience.

The range of media capabilities and communicational tools available to public health and primary care practitioners is as diverse as the health care field itself. Regardless of whether you have access to the teams of communicators at organizations like the American Public Health Association and the American Medical Association or the bare minimum of resources typically available for local health departments, you have the ability to engage with the media on behalf of the work you're doing. This chapter provides an overview of the different types of media as well as the tools and resources you need to start leveraging them.

WHAT IS MEDIA?

Simply put, media is any means of mass communication. For you and your colleagues, media may be a local television program, a radio station, your local newspaper, a digital journal, or a variety of social media outlets. These distribution channels can play a crucial role in moving your integration project forward by raising public awareness of the work you're doing, establishing channels of communication between you and your community, and documenting your progress in improving population health.

WORKING WITH THE MEDIA

The term "media relations" describes both your strategy for working with the media and the relationships you build with reporters, producers, editors,

NACCHO offers a communications toolkit that provides media outreach guides and templates for local health departments. For more information, see: http://www.naccho. org/advocacy/marketing/ toolkit/

bloggers, and more. Before you send an email or direct a tweet to the editor-in-chief of your local newspaper, check with your organization and its partners to get an idea of what resources are available to you as well as any rules you need to follow (most often regarding who has to clear external communications or how certain projects can be described). Most primary care networks and state health departments have well-established news and communications offices that can lend their experience and their existing media relations to help you. If you're not sure who to contact in a partner organization, look for a news or communications page on their website. In the health industry, the primary contact for media relations is usually a communications director.

Local public health departments and community programs may have limited personnel dedicated to media relations, if they have any at all. If this is the case, don't worry. There are numerous resources that can help guide you and your team. The next two sections of this chapter outline the different ways you can leverage traditional and social media on your own.

TRADITIONAL MEDIA

What Is Traditional Media?

Traditional media includes types of mass communication that do not provide a platform for social interaction. This includes television, radio, newspaper, and magazine outlets. By working with traditional media, partnerships can build name recognition and credibility.

Getting Started

Start by considering your target audience and the media it consumes. Which newspapers, magazines, television shows, and radio stations might they be reading, watching, or listening to? It's important to think in terms of geographic scope as well—if your program is operating on a local level it is best to reach out to local media, whereas statewide programs may garner media attention from regional or national organizations. In addition, consider news outlets that serve primary care or public health organizations. For example, if your audience includes family physicians, you could send your news to the communications team at the American Academy of Family Physicians (AAFP). If you're working with a program run out of a local health department, you can be in touch with the National Association of County and City Health Officials (NACCHO). Organizations like the AAFP and NACCHO usually have newsletters and social media outlets that reach a large audience.

Once you know who you are trying to reach, you can build your press list. A press list is exactly what it sounds like—a list of journalists, reporters, bloggers, producers, and editors to help you keep track of who you would like to cover your story and what contact you have had with them. Public relations and marketing professionals often buy access to media databases, but if you don't have that tool at your fingertips, your best bet is to put your detective hat on and use the Internet to search for contacts. When building your media list, it's helpful to include the outlet or publication name, the individual's contact information, and the topics that individual most often covers (his or her beat).

It can be tempting to blast an email out to everyone at a newspaper, but you will do your project more favors if you focus on the individuals responsible for producing the material relevant to you. Journalists hate getting pitches that are completely unrelated to their beat. Some of this is just common sense: If you are working on a project that has reduced repeat hospitalizations in your county, you should contact the journalists and editors who work with the "Metro," "Region," or "Health" sections—not the editor-in-chief of the whole newspaper. You can also reach out directly to bloggers and columnists, but when it comes to radio and television, you'll want to be in touch with producers, not the hosts.

Tips

The following are some tips for jump-starting your media outreach:

- ✔ Ask a local personality, political figure, or an influential member in your field to publicly endorse your work, and share the endorsement in your newsletter or on social media.

- ✔ Contribute an opinion article to a professional journal or newsletter in your field.

- ✔ Report your success at a meeting or event with people outside your field.

- ✔ Distribute a media advisory or press release (see Figs. 11-1 and 11-2 for examples).

- ✔ Produce a promotional video.

- ✔ Start a blog (some examples include the CDC Director Blog, the Association of American Medical Colleges' (AAMC) Wing of Zock blog, and the PLOS Blogs Network).

- ✔ Release a report analyzing your program's impact and its plans for the future.

- ✔ Host an event like a seminar or a panel discussion to discuss a big picture topic related to your organization's work.

- ✔ Celebrate an important milestone or anniversary for your project with stakeholders and take the opportunity to discuss the impact you are having.

What Is Newsworthy?

When contacting the media, you'll constantly be asked different versions of, "What makes your story newsworthy?" You can think of this as a respectful, "So what?" Before you send any news to the media, you need to know the answer to this question.

You: Hi, I wanted to tell you about the new partnership we've created between our local health department and the largest health system in our area.

Journalist: *Mmm-hmmm.* (So what?)

You: We are working together to improve asthma services for children in our area.

Figure 11-1 ▼

Annotated press release.

COMMENT 1:

The press release serves as an official record of what your news is, and some reporters and bloggers will write an article based on just the release. That's one reason to include quotations! You should send this out to your entire media list. If reporters ask for the press release ahead of the event, you can share it with them "under embargo," which means they can't write about it until the scheduled release.

PRESS RELEASE

COMMENT 2:

Make sure to include the following key elements so reporters know who to contact for more information:

For Immediate Release

Date

Contact Name

Contact Info

For Immediate Release
March 5, 2014

Contact: Kate Reuterswärd
[o] 202-555-1234

PRACTICAL PLAYBOOK FOR PUBLIC HEALTH AND PRIMARY CARE AIMS TO IMPROVE POPULATION HEALTH; CUT HEALTH CARE COSTS

THE DE BEAUMONT FOUNDATION, DUKE COMMUNITY AND FAMILY MEDICINE, AND THE CDC LAUNCH "PRACTICAL PLAYBOOK" INITIATIVE TO INTEGRATE PUBLIC HEALTH AND PRIMARY CARE

COMMENT 3:

A press release always starts with the location of the announcement

Washington, DC – For decades, the medical and public health communities have struggled to stem the rise of illnesses that have led to a dramatic decline in population health. Today, chronic diseases such as asthma, obesity, heart disease, and diabetes have replaced acute infectious diseases like polio and smallpox as the leading drivers of illness in this country.

This trend, which appears to have been initiated in the early to mid-twentieth century, is not only leading to a lower quality of life and reduced economic productivity, but is a primary contributor of this country's astronomical health care costs. Chronic diseases account for 80% of all health care costs today compared to only 20% in 1900.

In accordance with generations of studies citing a need for more effective preventative care, the de Beaumont Foundation, Duke Community and Family Medicine, and the Centers for Disease Control and Prevention have created a new initiative – **A Practical Playbook: Public Health & Primary Care Together** – to support the project-based integration of public health and primary care.

COMMENT 4:

Bolding sections of a press release is a style decision. We decided to do it in this case because our press release was running on the long side. Generally, a press release runs 1-1.5 pages.

The Practical Playbook is designed to achieve three objectives: to improve population health, to better manage illness – especially chronic disease, and to mitigate health care costs. In practice, it gives local health administrators, public health officials, and primary care providers the means to offer more comprehensive health care both within and beyond a clinical context.

"We developed the Practical Playbook based upon years of research and anecdotal evidence that show that when local health departments and primary care providers work together, they can help communities get healthier and help both patients and insurers save on preventable illnesses," said Dr. Lloyd Michener, Professor and Chair of Duke Community and Family Medicine. "Our goal now is to take these local successes and apply them on a national scale."

Consider chronic asthma, which is growing every year and at last count (in 2007), cost the United States $56 billion in medical costs, lost school and work days, and early deaths. Today, the best that primary care providers can do is treat an individual patient's repeat episodes (or flare-ups). If there is an ongoing collaboration with the local health department, however, public health officials can collect real time data from multiple practices and emergency rooms and compile information that would identify asthma clusters. This would allow the health department to take immediate action to investigate whether there is an environmental cause that can be addressed to control the ongoing cases and to prevent the development of new ones.

To promote this kind of public health and primary care collaboration, the Practical Playbook initiative has developed a web-based tool in three parts. Part one, "Learn," explains the theoretical background of public health and primary care integration. Part two, "Do," outlines action steps for starting your own collaborative project to engage with a health concern in your community, like heart disease, obesity, or asthma. Part three, "Share," provides case studies of successful collaborative projects, complete with direct contacts to the project leads.

"Despite years of conferences, seminars, and reports from the medical community lauding the merits of public health and primary care integration, we have yet to see any meaningful progress towards improving population health," said Dr. James Sprague, CEO of the de Beaumont Foundation. "Facilitating collaboration between primary care providers and local health departments is a crucial element in addressing the social determinants of health and working long term to make all Americans live longer, healthier lives."

Dr. Denise Koo, Senior Advisor for Health Systems, Centers for Disease Control and Prevention added, "The Practical Playbook will be a game-changing tool for helping communities deal with the unchecked rise of chronic diseases like obesity, diabetes, and heart disease. It will be a cornerstone in our efforts to shift to a system focused on keeping our communities healthy rather than putting a bandaid on after they get sick."

COMMENT 5:

If you're using quotations, you have to be mindful of the appearance of a hierarchy: most important people speak first, less important speak last. In addition to project heads, you may also want to include quotations from important funders, community leaders, local politicians, people impacted by your health project, and more.

Figure 11-2 ▼
Annotated media advisory.

COMMENT 1:

A media advisory is an official communication from your project, so it should be polished and professional without providing excessive detail. Just the facts! Hopefully, you've already done the legwork of reaching out to reporters and pitching them on your news story. The media advisory is intended to serve as one last, final reminder of what's happening and when.

COMMENT 2:

You can put media contact information at the top or bottom of your media advisory, but make sure to include:

For Immediate Release

DATE

The name of your contact person

Their contact information (with email if they are not sending out the media advisory themselves)

COMMENT 3:

Obviously, catchy headlines and sub-headlines are better than boring ones! Try to use action verbs and, as appropriate, adjectives like "first," "biggest," "groundbreaking," etc. If your project can be quantified in some way (especially with impressive numbers), that is helpful to add as well.

COMMENT 4:

You always start off with marking the location.

COMMENT 5:

The media advisory should be as short and condensed as possible. You need to give the press the quick and dirty: who, what, when, and where. No quotations; no fluff!

MEDIA RELEASE

For Immediate Release
March 3, 2014

Contact: Kate Reuterswärd
[o] 202-555-1234

Media Alert *** Media Alert *** Media Alert

BRINGING PUBLIC HEALTH AND PRIMARY CARE TOGETHER

DE BEAUMONT FOUNDATION, DUKE COMMUNITY AND FAMILY MEDICINE, AND CDC LAUNCH PRACTICAL PLAYBOOK INITIATIVE

(Washington, DC) The de Beaumont Foundation, Duke Community and Family Medicine, and the CDC are launching **A Practical Playbook: Public Health and Primary Care Together**, a health care initiative to facilitate greater collaboration between public health and primary care in targeted health interventions. Founding partners at de Beaumont, Duke Community and Family Medicine, and the CDC are joined by NACCHO, ASTHO, the American Academy of Family Physicians, and the Institute of Medicine to discuss public health and primary care integration – how it works, what successes have been achieved, and the roadmap for effecting systemic change.

When implemented, Practical Playbook-style integrated public health projects are showing evidence of better management of chronic disease, reduced health care costs, and better population health outcomes.

WHAT: Presentations and panel discussion on public health and primary care integration

WHEN: 9:00 am on Wednesday, March 5, 2014

WHERE: National Press Club, 1st Amendment Lounge

WHO: **Harvey Fineberg**, MD, Institute of Medicine
James Sprague, MD, de Beaumont Foundation
Brian Castrucci, MA, de Beaumont Foundation
Lloyd Michener, MD, Duke Community and Family Medicine
Denise Koo, MD, MPH, Centers for Disease Control and Prevention
Jose Montero, MD, MHCDS, New Hampshire Public Health Services
Julie Wood, MD, FAAFP, American Academy of Family Physicians
Claude-Alix Jacob, MPH, National Association of County and City Health Officials

Journalist: *Mmm-hmmm.* (So what?)

You: Well, our partnership has reduced ER admissions, cut parent absenteeism from work by an estimated 7%, and, most importantly, improved the quality of life for 1500 children so far this year.

Journalist: Wow! (BINGO!)

When you are passionate and dedicated to your cause, it can be hard to distinguish between what's newsworthy and what's not. Think from the perspective of someone who's not familiar with you and your cause. What is there to know about your organization that can't be found on the website? Is there anything new and different happening that would interest others? Good intentions and hypotheses about your project outcomes are one thing, but you have to be ready to share a concrete story with a concrete impact. Still unsure? If a story includes at least one of the following characteristics, it might be newsworthy:

- Timing—your story relates directly to a current news story.
- Significance—your project affects the majority of the outlet's audience, or the outlet's audience was directly involved in your project.
- Proximity—your project took place in the outlet's audience's community.
- Prominence—your project involves someone (like a mayor or a major donor) or something (like political action or large amounts of money) important.
- Human interest—your project can be represented with or through a moving personal story.

Above all, it is important to understand the distinction between *news* and *message*. Your opinions about your project and its importance constitute the message. The qualitative or quantitative impact of your project is news. Yes, the work you are doing is important, but unless it has one of the elements listed earlier, your message alone is not enough to reach out to the traditional media.

Not sure what to share with the media? The Centers for Disease Control and Prevention (CDC) provides an outline of characteristics that make something newsworthy as well as helpful tips for pitching your story to the media. Available at http://www.cdc.gov/injury/anniversary/media-pitch.html

Pitching

Journalists will not typically commit to covering your story much in advance of its actually happening. At the same time, you want to try to keep them from missing your news on the day of the announcement. If you're planning an event, a good strategy is to send a concise email a month in advance to alert the media that the event is going to take place. The email should provide a simple rundown of the who, what, where, when, and why of your news. If the media is interested, they'll ask for more. Two weeks before your event, follow up with details handpicked to fit their interests by email or phone. If you don't get a response, don't consider that tantamount to a no. You have to be persistent! Most reporters are inundated with email. Sometimes, a quick phone call is the best way to cut through a cluttered inbox.

Press Releases

A press release is an official announcement made on behalf of your partnership. It makes it as easy as possible for a print or broadcast outlet to share your news because anything in the release can be quoted or reprinted. Consequently, you need to make sure your press release has been approved by the project leads. If you are partnering with a primary care network or state public health department, you'll need to secure their approval as well.

A press release should be about one to two pages, written using the inverted pyramid organizational structure, with the most important information at the beginning of the press release and the less important information saved for the end of the release. A typical press release includes:

- Your contact information (in case a journalist has follow-up questions)
- The date of your release
- An attention-grabbing headline
- A "hook" within the first paragraph (the hook summarizes the pitch and tells the journalist why he or she should cover the story)
- The who, what, when, where, and why of the story
- A quote that falls within the first three paragraphs (you can add as many additional quotes as you'd like—it's typically good to include the project leads and any major partners or funders)
- A boilerplate statement at the end that summarizes the organization's mission

When in doubt about what to include in your press release, favor being concise. Avoid the temptation to add unnecessary details and focus on the most important elements: an irresistible headline and hard-hitting quotations and/or statistics.

If you'd like to share the press release before your announcement goes live, you can do that—just make sure to tell the media that the release is "under embargo," which means they can't share it until the embargo lifts. Being clear about when your announcement goes public allows you to help reporters get a step ahead of the news by giving them a preview without having them let the cat out of the bag before you're ready. Along those lines, a press release should not be used to announce an event; you can use a media advisory (the simpler version) for that purpose. Don't forget to indicate that the event is open to the press!

Staying in Touch

If you're working on a long-term project, stay in touch with the connections you've made. Building a relationship with journalists whose work is relevant to yours can open up new opportunities for your organization. Staying on the editors' radar can also establish you as a go-to source of information if the editor is writing a story pertinent to your field.

SOCIAL MEDIA

What Is Social Media?

Social media is a form of mass communication that involves social interaction. Integrating social media into health communication campaigns and activities allows health communicators to leverage social networks to encourage participation, conversation, and community—all of which can help spread key messages and influence health decision making. Some health communicators are having an incredible impact on their communities through social media, but this requires a thoughtful strategy and ongoing manpower to maintain.

Getting Started

The advantage of social media is that there are no gatekeepers—all you have to do is sign up for a blog, a Twitter account, or Facebook to get started. The disadvantage is that you are responsible for content creation, so it requires you to allocate time and energy to maintaining whatever account you create.

The most important thing you should do before starting to participate in social media is to think carefully and strategically about what platforms will work best for you. You can tweet, blog, upload videos to YouTube, join a group on LinkedIn, share images on Instagram and Pinterest, or host Google Hangouts, to name a few options, but not all public health projects will naturally translate to photos or videos, just as not all projects will generate the ongoing updates that work best on Twitter. There is no right or wrong—you just have to imagine what kind of content you'll be able to generate and what kinds of interactions you want to have with the rest of the online world.

Note that all of these forms of social media have their strengths and weaknesses—Facebook and Twitter are great for direct engagement, for example, whereas Instagram and Pinterest are more focused on still images, and LinkedIn commentary and blogs are good for a more thorough treatment of an idea or news item. There are lots of resources available online to help you understand the difference between all of these tools. If you start searching for terms like "best social media platforms for nonprofits" or "social media public health," you'll find helpful resources from public health organizations and social media gurus alike. If you'd like to see some public health and primary care social media accounts in action, check out the range of platforms in use by the AAFP (newsletter, Twitter, and Facebook), the CDC (multiple Twitter and Facebook accounts), and the AAMC (their blog, "Wing of Zock," is widely followed).

Like all things technology related, it's important not to let the decision-making process prevent you from taking action. "Analysis paralysis"

Not sure which social media platform is right for you? Check out this online resource: http://www. examiner.com/list/how-to-pick-the-right-social-media-platform-for-you

describes the state of limbo that so commonly afflicts someone confronted with an overwhelming number of options. If you're completely new to social media, rope in a trusted millennial to walk you through the basics and spend a few hours continuing your education with reading online. Then start outlining a plan.

As you get started, keep in mind that it's very hard to "mess up" social media unless you publish content that is offensive or contrary to your organization's mission—short of that, it's all about building experience and getting better at using these online tools.

What's Worth Sharing?

Unlike traditional media, social media gives you complete agency over what information is shared. However, you should still be conscious about what will be interesting and engaging to your audience. Short anecdotes, pictures and updates from your project, and notable milestones are examples of appropriate social media content. Additionally, social media is a great platform for directly engaging with your audience: Starting conversations and creating relationships can benefit both you and your followers.

Some general guidelines for using social media include being consistent, using up-to-date information, and optimizing scheduling and posting times based on when your target audience is online. If you're not sure—and you have the time—experiment. Do people respond more in the morning or evening? During the workweek or on the weekends? To open-ended questions or a factoid? There are lots of ways to interact with your community, and it's up to you to discover what works best for your organization.

Monitoring

When monitoring engagement, remove spam and highly inappropriate content, but never delete comments simply because they are negative. Instead, respond to these comments head on and try to improve the relationship. Censoring or adopting a defensive attitude toward a negative comment will only attract more attention. Responding thoughtfully and constructively allows you to publicly make things right—and lays the bad experience to bed. Free software like HootSuite (https://hootsuite.com) can assist with both management and monitoring of social media accounts.

CONCLUSION

Traditional media coverage and social media outreach represents an opportunity for public health and primary care organizations to share the impact they're having on their communities. It takes time and some planning, but for the most part, common sense and strategic thinking—combined with some practice—will help your project get the attention it deserves. Keep in mind that although there is no trick or shortcut to getting media coverage, if you focus on building relationships on social media and delivering hard news to traditional media, you're well on your way to success.

Additional Resources
CDC. The Health Communicator's Social Media Toolkit. http://www.cdc.gov/socialmedia/tools/guidelines/pdf/socialmediatoolkit_bm.pdf

Chapter 12

The Practice of Public Health and How It Is Changing

BRIAN C. CASTRUCCI, HUGH H. TILSON, DENISE KOO, AND JONATHON P. LEIDER

Public health has been defined as "what we as a society do collectively to assure the conditions in which people can be healthy" (Institute of Medicine [IOM], 2003). This broad definition encompasses a wide range of activities targeted at social, environmental, behavioral, and other determinants of health. As a broad concept, public health is not a single service or product produced by a single profession, but it is a comprehensive set of activities provided or ensured by the public health system—a web of relationships that includes many people, organizations, and professions (Centers for Disease Control and Prevention [CDC], 2010) (Fig. 12-1). Governmental public health serves as the organization and coordinator—the "backbone"—of that public health system. The health care system, though vital, is only one of the dozens of interactive elements. The public health system also includes community-based organizations, school systems, and even businesses; every agency, group, and organization that contributes to a healthy community.

The public health system serves to protect and improve "population health," which may be thought of as an aggregation of health outcomes among groups of individuals, taking into account the distribution of health outcomes across and within those groups (Kindig, 2007). The public health system, and governmental public health especially, is responsible for the health and well-being of *all* individuals and groups in society. This is a significant departure from health care systems' traditional panel-based management, or "practice-based population health," which solely concerns the health outcomes of individuals under the care of providers in that system (Cusack et al., 2010).

ORGANIZATION OF GOVERNMENTAL PUBLIC HEALTH

The governmental public health enterprise in the United States consists of operations at the federal, state, and local levels. At the federal level, most public health functions are included in the U.S. Department of Health and Human Services (DHHS). Key public health agencies within DHHS include the CDC, the Health Resources and Services Administration (HRSA), the Substance Abuse and Mental Health Services Administration, the Centers for Medicare and Medicaid Services (CMS), the Food and Drug Administration, Environmental Protection Agency (EPA), Agency for Toxic Substances and Disease Registry, and the Agency for Healthcare Research and Quality. In addition to DHHS, the U.S. Department of Agriculture administers the Supplemental Nutrition Assistance Program and the Supplemental Nutrition Program for Women, Infants, and Children and the EPA conducts many environmental health-related activities. These federal agencies provide national leadership in establishing and achieving the nation's health goals and provide a significant amount of program-specific public health funding to state and local agencies. This "categorical" funding is specific funding for a narrow range of eligible activities. For example, a health department might receive a significant amount of categorical funding for HIV/AIDS. However, these funds may only be applied to HIV prevention and treatment, but not to prevention of other diseases transmitted in a similar fashion, such as syphilis or *Chlamydia*, and cannot generally be used for building the infrastructure for other communicable or chronic diseases.

Figure 12-1 ▼

The web of relationships among many people, organizations, and professions that constitute the public health system.

(From CDC. Ten Essential Services of Public Health. 2010. Available at: http://www.cdc.gov/nphpsp/essentialServices.html.)

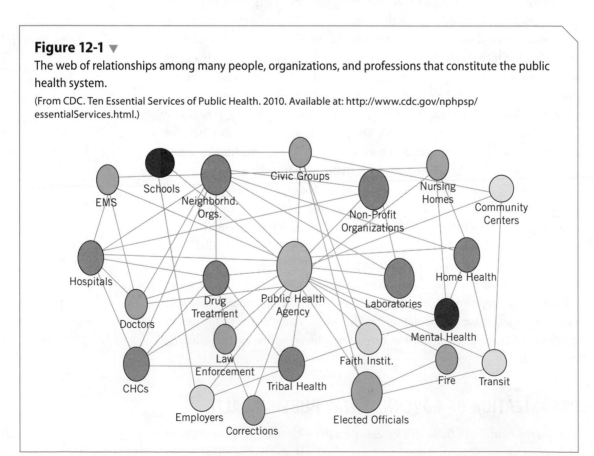

Public health as a governmental function is not specifically mentioned in the U.S. Constitution. Therefore, per the Tenth Amendment (Amendment X) to the U.S. Constitution, the majority of public health activities are organized and delivered under state direction and state police powers. Each of the 50 states, the District of Columbia, and seven U.S. territories has a lead health official. Although titles and reporting structures may change from state to state, the state health official typically directs the state health agency, serves as the public health authority in a state, promulgates rules and regulations, and is a resource for the governor and state legislators, among many other duties. Three-quarters of state health officials are appointed by their governors, with more than half of states requiring a medical degree (M.D. or D.O.) for the position (Association of State and Territorial Health Officials, 2014). Each state empowers, organizes, and funds its state health agencies differently. The majority of state health agencies are stand-alone departments of public health. However, over 20 umbrella health agencies also include other services to their state, for example, Medicaid, public assistance, and behavioral health care.

The most variability in governmental public health exists at the local level. There are roughly 2,800 local health departments throughout the United States (National Association of County and City Health Officials, 2014). Approximately three-quarters serve a county or a combined city-county area. Some have independent local authority and some report directly to the state. Local health departments can vary in jurisdictional size from a few hundred people to several millions. Variations in staff size can be equally as dramatic. Most local health departments (62%) serve jurisdictions of less than 50,000 people. More than half of the U.S. population is served by the 6% of U.S. local health departments that serve 500,000 people or more.

CORE FUNCTIONS OF PUBLIC HEALTH

The size, organization, priorities, and services of health departments vary by state, locale, local needs, the availability of services from other elements of the public health system, and the politics of those in charge. The core mission is typically constant. The IOM report *Future of Public Health* has defined three core functions of public health: (Institute of Medicine, 1988):

- Assessment—The ability to conduct public health surveillance and other monitoring activities to measure the health of the population and its determinants; investigate problems, and identify causes
- Policy development—The ability to inform leaders and the general population about health, to develop policy solutions, and mobilize support
- Assurance—The ability to ensure the health of the population by having a competent workforce to enforce laws; to have medical care available to all; and to evaluate progress as part of a cycle of quality improvement

In performing these core functions, governmental public health organizes around 10 essential services. The model presented in Figure 12-2 is a good general overview of public health functions and responsibilities at the state and local levels of public health (Institute of Medicine, 2003).

IMPACT OF PUBLIC HEALTH ON OUR POPULATION

Though one could look at all of the workers performing health-related tasks across all organizations participating in the public health system as "public health practitioners," those with full-time dedicated responsibility to the broad efforts to assure and protect public health generally work in governmental agencies. Governmental public health workers have positively impacted our collective health for centuries. Public health interventions, often carried out with multiple partners, are responsible for 25 years of the 30-year increase in life expectancy in the United States during the 20th century (CDC, 2000). From new health regulations and education campaigns to improved sanitation methods and vaccination programs, prevention services, especially those specific to communicable disease, have become second nature to public health. The CDC (1999) identified ten 20th-century achievements that contributed to this increase in life expectancy:

Figure 12-2 ▼

Overview of public health functions and responsibilities at the state and local levels.

(From Institute of Medicine (US). Committee on Assuring the Health of the Public in the 21st Century. The Future of the Public's Health in the 21st Century. Washington, DC: National Academy Press, 2003.)

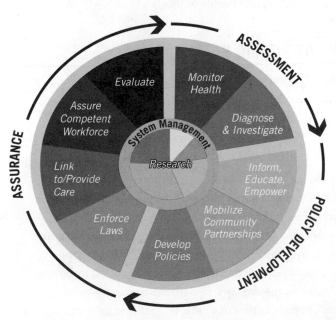

1. Childhood immunizations
2. Motor vehicle safety
3. Workplace safety
4. Control of infectious diseases
5. Declines in deaths from heart disease and stroke
6. Safer and healthier food
7. Healthier mothers and infants
8. Family planning
9. Fluoridation of drinking water
10. Recognition of tobacco as a health hazard

Several of these achievements—motor vehicle safety, workplace safety, safer and healthier food, and fluoridation of drinking water—were achieved through policy and regulatory changes. Improvements resulting from these achievements required minimal behavioral change on the part of the public, closely aligning with CDC Director Thomas Frieden's call to make healthy options the default choice (Frieden, 2010).

Local health departments are uniquely positioned to lead policy change. Local health departments can be innovators and advocates for health policy change because of their authority and focus at the local level (Pomeranz, 2011). For example, New York City's efforts have decreased childhood obesity substantially in recent years (New York City Department of Health and Mental Hygiene, 2012; Tsai et al., 2011). Nationally, local health departments were critical to drafting and implementing ordinances to restrict tobacco use in restaurants and bars in the early 2000s. Today, 80% of all Americans live in jurisdictions with limits on smoking in restaurants and bars, protecting them from this unhealthy exposure (Gostin, 2013). Policy development remains a growth area for LHDs. For example, the 2014 NACCHO Profile of Local Health Departments queried local health department activity for five obesity-related policies. The proportion of local health departments working on these policies ranged from 23% to 35% overall (Fig. 12-3) with local health departments serving larger jurisdictions overrepresented in this proportion (Hearne et al., 2015). Increasing these proportions for obesity-related policies and other issues will be vital to improving population health.

TODAY'S PUBLIC HEALTH CHALLENGES
Changing Disease Dynamics

Improved hygiene and sanitation, clean water, and the introduction of vaccinations and antibiotics contributed to a drastic decline in the burden of infectious disease. In 1900, 800 out of every 100,000 Americans died from infectious diseases (CDC, 1999). By 1960, there were only 100 deaths per 100,000 Americans attributed to infectious disease. Diseases that once plagued Americans, such as smallpox and polio, are no longer a concern, but as the United States worked to control infectious disease, chronic disease emerged as a threat to the public's health.

The United States has gone from a time in which the origins of diseases were largely microbial, physiologic, and biologic, to a time when they are mostly social and environmental. Lifestyle, living conditions, disparities, and other social determinants of disease are now disproportionately driving morbidity, mortality, and health care costs. There is no treatment, pill, or vaccine to address the lack of fresh fruits and vegetables to support a healthy diet, limited options for physical activity, exposures to environmental toxins, or the disproportionate distribution of alcohol and tobacco advertising and outlets.

By the year 2000, chronic disease accounted for four times the proportion of all U.S. deaths as compared to deaths in 1900 (Frieden, 2004). The annual costs of chronic disease are profound: when the costs for heart conditions ($107.2 billion), injuries ($82.3 billion), chronic obstructive pulmonary disease and asthma ($63.8 billion), diabetes ($51.3 billion), high blood pressure ($42.9 billion), and high cholesterol ($37.2B) are combined, they approach $400 billion (Smith, 2014).

Figure 12-3 ▼

The proportion of local health departments working on five obesity-related policies ranged from 23% to 35% overall, with local health departments (LHDs) serving larger jurisdictions being overrepresented in this proportion.

(Data from 2014 NACCHO National Profile of Local Health Departments.)

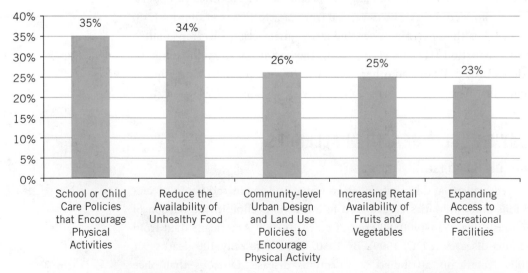

LHD Obesity-Related Policy Activity

Changing Data Needs and Availability

The increased burden of chronic diseases has had a significant impact on public health surveillance. Public health surveillance has long been an essential component of public health's assessment role. As disease dynamics changed and recognition of the role of individual behaviors in premature mortality increased, ongoing surveys—such as the Behavioral Risk Factor Surveillance Survey (piloted in 1981, initiated nationally in 1993), Youth Risk Behavior Survey (initiated in 1991), Pregnancy Risk Assessment and Monitoring System (initiated in 1988), National Health and Nutrition Examination Survey (first conducted in 1971, conducted annually since 1999), and others—have provided state-level data to improve identification and target behavioral risks.

However, state or county-level data might not be applicable to the conditions in a given community or neighborhood. Yet, for methodologic reasons primarily related to sample size and response rates, these surveys rarely provide any data below the county level, such as data from neighborhoods, census tracts, block groups, or other common sub-city geographic jurisdictions (Committee on Public Health Strategies to Improve Health and Institute of Medicine, 2010). Although most communicable diseases are reportable at the address level due to statutory reporting requirements, most chronic diseases are not reportable at all in most jurisdictions. Thus, local health departments do not have sufficient ability to accurately monitor the health status of their communities with geographically specific and timely data, to provide the necessary evidence-base to support programmatic and policy solutions, or to measure the impact of interventions (Castrucci et al., 2015). Even when data are available at the address level, as is the situation with mortality data, the delay in their availability limits their impact and places health departments in the position of implementing solutions today for problems documented more than a year in the past. Although local surveys similar to those implemented nationally provide community-level data, these surveys are quite costly.

Public health could benefit from embracing new, more comprehensive, and timelier methods of surveillance and data collection. Given the volume of health-related data now collected by the health care system electronically, the opportunities for collaboration between the health care enterprise and the official health agency have never been greater. For example, when the Boston Public Health Commission (BPHC) recently investigated an increase in deaths due to opioid overdose, data from the Boston Emergency Medical System provided real-time, address-level data that helped pinpoint sources of the problem, which enabled BPHC to take effective, targeted action (Ferrer, 2014). This would be impossible in most jurisdictions, because data are not shared, or shareable, between public health and health care systems. Although the federal government has supported the use of electronic health records (EHRs) by health care providers with incentives, including incentives for sharing data with public health (included in "meaningful use" standards), there are far fewer funds supporting the ability of public health agencies to accept and analyze these substantial amounts of EHR data. Public health agencies struggle to identify appropriate staff with the skills to gather and use "Big Data" to develop and implement data-driven programs and policies (Place et al., 2012). Please see chapter 7 for more specific information and tips regarding working with data and the use of EHRs for population health.

Budget and Workforce Reductions

The past decade has been difficult for the governmental public health system (Willard et al., 2012). After receiving monies to grow emergency preparedness capacities and capabilities in the wake of terrorist and bioterrorist attacks in 2001, state and local public health funding began to decline, and federal sources of revenue became increasingly important. This transition from mostly state and local government funding to federal sources accounting for the majority of state and local public health agency revenue accelerated after the onset of the Great Recession in 2007/2008 (Willard et al., 2012). Since 2008, over 90% of state health agencies (SHAs) have reported budget cuts (Association of State and Territorial Health Officials, 2011). Approximately 10,000 jobs have been lost from SHAs since 2008 (Association of State and Territorial Health Officials, 2014). Additionally, SHAs have resources only to try to fill about one-quarter of vacant positions. In combination with an aging workforce—one-quarter of which is eligible to retire beginning in FY16—workforce shortages appear imminent at SHAs. The situation may be worse at the local level. Many local health departments also saw significant budget decreases between 2008 and 2013. Overall, the local public health workforce decreased from approximately 190,000 to 170,000 between 2008 and 2013 (National Association of County and City Health Officials, 2014).

Changing Role in Clinical Care

In addition to its broad role as convener and coordinator of the overall public health system, the public health agency must also assure that needed clinical services are present in every community—the "assurance" function outlined by Essential Service 7 of the CDC's *Ten Essential Services*: "Link people to needed personal health services and assure the provision of health care when otherwise unavailable" (CDC, 2010). When others cannot or will not provide medical care to some or all of the population, public health plays the role of "safety net provider." The provision of clinical services is critical, but also complicates the provision of population-based services. Although the former might be provided by private or other public health care providers in the community, population-based activities, such as disease investigation and control, regulation, and health policy development, lie solely within the purview of governmental public health. Where more time and effort are spent on the provision of clinical services by public health agencies, less time might be spent on population-based activities (Institute of Medicine, 1988). More than 25 years ago, the IOM recommended public health agencies extricate themselves from providing direct services to their populations. However, state law, local ordinances, and continuing unmet health care needs lead the majority of LHDs to continue to provide some clinical services (Scutchfield et al., 1997).

In the third quarter of 2013, 18% of the U.S. population was without health insurance, a 6-year high. In raw numbers, this counted for more than 50 million Americans. The uninsured rely on an economically fragile, geographically inconsistent health care safety net consisting of "institutions, programs, and professionals that–either by legal mandate or explicitly adopted mission–offer care to patients regardless of their ability to pay for services" (Abramson, 2009). Governmental public health has been a significant part of that system providing care for the uninsured and underinsured, often without seeking reimbursement. Between 2005 and 2013, approximately one-third of health departments directly provided prenatal care and well-child checkups (National Association of County and City Health Officials, 2014). Approximately one-quarter of local health departments provided home health services and oral health services. Slightly more than 10% provide direct primary care, but this proportion climbs to one in five among medium (jurisdiction sizes of at least 50,000 people) and large health departments (jurisdiction sizes of at least 500,000 people). Nearly all health departments provide adult and child immunizations.

The passage of the Patient Protection and Affordable Care Act (ACA) has allowed state and local health departments to re-examine their roles in providing individual clinical care services (Burke, 2014). By the first quarter of 2014, the percentage of Americans without health insurance was the lowest it had been since 2008, at 13.4% (Grace Carman and Eibner, 2014). As the number of Americans with health insurance continues to increase, demand for safety net services might decline, although having health insurance does not guarantee access. In 2014, there were 6,100 designated Health Professional Shortage Areas throughout the United States, where there were not enough primary care providers to serve the number of people needing services (HRSA, 2013). In addition, clinical care needs exist for those who are not legally residing in the United States, those who cannot find providers, those who are uninsurable, and refugees. There are also services—like STD screening and treatment and family planning—for which patients might not want to engage their primary care provider or pay for through insurance.

The increase in the number insured might also present an opportunity for local health departments to capitalize on a revenue stream. According to the 2013 NACCHO Profile survey, local health departments receive a median of $5 per capita from billing public and private insurance for clinical services and fees. Revenues vary by the size of the jurisdiction served, ranging from $2 per capita in local health departments serving 1,000,000 people or more to $7 per capita in local health departments serving fewer than 25,000 people (National Association of County and City Health Officials, 2014).

Although focus and resources in providing clinical services may need to be balanced with providing population-wide services, each health department will need to assess its safety-net role and make a decision based on a thorough analysis of the factors discussed here as well as others (Georgia Health Policy Center, 2014; McGill, 2014). The decision each jurisdiction makes will influence the operations of the health department and local health care delivery system.

MOVING FORWARD

In the context of changing disease patterns, new availability and methods for collecting data, budget and resource challenges, and health care reform, public health agencies are reassessing the role of public health. This is especially the case relative to the health care system but also in relation to the community. A series of recent IOM reports highlights the role of the governmental public health system in the following areas: 1) measurement and accountability in public health and health care for attainment of desired health outcomes, 2) the leveraging of law and policy to achieve improved health, and 3) the definition and investment in a core package of public health services and supporting infrastructure as foundational for addressing public health needs across the country (Committee on Public Health Strategies to Improve Health, Institute of Medicine, 2010, 2011, 2012). The need for health departments to engage with the clinical care delivery system and vice versa is explicitly addressed in these reports, as it has been consistently in prior IOM reports on public health (Institute of Medicine, 1988, 2003). Several health departments and emerging organized systems of direct medical care delivery, including accountable care organizations, have emphasized the imperative for an integrated approach (Kaufman et al., 2015), in which clinical care and public health efforts are effectively complementary. This requires each to actively have a "seat at the table" as the health care system changes, to ensure inclusion and leveraging of governmental public health's strengths in health care and, conversely, for the clinical system to work with public health to assure the provision of health and health care in every community (Committee on Integrating Primary Care et al., 2012). National voluntary accreditation of public health agencies also holds the potential to increase the focus on accountability and evidence-based public health practice (Riley et al., 2012). Public health accreditation standards include requirements to conduct a community health assessment and to develop a community health improvement plan, and they underscore the need for community engagement in the work of the health department.

There is growing recognition that all health-related organizations in a neighborhood—which includes clinical providers, public health departments, and organizations that impact the ability of people to be healthy—must coordinate and collaborate to protect and improve population health. Public health skills such as convening, facilitating, and mobilizing multi-disciplinary, multi-stakeholder community initiatives will undoubtedly be in high demand.

"I have a sign over my desk that reads, 'What did you do to improve the public's health today?' Many days you wonder because policy change often comes so slowly. But then you watch the number of smokers going down for another year, and you know it's because of the work we did. Now that is truly satisfying."

—Kate O'Leary, MPH, Recently retired Public Health Administrator, Washington County, Oregon

REFERENCES

Achievements in public health, 1900–1999: Changes in the public health system. (Reprinted from MMWR 1999; 48: 1141–1147) JAMA 2000; 283(6): 735–738.

Abramson, SS. Holes in the Net: Surveying the Impact of the Current Economic Recession on the Health Care Safety Net. APHA, Washington, DC, 2009.

Association of State and Territorial Health Officials. ASTHO Profile of Health 2014; 3.

Association of State and Territorial Health Officials. Budget Cuts Continue to Affect the Health of Americans: May 2011 update.

Burke T. Federally facilitated insurance exchanges under the affordable care act: Implications for public health policy and practice. Public Health Rep 2014; 129(1): 94–96.

Castrucci B, Rhoades E, Leider JP, Hearne S. What gets measured gets done: An assessment of local data uses and needs in large urban health departments. J Public Health Manag Pract 2015; 21(Suppl 1): S38–S48.

Centers for Disease Control and Prevention. Ten Great Public Health Achievements—United States, 1900–1999. MMWR 1999; 48(12); 241–243.

Centers for Disease Control and Prevention. Ten Essential Services of Public Health. 2010. Available at: http://www.cdc.gov/nphpsp/essentialServices.html. Accessed August 3, 2014.

Committee on Integrating Primary Care, Public Health, Board on Population Health, Public Health Practice & Institute Of Medicine. Primary Care and Public Health: Exploring Integration to Improve Population Health. Washington, DC: National Academies Press, 2012.

Committee on Public Health Strategies to Improve Health & Institute of Medicine. For the Public's Health: Investing in a Healthier Future. Washington, DC: National Academy Press, 2012.

Committee on Public Health Strategies to Improve Health & Institute of Medicine. For the Public's Health: Revitalizing Law and Policy to Meet New Challenges. Washington, DC: National Academies Press, 2011.

Committee on Public Health Strategies to Improve Health & Institute of Medicine. For the Public's Health: The Role of Measurement in Action and Accountability. Washington, DC: National Academy Press, 2010.

Cusack CM, Knudson AD, Kronstadt JL, Singer RF, Brown AL. Practice-Based Population Health: Information Technology to Support Transformation to Proactive Primary Care. Rockville, MD: Agency for Healthcare Research and Quality, 2010.

Ferrer B. Lessons from the Big City Health Coalition. Conference presentation at Health Datapalooza, Washington, DC, 2014.

Frieden TR. Asleep at the switch: Local public health and chronic disease. Am J Public Health 2004; 94(12): 2059–2061.

Frieden TR. A Framework for public health action: The health impact pyramid. Am J Public Health 2010; 100(4): 590–595.

Georgia Health Policy Center & National Network of Public Health Institutes. Leading through Health System Change: A Public Health Opportunity. 2014. Available at: http://www.acaplanningtool.com. Accessed August 3, 2014.

Gostin LO. Bloomberg's health legacy: Urban innovator or meddling nanny? Hastings Cent Rep 2013; 43(5): 19–25.

Grace Carman K, Eibner C. Changes in Health Insurance Enrollment since 2013. Santa Monica, Rand Corporation, CA, 2014.

Hearne S, Castrucci B, Leider JP, Russo P, Rhoades E, Bass V. The future of urban health: Needs, barriers, opportunities, and policy advancement at big city health departments. J Public Health Manag Pract 2015; 21(Suppl 1): S4–S13.

Health Resources and Services Administration, Health Professional Shortage Areas. Available at: http://www.hrsa.gov/shortage/. Accessed August 6, 2014.

Institute of Medicine (US). Committee on Assuring the Health of the Public in the 21st Century. The Future of the Public's Health in the 21st Century. Washington, DC: National Academy Press, 2003.

Institute of Medicine (US). Committee for the Study of the Future of Public Health. The Future of Public Health. Washington, DC: National Academy Press, 1988.

Kaufman NJ, Castrucci BC, Pearsol J, Leider JP, Sellers K, Kaufman IR, et al. Thinking beyond the silos: Identifying foundational training and development needs for the public health workforce. J Public Health Manag Pract 2014 Nov-Dec; 20(6): 55–565. doi:10.1097/PHH.0000000000000076

Kindig DA. Understanding population health terminology. Milbank Quarterly 2007; 85(1): 139–161.

McGill N. Planning tool helps agencies adapt to health service reform. The Nation's Health 2014; 44(6): 25.

National Association of County and City Health Officials. National Profile of Local Health Departments. 2014.

National Research Council (US), Committee on Health Impact Assessment. Why We Need Health-Informed Policies and Decision-Making. 2011.

New York City Department of Health and Mental Hygiene. Reversing the Epidemic. 2012

Place J, Edgar M, Sever M. Assessing the Needs for Public Health Workforce Development. Health Resources and Services Administration, Rockville, MD, 2012.

Pomeranz JL. The unique authority of state and local health departments to address obesity. Am J Public Health 2011; 101(7): 1192–1197.

Riley WJ, Bender K, Lownik E. Public health department accreditation implementation: Transforming public health department performance. Am J Public Health 2012; 102(2): 237–242.

Scutchfield FD, Hiltabiddle SE, Rawding N, Violante T. Compliance with the recommendations of the Institute of medicine report, The Future of Public Health: a survey of local health departments. J Public Health Policy 1997; 18(2): 155–166.

Smith M. Top 11 Medical Expenses. Available at: http://www.webmd.com/healthy-aging/disability-cost-13/slideshow-medical-expenses. Accessed August 3, 2014.

Tsai AG, Williamson DF, Glick HA. Direct medical cost of overweight and obesity in the USA: A quantitative systematic review. Obesity Rev 2011; 12(1) 50–61.

Willard R, Shah GH, Leep C, Ku L. Impact of the 2008–2010 economic recession on local health departments. J Public Health Manag Pract 2012; 18(2): 106–14.

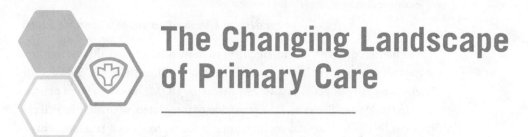

Chapter 13

The Changing Landscape of Primary Care

ANDREW BAZEMORE, RUSSELL PHILLIPS, AND ROBERT L. PHILLIPS, JR

PRACTICE OF PRIMARY CARE AND HOW IT IS CHANGING

The Patient Protection and Affordable Care Act (ACA), the rise of "Big Data," and increasing recognition that the return on current investment in health care is poor have returned attention to the potential of effective primary care in the United States. At the same time, there is a call for radical reinvention of the way in which it is currently delivered. National initiatives are underway to transform its practice platform into patient-centered medical homes (PCMHs), to transform its providers into data denizens and leaders of complex care teams, and to charge these teams with the simultaneous responsibility of building personal relationships with patients and for the outcomes of entire populations. These initiatives come after more than a decade of atrophy in interest, amid increasingly unfriendly payment structures and training environments; in addition, more complex patients create barriers and stress points. This chapter explores both the challenges and potential of primary care as demonstrated in its history and current prospects. It also tackles its imperative to partner with public health to improve health in our communities, and the individuals living therein.

PRIMARY CARE ASPIRES TO AND SHARES POPULATION HEALTH AS A GOAL

Primary Care Is Intended to Be Integrative and Essential

"Primary care is essential health care based on practical, scientifically sound and socially acceptable methods and technology made universally accessible to individuals and families in the community through their full participation and at a cost that the

community and country can afford … It forms an integral part of both the country's health system, of which it is the central function and main focus, and overall social economic development of the community"

—World Health Assembly, Declaration of Alma-Ata, 1978

Those gathered at the World Health Assembly who crafted this aspirational statement saw primary health care as a pathway to "health for all." Two decades later, an equally hopeful Institute of Medicine (IOM) report defined primary care in the United States as, "the provision of integrated, accessible health care services by clinicians, who are accountable for addressing a large majority of personal health care needs, developing a sustained partnership with patients, and practicing in the context of family and community" (Donaldson et al., 1996). And indeed, as Starfield and others (2005) went on to demonstrate, where primary care is most present or embraced, it is also the case that higher quality, lower costs, and better access are also found. However, Starfield also demonstrated how far the United States was from achieving these aspirations for primary care, lagging peer nations in support of its payment structures, training pipeline, workforce, infrastructure, and other features required for its robust functioning.

PRIMARY CARE: SHARED SETTINGS AND CHALLENGES

Most health care in the United States that addresses the majority of the problems facing its population is delivered outside of large academic health centers (Green et al., 2001). However, the vast majority of training for primary and specialty providers occurs in academic centers, despite evidence of the advantages of decentralized and team-based training in the community (Fagan et al., 2013; Phillips et al., 2013). Like their potential partners in public health and the community, primary care providers also face growing expectations and service demand on budgets that are proportionally small relative to overall U.S. health care spending. Some estimate that only 5% to 7% of health care spending is on primary care (Goroll et al., 2007) compared to 10% to 15% in countries that have succeeded in supporting systems for primary care that improve population health while reducing overall costs of care. Presenting at the 2014 American Association of Medical Colleges Annual Health Workforce Research Conference, Joseph Thompson, Surgeon General of the State of Arkansas, noted that just 2% of Medicaid spending in Arkansas is in primary care (Thompson, 2014).

Primary care providers are expected to care for patients with increasing complexity, not adequately accounted for in existing payment structures. In fact, current payment incentives often encourage less time for patient encounters and prioritizes procedures over prevention. Providers have, on average, 15 minutes per visit because delivery and payment models incent volume of visits over value of interaction. This allows clinicians to explore one issue for 5 minutes with their patients and have 2 remaining minutes for each additional need (since there are, on average, six topics raised per visit). Given that primary care providers would need 21 hours each day to provide all recommended acute, chronic, and preventive care for an average panel of patients, it is easy to understand how additional efforts at integration with public health and community stakeholders seem daunting.

Comprehensiveness, or capacity to deliver a breadth of services across a variety of settings, and including preventive, acute/undifferentiated, and chronic care, is a long-held core principle of primary care and one of its strengths in addressing whole populations. As recently as 2004, leaders of one primary care provider group declared the Future of Family Medicine to be one "committed to providing the full basket of clinical services offered by [that discipline]" (Martin et al., 2004). Such comprehensiveness appears, however, to be diminishing in the face of increasing specialization nationally, consequent credentialing pressures and a fee-for-service payment system that rewards doing as many things to as many people as possible. Over the past decade, family physicians report decreasing inpatient and obstetrical care, as well as less care of children. General pediatrics and internal medicine continue to wane in favor of not only continued subspecialty growth, but also a growing hospitalist movement, whose providers work and see patients exclusively in the hospital setting. Although internal medicine still represents nearly 25% of residency positions, only 40% of these trainees are opting for careers as generalists, and of these, only half are becoming primary care doctors, suggesting that only 20% of internal medicine residents will become primary care providers. Primary care faces similar challenges across the primary care workforce, as only half of nurse practitioners and one-third of physician assistants are entering primary care fields. Although some argue that specialization improves professional lifestyle, little evidence exists associating this change with quality improvement, whereas considerable evidence exists suggesting that increased specialization will lead to increased costs of care. With these challenges, a mandate to better serve population health needs as well as the increased demands of an aging, growing, and increasingly insured population and persistent concerns over geographic maldistribution, primary care effectiveness will increasingly depend on health information technology and data-driven service delivery. Additionally, transformed practice infrastructure, broader care delivery teams, and community partnerships will be important components of the new model.

Opportunities for Shared Data and Analysis

Primary care has increasingly embraced health information technology (HIT) over the past decade, and has steadily increased its adoption of electronic health records (EHRs) at a pace ahead of subspecialty peers. However, the aim to use EHRs to streamline efforts, reduce costs, and enhance quality of primary care has fallen short of its promise. In some cases, EHR adoption is associated with reduced rather than increased quality and care efficiencies, and has led to significant "change fatigue" and frustration for providers (Crosson et al., 2007). Electronic health record design has supported higher billing rates, but it has reduced the amount of time for physician–patient engagement and delivering on more meaningful functions, such as patient registries and population health management.

Busy providers and practice administrators are just beginning to tap the potential of HIT to help them visualize, understand, and utilize community data and information quite familiar to most public health professionals. The next horizon for primary care providers is to use a growing array of publicly available information to understand their patients and panels in a community context. The idea of primary care providers identifying and adapting care to their community and understanding the local ecology and problems facing their patients is hardly a new one, having been branded "community oriented primary care" by South African Sidney Kark, MD, in the 1950s. These ideas expanded and were disseminated globally by disciples such as H. Jack Geiger, MD, MSciHyg, and early leaders of the American Community Health Center movement, which was born in the wake of the last major era of health reform, the1960s. They engaged community stakeholders as oversight boards for their clinics, regularly gathered community information and integrated it with their records, and directed clinical activities to match population needs. However, these pioneers could only dream of the opportunities available for public health-primary care data integration that are available in this age of Big Data, which includes nearly unlimited computing capacity, troves of publically available information, and geospatial and other technological advances. Additionally, growing evidence enumerating the importance of neighborhoods to health, emerging from social sciences and public health, offers the potential to guide practice and even individual level health decision making. One can imagine an age in which primary care providers enter a room armed not only with biometric measures of cardiovascular risk such as blood pressure, but also an array of "community vital signs" that offer greater context for providers to as they partner with their patients in pursuit of health. Such information might include local healthy food sources, walkability, social capital, and much more. The IOM has called for the development of a related IT platform that helped primary care clinicians integrate care with public health with the goal of improving population health. Information technology systems have matured enough that they can help physicians better manage their patient population and become partners in community health efforts.

Opportunities and Alignment with Population and Public Health Aims

Architects of the ACA, recognizing the perils of expanding insurance without policy aimed at access expansion and cost control, returned the spotlight to primary care. In the past 5 years, new thinking, new will, and new innovation has been seen on many health care fronts. The Institute for Healthcare Improvement Triple Aim initiative has provided a unifying goal that is leading to new models of care and systems of payment that will improve health outcomes, reduce costs, and enhance the health care experience for both patients and providers. New models requiring population health management, including accountable care organizations, are emerging, and discussions are under way about establishing alternative payment methodologies to traditional fee-for-service payments. But whether these new payment models will fully support a transformation of primary care remains to be seen. Patient-centered medical homes are intended to provide for accessible, continuous, and comprehensive care by providing capacity for teaming, proactively managing the needs of the population of patients served by the practice, care coordination, and patient partnership. Leaders revisiting the American Academy of Family Physicians' "Future of Family Medicine 2.0" (www.fmahealth.org) specifically embrace accountability for costs and outcomes for all of the patients they serve, and seek payment structures to accommodate a shift toward population health.

Efforts to transform primary care practices into PCMHs open doors to a new era of population health management and expanded access by 1) spreading what has traditionally been a relationship limited to doctor and patient across primary care teams, 2) capturing the power of health information technology to manage preventive and chronic care for whole panels and populations, and 3) expanding access, both face-to-face and via asynchronous or virtual communication with patients. However, such a radical evolution comes with significant costs and requires matching payment models to be sustained, such as those being tested in the Comprehensive Primary Care Initiative, a federally supported, multipayor effort to support population and chronic care management. Furthermore, to mitigate the change fatigue so often associated with rapid and ongoing transformation, practices will need coaching and facilitation specifically intended to support transformation. Grants to build infrastructure that supports transformation, such as regional extension centers for health information technology and the Primary Care Extension Program (PCEP) for practice transformation build on century-old models for disseminating and supporting best practices in agriculture from the land-grant universities to frontline farmers. Such infrastructure needs sustainable funding if transformation and practice improvement is to be a continuous process. Practices also need shared resources in the community that can support a broader scope of care, mental health, care management, and other functions that many practices cannot afford to maintain on their own. Vermont's community care teams and the Community Care of North Carolina's AccessCare are good examples of these models. The ACA authorized, but did not fund, the PCEP, but the Agency for Healthcare Research and Quality has slowly been developing and disseminating this model through strategic grants (Phillips et al., 2013). The PCEP and shared community infrastructure could support enhancement of primary care's capacity to support the Triple Aim and to integrate with public health functions.

BUILDING TEAMS IN PRIMARY CARE
Opportunities to Partner With Public Health and Community Stakeholders

To mitigate the expected shortfall of primary care providers, broader teams and coalitions are required. The new era of patient-centered primary care delivery requires tasks to be shared across a broader team. Primary care transformation is already expanding the roles of nurses, physician assistants, medical assistants, pharmacists, nutritionists, behaviorists, and care coordinators in the care of patients and populations.

However, broader community engagement and expansion of nonclinical team members is also needed. For primary care practices to contribute more broadly to patient health, they will need to increase their capacity to address social determinants of health and health behaviors. To address these factors more effectively, practices must better leverage and partner with community resources. One model for advancing community connection is through the training and effective deployment of community health workers and peer wellness coaches, who engage patients in pursuit of health in their natural milieu, also adding deep cultural competency and service navigation support. Community and public health involvement by primary care is hardly a new concept, but it is one well worth revisiting and refining. As Folsom and others noted in the National Commission on Community Health Services' landmark 1967 report "Health is a Community Affair," the primary care provider should play an essential role in building "communities of solution" to tackle local "problemsheds" that inhibit health locally. Primary care is a backbone of the health care system in communities, and to deliver on this framework, clinicians will need enhanced training in leadership and community. Still other care teams may be supported or delivered by virtual team members who serve multiple clinics, such as Vermont's community health teams and the health extension agents noted above.

The number of clinicians needed in these new models of care is not yet clear, but it is apparent that an aging, growing, and increasingly co-morbid population demands a shift from physician-centered to more patient- and community-centered models. And these models recognize the need to partner with, among others, local hospitals/health systems, "upstreamists," and, particularly, public health to produce the health, experience, and cost outcomes that all stakeholders seek.

REFERENCES

Crosson J, Ohman-Strickland P, Hahn K, et al. Electronic medical records and diabetes quality of care: Results from a sample of family medicine practices. Ann Fam Med 2007; 5(3): 209–215. doi:10.1370/afm.696.

Donaldson M, Yordy K, Lohr K, Vaneslow N. Primary Care: America's Health in a New Era. Washington, DC: National Academies Press; 1996. Available at: http://www.nap.edu/openbook.php?record_id=5152&page=R1. Accessed April 16, 2014.

Fagan EB, Finnegan SC, Bazemore AW, Gibbons CB, Petterson SM. Migration after family medicine residency: 56% of graduates practice within 100 miles of training. Am Fam Physician 2013; 88(10): 704.

Goroll AH, Berenson RA, Schoenbaum SC, Gardner L. Fundamental reform of payment for adult primary care: comprehensive payment for comprehensive care. J Gen Intern Med 2007; 22(3): 410–415. doi:10.1007/s11606-006-0083-2.

Green LA, Fryer GE, Yawn BP, Lanier D, Dovey SM. The ecology of medical care revisited. N Engl J Med 2001; 344(26): 2021–2025.

Martin JC, Avant RF, Bowman MA, et al. The future of family medicine: a collaborative project of the family medicine community. Ann Fam Med 2004; 2(suppl 1): S3–32. doi:10.1370/afm.130.

National Commission on Community Health Services. Health Is a Community Affair—Report of the National Commission on Community Health Services (NCCHS). Cambridge, MA: Harvard University Press; 1967.

Phillips RL, Kaufman A, Mold JW, et al. The primary care extension program: A catalyst for change. Ann Fam Med 2013; 11(2): 173–178. doi:10.1370/afm.1495.

Phillips RL, Petterson S, Bazemore A. Do residents who train in safety net settings return for practice? Acad Med 2013; 88(12): 34–40. doi:10.1097/ACM.0000000000000025.

Starfield B, Shi L, Macinko J. Contribution of primary care to health systems and health. Milbank Q 2005; 83(3): 457–502.

Thompson JW. Arkansas Innovations in Medicaid Delivery. 2014. Available at: http://www.cvent.com/events/2014-health-workforce-research-conference/event-summary-d440681a32e144de88325c47815cb496.aspx.

Chapter 14

Addressing Social Determinants of Health

MINA SILBERBERG AND BRIAN C. CASTRUCCI

SUMMARY

The distribution of health, disease, and disability within and among populations is to a great extent determined by social factors such as income, race, gender, sexual orientation, education, housing, and neighborhood of residence. This chapter explains the enormous importance of social determinants of health and provides an overview of ways in which public health and primary care can work independently, together, and with other sectors to address these factors.

THE ROLE OF SOCIAL FACTORS IN DETERMINING HEALTH

The United States ranks 53rd in life expectancy, behind such countries as Guam, Bosnia-Herzegovina, and Jordan (Geoba.se, 2014). At the same time, the United States spends more on health care than any other nation (Squires, 2014), with most of that cost going to the treatment of chronic disease (Centers for Disease Control and Prevention, 2014). Much of our attention has been focused on modifying the biologic processes of disease or individual lifestyle choices. However, there is growing agreement that effective disease prevention must focus even further upstream to address the social determinants of health. In fact, research indicates that among the nations included in the Organization for Economic Cooperation and Development, it is social spending, not health care spending, that is associated with improvements in infant mortality rates and life expectancy (Lobb, 2009).

The social determinants of health are defined in Healthy People 2020 as "the conditions in the environments in which people are born, live, learn, work, play, worship, and age ... [that] affect a wide range of health, functioning, and quality-of-life outcomes and risks" (US Department of Health and Human Services, 2013). They range from access to healthy foods to the stress associated with discrimination to social norms around diet and transportation barriers in accessing care. Primary care providers, public health professionals, and the patients and communities with whom they work experience the effects of social determinants of health on a daily basis, whether they are aware of such or not (Bond, 2014). For example, primary care providers regularly encounter patients who are unable to afford their prescriptions or patients with asthmatic events triggered by allergens in their homes. Similarly, despite new knowledge regarding nutrition and physical activity, public health professionals are likely to see a growing rate of obesity in their community because residents lack access to healthy foods and safe places to exercise or are overwhelmed by the stresses of their daily lives (Acevedo-Garcia et al., 2008; Diez Roux, 2001).

Centers for Disease Control and Prevention Director Thomas Frieden's health impact pyramid (Fig. 14-1) (Frieden, 2010) shows the relative impact of five different approaches to improving health. As illustrated by their

Figure 14-1 ▼

The five-tier health impact pyramid.

(From Frieden, Thomas R. A Framework for Public Health Action: The Health Impact Pyramid. American Journal of Public Health: April 2010, Vol. 100, No. 4, pp. 590–595.)

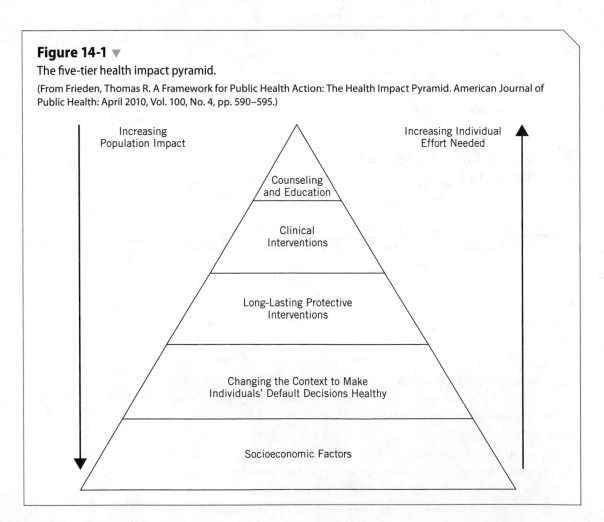

placement at the broad base of the pyramid, changing socioeconomic conditions, such as income, education, and housing, will have the largest effect on population health. Strikingly, the approaches we usually associate with health improvement—clinical care as well as health education and counseling—although clearly important, have the least impact on population health. Moreover, many of the actions that can be taken in the two pyramid strata above socioeconomic factors (changing the context to make individuals' default decisions healthy, and, to a lesser extent, providing long-lasting protective interventions) involve making changes in the social determinants of health. For example, it is much easier to incorporate walking into one's daily routine in communities with strong public transportation systems and low crime rates than in communities in which cars are the predominant mode of transit and/or crime is prevalent. In another example, cultivating social support can be described as a protective intervention given its known impact in buffering individuals against stressors that negatively affect well-being (Cohen & Wills, 1985).

One of the most important components of the social determinants of health is social status, the relative rank or position of a person or group within a society. Research indicates that no matter how social status is determined in a society, whether by age, "caste," race/ethnicity, or income, health will be strongly associated with status. In other words, as long as social inequalities exist, so will health inequalities (also known as health disparities). There are things we can do to lessen the impact of social inequalities on health (e.g., provide universal health care or put more resources into public health outreach), but on average, those at the top of the social ladder will always be in better health than those of lower social status. A stark illustration of this point comes from a recent assessment of the 15-year trend in black-white health disparities nationally and in one major metropolitan area. Disparities narrowed nationally for about half of the indicators examined, and the rest remained the same or widened; at the local level, the trend was overwhelmingly toward a widening gap. In the words of the authors, "With more than 15 years of time and effort spent at the national and local level to reduce disparities, the impact remains negligible" (Orsi et al., 2010).

Put simply, then, social determinants confound the efforts of primary care and public health to improve population health. Despite the great gains in knowledge surrounding the science and methods of medicine and prevention, social inequalities and unhealthy environments will result in unhealthy lifestyles, stress-induced disparities, and deficiencies in medical care and self-management. To make a significant change in population health, primary care and public health professionals will have to collaborate with each other and with other sectors of society to address social determinants.

THE ROLES OF PRIMARY CARE, PUBLIC HEALTH, AND INTEGRATION IN ADDRESSING SOCIAL DETERMINANTS OF HEALTH

Primary care and public health professionals have significant, sometimes overlooked, roles to play in addressing social determinants of health. However, neither public health nor primary care alone can address social determinants at the scale that is required. Such a significant challenge will require the coordinated efforts of primary care and public health as well as the engagement of other social sectors.

The Role of Primary Care

Gottlieb et al. (2013) suggest that primary care providers can address social determinants of health on three different levels: individual, institutional, and community. For example, a growing number of primary care clinics now employ social workers to whom primary care providers (PCPs) can refer individual patients in need of assistance with obtaining food or finding housing. Manchanda (2013), in his TED book, *The Upstream Doctors*, argues that doctors should be assessed in part by the extent to which their care plans take into account an individual patient's social and economic conditions. Similarly, the Health Leads program (http://healthleadsusa.org/) encourages providers to "prescribe" basic resources, such as food, to individual patients and trains college students to work with patients to connect them with those resources.

Integrating social determinants into individual-level patient care is a natural fit with the daily routine, skill set, and comfort zone of providers. Providers can also enhance their impact by taking action at institutional and community levels. At an institutional level, a clinical practice might encourage employees to walk by marking off a trail on their grounds. At a community level (local, state, or national), PCPs could advocate for building new public facilities for physical activity or keeping gym classes in low-resource schools, particularly in communities that have been identified as having a high prevalence of disease or disease risk factors.

Primary care providers have a number of assets in addressing social determinants of health. Their patient data can be used to identify patterns of health outcomes that indicate the need to explore social determinants (e.g., a pattern of uncontrolled pediatric asthma in one area of town may indicate substandard housing). The stories of individual patients are also powerful tools for raising the visibility of an issue. Primary care providers can leverage the respect afforded their profession and their expertise about health and illness to raise awareness among policymakers and the general public about the impact of social conditions on health. They are also aided in this effort by their resources as members of the professional class, their gatekeepers of access to health resources, and their ability to reach decision-makers. In one example, in the 1960s, the health council of the Tufts-Delta Health Center in Mound Bayou, MS, helped end discriminatory banking practices by promising local banks that the council's funding would be deposited with the first bank that opened a branch in a black neighborhood and engaged in fair employment and mortgage loan practices (Geiger, 2002).

The Role of Public Health

The social determinants framework is intrinsic to public health. The spread of an infectious disease, for example, may be exacerbated by crowded housing conditions. Targeting distribution of prophylactic treatment in crowded housing or to otherwise vulnerable populations is a standard part of the public health toolkit. However, many in public health see a need to enhance their efforts to address social inequality at its root and the institutional mechanisms that link social inequality and health inequality. For example, Sadana and Blas (2013), reviewing programs of the World Health Organization, found that most of those concerned with social determinants of health focused primarily on targeting treatment to vulnerable groups, rather than on addressing the upstream social determinants that shape differential exposure to health risk and protective factors.

Public health officials have significant resources for addressing social determinants of health. The public health sector has data that can place disease in a social context; respect and legitimacy as experts in health, illness, and their etiology; access to decision-makers; and access to colleagues whom they can inform about the issues; and contacts with whom they can work with to address social determinants. Moreover, public health departments are unique in that they are by definition responsible for the health of entire communities, legitimating and mandating their involvement with social determinants of health. Public health professionals engage in an ongoing basis with partners from outside the health system, such as the public housing authority and the schools, creating valuable relationships for addressing underlying social determinants of health, such as housing and education.

Working Together

The capacity of public health and primary care to address social determinants of health is greatly increased when they work together. Even identifying the challenges facing *one* individual (e.g., poverty, lack of housing, untreated mental health problems) and connecting that person to resources will be greatly facilitated by combining the access to clinic patients and medical referrals that are part of primary care with the access to individuals who don't go to clinics and the connections to social services that are part of public health. For example, within many of the regional networks of Community Care of North Carolina, the state's Medicaid care management program, care managers have the resources of primary care, public health, social services, and other sectors at their disposal to meet a range of patient needs.

Going beyond the individual to address health outcomes related to social determinants of health at the population level requires changing the mechanisms that connect social status and health (e.g., an employment-based insurance system, the distribution of healthy food), changing the social factors themselves, or changing fundamental environmental conditions, such as transportation systems or the industries creating pollution. Any of these requires effecting change in economic structures, political systems, cultural systems, social institutions, and/or social policies. The systems involved are complex, and the changes required take time. Moreover, these systems have costs and benefits, and there will sometimes be opposition to change from those who will lose their current benefits and/or pay the costs of system change—often among the most powerful members of society. Furthermore, issues of policymaking, culture, and system change are controversial, bringing into play conflicting perspectives on the reasons for social inequality, the role of government, and individual responsibility, to name just a few of the relevant contested issues.

The value of integration in meeting these challenges goes beyond the simple benefits of putting more hands on the job. In many ways, primary care and public health have different but complementary strengths For example, because of their daily access to patients and their real-time data, primary care providers might sometimes identify a pattern of illness that may indicate an underlying social cause. However, they will often lack the time and resources to identify those patterns, and even more often will lack the time and the resources to investigate the causes of the pattern. Public health departments, however, generally have the mandate and usually the capacity to analyze encounter data to reveal trends, carry out epidemiologic investigations, and identify determinants of health and illness, including the social determinants. They also generally have strong relationships with other governmental and community agencies that are concerned about these social determinants.

New Mexico provides one example of the collaborative efforts that can be made to address social determinants of health. The State Health Department and the Department of Family and Community Medicine at the University of New Mexico have partnered to create local "Health Commons" models of care in communities with large uninsured, minority populations (Kaufman et al., 2006). The Health Commons bring together stakeholders from a variety of sectors to address immediate health needs and the social determinants of health through collaborative health planning; one-stop shopping for medical, behavioral, and social services; employment of community health workers bridging the clinic and the community; and job creation.

For example, in the southwestern region of the state, the Health Commons is led by Hidalgo Medical Services, a network of federally qualified health centers. The Health Commons in that region has recruited providers to underserved communities; and developed a comprehensive service delivery system bringing together primary care, public health, behavioral health, and dental health, fitness resources, and individual assistance with medication costs. It has created the Hidalgo Area Development Corporation and made the Health Commons an essential part of the community's economic development strategy. The Health Commons model has led to statewide system changes as well, including a statewide telephone Health Advice Line that offers rural and urban uninsured individuals access to health and social service information and referrals 24 hours a day, 7 days a week. Health Commons creates jobs and has been sustained by attracting public and private investment.

How do public health and primary care professionals collaborate to arrive at approaches to addressing the social determinants of health that will be effective in our communities and states and even nationally? The next section of this chapter suggest four broad strategies.

STRATEGIES FOR ADDRESSING SOCIAL DETERMINANTS OF HEALTH

Creating the Conditions to Address Social Determinants of Health

A broad spectrum of resources on organizing in general, and organizing to improve health in particular, indicates the importance of taking on winnable battles when starting new initiatives or collaborations (Minkler, 2012). Earlier actions can help lay the foundation for addressing social determinants of health by 1) increasing a group's collective capacity to work effectively toward a common aim, 2) enhancing belief in collective self-efficacy and thereby the willingness to fight longer, harder battles, and 3) exposing the role of social determinants in health as well as the limitations that existing circumstances place on the group's ability to effect desired changes (Alinsky, 1969; Israel et al., 1998).

Avoiding Common Traps: Knowing Is Not Doing and Integration Does Not Equal Health

The World Health Organization study mentioned earlier found that we generally do not address social determinants of health at their most fundamental level, and thereby lose the opportunity to effect widespread, sustainable change in population health. Moreover, the call to integrate can inadvertently change our focus from our final end of social change to its means. In a 1980 study of the perspectives and practices of professionals working in local policy and planning agencies for the elderly, Estes (1980) found that although these professionals saw the problems of the elderly as being rooted in social structures, their actual practice was generally "accommodative" of these structures; they worked to provide their clients with services within the structural constraints they faced, rather than attempting to change those constraints. Many of their accommodative efforts were associated with integration: communication, coordination, information and referral, and collaborative needs assessment. This predominance of accommodative work is not surprising, given the difficulties of effecting change in social structures. Moreover, the activities Estes is describing are essential to improved population health and are often sorely lacking, and engaging in them is likely to have benefits. However, the juxtaposition of professional perspectives and practices that she describes highlights the danger for all of us of stopping at knowing and integrating, rather than figuring out how we can substantially address social determinants of health. This problem is augmented, no doubt, by the need to start with winnable battles. In fighting those battles, our goal should be not only to win, but to build the collective capacity (e.g., human and material resources, levers of influence, collective efficacy, issue-framing) necessary to expand what is winnable in the future.

Health in All Policies

One of the current strategies for addressing social determinants of health is the "Health in All Policies" movement, whose proponents (including the American Public Health Association) advocate that policymaking in all sectors take into account the implications for population health and health equity. An important tool for a "Health in All Policies" approach is the health impact assessment (HIA). The HIAs use a structured analytic methodology to provide a better understanding of the potential impacts of a proposed policy, regulation, or project while they are being developed to limit the adverse health effects and maximize opportunities for health promotion. For example, through funding from the Pew Charitable Trust and the Robert Wood Johnson Foundation, Michigan State University has created an interactive web-based tool that allows policymakers, planners, and the public to assess the potential impact of new construction and infrastructure development on access to public transportation, noise pollution, community walkability, and other social determinants of health. The Surgeon General's National Prevention Strategy, launched in 2011, reflects the approach of the Health in All Policies movement by highlighting the need to address housing, transportation, education, and the physical environment in order to improve health (National Prevention Council, 2011).

Communicating Effectively

If we are to effect change in the social and environmental conditions that promote poor health and health inequity, public health and primary care professionals must learn to communicate effectively with both the general public and decision-makers around these issues. Recent research sponsored by the Robert

Wood Johnson Foundation utilized focus groups and surveys with thousands of respondents and offers striking insights into effective communications around social determinants of health. It also models the types of considerations in which health professionals must become versed (Carger & Westen, 2010). It is interesting to note that among the respondents in the study, the very term "social determinants of health" did not register with most, and that participants reacted negatively to assertions that did not match their existing beliefs (e.g., "America is not among the top 25 countries in life expectancy"). Talking about equal opportunity to improve health resonated well with audiences, whereas pointing to disparities in health outcomes generally did not (with the exception of black audiences).

GOING BEYOND PUBLIC HEALTH AND PRIMARY CARE

Addressing social determinants of health generally requires engagement of the larger community beyond public health and primary care, including those involved in social justice, education, job development, housing, social services, parks and recreation, transportation, policy-making, business, the faith community, and advocacy groups. Involving more sectors increases challenges around shared goals, aligned leadership, communication, and data sharing. However, the deeper an initiative goes in addressing the social determinants of health, the more sustainable the health improvement gains. Collaborations can start with a small group of partners and expand as their capacity for effective collaboration grows.

Tips

1. Look for variation in health care and health status by race/ethnicity, gender, socioeconomic status, neighborhood of residence, and other Individual characteristics to identify ways in which social determinants of health are playing an important role in reducing population health.

2. Together, public health, primary care, and other partners should start with winnable campaigns that 1) increase their collective capacity to work effectively toward a common aim; 2) enhance belief in collective self-efficacy and thereby willingness to fight longer, harder battles; and 3) expose the role of social determinants in health.

3. Understand the perspectives of decision-makers and stakeholders whom you wish to influence, and learn the language that will allow for effective communication about the implications of the social determinants of health and how these might be addressed.

REFERENCES

Acevedo-Garcia D et al. Toward a policy-relevant analysis of geographic and racial/ethnic disparities child health. Health Affairs 2008; 27(2): 321–333.

Alinsky SD. Reveille for Radicals. New York: Vintage Books, 1969.

Bond A: Can you afford your medicine? Doctors don't ask. New York Times, May 1, 2014. http://well.blogs.nytimes.com/2014/05/01/doctors-not-asking-about-money/.

Carger E, Westen D. A New Way to Talk About the Social Determinants of Health. Princeton, NJ: The Robert Wood Johnson Foundation, 2010.

Centers for Disease Control and Prevention. Chronic Diseases: The Leading Causes of Death and Disability in the United States. Web page updated May 7, 2015. http://www.cdc.gov/chronicdisease/overview/index.htm Accessed July 4, 2014.

Cohen S, Wills TA. Stress, social support, and the buffering hypothesis. Psych Bull 1985; 98: 310–357.

Diez Roux AV. Investigating neighborhood and area effects on health. Am J Public Health 2001; 91(11): 1783–1789.

Estes, CL. Constructions of reality. J Soc Issues 1980; 36(2): 117–132.

Frieden, TR. A framework for public health action: The health impact pyramid. Am J Public Health 2010; 100(4): 590–595.

Geiger, J. Community-orietned primary care: A path to community development. Am J Public Health 2002; 92(11): 1713–1716.

Geoba.se. The World: Life Expectancy (2014)—Top 100+. Great Falls, VA, Canty Media. http://www.geoba.se/population.php?pc=world&type=15. Accessed July 4, 2014.

Gottlieb L, Sandel M, Adler NE. Collecting and applying data on social determinants of health in health care settings. JAMA Intern Med. 2013; 173(11): 1017–1020. doi:10.1001/jamainternmed.2013.560.

Israel BAA, Schulz AJ, Parker EA, Becker AB. Review of community-based research: assessing partnership approaches to improve public health. Ann Rev Public Health 1998; 19: 173–202.

Kaufman A, Derksen D, Alfero C, DeFelice R, et al. The health commons and care of New Mexico's uninsured. Ann Fam Med 2006; 4(Suppl 1): S22–S27.

Lobb A. Health care and social spending in OECD nations. Organization of Economic Cooperation and Development (OECD). Am J Public Health 2009; 99(9): 1542–1544.

Manchanda R: The upstream doctors: Medical innovators track sickness to its source. New York, TED Books, 2013.

National Prevention Council. National Prevention Strategy. Washington, DC: U.S. Department of Health and Human Services, Office of the Surgeon General, 2011.

Orsi J, Margellos-Anast H, Whitman S. Black–white health disparities in the United States and Chicago: A 15-year progress analysis. Am J Public Health 2010; 100(2): 349–356.

Sadana R, Erik B. What can public health programs do to improve health equity? Public Health Rep 2013; 128(Suppl 3): 12–20.

Squires D. The global slowdown in healthcare spending growth. JAMA 2014; 312(5): 485–486.

US Department of Health and Human Services. Social Determinants of Health: Overview. HealthyPeople.gov. http://www.healthypeople.gov/2020/topicsobjectives2020/overview.aspx?top. Updated Nov13, 2013. Accessed Jan 6, 2014.

Additional Resources

CDC. Health Impact Assessment. Available at: http://www.cdc.gov/healthyplaces/hia.htm

Health Impact Project. Available at: http://www.healthimpactproject.org/news/project/grantee-news-coverage-michigan-state-university-today

The Leading Change Network. Available at: http://leadingchangenetwork.org/mission/

Minkler M. Community building and Community Organizing for Health and Welfare, 3rd ed. New Brunswick, NJ: Rutgers University Press, 2012.

Minkler M, Wallerstein, N. Community-Based Participatory Research for Health: From Process to Outcomes. San Francisco: Jossey-Bass, 2008.

Policy Link. Equity Is. Available at: http://www.policylink.org/site/c.lkIXLbMNJrE/b.5136441/k.BD4A/Home.htm

Rudolph L, Caplan J, Ben-Moshe K, Dillon L. Health in All Policies: A Guide for State and Local Governments. Washington, DC: American Public Health Association and Public Health Institute, 2013.

WHO. Social Determinants of Health: The Solid Facts, 2nd ed. Edited by Richard G. Wilsons and M.G. Marmot. 2003. Available at: http://www.who.int/social_dcterminants/en/

Creating a Culture of Health in Cambridge, Massachusetts

CLAUDE-ALIX JACOB AND SUSAN FEINBERG

Cambridge, Massachusetts, is a city of the rich and the poor. It is home to Harvard and MIT, yet nearly half of the children in the public school system are growing up in low-income families.

Despite an abundance of private and public sector resources, this community faces challenges similar to those of urban cities elsewhere in the United States. Currently, 15% of all Cambridge residents live below the federal poverty line, and 17% of adult residents have a high school education or less (US Bureau of the Census, 2013). Poverty and low education are disproportionately experienced by black and Hispanic residents.

HEALTH OF THE CITY: A NEW BEGINNING

Cambridge city leaders recognized decades ago that factors such as income, education, gender, and race could impact health. In 1990, a citywide initiative called Health of the City launched as a joint venture between the city of Cambridge and Harvard University to improve the health of residents. Over time, physicians and public health leaders engaged civic and community partners in successful efforts to identify and develop innovative strategies to address the needs of the city's most vulnerable residents. These collaborative efforts resulted in the formation of two community advisory groups—which still exist today—that focus on the health and social burdens that impact children and men of color, respectively.

Meanwhile, the fiscal challenges of operating city-owned Cambridge Hospital, which housed the health department, led to the creation of a regional health care system in 1996 through a special act of the Massachusetts legislature. Today, the Cambridge Public Health Commission (doing business as Cambridge Health Alliance) operates three hospitals and numerous primary care practices and specialty centers in Cambridge, Somerville, and other communities north of Boston. Cambridge Health Alliance also oversees the administration of the Cambridge Public Health Department and the department's "upstream" population health functions.

Cambridge Health Alliance has a strong social justice mission and provides high-quality, cost-effective care to low-income and otherwise disadvantaged residents from over 200 communities in Massachusetts. Due to the uncertain economics of mission-driven health care, Cambridge Health Alliance has experienced the same trials

and tribulations as safety-net health systems across the country.

The Institute of Medicine, in its landmark 1988 report, defined public health as what we, as a society, do collectively to assure the conditions for people to be healthy. This vision drives the work of the Cambridge Public Health Department. Our staff are responsible for disease surveillance, health promotion, policy development, regulatory functions, and creating linkages between the community and the clinical and public health systems.

A great strength of our department has always been the ability to reach a large swath of the community by operating successful programs based at other institutions, including hospitals. For instance, we administer a regional tuberculosis program at Cambridge Hospital in which our public health nurses handle over 2,000 patient visits a year. Our department's school health program is based in the Cambridge Public Schools, with school nurses handling over 45,000 student visits annually. We also operate a children's oral health program that provides universal dental screenings to pre-K-3 students in Cambridge preschools and elementary schools. Most recently, we launched a navigated care program that links men at high risk for chronic disease to primary care providers at Cambridge Health Alliance.

NATIONAL ACCREDITATION: WHERE WE'RE GOING

Our department has set an ambitious agenda to become one of the first nationally accredited health departments in the Commonwealth of Massachusetts. Earning this designation will help identify community priorities while addressing the health needs of those who live, learn, work, and play in the City of Cambridge.

To accomplish this goal, we analyzed the health burdens, social and economic trends, and input from city residents and stakeholders. We conducted a comprehensive health assessment and engaged partners to chart the course for developing a health improvement plan for the city (Cambridge Community Health Assessment, 2014; Cambridge Teen Health Survey, 2012). The assessment reflects comments shared through focus groups, key informant interviews, and a citywide health survey. A number of themes surfaced in these conversations, including the importance of establishing strategic health partnerships with nontraditional players, and improving access and linkages to quality, affordable medical, dental, and behavioral health care.

Many residents expressed concerns about "upstream" issues impacting their health, such as safe and affordable housing, income inequality, the high cost of health insurance and deductibles, and stigma associated with mental illness. The affluent face of Cambridge often masks the profound issues faced by the city's middle-income and poor residents. As one survey respondent explained: "In a city that does have a high degree of economic wealth in some areas—young professionals, university students from wealthier backgrounds, wealthy universities—it is appalling to see certain issues related to poverty, homelessness, and discrimination (class- and race-based) are still rampant, and to see the vast disparities created by these economic divides in the city."

CREATING A CULTURE OF HEALTH

In many ways, Cambridge already is a healthy city. Cambridge fares better than the state and nation on many key measures of health. At the same time,

our health department is keenly aware that data in aggregate do not tell the whole story.

Fortunately, Cambridge is well poised to tackle the health and social inequities that do exist in our city. Looking back, Cambridge made a deliberate effort not to become an enclave for the wealthy when rent control ended in the 1990s. Civic leaders wanted to preserve the rich social fabric of Cambridge—a place where people of different socioeconomic and cultural backgrounds live, work, and thrive together.

This belief in equality has led to a substantial commitment by city departments and community organizations to ensure that less-advantaged residents not only have their basic needs met, such as affordable housing, but are also given opportunities, such as adult education and job training, to change the circumstances of their lives.

Investing in Children and Families

One of our city's biggest investments has been in children and families, because we know that early life experiences have an enormous impact on health, academic achievement, and future earnings. School health services make sure children are healthy through required immunizations and by providing linkages to primary care and other needed health care resources.

In addition, Cambridge offers an array of services that include parenting classes, play groups, an early literacy program, and other services that focus on a child's first 3 years of life—a time of rapid brain development. Many programs conduct special outreach to low-income and immigrant families with young children by linking residents to social services and family support programs.

These varied initiatives help parents build strong, nurturing relationships with their youngsters and empower them to be their child's first and most important teacher.

Making the Healthy Choice the Easy Choice

"I love living in Cambridge . . . I am thrilled with the public parks all over the city! I hope bike lanes continue to be added to city streets so people can feel safe and encourage their children to bike more."

—2013 Cambridge Health Survey respondent

Local government can have a significant impact on health. In Cambridge, participating city departments and community partners are addressing the burden of chronic disease among children by tackling obesity and changing the urban landscape.

Tackling obesity is one illustration of how the city has "moved the needle" on health through policy, systems, and environmental approaches.

City, school, and community partners in Cambridge have worked together for over a decade to improve the school environment so that kids eat healthier and are more active. These efforts include healthier and tasty school meals; innovative physical education activities like ballroom dancing; outdoor gardens in all elementary schools; health and fitness progress reports sent home annually; and adopting model nutrition and wellness policies. In 2013, 30% of Cambridge students (grades K-8) were overweight or obese (Cambridge Public Health Department, 2013), down from 39% in 2004 (Institute for Community Health, 2004).

In 2011, our department established a citywide Food and Fitness Policy Council to explore policy, systems, and practices for making healthy foods and fitness opportunities available to more residents. The council's vision for creating a healthy, sustainable, and equitable food and fitness environment in Cambridge emphasizes community engagement, communication, policy development, and infrastructure development. In addition, the city's urban planners have created safer streets for

pedestrians and cyclists and implemented policies and programs that encourage alternative transportation. Today, nearly a third of residents either walk or bike to work, and the number of cyclists has tripled over the past 10 years (US Bureau of the Census, 2013).

A SHARED VISION

"Cambridge is a unique and wonderful city because of its diversity. As a minority, the open-mindedness, political access, the way we interact with one another are the qualities that attract me the most living here."

—2013 Cambridge Health Survey respondent

We believe Cambridge will be successful in improving the health and well-being of its residents because there exists a collaborative spirit in which local government, businesses, non-profits, and citizens come together to identify and address needs.

The diverse voices of the Cambridge community are helping shape the city's vision for health and develop a "compass" for guiding the city's health priorities over the next 5 years.

Not surprisingly, the "health" priorities that emerged from the community health assessment and subsequent community planning sessions were mostly issues that occur outside of the doctor's office. The priorities that will form the basis of the city's health improvement plan are: mental and substance abuse (including tobacco); violence; healthy, safe, and affordable housing, healthy eating and active living; health access; and health equity and social justice.

The city's investments in the social capital of the community will be measured over time through a variety of data reports and stories shared by residents, workers, visitors, and patients.

This health improvement planning process will allow us to strive for the *balance* that is referenced in the World Health Organization's definition of a "healthy" community by reexamining investments made in the past and putting the necessary systems in place to address the *health of the city* well into the future (World Health Organization, 1947).

REFERENCES

Cambridge Community Health Assessment, City of Cambridge, Massachusetts, 2014.

Cambridge Public Health Department, Cambridge Youth Weight Surveillance, 2012.

Cambridge Teen Health Survey, Grades 9–12, 2012.

Constitution of World Health Organization. In Chronicle of World Health Organization, vol 1. Geneva, Switzerland: World Health Organization (WHO), 1947: 29–43.

Institute for Community Health. Cambridge Youth Weight Surveillance, 2004.

Rudolph L, Caplan J, Ben-Moshe K, Dillon L. Health in All Policies: A Guide for State and Local Governments. Washington, DC: American Public Health Association and Public Health Institute. 2013.

US Bureau of the Census, Department of Commerce. American Community Survey, 3-Year Estimates, 2009–2011. 2013 Available at: https://catalog.data.gov/dataset/2009-2 011-american-community-survey-3-year-esti mates-summary-file

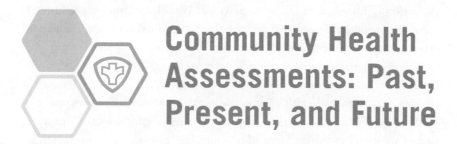

Community Health Assessments: Past, Present, and Future

KEVIN BARNETT AND SARA ROSENBAUM

Community health assessments (CHAs) are a key tool in identifying both health-related needs in defined geographic areas and populations as well as the resources and assets available to address those needs. The identified needs and assets serve as a starting point for the selection of priority areas of focus, and as markers to monitor progress toward measurable objectives. Many types of organizations conduct CHAs, often for similar populations in common geographic areas. The number of independent CHA and planning activities by public and private sector organizations often reflects a duplication of effort, resulting in squandering of precious resources. There is an immense opportunity—and some would suggest an imperative—for greater alignment of assessment and planning processes. This may require the formation of working relationships that did not exist previously, the negotiation of agreed upon geographic parameters that accommodate multiple sets of requirements, and adjustments in timing of processes. This chapter will: 1) provide a brief overview of the history of assessment practices by hospitals and public health agencies, 2) identify other organizations with similar processes, 3) examine how different organizations define the community of focus for their assessments, and 4) explore opportunities for partnership.

ASSESSMENTS BY HOSPITALS: A BRIEF HISTORY

For decades, assessing community health needs and community health improvement planning have been features of U.S. health policy and a key element of state and community public health activities. The enactment of the Hospital Survey and Construction Act of 1946 (also called the Hill-Burton Act) by the federal government elevated health planning to the national level, requiring assessments as a precondition for states seeking grants, loans, and loan guarantees. The Hill-Burton Act was a major factor in the dramatic expansion of hospitals in the wake of World War II, linking hospital investment to a regional determination of need for medical services. Public and private nonprofit hospitals built with Hill-Burton Act funds were required to provide a reasonable amount of uncompensated health care and to serve the needs of the entire community (Rosenbaum et al., 2012).

The explosion in health care spending that followed the enactment of Medicare and Medicaid in 1965 triggered extensive efforts by policymakers to find solutions to the problem of uncontrolled growth. Among the strategies introduced was the 1974 Health Planning Resources Development Act (reauthorized and expanded in 1979 and ultimately repealed in 1987). The act was best known for its provisions that gave states an incentive to tie capital investments in health care to planned development through the use of certificate of need (CON) authority. Certificates of need are legal documents required in many states, and are used to prove that any plan to expand or create a new facility will actually fulfill the needs of the community where it will be built. CON regulations were spurred in part by a concern that too many medical facilities in one community would lead to inefficiencies, such as patients paying prices that are higher than necessary or being persuaded to undergo nonessential procedures. As of 2013, 36 states maintained CON programs (National Conference of State Legislatures, 2013).

In 1969, the IRS updated the charitable requirements of nonprofit hospitals with the establishment of the community benefit standard. This initiative broadened public expectations beyond the provision of charitable medical services to the *promotion of health* in local communities (IRS Revenue Rulings 69–545 and 83–158). Beginning in the 1990s, states such as New York, Texas, and California passed statutes requiring hospitals to conduct community health needs assessments (CHNAs) (Box 15-1) and document actions taken to address identified unmet health needs. The introduction of the IRS' Revised 990 Schedule H in 2009 significantly

---

Box 15-1 | CHA and CHNA: Are They Different?

Community health assessments (CHAs) and community health needs assessments (CHNAs) are the same in general terms, but the CHNA term was formalized by the Internal Revenue Service and the Patient Protection and Affordable Care Act (ACA). Unfortunately, the CHNA moniker does not accommodate the philosophical (and practical) approach that ensures that we don't just focus on the *deficits* in communities, but that we also focus on the identification of community assets. This was best articulated in the seminal publication *Building Communities from the Inside Out* (Kretzmann & McKnight, 1993).

expanded reporting requirements for hospitals at the national level, and included a requirement to conduct a CHNA. This requirement was codified with the subsequent passage of the Patient Protection and Affordable Care Act (ACA). Beginning in the 2012 tax year, all nonprofit hospitals were required to conduct a CHNA and adopt an implementation strategy to address priority community health needs identified through the assessment. Hospitals that fail to meet the CHNA requirements were subject to an annual $50,000 annual excise tax. Implementing guidance published by the US Treasury Department/IRS in 2011 (Notice 2011–52) indicates that hospitals must conduct CHNAs every 3 years and must update their implementation strategies annually. A facility's implementation strategy must outline community health needs to be addressed as well as needs that the facility will not address. It must be a written plan that addresses each of the community health needs identified in the CHNA and must be specific to each particular facility, including its resources and programs. Hospitals are required to post CHNAs on their websites or use other methods to make them available to the public. As of late 2014, the U.S. Treasury Department/IRS had not formally finalized its regulations interpreting the ACA's provisions covering the expanded obligations of nonprofit hospitals that seek tax-exempt status under §501(c)(3) of the Internal Revenue Code. However, the ACA amendments do not depend on formal agency policy to take effect.

ROLES FOR PUBLIC HEALTH AGENCIES IN THE COMMUNITY HEALTH IMPROVEMENT PROCESS

The implementing guidance from the U.S. Department of Treasury/IRS permits hospitals to collaborate with other facilities and organizations, such as state and local public health agencies, in developing and executing the implementation strategy. These public health organizations also operate under an imperative to improve the health of their communities; in fact, it is one of their core functions. The launch of national accreditation standards in 2011 by the Public Health Accreditation Board provides a formal structure to encourage assessment and planning processes for tribal, state, and local health departments. The standards include a requirement for a CHA and the development of a community health improvement plan (CHIP) as a prerequisite for participation in the accreditation process. Revised standards released in January 2014 strengthen requirements for community health assessment and health improvement plans, provide additional guidance on measurement, and examine emerging issues such as health informatics, workforce development, and health equity. Health departments seeking accreditation are required to make their assessments publicly available (Public Health Accreditation Board, 2013).

An Example from California

A local and/or state health department can play numerous roles in the development and implementation of community health improvement strategies, especially when they partner with hospitals and other community organizations. In California for example, the San Francisco Department of Public Health (SFDPH) is pursuing accreditation. The department used the results of a recent CHA to create a CHIP for San Francisco using the Mobilizing for Action Through Planning and Partnerships (MAPP) framework (see Additional Resources). The SFDPH is a member of the San Francisco Community Benefit Partnership, which "seeks to harness the collective energy and resources of San Francisco's private non-profit hospitals, city departments (Public Health and Human Services), community clinics, health plans, and non-profit providers and advocacy groups to improve the health status of San Francisco residents" (San Francisco Health Improvement Partnership, 2014). The Community Benefit Partnership conducted the CHA from 2009 to 2010, and in so doing, completed the first steps of the MAPP process it would later use to for the CHIP (those first steps were: organizing the planning process, creating community vision and goals, and conducting four MAPP assessments).

ASSESSMENTS BY OTHER ORGANIZATIONS

There are a number of organizations that periodically conduct community health assessments to determine the best use for available funds. Organizations such as community health centers, community action agencies, United Way, and state and local municipalities are interested in some of the same issues as public health agencies and hospitals. Efforts to better align these assessments offer an immense opportunity to strengthen community health improvement practices in the coming years.

How can this alignment happen? The first step is to understand some of the reasons why the alignment *isn't* happening. In a follow-up to a recent CDC study (Barnett et al., 2014), hospitals, public health agencies, United Ways, and Community Action Agencies in review sites were asked about their knowledge of other assessments and interest in collaboration. Responses often reflected a lack of knowledge and awareness of the opportunities and potential payoffs associated with the alignment of efforts. Key initial steps would be to explore the alignment of geographic parameters and timing for future assessments, In the meantime, stakeholders can adjust current programs, services, and investments to better target and align them where health inequities are concentrated in a manner that they are mutually reinforcing and increase the potential to produce measurable outcomes.

Community health centers (CHCs) are located in communities with high-unmet need/medically underserved areas (MUAs). They provide comprehensive primary health care services and supportive services (education, translation, transportation, etc.). Community health centers are nonprofit health care organizations that receive funding through Section 330 of the Public Health Service Act. One of the requirements of Section 330 is for health centers to conduct a community health needs assessment "when appropriate" (Bureau of Primary Health Care Health Resources and Services Administration, 2014).

As safety net organizations in low-income communities, CHCs play an important role in linking primary care and prevention. Much of established experience in the engagement of community health workers and promoters resides within these organizations. These workers, who most commonly reside in the communities they serve, possess the critical knowledge and understanding to serve as a bridge between primary care and community health improvement. Both community health workers and the primary care providers who engage them are well positioned to work with public health agencies and other stakeholder organizations to both assess and design comprehensive strategies to improve health in local communities (Box 15-2).

There are 1,100 Community Action Agencies (CAAs) that were established as part of the Community Action Program, which was founded by the Economic Opportunity Act of 1964. Their primary purpose is to provide support for people who live in poverty. Whether through Head Start programs, job training, housing, food banks, energy assistance, financial education, or any of the other 40-plus distinct programs, CAAs serve more than 17 million people per year, the majority of whom have incomes below 75% of federal poverty level. Their primary source of funding is the Community Services Block Grant (CSBG) program through the Administration for Children and Families. Community Action Agency core funding shifted to a block grant model in 1981, and the CSBG Act requires a community needs assessment as part of the development of an action plan. The CSBG Act indicates that the assessment "may be coordinated with community needs assessments

---

Box 15-2 | CHC in Pendleton County, West Virginia

Pendleton County is a rural area in West Virginia's Allegheny Mountains. In 1981, more than half of its residents sought primary care in another county. Conceived as an intentional application of Community-Oriented Primary Care (COPC), Pendleton Community Care opened in 1982. The clinic partners with academic institutions, the state health department, local health care providers, and community volunteers to address community health issues. After extensive community assessments, Pendleton Community Care gained Community Health Center status in July 2000. For more of this story, see https://practicalplaybook.org/success-story/primary-care-practice-leads-community-wide-health-assessment-pendleton-county-west]

conducted for other programs" (Community Services Block Grant Act, §676(b)(11)).

To find CAA in your area, visit the Community Action Partnership website (see Additional Resources at the end of this chapter).

United Way has provided services and partnership with various organizations to aid underserved communities for over 125 years, with a focus on promoting financial stability, improving health conditions, and improving educational attainment. There are 1,800 United Ways worldwide. All United Ways certify their compliance to standards, which include comprehensive requirements for financial reporting, governance, ethics, diversity, and operations. One of these requirements—unique for United Ways—includes conducting "individual self-assessments" every 3 years, which are retrospective evaluations of whether their investments yielded expected impacts.

Municipalities develop what are referred to as general plans or comprehensive plans that include status assessments of existing infrastructure as a baseline for planned investments. Although most cities do not have explicit responsibilities for health care and/or public health services, there is increasing attention to the explicit integration of actions to address the social determinants of health. The American Planning Association recently conducted a multiphase case study assessing the integration of health issues into comprehensive plans (Ricklin & Kushner, 2014). The most cited health-related topics that were identified in comprehensive plans include recreation, public safety, clean water, transportation, clean air, emergency preparedness, active living, physical activity, recreation, environmental health, food access, and public safety (Ricklin & Kushner, 2014).

DEFINING COMMUNITY

There are almost as many definitions of "community" as there are organizations trying to assess them. Understanding each other's definitions is crucial for those groups interested in partnering for the assessment process and for community health improvement planning in order to achieve economies of scale.

Hospitals

Guidance from the U.S. Department of Treasury/IRS permits hospitals to define communities in relation to geographic regions and population service areas, using a "facts and circumstances" approach (i.e., taking into consideration the geographic area served, target populations, and principal functions of facilities). At the same time, the agencies prohibit a community definition that "circumvents the requirement" to assess community health needs including the needs of "medically underserved, low income, or minority populations."

Public Sector Agencies and Municipalities

The geographic parameters and/or populations of focus for assessments are determined in part by the jurisdictional responsibilities of public sector agencies or the mission and core functions of organizations in the private sector. As such, local health department assessments are conducted at the county level or other established jurisdictional boundaries, and municipal general plans are typically confined to city boundaries.

Community Health Centers and Community Action Agencies

The defined communities for community health centers and CAAs vary, determined in part by criteria established by the Federal Health Resources and Services Administration. They include Health Professions Shortage Areas (HPSAs), which are determined by the ratio of physicians to population (i.e., 3,500 or more population per physician qualifies as an HPSA), and MUAs, which are determined by an index of four variables:1) physicians per population, 2) infant mortality rate, 3) percentage of population under the federal poverty level, and 4) percentage of the population age 65 years or older. Geographic parameters can range from multiple counties in rural areas to one or more census tracts in urban metropolitan areas. Similarly, the geographic parameters of local United Way agencies can vary significantly, driven in part by population density, as well as historical roles and capacity.

Other Considerations for Defining Communities

Consideration of several other important issues could encourage a more thoughtful approach to defining community that ensures a focus where health disparities are concentrated, brings stakeholders together to make optimal use of limited resources, and closely examines the social and physical environmental context. These other considerations include the following:

- **Health Disparities.** Most regions have sub-county geographic areas with concentrations of health disparities. Although the lack of sub-county health statistics (particularly in rural areas) makes it difficult to measure disparities in these terms, census tract level data such as the concentration of populations under the federal poverty line and high school noncompletion rates are excellent proxy metrics for health disparities. There is a public access resource entitled the Vulnerable Populations Footprint (VPF)/Target Intervention Area tool available through Community Commons that automatically uploads these metrics into a geographic information system map for any city, county, or region in the United States. (For a link to the VPF and other helpful tools and websites, see Additional Resources at the end of this chapter.)
- **Cross-Jurisdictional Dynamics.** Geographic areas with concentrations of health disparities may be situated near health care facilities that are

across jurisdictional boundaries. As a result, those populations may naturally cross those boundaries to seek most of their services from those facilities. In these situations, it is important to consider the establishment of geographic parameters that cover multiple jurisdictions.

- **Organizational Capacity.** Smaller health care facilities or public health agencies serving more rural populations may lack the capacity to conduct extensive assessments. The smallest health care facilities, such as critical access hospitals (representing over 1,300 of the approximately 3,000 nonprofit hospitals), are typically tied to one or more larger regional health care facilities to handle referrals for specialty services. In these cases, stakeholders should consider regional assessments across two or more counties.

- **Social Determinants.** In conducting an assessment, it is critically important to examine the characteristics of populations in the context of the social and physical environmental conditions that influence health behaviors and impact health status. Housing quality, transportation, access to healthy food and sites for physical activity, neighborhood safety, economic opportunity, and affordable childcare and child development resources are all important social determinants to include in the assessment process.

OPPORTUNITIES FOR PARTNERSHIP

The U.S. Department of Treasury/IRS requires that nonprofit hospitals "consider the input" of diverse community stakeholders in the assessment process, but is silent on engagement in other stages of the community health improvement process. Typical approaches to the solicitation of input during the assessment stage include public surveys, focus groups, key informant interviews, and town hall meetings. However, providing input in this context tends to reduce community to a more passive role as "consumers" or "patients," rather than as organizations and individuals with a direct stake in not only undertaking the assessment, but also in producing results. A growing number of hospitals are engaging diverse community organizations and individuals as ongoing partners in the community health improvement process. Community stakeholders participate in the selection of priorities, the design of interventions and evaluation strategies, and in the implementation of programs, activities, and advocacy efforts. This approach reflects an ethic of shared ownership, where all have something to contribute in the improvement of health in local communities.

Local health departments have a more robust history in the engagement of diverse community stakeholders in assessment processes, and many tax exempt hospitals have engaged them to provide health statistics and to secure community stakeholder input as part of their assessments. Local health departments may lack the resources and capacity, however, to sustain community engagement beyond the assessment and to design comprehensive implementation strategies that leverage the resources and contributions of diverse stakeholders with mutually reinforcing interventions and investments. In this context, ongoing engagement of diverse community stakeholders is essential (Box 15-3).

There is a clear imperative for greater alignment of assessment processes, and for sustained engagement of diverse stakeholders into priority setting, planning, and implementation of comprehensive community health improvement strategies. Education and financial incentives are needed to move stakeholders beyond a "check the box" approach to community health assessments, and toward an ongoing process that is informed by a shared commitment for measurable and sustainable improvement of health in communities.

The alignment of resources across organizations has been informed in recent years by a "collective impact" approach developed by FSG (established in 2000 as the Foundation Strategy Group), a nonprofit consulting firm based in San Francisco and Boston. The "collective impact" approach identifies the following five conditions, or principles, to support partnership approaches to addressing social problems:

1. A common agenda: coming together to collectively define the problem and create a shared vision to solve it.
2. Mutually reinforcing activities: coordinating collective efforts to maximize the end result.
3. Continuous communication: building trust and relationships among all participants.
4. Shared measurement systems: agreeing to track progress in the same way, which allows for continuous improvement.
5. A "backbone organization": having a team dedicated to orchestrating the work of the group.

Collective Impact Forum has several success stories available at: http://collectiveimpactforum.org/initiative-stories

---

Box 15-3 | Project Lazarus in North Carolina

The Wilkes County Health Department in western North Carolina was an essential player in reducing the number of prescription drug overdoses in the area. After a CHA tipped them off to the problem, and relying on funding from Northwest Community Care Network (the regional Medicare/Medicaid provider), a model called Project Lazarus was developed through partnerships with the local hospital, law enforcement, educators, and nonprofit agencies. This model was recently taken from the local level to become a statewide initiative. For a comprehensive description of this project, see chapter 28.

A more recent set of guiding principles (Rosenbaum, 2013) for CHNAs provides more targeted insights for hospitals, local health departments, and other stakeholders, consisting of the following:

1. A call for shared ownership
2. Ongoing engagement of diverse stakeholders
3. A broad definition of community that ensures a focus on disparities
4. Maximum transparency
5. A focus on evidence-based approaches and evaluation of innovations
6. A quality improvement approach that accommodates the need for periodic refinement
7. The pooling and sharing of data across organizational lines

Moving Forward

The national health reform agenda will require a shift in the financial incentives of health care toward reducing the demand for high cost care for preventable conditions, and keeping people healthy and out of inpatient settings. In this context, it is increasingly in the interests of hospitals to partner with local health departments, primary care providers, and the full spectrum of local stakeholders in CHNAs to address the social determinants of health.

Primary care practitioners can play an important role in connecting the dots by helping to make the case for linking traditional care coordination to strategies that address the social determinants of health. For example, increasing attention is being given to the role of community health workers

---

Box 15-4 | Community Health Workers as "Patient Navigators"

In New Mexico's Medicaid Managed Care, community health workers (CHWs) serve as patient navigators for the most high-cost, at-risk patients, addressing health literacy and social determinant needs of the assigned enrollees. In a program modeled after the U.S. Department of Agriculture's Cooperative Extension Service, the CHWs operate from Health Extension Rural Offices (HEROs) located in rural communities across New Mexico. Their roles range from helping newly insured patients navigate the complex health system to attracting local youth to health careers to helping disseminate best practices via telehealth links to the Health Center. The program has resulted in a reduction of claims and payments for individuals, increased visits to primary care, and improvements in quality measures of care.

For more information on the HERO program and to access a The Health Extension Tool Kit, see https://practicalplaybook.org/success-story/new-mexico-health-extension-rural-offices-address-community-priority-health-needs]

> **Box 15-5 | Make Sure to Meet Expectations**
>
> One of the most important considerations for organizations planning to conduct a community health assessment (CHA) is whether there is sufficient commitment to take action. CHAs are complex and often time-consuming processes, and expectations are raised among community stakeholders who participate in the process. As such, assessments should be viewed as a means to an end, rather than a completed product. In this regard, conducting a community health assessment without setting priorities, without the strategic allocation of resources to address unmet needs, and without a commitment to monitor progress toward measurable objectives is less than a fruitless exercise; it is a process that contributes to cynicism and hopelessness in communities in which there is a need for definitive action.

(CHWs) in serving as a bridge between primary care and place-based population health improvement. A significant proportion of the projects across the country funded by the Center for Medicare and Medicaid Innovation involve the engagement and evaluation of the impact of CHWs. Primary care practitioners with experience in the engagement of CHWs are well positioned to make the case for expanding engagement as well as building operational links between primary care, social services, and actions that address environmental obstacles to health improvement (Box 15-4).

The scope and scale of the transformation that is needed in the U.S. health care delivery system is daunting, and will require many, if not most, of our public and private sector organizations to change the way they do business. Engagement of diverse stakeholders in the full spectrum of community health improvement activities is both appropriate and necessary to achieve success (Box 15-5). The community health assessment is only one step, but nevertheless a critically important one, in that process.

REFERENCES

Barnett K., et al. Supporting Alignment and Accountability in Community Health Improvement: The Development and Piloting of a Regional Data-Sharing System. Public Health Institute, through a Cooperative Agreement with NNPHI and the CDC, April 2014.

Kretzmann JP, McKnight JL. Building Communities from the Inside Out: A Path Toward Finding and Mobilizing a Community's Assets. Evanston, IL: Institute for Policy Research, 1993.

National Conference of State Legislatures. Certificate of Need: State Health Laws and Programs. 2013. Website updated July 2014. Available at: http://www.ncsl. org/research/health/con-certificate-of-need-state-laws.aspx

Public Health Accreditation Board. Standards and Measures: Version 1.5. Adopted December 2013. Available at: http://www.phaboard.org/wp-content/uploads/ SM-Version-1.5-Board-adopted-FINAL-01-24-2014.docx.pdf

Ricklin A, Kushner N. Healthy Plan Making. Integrating Health into the Comprehensive Planning Process: An analysis of seven case studies and recommendations for change. American Planning Association. February 2014.

Rosenbaum S. Principles to Consider for the Implementation of a Community Health Needs Assessment Process. Washington, DC: George Washington University, 2013. Available at: http://nnphi.org/CMSuploads/PrinciplesToConsiderForTheImplementationOfACHNAProcess_GWU_20130604.pdf

Rosenbaum S, Frankford D, Law SA, et al. Law and the American Health Care System. New York: Foundation Press, 2012.

U.S. Treasury Department/IRS. Notice and Request for Comments Regarding the Community Health Needs Assessment Requirements for Tax-exempt Hospitals (Notice 2011–52). 2011. Available at: http://www.irs.gov/pub/irs-drop/n-11-52.pdf

San Francisco Health Improvement Partnership. The Community Benefit Partnership. Available at: http://www.sfhip.org/index.php?module=htmlpages&func=display&pid=56. Accessed Sept 7, 2014.

Additional Resources

Mobilizing for Action through Planning and Partnerships (MAPP) is a community-driven strategic planning tool for improving community health, developed by the National Association of County and City Health Officials (NACCHO) and the Centers for Disease Control and Prevention (CDC). The MAPP framework consists of six phases: Organizing; Visioning; Assessments; Strategic Issues; Goals/Strategies; and Action Cycle. Available at: http://www.naccho.org/topics/infrastructure/mapp/

The Community Action Partnership is the nonprofit, national membership organization representing the interests of the 1,100 (CAAs) across the country. In addition to resources such as webinars, online tools and toolkits, and a job line, there is a searchable database for CAAs by state. Available at: http://www.communityactionpartnership.com/research/index.php?option=com_spreadsheets&view=search&spreadsheet=cap&Itemid=188

Community Commons is an interactive mapping, networking, and learning utility for thebroad-based healthy, sustainable, and livable communities' movement. In addition to the Vulnerable Populations Footprint (VPF)/Target Intervention Area Tool mentioned in this chapter, registered users have access to many tools, articles, and other related content. Available at: http://www.communitycommons.org/

The VPF tool can be accessed directly at: http://assessment.communitycommons.org/footprint/targetarea.aspx

The Action Center at the County Health Rankings & Roadmaps website provides an interactive **Action Cycle**. Steps of the Action Cycle include: 1) Assess Needs & Resources; 2) Focus on What's Important; 3) Choose Effective Policies and Programs; 4) Act on What's Important; and 5) Evaluate Actions. There is a guide that describes key activities within each step and provides suggested tools, resources, and additional reading. Guides are also provided on eight community members, such as Public Health, Healthcare, Business, and Government. These guides provide information on the role that each can play in improving the health of communities along with guidance on what they can do during each action step. Available at: http://www.countyhealthrankings.org/roadmaps/action-center

The Centers for Disease Control and Prevention's (CDC) Office of the Associate Director for Policy offers many resources related to Community Health Needs Assessments, including:

- Background material (e.g., logic models, best practices)
- Principles to Guide a CHNA Process
- Planning Resources
- Data Resources

Available at: http://www.cdc.gov/policy/chna/

The Centers for Disease Control and Prevention's (CDC) Office of State, Tribal, Local and Territorial Support (OSTLTS) has a website that helps health departments as they develop community health assessments and health improvement plans, whether for accreditation preparation, nonprofit hospital collaboration, or other reasons. Resources include:

- Assessments and Plans
- Drivers
- Models, frameworks, and tools
- Data and benchmarks
- Stories and examples

Available at: http://www.cdc.gov/stltpublichealth/cha/index.html

Chapter 15

Community Health Needs Assessments Benefit Communities and Hospitals Alike

PHILIP ALBERTI AND IVY BAER

BACKGROUND

Hospitals that have a 501(c)(3) tax status are mission driven. For many, especially teaching hospitals, those missions include patient care, teaching, research, and improving the health of their community. Although many hospitals have a longstanding commitment to community health improvement activities, hospitals now have additional reasons to focus on that commitment, as well as federal requirements to ensure that they do.

The Patient Protection and Affordable Care Act (ACA) introduced a powerful lever to identify community health needs and to develop and adopt strategies addressing those needs: the community health needs assessment (CHNA) and implementation strategy that every 501(c)(3) hospital is required to conduct every 3 years, beginning in 2012. The ACA mandates that the CHNA "takes into account input from persons who represent the broad interests of the community served by the hospital facility, including those with special

knowledge of or expertise in public health" (U.S. Tax Code §501[r]), thus laying the groundwork for collaborations among hospitals, public health departments, communities, and others, to improve the health of their local populations. Despite the intention that the CHNA be a collaborative process, and that needs assessments are part of the voluntary accreditation process for health departments, only hospitals are under a statutory mandate to conduct a CHNA, and they are the only organizations at risk for a fine and possible loss of tax-exempt status if they fail to comply.

A collaborative, well-designed CHNA confers benefits that extend far beyond meeting statutory requirements to maintain 501(c)(3) status, however. The process of identifying, prioritizing, and intervening on important, local community health needs can empower community residents, strengthen the missions of all hospitals, and forge strong relationships among hospitals, local and state public health organizations, and communities. Teaching hospitals in particular could weave the CHNA into their research, clinical care, and

education missions in ways that benefit those hospitals, their communities and the nation as a whole.

COMMUNITY HEALTH NEEDS ASSESSMENT AS KEY TO IMPROVING THE HEALTH OF THE COMMUNITY

Although the CHNA directly informs hospital efforts to improve a community's health by providing information that can be used to tailor evidence-based interventions and implementation strategies to meet identified health needs, other advantages can accrue to communities through their engagement with the CHNA process. Partnering with hospitals and public health organizations on primary data collection and during the health needs prioritization process builds community residents' and community-based organizations' (CBO) own capacity to collect, analyze and understand data. Not only does this result in a more informed community, but a CBO engaged in this way will be better positioned to seek and secure grant funding and other support for its own initiatives, which can be tailored to relevant community needs and bolstered by substantiating data. By working with hospitals and public health organizations to identify local assets and resources, communities can more easily avail themselves of community-driven, public health-initiated, or hospital-based efforts to improve the health of residents and neighborhoods.

This kind of community capacity building has additional benefits for everyone involved. As local residents learn about hospital-based community health initiatives, and as hospitals learn about how prevalence and incidence statistics translate into the lived-experience of a community, trust and good will are likely to increase, easing the path for future collaborations. As community members grow to appreciate the hospital's partnership in researching local health needs, the likelihood that residents of the community will participate in other aspects of a hospital's research mission, for example by enrolling in clinical trials or other hospital-based research projects, increases. As hospitals and public health agencies coordinate their needs assessment efforts, communities will benefit from the efficiencies and synergies found in an increasingly unified approach to understanding and intervening on local health needs. Finally, a CHNA that engages community residents and public health agencies as partners serves to empower the community and develop residents' capacity to advocate successfully—bolstered by data and evidence—for their neighborhood's health.

INCORPORATING THE COMMUNITY HEALTH NEEDS ASSESSMENT ACROSS THE RESEARCH, CLINICAL CARE, AND TEACHING MISSIONS OF ACADEMIC MEDICINE

Although the main focus of the CHNA is rightly on the community context outside of the hospital's walls, the CHNA can also support and enhance the research, clinical care, and teaching missions central to teaching hospitals.

Comminity Health Needs Assessment and the Research Mission

A CHNA could be considered a piece of community-engaged health equity research that asks the research question "What are the most pressing health needs of the community our

hospital serves?" It uses multiple methodologies and primary and secondary data collection and analysis to identify and prioritize those health needs, including health and health care inequities. Finally, the CHNA requires collaborative team science, specifically with public health agencies and scientists, and members of the local community.

Because a CHNA is science- and data-based, an institution that has an existing research enterprise can deploy scientists, such as clinical researchers, quality improvement (QI) researchers, and community-based researchers, both hospital-based and at local public health departments, in service of crafting CHNAs that capture community data and perspectives in scientifically rigorous ways. The resulting data also can benefit hospital researchers' own science by providing rich contextual information in which they can couch their own analyses and models (Alberti, 2015). This interface between CHNA data and hospital-based QI, electronic health records (EHRs) or other health information technology data not only has research implications, but also clinical ones that are explored herein.

Finally, if hospitals use the CHNA as an evaluation instrument to ascertain how effectively the implementation strategies worked, for example, it becomes an invaluable research tool that can help refine and improve community health efforts on a regular basis.

Community Health Needs Assessment and the Clinical Care Mission

Our nation is moving from a fee-for-service system that bases payment on the volume of services provided toward new models of care that stress value, outcomes, and coordination. In other words, these new models embrace the "triple aims" of improving the patient experience, improving the health of populations, and reducing the per capita cost of health care (Institute for Health Care Improvement, 2014). This new way of approaching health care incorporates improvement in population health as one measure of quality and uses financial incentives and penalties to encourage providers. Data from a CHNA can provide important contextual information to help make these efforts successful.

In section 1886(q) of the ACA, Congress imposed financial penalties on hospitals that have high levels of Medicare patients who are readmitted during the 30 days following an inpatient discharge for certain conditions, such as pneumonia and congestive heart failure. Recent evidence suggests that community-level factors significantly increase the likelihood of readmissions. Although hospitals alone cannot control the sociodemographic factors in their communities, deploying CHNA data in service of understanding the communities into which our patients are discharged can provide essential information for understanding how to lessen the impact of these factors, an important step toward improving patient care (Herrin et al., 2014; Hu et al., 2014). Gathering these contextual, community-level data in partnership with local and state public health agencies can simultaneously decrease readmissions and the use of a hospital's own resources.

Data from CHNAs can aid hospitals as they develop strategies to avoid readmission by providing data about local resources and assets that can help patients and their families adhere to treatment and keep appointments; identifying patients most "at risk" for readmission based on the known prevalence of community-based needs; and suggesting hospital- and community-based implementation strategies that specifically target evidence-based programs likely to decrease readmissions for CHNA-prioritized health needs.

According to the Centers for Disease Control and Prevention, more than 75% of health care costs are due to chronic conditions (CDC, 2014), which are likely to be identified and prioritized by the CHNA. To the extent this is true, CHNA data can improve the population health management efforts of accountable care organizations and patient-centered medical homes by helping focus the design of coordinated care and by allowing the alignment of patient data, patient panel data, and community-level data.

To this end, there is growing interest in the incorporation of social, demographic, and community-level data into EHRs. A pair of recent IOM reports call for the inclusion of social and behavioral domains in EHRs (IOM, 2014), specifically sociodemographic data like sexual orientation, financial resource strain, and food and housing insecurity; psychological data such as health literacy, stress, and depression; behavioral data like physical activity and dietary patterns; data about relationships such as social isolation and exposure to violence; and community-level data like economic information and racial and ethnic composition, which are data that the CHNA gathers (IOM, 2014). The Office of the National Coordinator for Health Information Technology extended the IOM's recommendations to include elements like occupational and military service information, also important determinants of health status, as additional certification criteria for EHRs in service of meaningful use stage 3 (DHHS, 2015).

The IOM posits that, "Knowledge of the distribution of community resources and environmental factors that can affect the risk of disease may well become just as important for managing patients' health as knowledge of clinical indicators such as body mass index."

The CHNA provides that exact kind of knowledge and could become an invaluable tool as not-for-profit hospitals experiment with these new care delivery and payment models.

Finally, there is an increasingly loud call to include individual- and community-level socioeconomic, race/ethnicity, and other factors in risk adjustments for outcome and performance measures (National Quality Forum, 2014). The kind of information collected in the CHNA regarding community needs, assets, and aggregate sociodemographic data could inform these kinds of adjustments to ensure that safety net hospitals caring for the sickest among us are not penalized for the geographic and demographic characteristics of the patients they serve (Alberti et al., 2013).

Community Health Needs Assessment and the Medical Education Mission

Given the shifting health care landscape that includes the expanded use of team-based care, it is crucial to educate medical students, residents, allied health profession trainees, and faculty on the importance of community context and the social correlates of health for patient and population health management. Beginning in 2015, medical school aspirants taking the MCAT exam will be expected to demonstrate knowledge of the social, cultural, and behavioral contributors to health. Further developing this knowledge base into related competencies is essential if we are to meet the challenges of population health management and caring for an increasingly diverse patient population.

The CHNA offers numerous opportunities to engage learners in the principles of community health and its relationship to patient-centered care and population health management. Undergraduate medical students and residents/fellows could participate in the collection and

analysis of CHNA data in order to give them first-hand experience at community-engaged research and in partnering with local residents and public health practitioners. Undergraduate medical education curricula could incorporate findings from the most recent local CHNA in order to ground lessons in the prevalence and incidence of disease within the communities in which students learn. As the Accreditation Council for Graduate Medical Education (the organization responsible for the accreditation of roughly 9,200 residency education programs) conducts its Clinical Learning Environmental Review site visits to encourage clinical sites to educate trainees to provide safe, high-quality patient care, there is an expectation that residents and fellows learn about and develop competency in identifying and reducing health care disparities (ACGME, 2014). The juxtaposition of stratified QI data with CHNA data can be instructive for residents as they learn how to develop strategies and workflows that address health care disparities in a way that is responsive to the health disparities and prioritized health needs of the community in which they train.

CONCLUSION

The CHNA and related implementation strategies proffer numerous benefits for the communities that hospitals and public health agencies serve, and can enhance the ways in which hospitals incorporate community and population health into the research, clinical, and teaching missions of academic medical centers. The CHNA can be seen as one part of a puzzle that, when properly assembled, can make a difference in the health of communities. By wrapping the work that takes place inside a teaching hospital's walls in a deep understanding of the assets and needs that exist outside of those walls—and pairing that information with resources available from the hospital, local public health agencies, and other sources—current and future physicians, researchers, and educators will be positioned to develop effective, evidence-based strategies that successfully improve the health of all.

REFERENCES

Accreditation Council for Graduate Medical Education. CLER Pathways to Excellence: Expectations for an Optimal Clinical Learning Environment to Achieve Safe And High Quality Patient Care. Chicago: ACGME, 2014.

Alberti PM: Community health need assessments: Filling data gaps for population health research and management. eGEMS 2015;2(4): article 5.

Alberti PM, Bonham AC, Kirch DK. Making equity a value in value-based health care. Acad Med 2013; 88(11): 1619–1623.

DHHS: Health Information Technology Certification Criteria. 2015. http://www.healthit.gov/policy-researchers-implementers/certification-and-ehr-incentives. Accessed June 29, 2015.

Federal Register. Available at: http://www.healthit.gov/sites/default/files/2014-03959_pi_2015ednprm.pdf. Accessed 3/17/2014.

Herrin J, St. Andre J, Kenward K, Joshi, MS, Audet AMJ, Hines SC. Community Factors and Hospital Readmission Rates. Health Services Research, published online April 9, 2014. Available at: http://www.cdc.gov/chronicdisease/resources/publications/aag/chronic.htm. Accessed 5/14/2014.

Hu J, Gonsahn MD, Nerenz DR. Socioeconomic status and readmissions: Evidence from an urban teaching hospital. Health Affairs 2014; 33(5): 778–785.

Institute for Healthcare Improvement. The IHI Triple Aim. Available at: http://www.ihi.org/Engage/Initiatives/TripleAim/Pages/default.aspx. Accessed 5/20/2014.

Institute of Medicine. Capturing Social and Behavioral Domains in Electronic Health Records: Phase 2. Washington, DC: The National Academies Press, 2015.

National Quality Forum. 2014. Risk Adjustment for Socioeconomic Status or Other Sociodemographic Factors. Washington, DC: NQF, 2014.

Leveraging the Affordable Care Act for Population Health

EDUARDO SANCHEZ

The Patient Protection and Affordable Care Act (ACA) contains provisions that align with those of *The Practical Playbook: Public Health and Primary Care Together* and that can be leveraged to build health systems that effectively integrate public health and primary care to optimize population health improvement, prevent avoidable medical conditions, better manage chronic diseases, and lower health-care costs. The notion of integrating primary care and population health has its origins in community-oriented primary care, derived from traditional public health (including epidemiology, health promotion, and preventive medicine) combined with primary medical care (Longlett et al., 2001). More recently, the Institute of Medicine report, Primary Care and Public Health: Exploring Integration to Improve Population Health, proposed recommendations to foster broader integration of primary care and public health within the U.S. Department of Health and Human Services (Institute of Medicine, 2012).

THE AFFORDABLE CARE ACT

The ACA, signed into law on March 23, 2010, has promised health insurance reform and health insurance availability and affordability to increase the numbers of Americans with health insurance and access to medical care and to decrease the numbers of Americans who lose or do not have insurance coverage or medical care (Patient Protection and Affordable Care Act, 2010). The ACA will make *The Practical Playbook* all the more relevant as increasing numbers of Americans will seek primary care after gaining access to medical care through the increased availability and affordability of public and private health insurance coverage. In addition, the law contains numerous provisions that may serve as catalysts or accelerants for integration.

Only time will tell if the ACA will be considered, along with the Social Security Act of 1935 and the 1965 Medicare Amendment to the Social Security Act, a United States domestic policy watershed. In the years preceding the ACA, the increasingly poor health status of Americans, the increasing cost of medical care, and the high percentage of uninsured Americans created a crisis and an opportunity for serious consideration of policy options. According to the U.S. Census Bureau, in 2009, approximately 49 million, or 16% of, Americans lacked health insurance coverage (U.S. Census Bureau, 2014). As recently as November 2014 (Doty et al., 2014), the health status of Americans and costs associated with medical care did not compare favorably with peer countries (National Research Council and Institute of Medicine, 2013).

The ACA is a comprehensive law that addresses multiple facets of health and health care for American citizens, health insurance companies, and for U.S. government agencies. The law represents the culmination of years, if not decades, of discussion and deliberation. The law addresses key areas of policy, programming, regulations, and financing to make health insurance accessible to more Americans, to specifically direct health insurance companies, and to provide detailed guidance to existing health-related government programs (such as, but not limited to, Medicare, Medicaid, and the Children's Health Insurance Program) and on new programs and responsibilities enumerated in the law. The law provides a framework for action with the creation of councils and new advisory bodies, milestones, timelines, and deadlines; the law also lays the foundation for future policy and programming considerations. In what is a complex, comprehensive, multifaceted omnibus law, there is much in the ACA of 2010 that is germane to the aims of the *Practical Playbook*. This chapter will touch on how primary care and public health partners can leverage relevant policies and programs contained in the ACA.

INCREASING THE NUMBER OF PERSONS INSURED

One of the primary objectives of the ACA was to reduce the high percentage and number of persons in the United States without health insurance. Not having health insurance is due, in part, to the growing unaffordability of health insurance (Bundorf & Pauly, 2006). In addition, growing numbers of Americans were the subjects of rescission, the involuntary termination of insurance coverage, prior to the passage of the ACA. Others were being denied new policies, despite the resources to do so, because of previously diagnosed or treated medical conditions, so-called "pre-existing conditions." Some persons faced unplanned for and unexpected out-of–pocket costs on reaching annual or lifetime limits on insurance payments. A 2005 study suggested that 46.2% of personal bankruptcies were attributable to major medical expenses (Lavarreda et al., 2008). Those who are uninsured are less likely to seek regular primary care.

The ACA put into law specific measures to increase the number of Americans with health insurance by two major mechanisms: 1) by authorizing the expansion of Medicaid eligibility for previously ineligible low-income working-age individuals and 2) by the creation of health insurance purchasing platforms ("exchanges" or marketplaces) for individuals who are not eligible for Medicaid and otherwise do not have or cannot afford private health insurance. The ACA provides for subsidization of health insurance policy costs on the exchanges based on "sliding scale" income-specific criteria that reduces subsidies as income increases from 100% to 400% of the federal poverty guideline. This particular provision is meant to better assure the availability and affordability for all who qualify to buy insurance from one of many qualified public "exchange" health plans. The opportunity to "get" public health insurance or purchase affordable "private" health insurance was accompanied by a mandate in the ACA that all Americans have health insurance ("maintain minimum essential coverage"), a legal, personal responsibility.

OUTCOMES OF LEGAL CONTESTS: CONSTITUTIONALITY AND STATE EXCHANGES

Following the President's signing of ACA into law, two major components of the law were contested in the courts and ultimately settled by a U.S. Supreme Court ruling on June 28, 2012, that the mandate to be insured was constitutional and that, although Medicaid expansion was constitutional, states could not be coerced to expand Medicaid, but rather could opt to do so or not do so. This has resulted in some states expanding Medicaid and others electing to not expand. In addition, some states have implemented state government run exchanges, whereas other states have defaulted or chosen to use a federally administered exchange.

> **Tip**
>
> Know the specifics regarding Medicaid expansion and exchange specifics in your state. Assist persons to get insurance, by direct assistance or referral, if they are eligible to enroll in Medicaid or on an exchange.

HEALTH INSURANCE REFORMS IN THE AFFORDABLE CARE ACT

The law also codifies significant and protective health insurance reforms, including prohibiting refusal of coverage for pre-existing conditions, prohibiting lifetime or annual benefit limits, and prohibiting rescission, which is the discontinuation of an existing policy because of a new, potentially expensive medical condition or an expensive episode of care. One additional, important health insurance reform in the law is the requirement for health

> **Tip**
>
> **Primary care:** Inform individuals about the consumer protection provisions of the law that also pertain to private health insurance.

Table 16-1 ▼ Sections of the Patient Protection and Affordable Care Act
TITLE I—QUALITY, AFFORDABLE HEALTH CARE FOR ALL AMERICANS
TITLE II—ROLE OF PUBLIC PROGRAMS
TITLE III—IMPROVING THE QUALITY AND EFFICIENCY OF HEALTH CARE
TITLE IV—PREVENTION OF CHRONIC DISEASE AND IMPROVING PUBLIC HEALTH
TITLE V—HEALTH CARE WORKFORCE
TITLE VI—TRANSPARENCY AND PROGRAM INTEGRITY
TITLE VII—IMPROVING ACCESS TO INNOVATIVE MEDICAL THERAPIES
TITLE VIII—CLASS ACT
TITLE IX—REVENUE PROVISIONS
TITLE X—STRENGTHENING QUALITY, AFFORDABLE HEALTH CARE FOR ALL AMERICANS

insurance companies to allow policyholders to include "dependent" children up to 26 years old on their policies.

The ACA contains ten sections, or Titles (Table 16-1). The ten sections cover major topics such as "quality, affordable health care for all Americans" (Title I), "prevention of chronic disease and improving quality health" (Title IV), and "health care workforce" (Title V). Each section contains numerous subsections with principles, rules, regulations, timelines, policies, and procedures, in remarkable detail, directed at the responsibilities and operations of health insurance companies related to pricing, profit margins, and reporting requirements. For the purposes of this chapter, however, the focus is on the health-promoting elements of the law that improve the health of individuals and populations, rather than the mechanics, the administrative aspects of the law, or the regulatory and definitional aspects related to operations.

THE AFFORDABLE CARE ACT AND POPULATION HEALTH

Arguably, the two most important elements of the ACA from the standpoint of furthering the aims of integration (of primary care and public health) are provisions to increase the number of Americans with health insurance, which should increase the utilization of primary care, and provisions to improve public health and create and fund the Prevention and Public Health Fund. This is not to suggest that there aren't other important provisions that will accelerate or be accelerated by better integration of primary care and public health. However, from an impact perspective and a sequencing-of-stages perspective, health insurance coverage enables primary care services and the coordination with public health to improve individuals' health, and the Public Health and Prevention Fund and other public health provisions of the ACA enable services to protect and improve the public's health, some of which might complement or be complemented by quality primary care.

INCREASED DEMAND FOR PRIMARY CARE

Increasing the number of Americans with health insurance will predictably increase the demand for medical care and, presumably, primary care. Starfield and others (2005) have described the value as well as the following four important features of primary care: 1) contact access for each need, 2) long-term person-focused care, 3) comprehensive care for most health and medical care needs, and 4) coordinated care when it involves referrals to specialists or other providers. According to Starfield, the benefits of primary care-centered health care include improved health, reduced population health inequities, and lower cost of care. For those individuals diagnosed with or presenting with chronic conditions such as diabetes, hypertension, and congestive obstructive pulmonary disease (Sharma et al., 2014), primary care delivered using the chronic care model (Wagner et al., 1996) through patient-centered medical homes (Patient-Centered Primary Care Collaborative, 2007) will be the likely delivery mechanisms to address their medical needs. The establishment of community-based health teams to support patient self-management and other chronic disease care management activities for persons in patient-centered medical homes is addressed in the section of the ACA that establishes the Center for Medicare and Medicaid Innovation (CMMI).

> ### Tips
>
> Connect all new and existing health insurance-covered individuals with primary care medical homes.
>
> **Primary care:** Establish community health teams to support primary care and better coordinated care in your practice setting.

PREVENTIVE SCREENING

Lack of or loss of insurance coverage is associated with lower preventive screening rates (King et al., 2014). One of the provisions of the ACA assures that certain recommended clinical preventive services be provided with no additional out-of-pocket costs to individuals receiving those recommended services. The newly insured will likely benefit from increased utilization of recommended clinical preventive services for health promotion, counseling, screening for unhealthy behaviors such as tobacco use, screening for conditions such as obesity or hypertension, cancer screening, and appropriate vaccinations.

The Affordable Care Act and Innovation

Tip

Primary care: Because of ACA-related support of clinical preventive services, put policies and procedures in place to assure that all patients are up to date on U.S. Preventive Services Task Force and Advisory Committee on Immunization Practices' recommended clinical preventive services.

As previously mentioned, the CMMI was established by the ACA. The CMMI is directed to develop and test innovative health care payment and service delivery models. One CMMI innovation model is the accountable care organization, defined as health care providers, including clinicians and hospitals, that formally organize to coordinate care delivery to Medicare patients. In addition, the CMMI includes primary care transformation innovation models. Among the primary care models being tested, the CMMI website lists the Comprehensive Primary Care Initiative, the FQHC Advanced Primary Care Practice Demonstration, and the Multi-Payer Advance Primary Care Demonstration (Center for Medicare and Medicaid Services, 2014). Twenty models that are testing the ability of health care organizations and clinicians to manage population health and to manage health care resources have been funded by CMMI. One important distinction between this CMS effort and previous efforts is to engage multiple payers with the expectation of success (or, at least, a more complete understanding of what works and does not work) if multiple players, public and private, adopt the same, new payment models in a particular setting. These payment models reflect a shift from fee-for-service payments that incentivize volume over value to value-based reimbursement that incentivize quality care and optimal outcomes. Multi-payer approaches reduce administrative complexity for medical care providers and simplify evaluation for payers of care (Rajkumar, 2014) and health services researchers.

Tip

Play the role of convener to push for multi-payer collaboration and to push for primary care and public health integration.

The CMMI, through the State Innovation Models Initiative, provides funding to states to develop and test state-based models for multi-payer payment and health system transformation.

PATIENT-CENTERED OUTCOMES

The ACA also established the Patient-Centered Outcomes Research Institute (PCORI) to promote research and analysis in five priority areas: 1) medical care, 2) health care systems, 3) communication and dissemination, 4) health disparities, and 5) a patient-centered health services research agenda. The findings from the CMMI and PCORI will inform inform the evolution of primary care and public health.

Tip

Primary care: Be on the lookout for reports of findings as well as funding opportunity announcements from the CMMI and PCORI.

THE AFFORDABLE CARE ACT AND STATE HEALTH HOMES

The ACA contains provisions for states to use the Medicaid state plan amendment process to provide health homes for enrollees with chronic conditions that "shall" include, but are not limited to, mental health disorders or substance abuse disorders, asthma, diabetes, heart disease, and overweight or obesity. A health home is defined as a provider working with a team of health care professionals in the ACA: The "health home" and the ACA designated services are strikingly similar to the patient-centered medical home (Patient-Centered Primary Care Collaborative, 2007); standards for health home qualifications are detailed in the law.

> **Tip**
>
> Know the ACA "health homes" provisions and work to amend your state's Medicaid plan to achieve Medicaid health home designation for interested practices in your state.

NATIONAL PREVENTION STRATEGY

Title IV of the ACA, Prevention of Chronic Disease and Improving Public Health, contains significant provisions that will enable public health, community health, and population health improvements in infrastructure, funding, and capacity. The National Prevention, Health Promotion, and Public Health Council created in the ACA is chaired by the U.S. Surgeon General and is made up of administrators from multiple federal agencies and departments, including health, agriculture, education, transportation, labor, and others. Its charge is to provide federal-level leadership and coordination related broadly to health matters, including prevention and health promotion. In addition, the ACA establishes an advisory group to the Council; the advisory group works with the Council to develop a national prevention and health promotion strategic plan, known as the National Prevention Strategy, that is to be updated annually.

> **Tip**
>
> Know and participate in the deliberations of the advisory group to the National Prevention, Health Promotion, and Public Health Council and stay apprised of the National Prevention Strategy (http://www.surgeongeneral.gov/initiatives/prevention/advisorygrp/).

TWO EXPANDED FUNDING INITIATIVES IN THE AFFORDABLE CARE ACT

The Prevention and Public Health Fund was established in the ACA to provide expanded and predictable funding to address public health and population health issues. The additional funding is spelled out to include prevention, wellness, prevention research, health screenings, and immunization programs. The number of initiatives that are specified for funding and the details related to the funding preclude an exhaustive listing. Two examples, however, are funding of public awareness programs designed by "each state" to educate Medicaid enrollees about obesity-related and prevention services and a grant fund for states to provide incentives to Medicaid enrollees to stop tobacco use, manage weight, lower blood pressure, lower cholesterol, and prevent diabetes.

The "Creating Healthier Communities" section of the ACA established the Community Transformation Grants (CTG) program, which awarded competitive grants to state and local government agencies and community-based organizations to improve community health and, specifically, address health disparities. However, the 2014 omnibus federal budget bill does not fund CTG; funds are allocated for a new Community Prevention Grants program and to the Diabetes and Heart Disease and Stroke Prevention programs at the Centers for Disease Control and Prevention (The Prevention Institute, 2014). Activities to make communities healthier are listed in the Creating Healthier Communities section and include "creating the infrastructure to support active living and access to nutritious foods in a safe environment."

> **Tip**
>
> Engage your community and relevant stakeholders (which might include the state or local health department) in pursuing "healthier communities" opportunities.

QUALITY OF CARE

In addition to health insurance coverage expansion and protection and public health measures, the ACA also addresses quality of medical care and workforce issues. For example, Title III addresses the linkage of quality outcomes to payment in Medicare as well as the development of a national strategy to develop quality metrics and to improve the quality of medical care. The workforce section addresses issues related to the public health workforce and the primary care workforce, including training, recruitment, and retention.

> **Tip**
>
> Carefully study the law and how it has evolved and how it should be best leveraged in your community.

THE AFFORDABLE CARE ACT: A WORK IN PROGRESS

The ACA contains provisions that align the integration of primary care and public health to improve and, ideally, optimize the health of individuals and populations (Shaw et al., 2014). The ACA is a work in progress, subject to the vagaries of the law-making and law-fixing process of the U.S. Congress and subject to the pace of and capacity to change in the public and private sector. This chapter touches on some of the more relevant elements of the law, but there is much more to the law with implications for realizing the integration of primary care and public health. Fully leveraging the ACA to integrate public health and primary care will take continued study and understanding of the law, its components, and its nuances; discovering new elements of interest or relevance; following rule promulgation and finalization and appropriation of funds related to components of the law of interest; and understanding and communicating how the law and resources can be harnessed to support the objectives of *The Practical Playbook*, namely, the integration of primary care and public health to optimize people's health.

REFERENCES

Bundorf MK, Pauly MV. Defining health insurance affordability? J Health Econ 2006; 25: 650–673.

Center for Medicare and Medicaid Services. Innovation Center. 2014. Available at: http://innovation.cms.gov/initiatives/state-innovations/

Doty MM, Blumenthal D, Collins SR. The Affordable Care Act and health insurance for Latinos. JAMA 2014; 312: 1735–1736.

Institute of Medicine. Primary Care and Public Health: Exploring Integration to Improve Population Health. Washington, DC: Nationa Academies, 2012.

King CJ, Chan J, Garza MA, Thomas SB. Breast and cervical cancer screenings by race/ethnicity: Comparative analysis before and during the great recession. Am J Prev Med 2014; 46(4): 359–367.

Lavarreda SA, et al. Switching health insurance and its effects on access to physician services. Med Care 2008; 46: 1055–1063.

Longlett SK, Kruse JE, Wesley RM. Community-oriented primary care: Historical perspective. J Am Board Fam Pract 2001; 14(1): 54–63.

National Research Council and Institute of Medicine. Woolf SH, Aron L, editors. U.S. Health in International Perspective: Shorter Lives, Poorer Health. Washington, DC: National Acadamies Press, 2013.

Patient Protection and Affordable Care Act. Pub.L. 111–148. 2010. Retrieved from http://www.healthcare.gov.

Patient-Centered Primary Care Collaborative. Joint Principles of the Patient Centered Medical Home. 2007. Retrieved 2014 from: https://www.pcpcc.net/content/joint-principles-patient-centered-medical-home

The Prevention Institute. (2014). Community Transformation: Maintaining the Vision as Critical Funding Shifts. 2014. Available at: http://www.preventioninstitute.org/press/highlights/1117-community-transformation-maintaining-the-vision-as-critical-funding-shifts.html

Rajkumar R. CMS—Engaging multiple payers in payment reform. JAMA 2014; 311(19): 1967–1970.

Sharma MA, Cheng N, Moore M, Coffman M, Bazemore AW. Patients with high-cost chronic conditions rely heavily on primary care physicians. JAMA 2014; 27(1): 11–12. doi:10.3122/jabfm.2014.01.130128

Shaw FE, Asomugha CN, Conway PH, Rein AS. The Patient Protection and Affordable Care Act: Opportunities for prevention and public health. The Lancet 2014; 384(9937): 75–82.

Starfield B, Shi LY, Macinko J. Contribution of primary care to health systems and health. Milbank Q 2005; 83(3): 457–502. doi: 10.1111/j.1468-0009.2005.00409.x

U.S. Census Bureau. 2014. Available at: http://www.census.gov/hhes/www/hlthins/data/incpovhlth/2010/highlights.html

Wagner EH, Austin BT, VonKorff M. Organizing care for patients with chronic illness. Milbank Q 1996; 74(4): 511–544.

Chapter 17

Partnering With Medicaid, Medicare, Public Health, and Primary Care to Improve Health Outcomes

SHARON G. MOFFATT, MONICA VALDES LUPI, AND KATHLEEN NOLAN

A strong partnership among primary care, public health, Medicaid, and Medicare is essential if we are to improve health outcomes in the United States. The reach of Medicare and Medicaid is significant, as together they cover services for over 100 million Americans. Medicare covers over 49 million Americans who are over the age of 65 years or have an eligible disability. The 50-state Medicaid programs cover over 60 million Americans. For example almost 50% of all births, 42% of national spending on long-term services and supports (LTSS), and 25% of all mental health and substance abuse treatment spending is provided by Medicaid (Mitchell et al., 2014). There is a great opportunity for health promotion and disease prevention by keeping these Americans in optimum health. As a guide, we can look to the focus of the Centers for Medicare and Medicaid Services (CMS) on delivery models that aim to achieve better care for patients, better health for our communities, and lower costs by improving our health care system (Center for Medicare and Medicaid Innovation, 2014).

Heightened attention has been paid to opportunities to improve population health through the integration of primary care and public health, as described in the 2012 Institute of Medicine report *Primary Care and Public Health: Exploring Integration to Improve Population Health* (Institute of Medicine, 2012). Beyond this partnership, an increased awareness has developed of the importance for primary care and public health to develop a strong partnership with payers, notably Medicaid and Medicare.

Medicaid plays a large role in paying for the delivery of care to low-income individuals and in influencing the state's health care system. Medicaid is jointly funded by states and the federal government and provides health services for low-income children, pregnant women, and, in some states, childless adults and parents. Medicaid also provides health and long-term care services for adults with disabilities who are also low-income Medicare enrollees (i.e., dual eligibles). In every state, Medicaid is a major purchaser of health care services and and provider of community supports for a substantial portion of the population. Opportunities for collaboration abound at the state, health plan, and provider level to improve the care and health of Medicaid enrollees through Medicaid policy changes and health system reforms. (See more detailed descriptions in Opportunities for Partnership, later in the chapter.)

Medicare, serving seniors regardless of health disability status or income, is a federally funded and operated program with little state or local flexibility. However, its influence on state and local health systems is substantial. It is a major payer for many health care services and for hospitals and long-term care, and commercial payers often follow its lead in payment policies. Therefore opportunities for collaboration with public health come not only at the policy and program level, but also at the provider and insurance plan level, where collaborations can benefit Medicare enrollees. Also, a small but expensive fraction of Medicare enrollees are also receiving Medicaid; these cases offer an important focus for care improvement and collaboration with the goal to reduce health care costs to both the state and federal government. Managing Medicaid and Medicare beneficiaries at the state or local level offers an opportunity, not yet realized, to coordinate and redesign care around the need of individuals based on where they live, rather than on who pays for their care.

As rising health care costs reverberate throughout the health care system, ensuring sustainability of the public programs will require increased effectiveness and efficiency of health care as well as improved health outcomes. The effort will require strategic planning, optimizing data sharing, understanding and addressing barriers, implementing effective policies, and replicating successes in other settings. A dynamic collaboration with public health and primary care offers promise (for specific illustrations, see Examples of Successful Partnerships, later in the chapter).

Each entity brings a unique set of attributes and knowledge to improving health outcomes. For example, primary care brings medical expertise and in-depth understanding of individuals' health; public health brings expertise in addressing and targeting population health needs using data, policy, and programs; and Medicaid and Medicare bring the policy tools to cement change and operate the levers of market power. It will be through a collaborative partnership between primary care, public health, Medicaid, and Medicare that we can more rapidly achieve better care, better health, and lower costs.

WHY IS COLLABORATION IMPORTANT?

Two critical factors make essential the formation of strong partnerships among Medicaid, Medicare, primary care, and public health. These include both the increased number of Americans eligible for Medicaid and Medicare and the escalating health care costs, which particularly impact state and federal budgets.

Increased Eligibility for Medicaid

Historically, Medicaid eligibility has generally been limited to low-income infants and children, pregnant women, parents of dependent children, the elderly, and individuals with disabilities; however, the Patient Protection and Affordable Care Act (ACA; P.L. 111–148, as amended) included the ACA Medicaid expansion, which expands Medicaid eligibility to individuals under the age of 65 with income up to 133% of the federal poverty level (FPL) (effectively 138% FPL) at state discretion (states can opt out of the expansion) (Mitchell et al., 2014).

The ACA changes to Medicaid eligibility are projected to add 8.6 million people to Medicaid in FY2014 and 18.3 million people by FY2021. About 83% of new adult enrollees are projected to be "newly eligible" (i.e., eligible for Medicaid through the ACA Medicaid expansion), whereas 17% are projected to be individuals who would have been eligible for Medicaid prior to the ACA changes, but were not enrolled (Mitchell et al., 2014).

Roughly half of Medicaid enrollees were children without disabilities, who accounted for 20% of Medicaid's total benefit spending. The next largest enrollee group—adults—accounted for 24% of all enrollees, but only 15% of benefit expenditures. In contrast, individuals with disabilities represented 17% of Medicaid enrollees, but accounted for the largest share of Medicaid benefit spending (about 44%). Finally, the elderly represented about 9% of Medicaid enrollees, but about 20% of all benefit spending. While these statistics vary somewhat from year to year and state to state, the patterns described generally hold true across years (Truffer et al., 2012). Each state has made its own decision on Medicaid expansion, yet the opportunity for partnership with Medicaid is essential, given the increasing number of enrollees and the varied nature of their current and future health needs (Fig. 17-1). Strategic partnerships between Medicaid, primary care and public health can be a key to successfully addressing the health needs of increases in Medicaid participants. This can include public health and Medicaid outreach, primary care working with public health to identify and address barriers to health care services, and Medicaid and public health working with primary care to assure early screening, referrals, and follow up.

Cost Drivers: Medicaid and Medicare

Medicaid funding in states continues to be a serious cost driver of state funds. Medicaid budgets in states have grown at a much higher rate than general revenues year after year. With the growth in program enrollment—both recent and pending—the search continues for ways to control Medicaid spending (National Governors Association, 2014). Improving health outcomes via appropriate and timely uses of preventive services, screening, and timely diagnosis and treatment of conditions will improve the overall health status of Medicaid enrollees while decreasing expenditures for management of chronic conditions and unnecessary emergency room utilization (Institute of Medicine, 2012). Primary care, public health, and Medicaid working in tandem can focus on interventions that promote healthy lifestyles and assure preventive care, to contain or reduce costs.

Over the long term, Medicare will face significant financing challenges. Among these challenges is the aging of the American population. The first of the baby boom generation turned 65 and became eligible for Medicare in 2010. Between 2001 and 2030, the number of Medicare beneficiaries is projected to almost double, rising from 40 million to 77 million. The number of beneficiaries over age 85 (the "oldest-old") is projected to grow from 4.3 million individuals today to about 8.5 million in 2030 (Henry J. Kaiser Family Foundation, 2001). As this population is more likely to need health care services

Figure 17-1 ▼

Past and projected Medicaid enrollment, by population, FY2000–FY2021. Enrollment is measured by "person-year equivalents," which is the average enrollment over the course of the year. For purposes of this figure, "Newly Eligible Adults" are adult enrollees who are newly eligible in 2014 and later, as a result of the expanded eligibility criteria in the ACA. "Children of Newly Eligible Adults" are defined here as the dependent children of newly eligible adult enrollees, even if these children were eligible under current criteria.

(From Truffer CJ, Klemm JD, Wolfe CJ, Rennie KE, Shuff JF. 2012 Actuarial Report on the Financial Outlook for Medicaid. Washington, DC: Centers for Medicare & Medicaid Services, U.S. Department of Health & Human Services, 2012.)

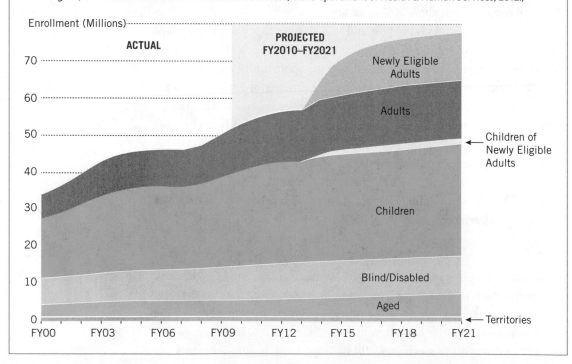

than younger beneficiaries, these projections raise particular concerns for Medicare's long-term financing challenges. The aging of the population also has significant implications for Medicare financing, as does the condition of the population's health when they become Medicare-eligible. Public health working with primary care providers and community partners can identify gaps in services, opportunities to link adults to community resources, and evidence-based interventions. This collaboration can focus on early preventative health interventions with an aim for a healthy aging Medicare population. Primary care and prevention now means healthier Medicare enrollees in the future, and reduced health care costs.

EXAMPLES OF SUCCESSFUL PARTNERSHIPS

As the collaborative partnership among public health, primary care medicine, Medicaid, and Medicare builds, we can draw from early examples of success to learn both the opportunities and challenges to sustaining success. The follow are examples of emerging promising partnerships at the state and national level.

Asthma Initiatives in Massachusetts

The Massachusetts Asthma Advocacy Partnership (MAAP) focuses on improving the health of children with uncontrolled asthma. MAPP consists of more than 78 partners, including community groups, health care providers, school officials, daycare providers, housing agencies, environmental groups, state agencies, and local governments. As a part of the services provided by MAAP, a community health worker/educator (CHW) visits the home to assess in-home asthma triggers and to equip families with educational tools to reduce environmental asthma triggers (i.e., vacuum cleaners and mattress covers). The CHW is based in the child's medical home, which enables the worker to easily link to the child's primary care provider and provide assistance in obtaining and taking medication when needed.

State Medicaid and public health leadership collaborated with MAPP to identify funding support for this statewide pediatric asthma home visiting program. State Medicaid programs may use a process of requesting a waiver from existing Medicaid program rules from the Centers for Medicare and Medicaid Services (CMS) for programs aimed at promoting health. A formal state request is made to CMS to waive federal Medicaid program rules in order to test new or existing ways to deliver and pay for health care services. Massachusetts received a CMS waiver in 2011 to support the statewide implementation of the pediatric asthma home visiting program. This program provides a bundled payment to health care providers to support pediatric home visits. Since asthma hospitalizations are considered preventable, the program aims to enable health care providers to focus on the prevention of asthma in high-risk children, with the intent of avoiding costly hospitalizations.

The pediatric asthma home visits model of bundled payments for clinicians, home visitors, and housing experts could be applied to older adults and serves as an excellent model for engaging community and housing experts and strengthening their linkages to clinical care providers.

Pregnancy Medical Homes in North Carolina

The North Carolina Division of Public Health (NCDPH) together with the North Carolina Division of Medical Assistance (NC Medicaid) have led the creation of a pregnancy-care model that establishes pregnancy medical homes (PMHs) for Medicaid recipients in North Carolina. The PMH initiative links community resources with health care providers to give essential support to pregnant women and provide the best chance for healthy pregnancies, deliveries, and newborns.

Care managers (nurses and social workers) from local health departments are assigned to PMH practices to provide case management for Medicaid recipients in the practice with high-risk pregnancies. The care manager completes a comprehensive assessment on each recipient who screens as a high risk for poor birth outcomes. The level of services provided to recipients is based on their needs and risk level. Care managers closely monitor high-risk pregnant women through regular follow-up with the physician and patient to promote a healthy birth outcome. This is a model of population health improvement that could be applied to other targeted high-risk individuals with diabetes, heart disease, or cancer. It provides an excellent model of collaboration between state and local public health, the state Medicaid agency, and primary care providers. The payment model is structured to support optimum quality of care and it funds both clinical care providers and community care managers.

Decreasing Hypertension: Maryland Million Hearts Initiative

The Maryland Million Hearts Initiative is led by the Maryland Department of Health and Mental Hygiene (DHMH) in partnership with the state Health Quality and Cost Council. The DHMH is one of nine states in which Medicaid and public health are in the same agency, thus providing important opportunities for linkages. This project moved beyond the state governmental agency structure to bring together primary care providers, local communities, health systems, nonprofit organizations, federal agencies, and private-sector businesses to work together on strategies for treatment and prevention of hypertension. Since the program began, the state has seen a 27% increase in blood pressure control at participating clinical settings.

The commitment of the DHMH to the Million Hearts Initiative has five core components:

1. Improving clinical care within public and private health care settings.
2. Strengthening tobacco control through promoting the State Tobacco Quit Line.

3. Promoting a healthy diet.
4. Encouraging workplace wellness.
5. Incentivizing local public health action.

The DHMH also reached out to providers, insurance professionals, and academics who helped link the initiative to local organizations, such as community and faith-based organizations, coalitions, federally qualified health centers, local health departments, employers, and others.

Importantly, the Maryland Million Hearts Initiative leveraged several federal funding sources, including a Centers for Disease Control and Prevention (CDC) Preventive Health and Health Services grant, a CMS State Innovation Models Testing grant, Maryland's Community Transformation grant, and the State Public Health Actions to Prevent and Control Diabetes, Heart Disease, Obesity, and Associated Risk Factors and Promote School Health grant. Maryland Million Hearts is not simply one program, but instead is a collaboration among a number of state and local initiatives for chronic disease control and management.

This initiative has demonstrated improved health outcomes, the value of state and community partnerships across the health system, and creativity to leverage multiple resources to sustain success.

OPPORTUNITIES FOR PARTNERSHIPS

1. State health agencies as conveners can conduct joint planning efforts that bring the voices, concerns, and assets of each group to a strategic process. State public health can lead this convening to include Medicaid, primary care providers, and other key stakeholders.
   For example: Identify local and state primary care and public health champions as key informants and vested stakeholders for inclusion in all state planning coalitions for Center for Medicaid and Medicare Innovation—State Innovation Model grants. As these grants are led by the governor's office, a formal request to the governor may be indicated. Primary care providers can identify experts and champions to participate in these state planning efforts.
2. State health departments and Medicaid offices can support joint training opportunities for the primary care and public health workforce to identify prevention opportunities, improve care, and connect to local/community-based services.
   For example: Engage state/local public health and state Medicaid officials to partner with state medical chapters for joint learning sessions. Identify opportunities to create linkages, such as state annual meetings, and joint online training sessions for continuing education credits. Primary care providers can have a key role in identification of learning needs, decision-making about how information is best

presented and disseminated, and identification of national, state, and local experts.

3. Use the combined data analytics resources of state and local public health, Medicaid, and Medicare to inform the development of strategies that best deploy health promotion and care services to vulnerable populations in targeted geographic areas, and decrease duplication of efforts.

For example: Partner with Medicaid and with Medicare to identify new enrollees and develop plans for targeted outreach, identification of areas of gaps in services, and opportunities for linkages with care providers. Georgia State Health Agency used geographic information system mapping to identify neighbor areas with high rates of infant morbidity and mortality, then worked with care providers and community partners for targeted outreach to assure access to timely care. Primary care providers can work with state and local public health workers to identify requests for analysis and opportunities to use the information for outreach and support of their patients.

4. State health agencies may identify policies that build on standards of practice to improve health outcomes. Policies can include payment policies, process policies, and evidence—based program policies.

For example: The Texas Department of Health partnered with Medicaid to develop a policy of nonpayment for non–medically necessary late preterm deliveries. This policy is consistent with the standards of practice of the American College of Obstetrics and Gynecology. Primary care providers can partner to identify and prioritize the policy needs, identify colleagues who are national, state, and local experts to contribute to the development and dissemination of state policies.

5. Since nearly half of all births in the country are covered by Medicaid, partnerships between state health agencies and Medicaid offices can enhance efforts to improve maternal and birth outcomes.

For example: Link public health programs that support maternal child health with primary care providers. In the Special Supplemental Nutrition Program for Women, Infants, and Children (WIC), as many as 95% of participants are also eligible for Medicaid. Co-location of WIC clinics in primary care settings links families with a medical home, Medicaid benefits, and community resources. Opportunities include increased access to ongoing preventative care, such as immunizations, oral health, and early pre- and postpregnancy care. Primary care providers can provide an essential linkage between state and local public health maternal child health programs, serve as pilot sites to test new models of linkages, and identify emerging health issues and recommend solutions.

6. State health agencies and Medicaid offices can increase understanding of the state's Medicaid service delivery models and work together to identify and implement optimum statewide approaches to improve health outcomes and lower costs.

> For example: State and local public health and state organizations representing clinical providers can work with Medicaid to increase knowledge of payment and policy methods. Examples include efforts to address prescription drug abuse through Medicaid policies that allow a patient to fill an opioid prescription through only one pharmacy. Primary care providers can identify policies that are barriers to optimum health care delivery and identify national, state, and local experts to work with Medicaid and state public health.

7. Federal partners, including CMS, CDC, US Health Resources and Services Administration, and Substance Abuse and Mental Health Services Administration can engage state Medicaid officials and Medicaid medical directors and state health officials by focusing on critical prevention opportunities, such as tobacco cessation, medical nutrition therapy, behavioral health assessments, and dental health.

> For example: In 11 states, state health agencies have worked with their Medicaid offices to allow for an administrative match to support state tobacco quit lines. This has resulted in increasing state quit-line capacity by creating a stronger support for primary care providers' referrals of individuals motivated to quit. Primary care providers can identify the challenges and opportunities for solutions to implement prevention strategies in their practice settings, as all partners work toward effective, practical, and affordable models.

8. State health agencies can work with their Medicaid offices to develop, pilot, and spread models of linking patients with primary care and community resources. This collaboration occurs both within states and across states and regions, with the aim of spreading best practices to all states.

> For example: Community health workers are utilized in Vermont housing for older adults and disabled individuals to provide linkages with community supports and primary care providers. An outcome of this linkage has shown decreased use of emergency departments. States now have the option to reimburse for CHW services. Primary care providers are a key partner in ensuring that these linkages will be effective by identifying colleagues who are willing to test new models of linkages and to identify the challenges and solutions for spread and sustainability.

9. State health agencies are uniquely positioned to identify needs, gaps in services, and opportunities for linking adults to community resources through partnerships between primary care and public health. Focus can be around identification, outreach, and engagement of high-risk adults to

provide such services as immunization, chronic disease self-management, and identification and treatment of infectious diseases.

For example: Through a 10-state Million Hearts collaborative, primary care, public health, and public and private payers have identified hypertensive-specific data in electronic health records, payer claims data, and public health survey and registry information. Working together, care providers, payers, and public health workers can identify individuals and population groups with undiagnosed or uncontrolled hypertension. Collectively they identify barriers to care and link with community resources. Primary care providers can contribute in multiple ways, including sharing their clinical best-practice algorithms and their successes using electronic health records (EHRs) and registries to identify and treat high-risk patients, thereby helping to spread best practices across communities and states.

10. State health agencies and Medicaid offices can work together to improve medication adherence through partnerships, including review of health and pharmacy data, outreach, and policies.

For example: Public health, primary care providers, and payers are focusing on identification of medication adherence for hypertensives. An in-depth utilization review of medication is done through review of EHRs in the primary care setting, and review of payers' pharmacy benefits claims data. Medicaid can work with community pharmacists and care providers on utilization review to identify the challenges and partner with public health to identify solutions and work with patients to strengthen medication adherence. Primary care providers can provide expertise on the barriers and solutions they identify in medication adherence; they can also identify educational outreach opportunities and examples of successful use of EHRs to identify individuals who need specialized support.

CONCLUSION

Primary care, public health, Medicaid, and Medicare each brings a unique set of skills and different leverage points for improving health outcomes. It will be through a collaborative partnership that we can more quickly achieve better care, better health outcomes, and lower costs.

The opportunities before us should catalyze efforts to replicate current successful partnerships and identify newly emerging opportunities and best practices. A few of these immediate opportunities are the Massachusetts pediatric asthma home visiting program, which demonstrates model partnership of the state health agency with Medicaid, housing, community partners, and community health providers, to improve health outcomes for at-risk children with asthma. The Maryland Million Hearts initiative, with collaboration of public health, Medicaid, primary care, and community partners, demonstrated a 27% increase in blood pressure control. National partnerships such as the ASTHO-S supported Primary Care and Public Health Collaborative (http://www.astho.org/Programs/Access/Primary-Care-and-Public-Health-Integration/give) provide an important structure for representatives from public health, clinical care, and insurers to identify opportunities to collectively improve the health of our nation.

Importantly, new investments to states and health systems innovators, through CMMI, provide significant opportunities to build collaborative partnerships. Primary care and public health should assure they are actively involved in developing new payment and service delivery models with Medicare and Medicaid, with the aim of better care for patients, better health for our communities, and lower costs.

REFERENCES

Center for Medicare and Medicaid Innovation. Innovation Models. http://innovation.cms.gov/initiatives/index.html#views=models. Accessed May 15, 2014.

Henry J. Kaiser Family Foundation. Fact Sheet: Medicare Spending and Financing. http://kff.org/medicare/fact-sheet/medicare-spending-and-financing-fact-sheet/. Accessed July 28, 2014.

Institute of Medicine. For the Public's Health, Investing in a Healthier Future. Washington, DC: The National Academies Press, 2012.

Institute of Medicine. Primary Care and Public Health: Exploring Integration to Improve Population Health. Washington, DC: The National Academies Press, 2012.

Medicare Chart Book. Henry J. Kaiser Family Foundation, 2001.

Mitchell A, Baumrucker EP, Herz EJ. Medicaid: An Overview. Congressional Research Service, U.S. Library of Congress, 2014. http://mspbwatcharchive.files.wordpress.com/2014/01/20140110_medicaid-an-overview.pdf. Accessed May 15, 2014.

National Governors Association. State Roles in Delivery System Reform. 2010. http://www.nga.org/files/live/sites/NGA/files/pdf/1007DELIVERYSYSTEMREFORM.PDF. Accessed May 5, 2014.

Truffer CJ, Klemm JD, Wolfe CJ, Rennie KE, Shuff JF. 2012 Actuarial Report on the Financial Outlook for Medicaid. Washington, DC: Centers for Medicare & Medicaid Services, U.S. Department of Health & Human Services, 2012.

Working With Accountable Care Organizations

JOANNE M. CONROY, CLESE ERIKSON, AND COLEEN KIVLAHAN

Public health leaders have long known that addressing social determinants of health such as housing, transportation, poverty, and nutrition can have a dramatic impact on patient health and utilization, but they have often struggled to effectively integrate community resources into medical care models. Now that new payment and care delivery models, such as accountable care organizations (ACOs), are providing a business case for thinking more holistically about patient care outside the clinical setting, there is an opportunity for public health to become a valued partner in redesigning care. Given their knowledge of community needs and available resources, local health departments and other public health officials are well positioned to partner with providers who are looking to enhance their population management efforts and help ensure that efforts are aligned and coordinated across the health care continuum.

Accountable care organizations are groups of providers taking responsibility—being accountable—for performance risk (quality and overall outcomes) and financial risk (costs) for a defined patient population. The ACO model encourages modification of traditional care processes and investment in infrastructure that promotes and monitors health improvements in order to deliver high-quality, efficient, and cost-effective health care. The ACO concept quickly moved from a "glimmer" to a legislated Medicare initiative in 2012 (Fisher et al., 2006; Public Law 111–148, 2010). The rationale and philosophy for ACOs is based on recognizing the "importance of shifting the payment system from a focus on volume and intensity to a focus on value and performance," according to a seminal 2009 article published in the journal *Health Affairs* and written by former Centers for Medicare and Medicaid Services (CMS) Administrator Mark McClellan, M.D, Ph.D., and Elliott S. Fisher, M.D., M.P.H., director of the Center for Health Policy Research at the Dartmouth Institute for Health Care Policy and Clinical Practice (Fisher et al., 2009). Unlike health maintenance organizations (HMOs), which traditionally focused more on cost control from an insurer perspective, in the ACO model, providers and patients determine diagnostic and treatment paths that encourage prudent and efficient use of health care services. The ACO concept continues to evolve. The CMS issued a request for information in the spring of 2014 to generate suggestions for new ACO models that encourage multiple-payer integration and greater accountability for financial and quality outcomes. Accountable care, in any form, ideally aligns health care providers' and patients' interests. Its promise to providers and to the public is that there are finally financial rewards for keeping people healthy. This is new territory for many health care organizations, which will only be successful if they effectively partner with community organizations including: 1) local health departments, which can help develop new programs or adapt existing programs to positively impact the health of their communities; 2) diverse and representative community groups that are far more effective than traditional medical providers in identifying barriers to care and understanding where real disparities exist; and 3) rural and physician providers who may be eligible for advance payment startup costs.

As of February 2013, ACOs covered 37 million to 43 million Medicare and commercial patients (Gandhi & Weil, 2012) and well over 600 healthcare entities are practicing accountable care, half of these with commercial carriers (Leavitt Partners, 2013). An estimated 11% of Medicare beneficiaries and 14% of the U.S. population is now being served by an ACO (Gandhi & Weil, 2012). Commercial ACOs are very similar to their Medicare cousins, but the commercial insurers generally set their own quality metrics. Risk and length of ACO contracts vary from payer to payer. The major commercial payers involved are Aetna, Blue Cross Blue Shield affiliates, Cigna, and United Healthcare.

THE PROBLEM

Unfortunately, most health care in the United States is still delivered under a system of reimbursement that pays for the volume of medical services provided without regard to the value that patients receive. This drives a level of health care spending that is unsustainable for federal payers, employers, and patients, which has created the tremendous interest in alternative payment models at the health system, provider, and payer levels. We have seen the rapid emergence of commercial ACOs and the deployment of Medicare and Medicaid ACOs. These models are far from perfect, however. For Medicare ACOs, the assignment of patients to the ACO is a work in progress, the startup costs are significant ranging from $300,000 to over $6 million per institution (National Association of ACOs, 2014), and apparently Medicare is struggling to deliver data in a timely way that allows organizations to assess their own performance. Most importantly, organizations are operating both fee-for-service and accountable care on the "same institutional chassis," which creates competing incentives.

HOW ACCOUNTABLE CARE ORGANIZATIONS WORK

Primary care providers, who deploy a team-based medical home approach with supportive organizational infrastructure from a health system or group practice, are at the core of the ACO. An ACO may be organized around a large primary care practice, a multi-specialty group, a fully integrated delivery system encompassing practitioners and facilities, a physician-hospital organization, or an independent practice association. Unlike HMOs, patients do not join ACOs; the health care providers do. Patients are attributed to the ACO according to the provider/site at which they received the majority or plurality of primary care services. Patients can refuse to participate in the ACO if they chose to receive care from a provider outside of the ACO. The health care provider is responsible for the patient's cost and quality of care, regardless of which providers actually deliver the services. The ACO is successful when they meet both cost and quality benchmarks. The cost benchmarks are met by delivering a total cost of care for the attributed patients below the historical, risk-adjusted benchmarks. The Congressional Budget Office has estimated that the impact of ACOs could reduce Medicare expenditures by nearly $5 billion between fiscal years 2013 and 2019 (Newman, 2011). The quality benchmarks are based on 33 nationally recognized quality measures in four domains: 1) patient/caregiver experience (7 measures), 2) care coordination/patient safely (6 measures), 3) preventive health (8 measures), and 4) at-risk populations (12 measures) (Centers for Medicare and Medicaid Services, 2013). There is real opportunity for collaborative approaches between public health and providers around care coordination measures focused on avoiding admissions for COPD, heart failure, and asthma in older adults, medication reconciliation, and screening for fall risk and depression, to name a few. A participating ACO that meets these predetermined quality and cost performance benchmarks can earn a share of Medicare's savings, which are then distributed among the providers who deliver care.

Ideally, this is achieved by deploying a physician-led team of providers across multiple disciplines to treat patient care as a continuum that can be managed more effectively with prevention and early treatment, rather than a series of fragmented individual units of disease-based services. This entails the use of technology, care coordinators, data, feedback, and a community of committed and connected providers. The care team strives to provide and properly manage the right level of resources, at the right time, and at the right intensity to keep healthy patients well and to effectively manage the care of patients with disease.

The intensity of monitoring and medical management depends on patients' individual needs. Most healthy patients need infrequent care with a focus on access, information, and prevention. For patients with chronic disease, directed, proactive office visits that link patients to supportive community programs can reduce the need for expensive—and for patients, unwelcome—hospitalizations. Providers actively monitor patients with chronic disease using e-mail, telemedicine, home monitoring, phone calls, and support groups in order to identify those at risk for poor health outcomes, so that prompt intervention can prevent erosion of their health status.

MOVING FROM "GLIMMER" TO NATIONAL INITIATIVE

Section 3022 of the Patient Protection and Affordable Care Act (ACA) established the Medicare Shared Savings Program (MSSP) to manage and coordinate all patient services provided under Medicare (including primary, specialty, and hospital care services) and to encourage investment in infrastructure and care process design to support high quality, efficient service delivery that reduces unnecessary costs. The Center for Medicare and Medicaid Innovation also launched the Pioneer ACO Model program in 2012. The CMS reported that 343 MSSP ACOs were in operation as of January 2014, with 23 Medicare Pioneer ACOs still in enrolled in the program (Centers for Medicare and Medicaid Services, 2014). Since then, others have dropped out of the Medicare Pioneer ACO Model program and moved to shared savings because of looming downside risk in year 3. And in August and September 2014, four more left the program, leaving only 19 of the original 32 Medicare Pioneer ACOs.

Medicare Pioneer Accountable Care Organization Model

The Pioneer ACO Model is similar to that of ACOs in the Medicare's Shared Savings Program, but there are important differences. Both models are intended to further the "triple aim" of improving care for individuals, achieving better health for populations, and reducing expenditures for Medicare. The Pioneer ACO Model, however, was designed for organizations to move more rapidly from a shared savings payment model to a population-based payment model (capitation). In the first 2 years, Pioneer ACOs will operate under a shared payment arrangement featuring higher levels of savings and risk than in MSSP; in year 3, Pioneer ACOs that have achieved certain minimum savings goals in the first 2 years will be eligible to transition away from fee-for-service payment to capitated payments, and to full-risk arrangements for years 4 and 5. Minimum at-risk Medicare fee-for-service population enrollment for a Pioneer ACO generally is 15,000 persons (5,000 in rural areas), compared to the MSSP minimum of 5,000 beneficiaries. In addition, Pioneer ACOs are expected to engage with purchasers other than Medicare (e.g., private health plans, state Medicaid agencies, and/or self-insured employers) in outcomes-based payment arrangements, and to commit to deriving a majority of revenues from outcomes-based payment arrangements by the end of their second performance period (December 2013).

Private Accountable Care Organization Models

Health care organizations and payers in the private sector are also operating ACOs, often associated with private health plans. The ACA's accountable care provisions for Medicare have influenced private ACO design, operations, payment incentives, and reporting mechanisms. Some private health insurers contract with providers under a shared-risk model that puts providers at risk for both shared savings and shared losses. Others have developed agreements with ACOs in which providers are eligible for shared savings, but bear no downside risk of shared losses. Because there is no formal method for tracking the formation of private ACOs, the growth of private ACOs is difficult to quantify.

ROLE FOR PUBLIC HEALTH IN ACCOUNTABLE CARE

Under new value-based care models, such as ACOs, providers are thinking much more expansively about population health and strategies for comprehensively addressing patients' health needs. Local health departments have a lot to offer provider organizations that are adopting new care models. It will be important for the public health workforce to be well versed in new payment models and how to demonstrate the business case for providers to engage in enhanced coordination with community resources. Involvement can range in scope from playing a leading role in designing and managing an accountable care model, such as the Hennepin Health model in Minnesota (Agency for Healthcare Research and Quality, 2013), to simply being familiar and knowledgeable enough about the concept to identify potential collaborations with local community organizations, such as churches and Meals on Wheels programs, or even the local fire department. For example, Bellin-ThedaCare ACO in Wisconsin is experimenting with having EMT personnel do home visits for patients recovering from congestive heart failure and other conditions as a way to prevent re-hospitalizations (Murray, 2013). The goal is to make sure that resources are aligned and well integrated. Do providers have up-to-date contacts for housing programs and other social service programs in the community? Do they have good working relationships, and see each other as allies? Health departments can be a valued partner in the transition by making these important connections and helping to coordinate resources across the care continuum.

CHALLENGES TO ACCOUNTABLE CARE ORGANIZATIONS SUSTAINABILITY

Early analysis of ACO performance is mixed, and there are a number of operational challenges (Centers for Medicare and Medicaid Services, 2014), which are listed below.

Providing Institutions with Timely and Actionable Data

Institutions continue to have difficulty getting accurate data from Medicare in a timely way in order to assess progress against their goals. Sophisticated organizations have created their own internal systems at significant expense to gauge their progress and make midcourse corrections.

Maximizing the Opportunity for Seamless New Model Implementation

In order to maximize the positive impact of the new models of care, such as ACOs and bundled payment, there must be a systematic process to quickly and fairly resolve clinical and operational conflicts in all overlapping federal programs. Such a process should focus on ways to align financial reconciliation, quality reporting, and beneficiary assignment across the various programs.

Connecting Patients More Closely to the Accountable Care Organization; Shared Accountability to Each Other

Because many of the new models are voluntary for the patients, population management becomes very challenging. Capitation within the current fee-for-service Medicare program, without the design features of Medicare Advantage (patients enroll instead of being attributed), must engage patients in managing their own health by seeking care from the capitated ACO, recognizing that they have freedom of choice in selecting a provider. Providers taking on additional risk through capitated payments need immediate and accurate information about who is covered and what services they are using. The current claims-based algorithms are not stable enough to do this. Allowing patients to proactively align themselves with an ACO would help both patients and providers have a common understanding of accountability and alignment. Under a purely claims-based attribution model, patients may not be aware of their assignment to an ACO, which limits the providers' ability to explain the ACO and its goals and delays enactment of patient incentives, such as enhanced case management or home visitations.

Extending Contract Time

Three years is inadequate to demonstrate real change. Providers recommend that that CMS extend the initial ACO contract period from 3 years to 5 years.

It takes time for the new care redesign efforts to develop and for ACOs to see savings from these efforts. ACOs should have at least 5 years to capture these savings before they are rebased.

CONCLUSION: REAL TRANSFORMATION

Recently both public and private payers have experimented with a variety of payment models designed to "bend the cost curve" downward by restraining ever-rising health care expenditures. In addition to ACOs, other examples include value-based purchasing, bundled payment models, penalties for excess hospital readmissions, and nonpayment for treatment of hospital-acquired and provider-preventable conditions (Centers for Medicare and Medicaid Services, 2010). However there is some confusion around the creative use of the term "population health" in all of these payment models. From the current provider perspective, they see their responsibility as preventing and caring for disease for those patients attributed to them. This falls short of an effort to improve population health, improving the health of a population in a geographic area. Nobel and Casalino (2013) posited that effective population health depends not only on medical care, but on partnership with social services, the public health system, and the social determinants of health (housing, education, poverty, and nutrition). They point out that ACOs currently lack the incentives, and in most cases the capabilities, to improve population health, and that even the ACO quality metrics do not have a clear link to the health of populations. Eventually ACOs, or the next iteration of health system models, should assume this more comprehensive role as payers align incentives across populations, providers move from panel management to community care, and patients are expected to engage in their health as well as that of their families and communities.

How to accomplish this? Health departments can help facilitate this transition by actively engaging with providers, identifying opportunities to align and coordinate community resources, and making the business case that these investments are not just the right thing to do for patients but will lead to greater financial sustainability for their organization, too. Value-based purchasing is the future, and public health can be a valued partner in supporting this transition. The ACOs and their primary care practices should solicit state and local health department participation in proposed pay-for-performance partnerships. Similarly, local health departments should feel empowered to reach out to providers and initiate these conversations. Local health departments are typically skilled in generating and collecting existing health status measures and translating them into valuable baseline reports and targeted wellness programs. In its traditional role as a "convener," public health departments facilitate planning discussions with community partners, review community health needs, and recommend systematic solutions. Public health professionals know the community well and can identify community resources and agencies that should be part of the broader conversation. They understand the importance of contextual community factors on performance. Public health may also be part of the care intervention team and link patients to professionals trained in nutrition, mental health, and social services. Success in an ACO model that truly improves population health will include broad collaborations, the addition of community health indicators to the ACO dashboard, and direction of part of the global payment to support community public health improvement activities (Hacker & Walker, 2013).

ACCOUNTABLE CARE ORGANIZATIONS SUCCESSES

The following websites describe successes in several different ACOs:

- Primary Partners: A small physician group Medicare ACO composed of 55 physicians in Florida covering 7500 lives
  http://www.prweb.com/releases/2012/4/prweb9389811.htm
- Abington Health: A hospital-based commercial ACO in Eastern PA covering 30,000 lives
  http://abingtonhealth.org
- OSF Health System: A delivery network of hospitals and physicians in a Pioneer ACO
  http://www.osfhealthcare.org
- Colorado Community Health Alliance: A Medicaid ACO that includes 260 physicians serving the broader Boulder community
  http://cchacares.com

REFERENCES

Agency for Healthcare Research and Quality. How SIM grants, ACOs, and other developments in Medicaid can help to accelerate and inform integrated human service delivery. 2013. Available at: http://www.innovations.ahrq.gov/content.aspx?id=3835\

Centers for Medicare and Medicaid Services. Affordable Care Act Update: Implementing Medicare Cost Savings. 2010. Available at: http://www.cms.gov/apps/docs/aca-update-implementing-medicare-costs-savings.pdf

Centers for Medicare and Medicaid Services. Medicare Shared Savings Program Quality Measure Benchmarks for the 2014 Reporting Year. 2013. Available at: http://www.cms.gov/Medicare/Medicare-Fee-for-Service-Payment/sharedsavingsprogram/Downloads/MSSP-QM-Benchmarks.pdf

Centers for Medicare and Medicaid Services. News and updates, 2014. Available at: http://www.cms.gov/Medicare/Medicare-Fee-for-Service-Payment/sharedsavingsprogram/News.html

Fisher ES, Staiger DO, Bynum JPW, Gottlieb DJ. Creating accountable care organizations: The extended hospital medical staff. Health Aff 2007; 26(1): w44–w57.

Fisher ES, McClellan MB, Bertko J, Lieberman SJ, Lee JJ, Lewis JL, Skinner JS. Fostering accountable health care: Moving forward in Medicare. Health Aff 2009; 28(2): w219–w231.

Gandhi N, Weil R: The ACO Surprise. 2012. Available at: http://www.oliverwyman. com/content/dam/oliver-wyman/global/en/files/archive/2012/OW_ENG_HLS_ PUBL_The_ACO_Surprise.pdf

Muhlestein D. Accountable Care Growth In 2014: A Look Ahead. Posted on Jan 29, 2014. Available at http://leavittpartners.com/wp-content/uploads/2013/03/ Accountable-Care-Paradigm.pdf

Hacker K, Walker DK. Achieving population health in accountable care organizations. Am J Public Health 2013; 103(7): 1163–1167.

Murray P. Green Bay Hospital Enlists Fire Department to Visit Patients at Home. Wisconsin Public Radio, Broadcast Monday, April 29, 2013, 5:36 pm. Available at: http://www.wpr.org/green-bay-hospital-enlists-fire-department-visit-patients-home

National Association of ACOs. National ACO Survey, Conducted November 2013: Final January 21, 2014. Washington DC and Bradenton FL. Available at: https://www.naacos.com/pdf/ACOSurveyFinal012114.pdf

Newman D. Accountable Care Organizations and the Medicare Share Savings Program. 2011. Congressional Research Service, http://www. hklaw.com/files/Uploads/Documents/HealthcareReformCenter/ ACOandMSSMemorandumApr252011.pdf

Nobel D, Casalino L. Can accountable care organizations improve population health? Should they try? JAMA 2013: 309(11): 1119–1120.

Public Law 111–148, 111th US Congress: 2010. http://www.gpo.gov/fdsys/pkg/ PLAW-111publ148/pdf/PLAW-111publ148.pdf

Local Health Departments and a Primary Care Safety Net

ROBERT M. PESTRONK

INTRODUCTION: FORCES FOR CHANGE

Periodically, the work of local health departments (LHDs) has been reexamined by those in governmental public health practice, think tanks, and academia, as well as by policy makers and residents of communities served by LHDs. One aspect of this reexamination has been defining the "proper" role for the LHD in relation to primary care and clinical services. The conundrum is illustrated by conversations I had as a young LHD director with two more senior colleagues, during which I received contradictory advice: on the one hand, steer clear of involvement with the direct delivery of primary care, because it would drain resources from other "public health" activity; on the other hand, deliver services, since many people lack access and it's a way to reach people in need.

Reexamination has resulted in models and recommendations based on opinion and an expectation that the dedicated people of LHDs will heed expert advice. Less often are the recommendations accompanied by funding to incentivize movement in a particular direction. Yet, we only have to look at what LHDs have accomplished with public health preparedness funding to understand how powerful the combination of recommendations and funding can be. I hope that work now under way to describe foundational capabilities and areas for LHDs, to calculate the cost for these, and to generate consensus regarding adoption, appropriation, and operationalization will prove fruitful.

Reexamination is afoot again for many reasons. The Great Recession forced cuts in state and local government budgets. In response, LHDs laid off or lost through attrition tens of thousands of staff. With fewer staff, scope and scale of service decreased. In some cases, entire areas of programming were eliminated.

Other forces have been at work, too. Partisan forces encouraged privatization of process and practice with the assumption, proven or not, that service would improve and be less costly. Technology opened data and information to members of the public formerly without access, breaking a monopoly on assessment and interpretation. Models of organizational consolidation and sharing have been pursued. Long-time "baby boomers" began to be replaced by a new generation of LHD leaders unexposed to decades of prior practice.

The Patient Protection and Affordable Care Act (ACA), signed into law in 2010, also

introduced uncertainty about the continuing need for categorical funding of certain clinical services. Immunization, breast and cervical cancer screening, family planning, and infectious disease treatment, for example—staples of LHD programming for decades—fell into this category. If everyone has insurance, so the reasoning goes, why fund these services separately? Have them delivered as part of a comprehensive episode of timely care delivered in a "doctor's" office when required, notwithstanding the fact that in some cases physicians are reluctant to provide the services, serve only some community members, or that there may be no clinicians geographically proximate to serve them.

Needless to say, access to care is unevenly distributed within and among states and communities for many reasons and will continue to be so. Different responses to the ACA by state governments has in some cases widened, rather than narrowed, access gulfs. In some cases, experiments in reorganizing and recombining elements of the care delivery process have deliberately, through oversight or by habit, excluded LHDs from re-forming networks.

Unlike government-funded primary care clinics, which received increased financial support to expand capacity nationwide following ACA passage, no such sustainable funding for work associated with clinical care or "a new public health" reached large numbers of LHDs. No single federal office benefits from the work of LHDs and, therefore, LDH funding is not recognized as an essential priority by a particular federal agency. Financial and administrative sponsorship is diffused, instead, across multiple federal agencies and among local and state governments.

Finally, the publication of *Primary Care and Public Health: Exploring Integration to Improve Population Health* by the Institute of Medicine (IOM, 2012) presented still another force for local change, despite the fact that the recommendations in the report focused primarily on the need to integrate thought, program, policy, and process within the federal government in order to promote better "integration of public health and primary care." Surprisingly, the IOM recommendations did not address a third, most influential, and giant partner, the Centers for Medicare and Medicaid Services (CMS). The CMS is only just beginning to examine its legal authority to be part of the nation's public health department and thereby reimburse a wider range of nonclinical services, which could lower health care costs and make us healthier.

WHITHER PRIMARY CARE AND PUBLIC HEALTH INTEGRATION?

What is the role of LHDs in the medical care safety net? Should LHDs provide clinical care? Should LHDs compete with other providers of medical care in the community? Will "discretionary" LHD resources, if used for clinical care, mean less capacity for "population health" work? The answers will evolve over time and in response to local conditions.

Healthier people require both medical services and a nurturing physical, sociocultural, educational, and economic environment. Many LHDs are enabled through legal authority to affect the latter environments for all of the people within their jurisdiction, whereas those who are in the business of providing medical services are typically focused on a more exclusive panel of patients one at a time.

Nonetheless, the worlds of primary care and LHD can nestle closer together. The interests of primary care providers and LHDs overlap, offering

hope for closer relationships between the two worlds and, perhaps, both integrated and separate role delineation as access to care becomes universal.

Local health departments will always have a role to play in the *health* safety net. That net is woven with what is necessary for both the public's health, now fashionably referred to as population health, and clinical care. Information and action is needed from LHDs to keep people healthy in the first place, to make health easier, and to make healthier decisions easier to make by default (for example, by making sugary drinks more expensive, less calorie-laden, or less accessible as we have done with tobacco products), and to organize response to and participate in emergent and emergency events (as has been demonstrated, once again for example, in relation to Ebola infection). Clinical care discovers illness already present and treats those requiring care.

Given the current costs associated with clinical care, twice per person what any other industrialized nation spends, we are be able to afford both a more robust LHD presence and universal access to primary care. Current lack of universal access to excellent evidence—and experience-based clinical care and to enablers of the public's health represent a moral and civic failure. Interest now grows to ensure delivery of clinical care in the right way, at the right time, in the right amounts, and for the right reasons, regardless of personal circumstance. Over time, I hope, those in clinical care will become more interested in broader, jurisdictional populations and therefore in the capability of LHDs. As methods of reimbursement move from fee-for-service to episodes of care and to compensation for real health outcomes achieved, health, rather than disease can become a profit center, and treatment of disease an avoidable cost subtracting from the bottom line.

With access to care (in all its dimensions) still limited (sometimes by design), particularly in rural areas or inner city neighborhoods where primary care providers may be absent, it is not unreasonable for LHDs to consider providing direct clinical relief to a population-at-large, a subset of that population, or to special populations, while at the same time attempting to be engaged in the work of assessment and policy development and other forms of assurance-like care.

A local health department should deliver medical services to residents of its jurisdiction if it discovers that it can provide them at higher quality or more efficiently, or simply to fill gaps not met by others collectively. Excellent examples exist nationwide in which the delivery of primary care or elements of it by LHDs is seen as mission critical; the care is as good or better than that provided in the private sector and it fills essential gaps.

Obvious challenges present themselves. The role of LHDs and its choice of services offered depends on the administrative and managerial capabilities of the department, its financial and technological resources, the existing skills of its workforce, and the availability of the workforce needed to provide care. LHDs are competing with a variety of entities for staff who can organize, deliver, and account for clinical services efficiently and efficaciously.

Many clinical services, more so than LHD services, are currently reimbursable. The capacity to collect that revenue through third-party billing is complex but at least available. Sophisticated negotiation, legal, and partnership skills may be required to work effectively with both those in state and federal government as well as those working for nonprofit and for-profit organizations to become eligible for and capture that revenue. Another task is to determine whether that revenue will cover costs of service delivery.

The decision calculus also includes political and legal considerations specific to the locality. Currently, some state governments now direct their LHDs into, and others away from, the delivery of personal clinical services. Some members of local governing bodies have a much easier time understanding the immediate need for clinical care based on their personal or family situation or on constituent demands and may therefore be eager to have their LHDs deliver clinical services. Abstract notions of population health and of health-in-all-policies can be more difficult to operationalize under these conditions.

An LHD can hasten integration with local primary care by working together to collect and share data; to assess health status; to analyze and interpret the assessment data together with community members; and to evaluate whether medical care is accessible to all residents of the jurisdiction and is delivered at an appropriate standard of quality. Where gaps are found, goals and objectives can be set, plans enabled to address those objectives, metrics established to monitor change in illness, death, disparity, and inequality. Joint voices can articulate demand for improvements in local culture and policy necessary for better health and quality of life. Guidelines for care and practice can be developed, and a culture of continuous quality improvement mutually reinforced.

Unless some higher level of government or some combination of governments steps in to fund a consistent set of foundational capabilities nationwide, and until all people have access to clinical care through a nongovernmental delivery system, some LHDs will continue to provide clinical care for financial, logical, legal, and ethical reasons; to fill gaps left open by design or default; or to demonstrate better models of care. And the foundational capabilities of LHDs, perhaps more important for preventing illness and death and promoting health, will remain unsupported. This represents a tremendous missed opportunity in our land of plenty.

PERSONAL EXPERIENCES WITH INTEGRATION

Four experiences, two early on, a third in the middle, and a fourth in the last quarter of my career helped me first better understand and then operationalize a meaningful route to public health-primary care integration. The first two or these early experiences are no longer available to others. That's unfortunate.

The first was my selection by the National Association of County and City Health Officials as their representative in the early 1990s to the U.S. Department of Health and Human Services Primary Care Policy Fellowship. The Fellowship brought together representatives from several dozen national public health, medical, and professional associations. It assessed personal profiles; explained the history of primary care and the conflicts among its practice guilds; and introduced the federal resources, policies, and people responsible for federal health care policy. As a result, I knew a lot more as a LHD official about the promise of primary care, and I developed a network of relationships still in use today.

That same year, serendipitously, I participated in the Public Health Leadership Institute sponsored by the Centers for Disease Control and Prevention. At the Institute, with a small cadre of other mid-career professionals, I was exposed to ideas about leadership, scenario-building, risk communication, and public health practice. The ability to explore these ideas with public health department leaders before testing them with leaders from other community domains proved helpful.

In my local practice, I initially attempted to hire the staff and create the needed processes to deliver primary care within my department. I asked my governing board for, and obtained, a large appropriation with which to build that infrastructure. However, the following year, in response to a developing local recession, I was asked to cut my department's budget by the same amount appropriated the previous year. I asked to cut our primary care funding.

Local health department/U.S. Health Resources and Services Administration (HRSA) primary care center relationships can be challenging. From the start of my career as a local health official, I had tried to work jointly with the executive leader of such a center. Center leadership closely guarded their prerogative to be the place where primary care was delivered to those who could otherwise not afford to see a physician or who could otherwise not receive care. They saw no need for partnership.

Federal policy limits the number of local health departments that could receive a HRSA grant to fund a center. Center history and culture identified government with the original failure to provide access to health care to millions of citizens nationwide. The LHDs, as governmental agencies, were identified with part of that failure.

A change in leadership at the local center and a supportive regional HRSA administrator changed all that, recognizing the rare but complementary relationship that could be struck between the center and the health department. An effective partnership enabled health department and center staff to co-locate in a new, jointly designed building. The center obtained additional funding from HRSA to expand. As part of county government, the LHD was able to obtain low-cost loans to reduce the cost of construction. Initial antipathy

among staffs to be working together eroded beautifully over time as each came to appreciate the complementary roles and ease of access to each other's services that co-location made possible. So successful was the site that the center obtained additional funding to further expand its services in the area.

My fourth, and capstone, experience involved creation of a new, adaptable, nonprofit organization. Over a 3-year period it widened access to primary care, pharmacy, laboratory, and radiology services, referral to medical specialists, and financial resources to support expanded access to primary care county-wide at medical, hospital, mental health, and university clinic offices. Support from an influential state senator was essential.

A small pilot project serving 6,000 residents grew under a Section 1115 waiver, with the eventual backing of local community, public health, health care, and foundation leaders and consultants into a system of care that the people of the community have now supported twice with their votes; first to increase their taxes and later to maintain that increase. The new organization enabled regular and convenient access to care for nearly 26,000 of the 33,000 people in the county estimated to be ineligible for Medicare and Medicaid or without insurance through employment or by choice. Ultimately the nonprofit organization's governing body included representation from all three of the local hospital systems, the medical society, community-based organizations, human service organizations, and the health department.

CONCLUSION

The role of LHDs in the safety net will continue to vary from state to state, and from community

to community. It remains dependent on local, state, and federal policy decisions, preferences, and resources. Health could be easier than it is for all of us. We've made it harder than it needs to be—sometimes intentionally, sometimes inadvertently. Preventing much current illness that now requires treatment is possible by changing life circumstances and conditions and thereby channeling personal and professional behavior differently (of both unfortunate patients and policy makers!). We know more about this than we have put into practice. It's hard and complicated work and sometimes requires struggle.

Strong crosswinds buffet travelers seeking a more uniform role for LHDs, if that goal is desirable. If it is, supportive politics and politicians, helpful law, sufficient and sustainable funding, patience, creative application of circumstance, luck, and willing partners are essential.

More than just playbooks and wonderful examples of best practice to emulate will be needed, but that's a start. We will have to agree on a shared destination, and find ways to keep policy makers and others eager to reach and focused on this new destination. We will have to teach those who are now learning to practice both public health and primary care to aspire and analyze differently. We will have to provide the funding, technology, workforce, and other tools to better observe, analyze, interpret, understand, and change present ways of doing business. At 17% of the national economy, we have the resources for this.

REFERENCE

Institute of Medicine. Primary Care and Public Health: Exploring Integration to Improve Population Health. Washington, DC: The National Academies Press, 2012.

Co-Locating Primary Care and Public Health Services

Essay II

MICHELLE J. LYN

WHAT IS CO-LOCATION?

To improve access to services, communities across the country have long placed health and human services organizations in the same building or adjacent buildings. Typical models include the co-location of public health, social services, dental services, and mental/behavioral health services. Co-locating such services and others such as primary care in a central, easily accessible location often proves to be more convenient for individuals and communities to access services. Co-location, however, is not the same as collaboration or integration. Services that are co-located may be in the same or adjacent buildings, but they often operate independently and without coordination.

Getting Started

As in any community health improvement endeavor, the starting point for considering the co-location of services begins with community engagement.

What Are the Needs and Priorities Identified by the Community?

Use the identified needs and priorities as the basis for conducting an environmental scan of existing services that seek to address all or part of those needs. Delve deeply into exploring the services, and include the providers of those services and those served in the exploration.

What Is Working and What Isn't?
What Makes Sense and What Doesn't Make Sense in Terms of Information Flow, Convenience, Efficiency?
What Would Make the Service Comprehensive and Seamless?

Listen carefully to the responses from the leadership and staff of the organizations who deliver these services and from the people who seek the services. This process will indicate gaps that need to be closed and redundancies, which are an annoyance to those being served and inefficient for those providing the services. As a result, workflow will likely be redesigned, and antiquated policies changed.

Note that physically moving services may not be the first action on the solutions list; it may be one that results organically from considering collaboration and analyzing community needs. The first actions are focused on working through ways to collaborate to meet the expressed needs of the community and achieve the outcomes that the community

desires in ways that make sense in the context of the community and the collaborating entities. Such collaboration can bring about shifts in workflow as well as integration of IT systems, registration, and support services. If such changes shift space and staffing requirements, co-location may be the next logical step.

WHAT TO CONSIDER

While the potential benefits of exploring fragmented services and finding ways to collaborate may seem evident, there are a number of potential barriers that must be considered. The barriers are not insurmountable, but careful and persistent effort is required to work through the myriad of issues for collaborative services (co-located or not) to be successful.

Some of the barriers may be as follows:

- Each sector functions under a different funding stream, which leads to complex budgeting.
- Assumptions about how things should work differ between sectors.
- Infrastructure is different, which can create systems challenges.
- Discomfort with change should be anticipated when physically moving entities into the same location. What may be unexpected is the degree of challenge experienced by external partners and power brokers.
- The expansion of services can lead to physical constraints, as the building that initially served a new partnership may no longer support its growth.
- Mismanaging growth in a partnership can lead to breakdown.

While co-location does make it easier to have quick discussions and to resolve problems through hallway discussions, it does not directly address the cultural and operational differences between health and human services entities. In challenging times, starting from a situation of co-location can make collaborating more difficult, as it can be hard to for each entity to find respite from the other.

VALUE OF CO-LOCATION

Successful co-location models are likely to have the following attributes:

- Patients have easier access and more seamless referrals to an array of services.
- Leadership is encouraged to reach across their backgrounds, leading to better outcomes.
- Teams consisting of members from collaborating organizations are able to analyze joint data and develop creative approaches to shared challenges.
- Co-located entities can develop deeper collaboration, which leads to more efficient use of staff and resources.
- Providers can more easily participate in community health initiatives, including planning and mobilizing efforts with city officials and policy makers. (See https://practicalplaybook.org/success-story/benton-county-oregons-succeeds-co-locating-public-health-and-primary-care-services.)

EXAMPLES OF CO-LOCATION

The Center for Health Care Design produced a white paper for the California HealthCare Foundation (Xiaobo et al., 2011) in March 2011 detailing the characteristics of the physical environment design for new care delivery models; they cited a number of co-located services models:

Essay II

La Maestra Community Health Centers at City Heights, San Diego

This is a safety-net clinic that combines community spaces, such as retail shops, a pharmacy, and a health education center, with medical and dental clinics, a laboratory, and a mental and behavioral health center (www.lamaestra.org).

Native American Health Center's Seven Directions, Oakland

This is mixed-use facility with medical, dental, and WIC services as well as an outdoor community ceremonial space on the first floor, and 36 units of affordable housing on the second floor (www.nativehealth.org).

Hill County Health and Wellness Center, Round Mountain, CA

This center initially planned to expand its dental facility, but as a result of meetings with and surveys of staff, board, patients, and community members, it not only expanded its dental facility, but also added a library, children's play areas, and community gardens (www.hillcountryclinic.org).

CO-LOCATION PARTNERS

Typical partners in co-location models include departments of public health, Federally Qualified Health Centers, departments of social services, and mental health entities, as well as hospitals, health systems, primary care practices, and dental practices. As noted in the examples, co-location can include retail, housing, schools, and child-care, for example. In addition, county and/or city governments and the respective boards of the

co-located entities play a pivotal role in planning and developing co-located services. Having a single "service center" that offers one-stop service for social services, mental health, dental care, housing, and retail, as well as primary care and public health, can be a time-saver for those served, and can allow pooling of resources and shared infrastructure.

Tips

1. Co-location is not the same as collaboration or integration.

2. Co-location, collaboration, and even integration can happen with many health and human services partners—think about the social determinants of health and include housing, schools, farmers markets, for example, in your strategies for improving community health.

3. Using identified community needs and priorities and ongoing input from the community to guide you, find ways to collaborate or even integrate services before co-locating, rather than using co-location to drive collaboration or integration.

4. Create alignment and direction by outlining shared goals for population health, efficiency, and cost containment.

5. Expand your objectives and energies beyond your own entity to take advantage of new opportunities.

REFERENCE

Xiaobo Q, Anjali J, Keller A, Taylor E. Designing Safety-Net Clinics for Innovative Care Delivery Models. Oakland, CA: California HealthCare Foundation, March 2011.

Chapter 19

Return on Investment and Economic Evaluation

STEVEN M. TEUTSCH, DENISE KOO, AND SCOTT D. GROSSE

Government officials such as governors and mayors or chief financial officers of health care systems often ask, "What impact will this project have on our budget?" or, "What is the value proposition?" In fact, particularly in the private sector health care system, they specifically want to know their return on investment (ROI). A collaborative project's most significant outputs, however, are likely to be nonfinancial benefits that are realized by patients, communities, and society as a whole (e.g., improved quality of life, increased quality of care, prevention of illness, and improved provider/patient relationships). At the same time, some of these projects might also produce a financial ROI, and health care system leaders can use that return to incentivize their support of such projects with population health goals.

Different stakeholders—patients, payers, health care systems, clinicians—bring different perspectives and measure ROI in different ways. It is therefore important to agree on definitions of all costs and benefits, including projected cost savings and health outcomes, as part of the planning process. This ensures that stakeholders can fully understand their costs and returns, and secure ongoing support from decision makers (thus ensuring sustainability). This chapter provides an overview of the concepts of ROI, cost–benefit, and cost-effectiveness—and discusses who will be most interested in considering which aspect—as guide for this aspect of collaboration.

Tips

In thinking about, promoting, and evaluating the value produced by a collaborative health improvement project:

✔ Take into account not only direct financial benefits to investors, such as payers' lower health care delivery costs, but also the nonfinancial benefits provided to the community: the project's *social* return on investment.

✔ Keep in mind that the value of a community health improvement initiative largely depends on whether its benefits are considered from the perspective of the community as a whole (societal perspective); the patient, physician, local (public health) government; or the health services purchaser. Strive to identify project benefits that accrue to as many stakeholders as possible.

WHAT IS "RETURN ON INVESTMENT"?
The Right Question for the Payer to Ask

Return on investment is a useful tool for understanding a project's costs and benefits from the perspective of an investor. Analysis of ROI originally was developed in a commercial, business context to assess the performance of a financial investment. Its focus is the financial return that a specific investor receives from his/her own financial investment. A simple ROI equation, for example, shows that an investor who purchases goods for $1 and resells them for $3 receives a 200% return on the cost of the initial investment (Cavallo, 2014):

$$\frac{Proceeds\,of\,investment\,[\$3] - cost\,of\,investment\,[\$1]}{Cost\,of\,investment\,[\$1]} \times 100\% = ROI\,[200\%]$$

In health care, ROI usually refers to the financial costs to a specific payer or health care system, because it is the payer or institution that wants to know the value to itself of any investment. For many health care payers, the period over which ROI is calculated is short due to high rates of turnover in health plans; payers cannot recoup the costs of prevention or disease management if people are no longer enrolled in their plans. However, each plan may differ in terms of time frame. Medicare takes a relatively long time perspective, typically 10 years.

Return on investment can have multiple meanings. It can be used to refer to the financial return to a particular state agency, to all state/local agencies, or to government as a whole. The latter is sometimes referred to as the taxpayer perspective, even though it is not from the viewpoint of taxpayers as individuals. It includes spending on nonhealth services, such as public assistance and schooling, and also impacts on revenues from taxes paid by people who might otherwise not be able to work. A societal perspective ROI should include all financial costs and benefits regardless of who receives them or pays for them. It includes government programs, businesses, and individual consumers, and is therefore more complete.

Consider an asthma education program that costs $500/asthma patient and, on average, avoids a single emergency room visit at a cost of $1,500. Assume that the cost of the program is paid by the public health department and the benefit accrues to a payer. From the public health department's perspective, the cost is $500 per person served with a zero (0%) return. From the payer's perspective, there is no cost of the education program but a net savings of $1,500 per enrollee, all return. If Medicaid is the payer, the ROI in terms of total health expenditures is 200% [($1500 – $500)/$500]—a great investment! Similarly, if either Medicaid or a private payer were to pay for the asthma education program, the ROI to the payer would likewise be 200%. The societal ROI is difficult to calculate because other potential impacts besides reduction in emergency department visits would need to be considered (Table 19-1).

Table 19-1 ▼ Return on Investment from Different Perspectives

Perspective of Agency/ Individual	Cost of Educational Program	Emergency Room Cost Saved	ROI
Public Health Department (PHD)	$500	$0	0% (0–$500)/$500
Payer (PHD pays for the program)	$0	$1,500	ROI can't be calculated because there is no payer investment.
State health programs (PHD, Medicaid pay)	$500	$1,500	200% ($1,500–$500)/$500
Payer (Payer pays for the program)	$500	$1,500	200% ($1,500–$500)/$500
Societal (PHD pays for the program)	$500	$1,500	ROI can't be calculated without additional information on benefits.

It is usually clearer to think about societal ROI in terms of cost–benefit analysis (CBA) or cost-effectiveness analysis (CEA), as described in the following.

WHAT ABOUT COST–BENEFIT ANALYSIS?

The Right Analysis for Assessing any Program from the Perspective of Society as a Whole

The interests of investors in a public health project are different than those of individuals and entities that invest for the primary purpose of generating profits. Most public health projects are implemented because of their non-financial benefits (such as improved health or cases of illness prevented). These projects' benefits accrue to patients, communities, and society as a whole. In a CBA, though, the value of those nonfinancial benefits needs to be expressed in terms of their dollar value. In addition, public health projects may also have financial benefits, such as health care costs averted or increased productivity. When the project is considered from a societal perspective, rather than as a financial ROI, a simple CBA, which is equivalent to a societal ROI, can be used to assess whether the project's benefits justify its costs. If an intervention costs $1,000 to implement, for example, and achieves improved outcomes valued at $2,000, the project has a net benefit:

$$\text{Benefits}[\$2K] - \text{costs}[\$1K] = \$1K \text{ net gain}$$

A cost–benefit analysis attaches dollar values to all costs and benefits of a project. Costs are not limited to monetary outlays; they include costs relating to human effort (e.g., staff time devoted to the project), costs related to the project's use of physical resources (meeting space, equipment), and lost opportunity costs (forgoing potential gains from other possible use of the resources). Benefits, particularly in the case of health interventions, include not just the project's financial outputs, but, often more importantly, its nonfinancial social benefits (e.g., improved patient and population health, better health care quality, improved accountability for government resources). In a cost–benefit analysis, all nonmonetary costs and benefits, including these social impacts, are assigned a monetary value.

WHAT ABOUT COST-EFFECTIVENESS ANALYSIS?
The Right Analysis for Assessing the *Value* of a Health Program

The costs of a project involving public health and primary care integration are often shared among multiple sponsors with varying interests and perspectives. Its benefits might be diffused among patients, providers, payers, the community, and society. Depending on its goals and expectations, financial or social returns may be of more or less importance to a particular sponsor or stakeholder. A CEA examines the costs and outcomes of alternative intervention strategies (i.e., programs or policies), and can be used to facilitate decisions about potential approaches for a given health outcome. A CEA compares the cost of an intervention to its effectiveness as measured in health outcomes (e.g., cases prevented or years of life saved). The results of a CEA are expressed in cost per health outcome (e.g., cost per case prevented or cost per workday gained). A CEA is often expressed as a cost per quality-adjusted life year (QALY) gained, where QALYs are a combination of improved quality of life and number of years of survival gained; this is also called a cost utility analysis and allows comparison of different health outcomes. In contrast to CBA, CEA does not require a monetary value to be assigned to health outcomes.

When applied prospectively, CEA helps planners choose among different approaches to achieve a desired outcome by quantifying the value that each proposed intervention is likely to produce. By taking into consideration all of the project's costs and benefits, and the perspectives of all potential sponsors, the analysis can help answer questions such as:

- Do the project's expected benefits justify the cost of implementation?
- Which project will produce the greatest impact?
- Which potential sponsors are most likely to support the project?

Cost-effectiveness analysis also can serve as a powerful tool for policy development when used to demonstrate to stakeholders, decision-makers, and the public: 1) the financial costs or savings and social value to be gained from investments in population health, 2) health system transformation, 3) quality improvement, and 4) public health/primary care integration. Though some programs and policies save money, many do not. As in most things in life, the question is whether those programs and policies are worth the investment.

WHICH ECONOMIC EVALUATION METHOD TO USE?

A Comparison

For any economic analysis, it is critical to understand the costs and benefits that are included. Table 19-2 compares basic characteristics of different approaches. It is common for analyses claiming to take a societal perspective to include only a small subset of benefits. For example, an analysis of the financial return on investment for patients enrolled in the Boston Children's Hospital Community Asthma Initiative (https://practicalplaybook.org/content/boston-childrens-hospital-community-asthma-initiative) was described as a cost–benefit analysis even though it only included the avoided costs of hospital care as benefits, and did not include the monetary value of health outcomes or of other societal benefits. A similar analysis of another asthma disease prevention program was correctly described as an ROI analysis (Cloutier et al., 2009).

We conclude this important topic with an illustration of the use of ROI and CEA for the area of diabetes prevention.

Table 19-2 ▼ Overview of Types of Financial and Economic Evaluation					
Type of Analysis	**Definition**	**Typical Costs**	**Typical Outcomes**	**Metric**	**Typical Use**
Return on investment (ROI)	A financial analysis from the perspective of the investor	Dollars invested	Dollars saved	Net financial cost/dollars invested	To assess financial return
Cost–benefit analysis (CBA)	An economic evaluation that assesses the dollar value of all resources used and benefits achieved from the perspective of society	Dollar value of all resources used	Dollar value of all health and non-health outcomes	Net cost (dollars)	To compare the value of policies and programs with different outcomes, particularly when there are both health and non-health effects
Cost-effectiveness analysis (CEA)	An economic analysis that assesses the net cost of an intervention compared to the health outcomes achieved (perspective must be specified)	Dollar value of resources used	Health benefits (eg, deaths averted)	Cost per health benefit (eg, cost per life year gained)	To compare the value of policies and programs with the same health outcome

Case Illustration: Projected Value of Diabetes Prevention

Preventing diabetes is a major opportunity to reduce health care costs through a collaborative partnership. The Diabetes Prevention Program (DPP) is an effective model to prevent diabetes through intensive dietary and physical activity counseling, and illustrates the importance of including all perspectives when considering the costs and benefits of a collaborative project. The original DPP was an intensive clinic-based research study. The intensive lifestyle arm of the study was shown to be highly effective in leading to large weight reductions in overweight adults with prediabetes, and incidence of diabetes was reduced by 58% over a 3-year period (Diabetes Prevention Program Research Group, 2002). The intervention was found to be highly cost-effective from the long-term, societal perspective, costing a little over $1,000 per QALY gained, but from the short-term financial ROI perspective of a private health plan, it would return only 24 cents on the dollar within a 3-year time frame (Ackermann et al., 2006). An adaptation of the DPP intervention using group-based counseling delivered though a community-based organization (the YMCA) following clinician referrals of overweight patients with prediabetes was found to be feasible and to cost less than one-third as much as the clinic-based DPP (Ackermann et al., 2008). In 2010, Congress authorized the CDC to establish the National Diabetes Prevention Program (National DPP), which brings together community and health care organizations, insurance companies, employers, and government agencies to implement the lifestyle intervention across the United States (Albright & Gregg, 2013). The inaugural partners joining the CDC in the National DPP were UnitedHealth Group and the YMCA of the USA. They rolled out the adapted DPP in 46 communities between July 2010 and December 2011, and 1,723 participants completed the program at an average cost of $400/person (Vojta et al., 2013). UnitedHealth Group projected that avoided health care costs would exceed intervention costs within 3 years (Vojta et al., 2013). Currently, over 500 organizations have received CDC recognition as part of the National DPP.

Two simulation-models based on the YMCA DPP model calculated that this group-based lifestyle program is eventually cost-saving at a national level. One model projected the costs and benefits of adapted DPP to the U.S. health care system as a whole using conservative assumptions and concluded it would break even in 14 years; within 25 years it could produce societal savings of $5.7 billion nationwide (Zhou et al., 2012). That model, unlike other analyses, included the costs to detect prediabetes in adults through screening of overweight adults by primary care providers. Another simulation model concluded that referring overweight adults ages 60 to 64 years to such group counseling could be cost saving to the Medicare program in well under 10 years (Thorpe & Yang, 2011). A larger-scale study of the YMCA DPP program is currently underway to produce more robust estimates of costs, effectiveness, and cost savings (Ackermann et al., 2013).

Although the exact length of the payback period for the community-based DPP model to generate negative net health care costs remains to be determined, it is clearly cost-saving to the U.S. health care system overall, and to payers such as Medicare that take a relatively long-term (i.e., 10-year or longer) perspective. As such, it is a worthwhile priority for public health–health care collaborations aimed at improving population health and controlling health care costs.

CONCLUSION

Understanding the economic consequences of collaborative projects to each stakeholder, as well as to communities more broadly, can help in the design of programs and enhance the likelihood of success and sustainability.

REFERENCES

Ackermann RT, Finch EA, Brizendine E, Zhou H, Marrero DG. Translating the Diabetes Prevention Program into the community. The DEPLOY Pilot Study. Am J Prev Med 2008; 35(4): 357–363.

Ackermann RT, Holmes AM, Saha C. Designing a natural experiment to evaluate a national health care-community partnership to prevent type 2 diabetes. Prev Chronic Dis 2013; 10: E12.

Ackermann RT, Marrero DG, Hicks KA, Hoerger TJ, Sorensen S, Zhang P, et al. An evaluation of cost sharing to finance a diet and physical activity intervention to prevent diabetes. Diabetes Care 2006; 29(6): 1237–1241.

Albright AL, Gregg EW. Preventing type 2 diabetes in communities across the U.S. Am J Prev Med 2013; 44(4S4): S346–S351.

Cavallo D. Health Promotion Economics: Using Return on Investment Analysis to Evaluate Health Promotion Programs: Challenges and Opportunities. Research Triangle Institute website. http://www.rti.org/pubs/issuebrief_3.pdf Published November 2006. Accessed February 4, 2014.

Cloutier MM, Grosse SD, Wakefield DB, Nurmagambetov TA, Brown CM. The economic impact of an urban asthma management program. Am J Manag Care 2009; 15(6): 345–351.

Diabetes Prevention Program Research Group. Reduction in the incidence of type 2 diabetes with lifestyle intervention or metformin. N Engl J Med 2002; 346: 393–403.

Thorpe KE, Yang Z. Enrolling people with prediabetes ages 60–64 in a proven weight loss program could save Medicare $7 billion or more. Health Aff (Millwood) 2011; 30(9): 1673–1679.

Vojta D, Koehler TB, Longjohn M, Lever JA, Caputo NF. A coordinated national model for diabetes prevention: Linking health systems to an evidence-based community program. Am J Prev Med 2013; 44(4 Suppl 4): S301–306.

Zhuo X, Zhang P, Gregg EW, Barker L, Hoerger TJ, Pearson-Clarke T, Albright A. A nationwide community-based lifestyle program could delay or prevent type 2 diabetes cases and save $5.7 billion in 25 years. Health Aff (Millwood) 2012; 31(1): 50–60.

Additional Resources

Use the following tools and guides to assist with understanding and calculating return on investment and other economic evaluations for your collaborative project:

AHRQ's Asthma Return on Investment Calculator. Available at: (https://practicalplaybook.org/tool/ahrqs-asthma-return-investment-calculator)

Estimating Return on Investment for Public Health Improvements: Tutorial on Using the new Tool. Available at: (https://practicalplaybook.org/tool/estimating-return-investment-public-health-improvements-tutorial-using-new-tool)

Haddix A, Teutsch SM, Corso PS. Prevention Effectiveness: A Guide to Decision Analysis and Economic Evaluation, 2nd ed. New York: Oxford University Press, 2003.

Jamison DT, Breman JG, Measham AR, et al., editors. Cost-Effectiveness Analysis. In Priorities in Health. Washington, DC: World Bank, 2006. Cost-Effectiveness Analysis. http://www.ncbi.nlm.nih.gov/books/NBK10253/

Learn how to implement an integrated framework for assessing the value of community-based prevention policies and wellness strategies. Available at: (https://practicalplaybook.org/tool/integrated-framework-assessing-value-community-based-prevention)

Medicaid Return on Investment Template. Available at: (https://practicalplaybook.org/tool/medicaid-return-investment-template)

Rapid Response Team Return on Investment Calculator. Available at: (https://practicalplaybook.org/tool/rapid-response-team-return-investment-calculator)

Rochester Institute of Technology. Outreach and Education, S&H Management Systems—Module 5, Measurement of Performance—Supplementary Materials: Cost Benefit Analysis. Available at: https://www.rit.edu/~w-outrea/training/Module5/M5_CostBenefitAnalysis.pdf.

See this primary care–public health collaborative document outlining the value proposition for immunizations for examples of the value of immunization to various stakeholders. Available at: (http://www.astho.org/PCPHCollaborative/ValueProposition/Immunizations-case-study/)

Working with Data

Chapter 20

From Clinic to Community: The Promise and Power of Using Data Together

BRIAN C. CASTRUCCI, HUGH H. TILSON, AND DAVID A. ROSS

T he growing availability of data in electronic formats suggests that population health improvement efforts can be strengthened through an expanded cooperation and partnership between public health and primary care. From the public health side, these data range from state and nationally published health care encounter data, such as hospital discharge, all payer claims databases, and numerous public health program-specific surveillance and service delivery datasets covering infectious diseases, chronic, injury, environmental, and maternal and child health services. From the primary care side, clinical case data resulting from medical care encounters need to be aggregated within practices and linked across practices to yield valid population level incidence and/or prevalence estimates. Once aggregated, encounter data do not represent a longitudinal health record for a given patient but can be used in ways that can help describe population-level disease trends and service delivery patterns. Improving community health begins with better utilization and understanding of these data, but this begins with a commitment to share information.

PRIMARY CARE DATA

Electronic health records (EHRs) create the opportunity for clinicians to monitor trends within their panel of patients, track their practice's adherence to recommended disease management protocols, as well as collaborate with public health by sharing analysis of their patient data to contribute to population-based estimates specific to their locale and patient population. For example, using EHR data in tandem with public health, a primary care provider can compare his or her practice's immunization rates with state and/or local rates, identify patients needing blood pressure control, and track effectiveness of hemoglobin A1c interventions in comparison with those in similar patient populations. Additionally, other population-based metrics can be developed to gauge the effectiveness of treatment of the physician's patient panel. Analysis of practice data can lead to practice changes, which in turn should lead to improved health status metrics and outcomes. The work of the Primary Care Information Project (PCIP) provides a great example of how practice data collected through EHRs can be used to improve adherence to routine, evidence-based guidance (New York Department of Health and Mental Hygiene, 2015). Using data from EHRs, the New York City Department of Health and Mental Hygiene analyzes aggregated data from a citywide network of primary care providers to identify low adherence rates to interventions and screenings and to intervene at the practice level to improve clinical adherence and population health. The PCIP is unique in the United States, having had both the political will and support of the mayor and $60 million in city, state, federal, and private funds. The PCIP is a vision for others to emulate, but data exchange infrastructure is still emerging in most locales.

From a population health perspective, clinical data can be used to understand the geographic distribution of different diagnoses and conditions throughout a community. These data also have the major advantage of being real-time (when accessible) and providing the more geographically specific and timely information on chronic diseases than is available via typical public health survey datasets, such as BRFSS (Behavioral Risk Factor Surveillance System) or NHANES (National Health and Nutrition Examination Survey). Syndromic surveillance and laboratory reporting can facilitate quick identification of acute infectious disease outbreaks, although frequently after astute clinicians have detected and reported a cluster before syndromic systems can indicate a problem. However, such systems do not exist for chronic diseases. Near real-time analysis of clinical data can help target community level interventions, ultimately leading to targeted public health interventions that can help reduce the complexity and severity of disease, cost, and burden on the health care system. Because clinical data exclude those who do not access health care, are fragmented across different practices, don't necessarily encompass a complete longitudinal patient record, reside within different EHR systems, and encode data that may even be collected using different semantic definitions, both primary care practitioners and public health analysts confront challenges in translating EHR data into useful information. This fragmentation obstructs our view of the community and limits our ability to improve the health of individuals and the community. The increasingly widespread use of EHRs offers opportunity as a facilitator in the integration of primary care and public health efforts, but will require significant commitment by both parties to realize the promise held in these data repositories (see chapter 23).

PUBLIC HEALTH DATA

Public health agencies assess and monitor the health status of their community. Population surveillance data have the advantage of being gathered to measure prevalence and incidence by jurisdiction, thus depicting a more holistic and community-based view of specific health problems. Public health surveillance data often include not only clinical data, but also data on exposures and health behaviors. Public health data also can identify characteristics of the community that indicate direction for productive interventions. For example, public health data show restaurants that have failed inspections, locations of alcohol outlets, and locations of unsafe pools, each of these examples being associated with morbidity and mortality data captured in clinical records. Because of limitations on sampling and/or cost of data collection and processing, public health data are often not available at the appropriate level of geographic aggregation for community health work, with precision possible only at the state or even national level. In addition, there is often a significant temporal lag between their collection and their dissemination. These limitations must be considered when interpreting these data.

The following example portrays the kind of challenges to understanding public health intervention effectiveness that stem from traditionally gathered public health data. Consider a health department wanting to assess the impact of a state-funded project to reduce preterm births that was started in 2012 and implemented for 24 months. Although the endpoint of interest is 2014, the only available data are from 2012, when the intervention started. Further investigation reveals that the data used to justify the implementation of the project were from 2010. Unfortunately, despite the best of intentions, the data are not available to assess the impact of the project. However, if clinical data from EHRs were used appropriately, it could be determined if the intervention was, in fact, actually efficacious. If public health and primary care join forces in using data, these data can be used to know if public health interventions are working, which means that politically motivated and fallacious claims about programs that may not be valid can be avoided.

Although public health data help to provide context for a community, then, it is important to consider the date of data collection and the precision of data when using them to plan and evaluate population health efforts. Joining primary care data with public health data offers the opportunity to determine much more precisely which population-oriented interventions have merit.

IMPACTS OF WORKING TOGETHER

Working together, primary care and public health can improve patient outcomes and overall community health status by joining forces to use their data and analytic capabilities. Consider the scenario described in Box 20-1.

Unfortunately, in most places throughout the United States, this type of investigation is not possible, as most locales lack the information exchange infrastructure and active partnership with public health needed to identify these kinds of clusters. There are real-life examples in which just this type of analysis has led to population-level health improvement. The Cincinnati Children's Hospital Medical Center used geographic information systems to map the homes of re-admitted asthma patients (Beck et al., 2013; Waters, 2013). Once mapped, additional investigation revealed that many patients were living in substandard housing units owned by the same landlord. Action compelled the landlord to make necessary improvements (see chapter 24).

Box 20-1 | Using Data Aggregation to Track Outcomes in Pediatric Asthma

In a community, there are four primary care providers. Each has four patients with pediatric asthma that has not been controlled. These patients have good adherence to their medication and a mix of private and public insurance. Each provider has taken the appropriate treatment steps, and is stumped as to what else can be done. These children are caught in a loop in which they visit their providers and return home with little additional insight into their condition other than possibly new medicines or other ideas to try, but unfortunately they return to the emergency department. Although the health impacts are clear, the indirect impacts are also taking a toll on the family. Children miss school, fall behind in their classes, and can't participate in sports and other activities, while the parents miss work and exhaust their limited time off. Unfortunately, this community lacks an adequate data exchange infrastructure and/or partnerships with public health. Without this data-sharing infrastructure, prevention opportunities are missed.

However, if these data could be aggregated, the cluster could be identified, thereby leading to investigation and action. Governmental public health has an aggregation, analysis, and investigation role that can help identify the source of this problem. Public health could begin an epidemiologic analysis of these 16 cases. The health department could analyze these cases geographically and find them to be within a 7-mile radius of each other. Further investigation could reveal that these children are all in the same school, which is not surprising given their geographic proximity. Additional inquiry could reveal that these children ride the same school bus. Public health officials could conduct environmental testing of the school bus and find high levels of exhaust fumes. The bus could then be fixed, resulting in a decline in asthma attack incidence among these 16 students.

OBESITY: AN OPPORTUNITY FOR SHARED DATA AND SHARED ACTION

Nearly 80 million American adults are obese, as are nearly 13 million children (Ogden et al., 2014). That's more people than the combined populations of California, Texas, and New York. At the current rate of growth, it is estimated that 44% of Americans will be obese by 2030 (Levi et al., 2012). Overweight- and obesity-related conditions are now the second leading cause of preventable death (Mokdad et al., 2004). The annual health care costs of obesity-related illness are nearly $200 billion (Cawley & Meyerhoefer, 2012). For U.S. employers, the annual costs attributable to obesity among full-time employees are $73.1 billion (Finkelstein et al., 2010). Obesity is linked to more chronic illnesses than smoking, drinking, or poverty (Sturm, 2002; Sturm & Wells, 2001). By all measures, obesity is an epidemic with significant human and economic costs.

From a clinical perspective, the American Medical Association recognized obesity as a disease in 2013 (Frellick, 2013). Clinicians must now confront another disease with social and environmental origins and for which there are few clinical remedies. This amplifies the need for primary care practitioners to partner with public health practitioners who are skilled in influencing the spectrum of social determinants that lead to health change.

For public health, obesity surveillance has been primarily conducted through large national telephone surveys such as the BRFSS, National Study of Children's Health, and Youth Risk Behavior Survey. These surveys rarely provide data below the county level and frequently involve delayed release that further reduces their potential benefit for community health planning. Few mechanisms have been developed that provided the geographic precision and clinical accuracy necessary to monitor chronic conditions, like obesity, at the local level. Thus, local health departments have limited ability to monitor accurately the health status of their communities with geographically specific and timely data. Presently, survey-based obesity data do not have the precision to identify health problems at the census tract, neighborhood, or even ZIP code levels; to provide the necessary evidence-base to support programmatic and policy solutions; or to measure the impact of interventions.

Although public health relies on data that lags in time and only reflects large population status, the opportunity for secondary and tertiary preventive interventions is being captured and stored in medical records. In the past these were stored as paper-based data. Today, more data are digital and need to be accessible to serve the community health status surveillance goals. The use of EHRs offers hope that this situation will change. Most clinical encounters include routine collection of height and weight data. The Centers for Disease Control and Prevention in partnership with Health Level 7 and Integrating the Healthcare Enterprise (ILE) have developed and tested a body mass index data and message transmission standard (ILE, 2012, 2014). To unlock the information value of clinical data, the primary care and public health partnership needs data-sharing protocols, procedures, partnerships, and standards-enabled clinical data collection. If these data can be made accessible, they can be merged with data on the physical environment, housing, parks, and food access to facilitate the development of precise, targeted interventions and can be used to track the impact of community-level interventions, as well as clinical interventions. Without these data, even when states and cities have implemented policies, the evaluation of the impacts of interventions will lag. Today, changes in obesity rates can only be measured at the state or large population level, thereby obfuscating the impacts, or lack thereof, on more sharply targeted geographies or population groups. Neighborhood-based information that could support behavior change (e.g., locations of fresh fruits and vegetables or opportunities for low- or no-cost physical activity) could be included in EHR systems, providing information that otherwise may not be available during the clinical interaction (Institute of Medicine, 2014).

The obesity epidemic has had significant personal and economic costs. We will never know if these could have been avoided or lessened if the data were available to guide prevention and intervention actions. The obesity epidemic stands as an example of how today's health care problems are rooted in individual health choices, such as choices about diet and exercise, and shaped by the many contexts in which people live. Medicine and public health simply cannot afford to continue to work in their separate silos. Public health and primary care professionals need to see their work as components of an integrated health system—a health system that is challenged to address an increasing burden of chronic diseases, play a role in reducing the preventable injury morbidity and mortality, and partner with those that can support patient social service needs that extend beyond the reach of care providers directly. In effect, the emerging health system supported through EHRs can view its patients from clinic to community. In the past, clinical treatment alone has been unable to prevent or stem the obesity epidemic. Slow and very general public health surveillance has been unable to alert providers, public, and policy-makers of the growing problem. Going forward, primary care practitioners and public health can promote healthier lifestyles and reduce the burden and severity of disease by joining forces and using their collective data wisely.

HOW ELECTRONIC HEALTH RECORDS CAN BRING US TOGETHER

The ideal situation is one in which we have timely and geographically specific data. Data that are neither timely nor local fail to provide information for action of the type most policy-makers and community leaders need to act.

The growing availability of data in electronic formats supports expanded cooperation and partnership between public health and primary care. Available data range from encounter data to publicly available datasets that address issues of health behaviors, clinical status, and health expenditures. Analysis of these data can support new insights and may spark innovative interventions at each stage of health system integration. Many challenges need to be overcome to make this vision possible, and they can only be overcome if primary care providers work in partnership with public health. Improving community health begins with better utilization and understanding of these data and how they can be applied to improve population health, simultaneously reducing the demand on the health care system.

Tips

1. Remember that each practice provides a slice of clinical data—only when they are taken together can you see the whole community.

2. Data are only as good as the information gathered. Knowing about potential uses within your practice and among partners will sharpen your focus on what to record.

3. Remember when data are collected may be different from when they are reported. Just because data are included in a report labeled with a particular year does not mean that those data included in the report are from that same year.

4. Don't forget that clinical data are usually timelier than public health data, but such data still need context.

REFERENCES

Beck AF, Moncrief T, Huang B, et al. Inequalities in neighborhood child asthma admission rates and underlying community characteristics in one US county. J Pediatr 2013; 163(2): 574–580.

Cawley J, Meyerhoefer C. The medical care costs of obesity: An instrumental variables approach. J Health Econ 2012; 31(1): 219–230.

Finkelstein EA, DiBonaventura MD, Burgess SM, et al. The costs of obesity in the workplace. J Occup Environ Med 2010; 52(10): 971–976.

Frellick M. AMA declares obesity a disease. Medscape Medical News. June 19, 2013. Available at: http://www.medscape.com/viewarticle/806566. Accessed January 14, 2015.

Integrating the Healthcare Enterprise. Proposed Work Item: BMI Content Profile. November 26, 2012. Available at: https://www.google.com/search?ie=iso-8859-1&oe=iso-8859-1&domains=ihe.net&sitesearch=ihe.net&btnG=Search&q=BMI%20Message. Accessed January 14, 2015.

Integrating the Healthcare Enterprise. Proposed Work Item: Healthy Weight R2 Content Profile. September 26, 2014. Available at: https://www.google.com/search?ie=iso-8859-1&oe=iso-8859-1&domains=ihe.net&sitesearch=ihe.net&btnG=Search&q=BMI%20Message. Accessed January 14, 2015.

Institute of Medicine. 2014. Capturing Social And Behavioral Domains And Measures In Electronic Health Records: Phase 2. Washington, DC: The National Academies Press, 2014.

Levi J, Segal LM, St. Laurent R, et al. F as in Fat: How Obesity Threatens America's Future. 2012. Available at: http://healthyamericans.org/assets/files/TFAH2012FasInFat18.pdf. Accessed on January 14, 2015.

Mokdad AH, Marks JS, Stroup DF, et al. Actual Causes of Death in the United States. 2000. JAMA 2004; 291(10): 1238–1245.

New York Department of Health and Mental Hygiene. Primary Care Information Project. Available at: http://www.nyc.gov/html/doh/html/hcp/pcip.shtml. Accessed on January 13, 2015.

Ogden CL, Carroll MD, Kit BK, et al. Prevalence of childhood and adult obesity in the United States, 2011–2012. JAMA 2014; 311(8): 806–814.

Sturm R. The Effects of obesity, smoking, and problem drinking on chronic medical problems and health care costs. Health Affairs 2002; 21(2): 245–253.

Sturm R, Wells KB. Does obesity contribute as much to morbidity as poverty or smoking? Public Health 2001; 115: 229–295.

Waters R. It's All in the Data: Cincinnati Children's Hospital Gets Wonky to Transform the Health of Its Community. November 26, 2013. Available at: http://www.forbes.com/sites/robwaters/2013/11/26/its-all-in-the-data-cincinnati-childrens-hospital-gets-wonky-to-transform-a-communitys-health//. Accessed on January 15, 2015.

Chapter 21

Working With Data

MINA SILBERBERG, DENISE KOO, AND RAYMOND J. KING

SUMMARY

Data are a driving force behind all that we do in public health and in primary care, informing the decisions made to impact the health of individuals and populations. The public health and primary care sectors have generally used their own data sources. For example, primary care mainly utilizes data collected in the clinic or from patient laboratory tests, whereas public health primarily uses surveillance and other data collected for monitoring the public's health. By combining and sharing public health and primary care data, we strengthen our capacity for thoughtful, strategic, and evidence-driven population health improvement. The advances in health information technology increase the feasibility of sharing and integrating data in this way. Data not only can inform action, but also are a tool for the engagement of diverse actors in population health improvement: a way of communicating with partners, persuading stakeholders, and framing issues. This chapter provides some starting points for using data, along with some cautionary advice about data analysis and interpretation. Most importantly, it argues for collaboration and community engagement in using data for population health improvement.

DATA BASICS

What Are Data?

Although the term "data" (the plural of datum) generally brings to mind numbers on a page, data take many forms. Ackoff (1989) describes data as symbols representing what has been. Examples include:

- Numbers: blood pressure measurements
- Words: patient responses to provider questions
- Observations: whether or not passengers in cars passing the corner of Main and Grove were wearing their seatbelts

- Pictures: x-rays of the spines of elementary school children who have been carrying book bags
- Maps: locations of fast food outlets

Quantitative data take the form of numbers that tell us "how much" or "how often," for example. Qualitative data take the form of words or images and generally tell us "why" or "how." Using these data together can provide a more complete picture of a problem than either quantitative or qualitative data provide on their own. For example, the number, percentage, ages, and races of individuals lost to treatment for hepatitis C (quantitative data) will tell us how common that occurrence is and for whom, but not why it is happening. Open-ended interviews (i.e., interviews with no set response options) with subsets of patients will generate qualitative data about the reasons for this attrition (e.g., financial barriers, fear of treatment, active drug use); a survey of patients can then be designed to determine how often each reason has influenced a patient to leave treatment. Together these data provide a better understanding of drivers of inadequate care.

Moving From Individual-Level to Population-Level Data

For population health improvement, a crucial distinction is that between individual-level and population-level data. Clinicians are most often dealing with data about individuals: a person's height, weight, blood pressure, or blood sugar level, for example. Public health agencies often aggregate individual data to create population-level data (e.g., the frequency of obesity in a population, the number of new cases of tuberculosis per 100,000 individuals in a given year, the prevalence of tobacco smoking in a community). However, population health data go beyond aggregation of individual health indicators. Determinants of health such as air pollution levels, exposure to toxic chemicals, literacy levels, or access to grocery stores are also important population-level data.

Using Data for Collaborative Population Health Improvement

The use of data, particularly from multiple data sources, is integral to the enterprise of population health improvement. The authors of the report *Primary Care and Public Health: Exploring Integration to Improve Population Health* (Institute of Medicine, 2012) identified shared data and data analysis as one of the five principles of integration, underscoring its importance. Through data analysis, we are able to identify, understand, and act on the problems that face our communities, as well as measure the effect of our interventions. Moreover, data are a tool for engaging stakeholders: a way of communicating, persuading, and framing issues.

Traditionally, primary care and public health have utilized data separately to meet their respective needs. Health care professionals are generally focused on what disease or condition a given patient has, whereas public health professionals tend to focus on characterizing the distribution of a disease or condition and its risk factors within a given population. Primary care providers, for example, will use symptoms, pain assessments, vital signs, and laboratory tests to diagnose a patient's problem and create a treatment plan. Public health professionals, for example, will use public health surveillance data on disease incidence and prevalence and other community health data and priorities (for example, location of environmental health exposures or top community health concerns based on a local survey) to develop public health programs and to create a community health improvement plan.

Integration of public health and primary care work allows data to be shared and merged across sectors, potentially enhancing their impact, a process made easier and facilitated by the storage of data in electronic formats. Examples of how shared data and data analysis can enhance efforts to improve population health include:

- Aggregating data from lead poisoning incidence data across providers, thereby allowing the public health department to determine if affected children live in the same apartment building or housing development
- Sharing public health information about the prevalence of drug-resistant disease with local providers to inform their practice
- Combining clinical heart disease data with public health behavioral data to target community-based interventions to areas with high disease prevalence and poor diet and exercise

GETTING STARTED: USING DATA THROUGHOUT THE STAGES OF INTEGRATION

Overview

The use of data for collaborative population health improvement starts with engagement and alignment; public health and primary care can come together to review data to identify or explore a common concern, to discuss the data that each party has or can generate to support a common goal, and to create a unified information system to support coordinated work. This information system can utilize data to inform action and/or disseminate the data.

Data are a means to the end of population health improvement, not the end in and of itself. At all stages of health improvement, effective data use requires knowing the questions you want to answer. Those questions—Who? What? Where? Why? How?—must drive data collection and analysis, which are the means by which those questions will be answered.

Plan and Prioritize

Planning a project requires having a solid grasp on a community's health problems and their root causes. Triangulation of data (looking at health issues from multiple perspectives, with multiple datasets) can help identify and clarify these community health problems and their causes. For example, planning and prioritizing work on diabetes management at the population level can be informed by:

- Public health data on diabetes prevalence and incidence
- Clinical data on diabetes prevalence and management
- Pharmacy data on prescription refills
- Community data on food deserts, walkability, and neighborhood safety

Collectively, these data illuminate the importance of diabetes in the community, successes and failures in diabetes management at the population level, and the factors associated with diabetes incidence and adverse outcomes.

Data will be important in thinking about possible solutions as well. Scientific studies, community program results, and key informant interviews can tell you:

- What's worked before, what has not, and what it will take to achieve the extent, depth, and scale of effectiveness you seek
- How many people your intervention might reach in a given time period
- How many staff working how many hours/week it might take to reach that objective

Implement, Monitor, and Evaluate

A mix of qualitative and quantitative data will need to be generated on an ongoing basis to tell you:

- If your project is being implemented as expected (monitoring)
- What factors facilitate and impede implementation (process evaluation)
- Whether the results of implementation are what you expected (outcome evaluation) (Box 21-1)

Box 21-1 | Using Data to Guide Design

Pendleton Community Care (PCC), a clinic offering community-oriented primary care in West Virginia, was founded because of a survey demonstrating an inadequate local supply of primary care. PCC and its partners have used diverse forms of data—including stakeholder focus groups, a community survey, and epidemiologic data—to guide design of new programs and infrastructure to meet population health needs. For example, data indicating the need for a drug-free place where teens could be physically active led volunteers to build a bowling alley and snack bar. (For more information, see https://practicalplaybook.org/success-story/primary-care-practice-leads-community-wide-health-assessment-pendleton-county-west.)

When designing evaluation plans, it is crucial to consider the audience or audiences to be reached (Box 21-1). Program administrators, funders, legislators, community members, health care payers, providers, and other stakeholders will all be interested in different questions and be persuaded by different kinds of data presented in different ways. Payers, for example, are likely to want to know the impact of a program on their bottom line. Providers will care about the impact on patient and population health, but, if it requires their involvement, will also want to know if an intervention can be easily integrated into their current practice. Prior engagement with these audiences to find out what they want to know and how they want to know it will help here.

Celebrate and Share

Sharing data on project outcomes is vital to collaboration, but so is making sure that communication of findings is respectful of the permissions established in the data use agreements. Particular attention should be paid to the lessons learned throughout this process to facilitate more effective data sharing in the future.

Whenever possible, stakeholders should consider disseminating findings to a wider audience. In doing so, be sure to tailor the communication of the information in a manner appropriate to the target audience. For example, journal reviewers and editors may want to know the project's impact on health indicators, complete with statistics about effect size and statistical significance. Clinical providers might want to know what it would take for them to replicate a successful intervention in their practice; public health practitioners may be interested in replication across the broader community. The community might want to know what the change in health indicators means in terms of death, disability, and quality of life.

Even when interested in the same information, different audiences may prefer different ways of presenting information (e.g., figures vs. maps vs.

Box 21-2 | Two Examples of Sharing and Generating Data

By sharing existing data and generating new data, the partners in Indiana's Emergency Department Asthma Call Back Program have been able to demonstrate their program's value (see chapter 27).

Generating and sharing data might also be a large part of the intervention itself. For example, the South Bronx Community Referral Task Force encourages physicians to refer patients with diabetes and at risk for diabetes to community resources in part by tracking the providers' referral data and feeding information back to them on a regular basis (see https://practicalplaybook.org/success-story/new-york-city-promotes-primary-care-referral-programs-combat-diabetes-south-bronx)

tables) and different words (watch out for scientific jargon when you're not writing for a scientific population). The best way to find out what information your stakeholders want and in what format is to ask them!

COMMON DATA SOURCES

New data can be generated through "primary data collection," using surveys, focus groups, interviews, observation, and clinical testing. Existing data can also be analyzed ("secondary data analysis") for population health. Links to specific data sources are provided on the website of the *Practical Playbook* (https://practicalplaybook.org/). Some common types of useful existing data include:

Clinical Data

These are timely and (for clinicians) accessible. They tend to be less consistent or reliable than data collected for research purposes. Moreover, they exclude those who do not access the clinic and often have little to say about nonclinical factors that affect health. Sometimes, clinical settings, like others, will see data sharing as a threat to patient privacy and institutional reputation.

The increasingly widespread use of electronic health records (EHRs) has great potential to contribute to improved population health through the integration of primary care and public health and secondary use of these data for population health. Chapter 23 discusses the promise of EHRs and how to get started using them.

Local and Statewide Public Health Data

Public health agencies have a key function of monitoring the health of their community. Data from public health surveillance systems, community needs assessment data, and other data are often available on the local or state health department website. Some of these data are clinical data aggregated from multiple health care systems and providers. Hospital discharge data, for example, are commonly used in public health for injury and disease surveillance, quality assurance, consumer education, and other purposes. Other data include many variables not found in clinical data and have the advantage of attempting to characterize an entire geographic or jurisdictional area. Surveillance data include not only data on incidence and prevalence of diseases or determinants, but also birth and death records. Public health departments will also have data from programs they run, such as the Women, Infants, and Children nutritional program or family planning; and they will have collected data on specific topics for the purpose of applying for specific grants or fulfilling grant requirements. Be aware that when a public health entity collects community-based data, there can be a significant lag time from collection to use. Moreover, state data samples may not be specific enough to accurately characterize a smaller community.

Other Local Government Data

Government sources from outside your local health department will have important information that can help you understand a community and the determinants of community health. Examples include crime data, public housing statistics, electricity service disconnections, foreclosures, and free and reduced-cost school lunch programs.

National Data Sources

There are a number of important national data sources readily available, such as the Dartmouth Atlas of Health Care, UDS Mapper, Uniform Data System Mapper, Robert Wood Johnson/University of Wisconsin Mobilizing Action Toward Community Health (MATCH) data (Community Health Rankings), and Dignity Health's Community Need Index, to name but a few. The Centers for Disease Control and Prevention run a number of national public health surveys, including the Behavioral Risk Factor Surveillance System, the Youth Risk Behavior Survey (a related effort focused on adolescents), the Pregnancy Risk Assessment Monitoring System, and the National Immunization Survey. Other government agencies also sponsor relevant data collection, most notably, the U.S. Census Bureau; in addition to the American Community Survey for which it is best known, the Census Bureau also provides other data sources, including the Small Area Health Insurance Estimates. When using these data, it is crucial to understand how they were collected. Making inferences about a local community, for example, requires that the local sample be big enough, representative enough, and appropriately defined.

Program Data

Data from programs outside of the public health department can also offer a great deal of insight. If you want to understand why a clinic or community-based intervention did not work the way you thought it would, look at the program data. How many people actually were "exposed" to the intervention (e.g., attended events, used services)? Do they represent the target audience in terms of race, gender, health risk factors, and geography?

Data from Community-Based Organizations

Community-based organizations use data to plan and evaluate their activities or solicit grant funding. They may have unique information that cannot be found through the sources previously mentioned (e.g., data on the health priorities of local ministers, access to fruits and vegetables in select neighborhoods, or resident concerns about environmental hazards). Finding these data sources requires good community engagement.

Academic/Media Data

Has the local university been conducting research related to your community's issues? Have the media been polling residents about attitudes, knowledge, or needs? These sources can provide helpful data that the provider and public health communities don't have. Leads on these data sources can be found through Internet searches, by contacting the community relations office at the local university, or by searching archives of local newspapers.

TURNING DATA INTO MEANINGFUL INFORMATION

A dataset is nothing more than a list of numbers, pictures, or words. Without human judgment to make sense of it, a dataset tells us nothing. Furthermore, poor use of human judgment can lead us to erroneous understandings of data. This section addresses the process of turning data into meaningful information from three perspectives: the need to know your data source, the role of choice and values in making meaning out of data, and data display as a tool for making and conveying meaning.

Know Your Data

Data are often messy, ambiguous, or simply not what you think they are. How do we deal with this reality?

First, ask the following questions:

- How were these particular data collected? Do the data include the entire population of interest or is this a sample? If a sample, who was included? Who was excluded? Is the resulting sample representative of the population of interest?
- How consistent was the collection of these data? For example, one social worker assessing fall risk in an elderly person's home might ask the resident to identify situations in which she feels unstable, whereas another might ask about a list of specific situations. In another example, absence of a diagnosis in a medical record does not always mean an absence of disease; sometimes, it represents a failure to document.
- Are there outliers in the data? If so, were mistakes possibly made in data collection or entry? Did a survey respondent misunderstand which questions she was supposed to answer? Or did a transcriptionist make a typo? Perhaps the outlier is correct and offers an insight. In one diabetes improvement project, for example, researchers investigating one enormous drop in HbA1c found that the man in question had gone from consuming several sodas daily to eliminating all soft drinks.

Second, consider "cleaning" your data or having a skilled data manager do so. Data cleaning is a process by which data anomalies are identified and decisions made about whether and how to correct them. For example, if a dataset includes somebody whose birth year is listed as 1820, this is probably a data entry error! Now you must decide whether to track down the correct birth year, change the year to 1920, treat that piece of information as missing, or identify other resolutions.

Third, take what you know about your data into account when planning analysis and interpreting results. If you know that diagnoses are not always in the chart, then you might want to look for other indications that a person has a health condition. For example, you could collect information on use of glipizide (an oral medication that lowers blood sugar) or insulin for non-hospitalized patients without a recorded diagnosis of diabetes. Whether it is necessary to do this extra work depends on the purpose for which the data are being used. If the only question at hand is whether the prevalence of diabetes in a county exceeds a certain threshold, and the estimated prevalence based on diagnosis alone exceeds that threshold, then no further work is needed.

Finally, compare data from different sources to understand your dataset better and compensate for data deficiencies. For example, if survey data were collected only from people with land lines, it will be helpful to collect a small sample of data for cell phone users and those with no phones at all and see whether the results differ from those of landline users.

Making Meaning Out of Data Is a Process of Choice

Even when we know that our data are reliable and accurate, data (numbers, words, symbols) by themselves are meaningless. For example, what is the meaning of a spreadsheet containing spirometry readings and patient characteristics (spirometry is a test that measures lung capacity and function, and is used to characterize status of conditions that affect breathing)? These data have no meaning until they are understood, analyzed, and interpreted. Data collection, analysis, and interpretation are nuanced, value-driven work, and far from the technocratic "number-crunching" many think them to be. Analyzing data to create meaning involves choices, and those choices have implications. Even collecting data to analyze is premised on choices about what to collect and what to ignore.

How would we make meaning of the spirometry data? As a first step, we might identify how many people have spirometry readings within specified ranges. To make these ranges meaningful, however, we must identify criteria for "normal" based on, for example, age, body build, and fitness level. Once these criteria are identified, we might ask ourselves whether there is an association between specific patient characteristics and the status of their asthma. But which characteristics? To use an extreme example, you could analyze asthma outcomes by the eye color of the person with asthma, but this would be an odd choice. In contrast, it makes sense to analyze asthma outcomes by race, socioeconomic status, or living conditions of persons with asthma. Why? Because there is no reason to think that eye color has a meaningful effect on asthma outcomes, whereas we know that race and socioeconomic status are often associated with access to the resources for controlling chronic disease, and that living conditions can affect a person's level of exposure to allergens. Choosing not to look at living conditions when analyzing data (or not having the data to do so) doesn't make living situation unimportant. It just means you do not know how it might be affecting your results. Bring in relevant literature and theoretical/conceptual models when developing data plans so as to identify variables that are important for the analysis and analytic methods that are appropriate to the questions you want to answer.

We also make choices when we interpret the results of analyses. For example, many surveys collect metrics for health-related quality of life, some of which are designed to predict long-term health outcomes and therefore do not respond quickly to environmental changes. The fact that health-related quality of life has not changed for a population postintervention does not mean the intervention had no effect. It could mean that this metric is not able to pick up the kinds of changes that actually occurred.

Illness and injury are undesirable, but they are also a part of life. How do we decide how well we are doing? Comparisons or benchmarking against a standard can help us assign meaning to a rate. For example, we may be pretty sure that we could be doing better with infant mortality among babies born to teenage mothers because other states or counties or health plans have achieved better rates among this population. (More detailed information on metrics can be found in chapter 22.)

Applying relevant theoretical or conceptual models, including what we know about the etiology of illness, will also aid data interpretation. For example, when we look at data on multivitamin use and child birth defects among pregnant women, we might not see the positive effect we were expecting because of what we call a confounder—in this case, maternal age. Although maternal age might make women more likely to take multivitamins (a positive association, in the sense that as age increases so does the likelihood of taking vitamins), it is also associated with higher levels of birth defects (also a positive association), thereby "hiding" the relationship between taking vitamins and birth defect (a negative association, in the sense that taking vitamins lowers the risk of birth defects). That relationship is shown in Figure 21-1.

The Art of Data Display

Presenting information through tables and charts can help you see patterns and communicate about your information effectively with others. Edward Tufte (2001) notes that good displays will not only reflect but actually enhance the thinking process. Conversely, thinking can be impeded by visual clutter,

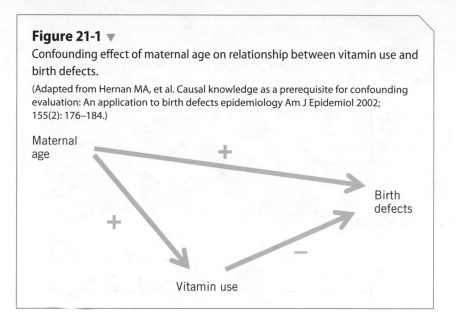

Figure 21-1 ▼

Confounding effect of maternal age on relationship between vitamin use and birth defects.

(Adapted from Hernan MA, et al. Causal knowledge as a prerequisite for confounding evaluation: An application to birth defects epidemiology Am J Epidemiol 2002; 155(2): 176–184.)

Maternal age

+

Birth defects

+

−

Vitamin use

inappropriate scales, poor comparisons, and failure to include key information. Data visualization can help us generate hypotheses or analysis plans or communicate with others. For example, compare Figures 21-2, 21-3, 21-4, and 21-5. Do you think that the anti-smoking media campaign initiated by (the fictitious) Warren County in 2012 might have reduced smoking rates?

A quick look at Figure 21-2, with its steep downward slope, suggests that smoking prevalence dropped dramatically from 2012, when the media campaign was initiated, to 2013, although it cannot tell us whether the change was a result of the campaign. Figure 21-3, providing more years of data, indicates that the drop in smoking prevalence preceded the media campaign. A causal connection between the reduction in smoking and the campaign seems less likely when we look at this graph. Figure 21-4, with its different scale on the vertical axis, brings into question whether the drop in smoking was as dramatic as we first thought. A look back at Figure 21-2 reveals that each line on the vertical axis represents a change of only .05%; in Figure 21-4, each line represents a change ten times that size, flattening out the trend line. Finally, when we add the statewide trend in smoking prevalence to our graph in Figure 21-5, we find that Warren County's downward trend mirrors larger trends in the state, suggesting that the factors behind the trend may not be unique to the county.

None of these figures represents the "final word" on the impact of Warren County's media campaign, of course. Each simply provides some information that can help us in our quest to assess that impact. The differences among the slides illustrate how data display influences our perception of what that information means.

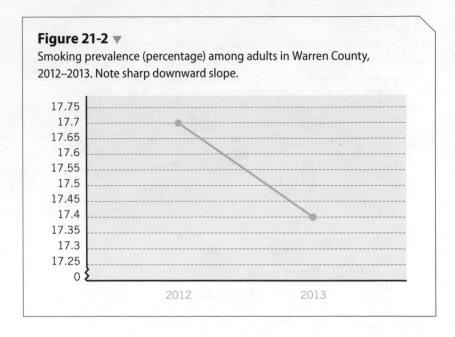

Figure 21-2 ▼

Smoking prevalence (percentage) among adults in Warren County, 2012–2013. Note sharp downward slope.

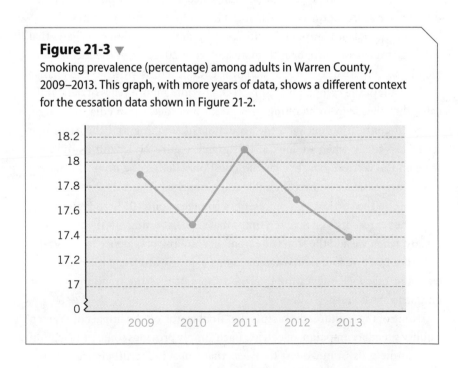

Figure 21-3 ▼

Smoking prevalence (percentage) among adults in Warren County, 2009–2013. This graph, with more years of data, shows a different context for the cessation data shown in Figure 21-2.

Figure 21-4 ▼

Smoking prevalence (percentage) among adults in Warren County, 2009–2013. Note different scale on vertical axis, which makes data in Figure 21-2 seem less dramatic.

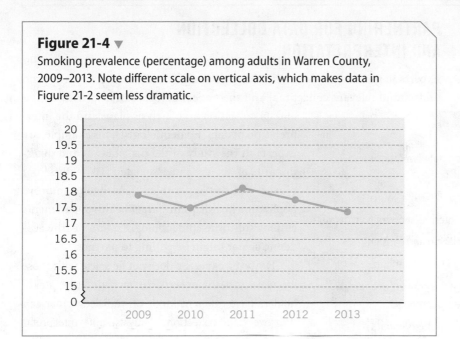

Figure 21-5 ▼

Smoking prevalence (percentage) among adults in Warren County, 2009–2013. Data compared with statewide prevalence data, suggesting that county trend may not be unique.

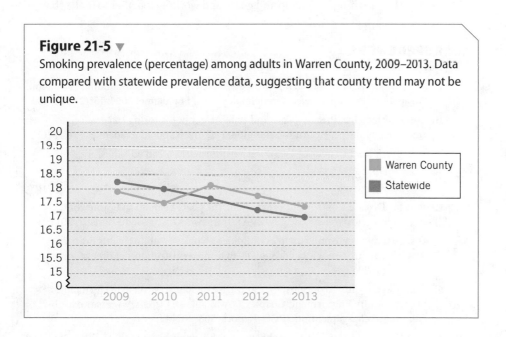

PARTNERING FOR DATA COLLECTION AND INTERPRETATION

Experts in methods of data collection and analysis and "content experts" who understand relevant conceptual and theoretical models can help with design of data collection and analysis plans and the interpretation of data. Epidemiologists, for example, are experts in the study of the distribution and determinants of disease and associated risk factors/root causes, and can apply this knowledge to improve population health. Many larger health departments employ full-time epidemiologists, or a nearby academic center might be willing to partner.

However, expertise does not lie solely with those we usually deem experts. In fact, different stakeholders have different kinds of knowledge that can improve data collection, analysis, and interpretation. Understanding of teen birth outcomes will be enhanced by engaging teenage mothers, their parents/guardians, and obstetricians in thinking about the data needed to understand these outcomes, how to best collect the data, what research questions to ask, and how to interpret findings. Collaborative data collection, analysis, and interpretation, and thus, agreement among partners, also lay the foundation for working together, aligning leadership and goals, and working together to make change.

Tips

✔ Account for common data limitations and challenges.

✔ Triangulate data from different sources.

✔ Consider alternative interpretations of your data.

✔ Don't confuse correlation and causality.

✔ Use comparisons and benchmarking.

✔ Interpret data within the context of a relevant theoretical or conceptual model.

✔ Involve multiple stakeholders in data interpretation.

REFERENCES

Ackoff R. From data to wisdom. J Appl Syst Anal 1989; 16: 3–9.

Hernan, Miguel A. et al. Causal knowledge as a prerequisite for confounding evaluation: An application to birth defects epidemiology. Am J Epidemiol 2002; 155(2): 176–184.

Institute of Medicine. Primary Care and Public Health: Exploring Integration to Improve Population Health. Washington, DC: The National Academies Press, 2012.

Tufte E. The Visual Display of Quantitative Information, 2nd ed. Cheshire, CT: Graphics Press, 2001.

Additional Resources

Centers for Disease Control and Prevention. The CDC Evaluation Framework. Available at: http://www.cdc.gov/EVAL/framework/ Accessed August 1, 2014.

CDC self-study course on Principles of Epidemiology in Public Health Practice. Available at: http://www2a.cdc.gov/TCEOnline/registration/detailpage. asp?res_id=2965

CDC and Agency for Toxic Substance and Disease Registry (ATSDR). Principles of Community Engagement: Chapter 7. Available at: http://www.atsdr.cdc.gov/ communityengagement/pdf/PCE_Report_508_FINAL.pdf

Rosling H. The Best Stats You've Ever Seen. Ted-Ed, published on July 13, 2013. Available at: http://www.youtube.com/watch?v=usdJgEwMinM. Accessed August 1, 2014.

SAGE Research Methods series provides assistance on data collection and analysis. Available at: http://www.srmo.sagepub.com

Chapter 22

Metrics: How to Select Them, How to Use Them

MINA SILBERBERG AND DENISE KOO

METRICS: HOW TO SELECT THEM, HOW TO USE THEM

Metrics are measures with meaning. They help us move from "how long," "how far," and "how much" to "where do we want to be?" and "how well are we doing?" Metrics are commonly used in primary care and in public health. The clinician has quality goals that are reflected in metrics, such as percentage of patients counseled to quit smoking or percentage who get their annual influenza vaccination. The public health agency has target metrics, such as the percentage of children in their jurisdiction who are fully immunized or the percentage of persons in their county who smoke. Working together requires identifying common outcome and process metrics that represent shared goals for population health and allow partners to assess joint progress toward those goals. Multiple considerations go into selecting metrics, such as validity, reliability, practicality, and how acceptable and compelling the metric is to stakeholders. Often one consideration will need to be balanced against another. When selecting metrics, review consensus-based metrics set by national organizations and consider the opinions of experts and partners.

WHAT ARE METRICS AND HOW ARE THEY USED?

A metric is a measure with meaning. For example, when we say that normal blood pressure is below 140/90, we have turned a measure of blood pressure (simply a count) into a metric of hypertension. One specific kind of metric is an indicator, which tells you where you stand relative to a goal. An indicator benchmark defines that goal, often relative to a comparison group or best practice. For example, if the "benchmark" is a normal blood pressure measurement among 80% of the population with known hypertension, then an actual metric of 60% normal in a particular community or practice indicates that the community has a ways to go. Indicators from multiple points in time will show a trend (if they are generally moving in a particular direction) or the lack thereof (if they are fluctuating).

Metrics are used to identify population health problems, to specify goals, to monitor and evaluate the progress of work together (using process metrics), and to evaluate project results (using outcome metrics). The metrics you choose should reflect your best thinking about what you want to achieve and what it is possible to achieve, because, once chosen, metrics can significantly shape future work. Metrics focus attention on specific tasks, as reflected in the frequently-quoted saying "What gets measured gets done." They also affect our perception of how well our work is going. For example, through Healthy People, the federal government has for three decades established a framework with benchmark metrics for the improvement of population health, for example, increasing the percentage of non-elderly Americans with medical coverage to 100% by 2020 (U.S. Department of Health and Human Services, 2014). Each time the government issues Healthy People, they modify metrics and benchmarks based on current thinking and priorities. For example, the 2020 metrics have a greater emphasis on health disparities and social determinants of health than do the metrics of previous decades. In developing these new metrics, the government has increased the focus on the need to reduce disparities (vs. using health promotion approaches to improve health overall but actually increase disparities) and address social determinants (in contrast to a more clinical focus).

METRICS FOR POPULATION HEALTH

Using Metrics in Population Health Improvement

Metrics are vital throughout all stages of population health improvement work. During the *planning and prioritizing* stage, metrics are used to describe the current situation, generate interest in the problem, set goals and milestones for getting there (with clear delineation of responsibilities and accountability), and create an evaluation plan. During *implementation, monitoring, and evaluation*, identified metrics serve as signposts for assessing progress toward agreed-on goals. These signposts include process metrics (e.g., whether you are meeting milestones on your work plan or how many individuals have been reached by your intervention), and outcome metrics (e.g., population-level changes in knowledge, attitudes, behavior, clinical status, or quality of life). When you *celebrate and share*, you will undoubtedly cite achievement of target metrics as evidence of success and will discuss lessons learned from targets not met!

The San Diego Healthy Weight Collaborative exemplifies all these uses of metrics (see chapter 26 for detailed information). The collaborative came about when a school district employee instituted a body mass index (BMI) surveillance project that determined that almost 40% of district elementary school students were overweight. They noted potential determinants associated with this problem, such as school proximity to fast-food restaurants and lack of green space, and recognized the need for a multidimensional approach to the problem. The metrics the collaborative uses to monitor and evaluate their work reflect the variety of their interventions, and the need to monitor success (or challenges) with steps along the way to outcomes, not just the outcomes themselves. These metrics range from targets for clinic-based documentation of BMI to the volume of messaging about healthy eating behaviors in multiple sites (clinics, schools, daycare sites) to adoption of school wellness policies. The collaborative is purposeful about sharing lessons learned and generating support for their work by disseminating results regarding key metrics to stakeholders, the local public, and the larger practice and research communities.

The Results-Based Accountability (RBA) movement has delineated useful principles for utilizing metrics to spur real change and communicate clearly, including the following:

- Start with where you want to go, then figure out how you will know when you're there and what it will take to get there.
- Be clear and specific.
- Use metrics to assess success, failure, and progress and drive decision-making.

As we do, RBA also emphasizes the importance of stakeholder involvement in selecting and tracking metrics.

Frameworks and Types of Population Health Metrics

Jacobson and Teutsch (2012) propose an *integrated* measurement framework that includes three domains: 1) population health, including total population health (health status, and outcomes for a defined geopolitical area) and the health of subpopulations; 2) determinants of health, including genetics/biology, clinical care, behaviors, and the social and physical environments; and 3) health improvement activities undertaken by the clinical system, the public health system, or multi-sectoral collaborations. This framework facilitates measurement across public health and clinical systems, and, thus, identification of the impact of collaborative activities.

Many of the metrics used for population health will be familiar to clinicians and public health officials from their daily work. For example, clinicians commonly use metrics that tell them about the state of an individual's health (e.g., cholesterol level) or that provide an aggregate picture of patient health (e.g., percent of patients with cholesterol in an abnormal range). Clinical indicators aggregated across all patients in a practice, or all practices in a plan are an example of measures of health status of subpopulations. Public health officials use metrics that refer to what Jacobson and Teutsch (2012) define as total population health, that is, incidence or prevalence of health outcomes (e.g., low birth weight or obesity) in a geopolitical or jurisdictional area, such as an entire county or state.

In an example from Jacobson and Teutsch's domain, public health officials commonly measure determinants of health, such as exposure to lead, air quality, and health behaviors. Metrics of clinical care (e.g., percentage of people with diabetes who have had their HBA1c measured in the last 6 months) and penetration of public health programs (e.g., numbers attending a health education event) facilitate monitoring of health improvement activities, Jacobson and Teutsch's third domain.

With increased collaboration between public health and primary care, and an increased focus on population and systemic change, there is a need to think about metrics that best capture what we are trying to accomplish and how we are trying to get there. Some of these may be different from those with which health professionals are now most familiar. For example, measurement of population health status can go beyond aggregation of individual-level data to characterize overall dimensions of population health, such as equity or progress. A Gini coefficient for a health indicator (e.g., the prevalence of cardiovascular disease) ranges from 0 (equal prevalence throughout the population) to 1 (maximum inequality in prevalence among subpopulations).

Identifying Potential Metrics

Review Existing Sources of Metrics

Many people have already traveled the road of identifying metrics for population health improvement. It is helpful to review the available literature or to consult with experts. Excellent sources include the World Health Organization Indicator and Measurement Registry, the National Quality Forum, Healthy People 2020, and the National Prevention Council's National Prevention Strategy, among others (please see Additional Resources at the end of this chapter). Such national indicator sets often use readily available data and incorporate input from multiple stakeholders. Using existing metrics saves time and energy and, when the data are collected in a comparable fashion, allows comparison of your community to other populations. On the other hand, existing metrics may not capture what you want or may be hard to generate. Even then, reviewing existing measures will provide an excellent starting point for thinking about how the metrics you develop might be similar to and different from what's already available.

Collaborative Identification of Metrics

It is critical that partners and stakeholders collaborate in selecting key metrics for your project. First, metrics are a reflection of goals and beliefs—what you think needs to be done and can be done. Often, the selection of metrics forces thinking through the specifics of what you want to do in a way that is not required when discussing such abstract goals as "improved health." Deciding as a team that you want to decrease your community's black–white racial gap in the prevalence of cardiovascular disease by 10% will take you much further in aligning goals and work than agreeing that you want to "address cardiovascular health disparities." Second, failure to align goals and work in this way risks later conflict and failure when partners realize that they are not working toward a common goal, and that key stakeholder voices were excluded from this important step in project planning. Third, because the discussion of goals and related metrics clarifies perspectives and beliefs, it represents an important opportunity to learn from one another. Fourth, generating the data for metrics has costs and implications for those involved in data collection and analysis; these individuals—who often include front-line program staff—need to be part of the deliberative process. Finally, metrics can be used to generate support for work, so the metrics chosen must matter to your stakeholders. For example, while health professionals are generally drawn to measures of clinical status such as HbA1c, community members often find little meaning in such measures, and instead are motivated by metrics such as quality of life or number of amputations avoided. Accountable care organizations or community care organizations offer important opportunities for primary care and public health partners to discuss and agree on metrics of mutual interest (Centers for Medicare and Medicaid Services, 2011).

CONSIDERATIONS FOR METRIC SELECTION

There are a number of considerations to keep in mind when selecting metrics. The following are among the most important:

1. **Validity:** Does this metric capture what you care about? While frequently used as a measure of access to care, does the ratio of providers to residents in your county really capture "access"? Does it need to be used in conjunction with other measures (e.g., use of emergency rooms instead of visits to primary care providers)?

2. **Reliability:** Will this metric give you the same "value" for the same unit no matter who is doing the measurement or when? Two observers of a health educator at work may rate the educator's effectiveness differently depending on the observers' expectations of and experience with health education.

3. **Practicality:** Are the data for the metric you're interested in already being generated for some other reason, making it easy to use? For example, providers already generate quality of care measures for required health plan reporting, such as percent of female patients receiving cervical cancer screening in accordance with guidelines. This measure could be useful for a cancer screening prevention initiative. If the metric is not already being generated, what would it take for you to generate it, and do you have the resources to do so? One crucial aspect of practicality is the potential burden on those involved in data collection and analysis.

4. **Standardization:** Will this metric allow you to compare your population to other populations? If you want to know whether access to care in your community has improved compared to access to care statewide, you will want to use the same access metric that is used at the state level.

Standardization is also important if you want to aggregate the work of multiple partners across a community. If you have a campaign to promote blood pressure screening across multiple clinical and community sites, you will want to have a common understanding of how you are measuring the denominator (who should have been screened), the numerator (who was screened), and the yield (who was diagnosed with hypertension). Without standardization, some sites might consider screening all adults, while others consider the denominator to be only those with risk factors; some might consider screening to be one reading of blood pressure, whereas others require three; and some sites might consider yield to include only individuals who have never been previously diagnosed, whereas others might include *anybody* whose blood pressure screened high or who reported being on antihypertensive medication.

5. **Accuracy for your population—and subpopulations:** Frequently, commonly used data sets providing data for metrics at the national or state level will not be useful at the community level. For example, the Behavioral Risk Factor Surveillance System pulls limited samples from most counties, such that the data are representative at the state level and not for smaller jurisdictions. Similarly, a sample that is appropriate at the county level might not be large enough to allow a look at specific racial, age, or socioeconomic groups.

6. **Relevance to your time frame:** Because of the effort required to collect them, many public health datasets are not collected annually. If you are conducting an intervention starting in 2013 that should realize measurable changes by 2015, you will want your baseline data to be from as close to 2013 as possible and your follow-up data to be as close to 2015 as possible. Public health datasets can be misleading in this regard. Often, data that are reported out in a particular year were actually collected 2 years previously.

7. **Timeliness:** If you are using metrics to make programmatic decisions, you will need to have those metrics available to you at the time the decision needs to be made. Researchers sometimes spend a lot of time to get the data "right" and do not have it available when needed.

8. **Importance and acceptability to stakeholders:** As noted above, metrics must speak to the stakeholders whose support you need. In fact, some metrics will be unacceptable to key stakeholders. The decision to disallow use of the metric "quality-adjusted life-years" in comparative effectiveness research funded by the Patient Centered Outcomes Research Institute was meant to counter concerns that this research would lead to rationing or would be used by Medicare for coverage and reimbursement decisions (Sorenson et al., 2014). It is not surprising that metrics can be controversial, since they reflect values and drive work.

9. **Realism:** Choose a metric that can be achieved by your intervention on its own in the time frame in which you will measure it. Using an unrealistic metric will either undermine support for your work when the metric isn't achieved (e.g., eliminating all racial health disparities in stroke incidence

in the next 5 years) or will lead you to ignore your metric, leaving you with no means of assessing actual progress against desired change.

Generally, it will be impossible to maximize metric "performance" on all of the considerations just outlined. How one consideration should be balanced against the others depends on the nature of the work and the preferences of stakeholders. For example, two common metrics for measuring medication adherence are: 1) self-reported adherence from surveys and 2) the gap between expected and actual prescription refills as derived from claims or pharmacy data. Self-report of behavior is generally less "valid" than more "objective" measures. However, accessing pharmacy or claims data may be difficult in a particular community; moreover, if the goal is to measure change over time, the reliability of the metric will be more important than the validity. Select metrics that reflect what you are trying to achieve and your priorities for measurement.

Tips

✔ Good metrics are generally not absolute numbers (e.g., number of deaths due to cancer), but rather proportions among a specified population within a given time frame (e.g., number of deaths due to cancer per 100,000 residents in a given year), allowing for meaningful comparisons.

✔ "Bean-counting" (e.g., number of handouts distributed) is good for process measures but generally makes for poor outcome measures.

✔ Sometimes a simple metric is all that is needed to provide stakeholders with the information they need to make a decision.

✔ Tables 22-1 and 22-2 provide some additional succinct tips for using metrics to drive performance.

Table 22-1 ▾ Guidelines That Can Help Ensure That Metrics Are Applied in Meaningful Ways for Rewarding Improved Population Health

Determine the problem that needs to be solved.
Create a visual model that explains the causes of the problem and potential solutions.
Use an acceptable metric to measure the problem over time so that change can be objectively documented.
Approach selection of the problem, the solutions to be attempted, and the methods associated with each keeping continuous quality improvement in mind.
Use a metric that can quantify the problem in real time at the beginning and end of the incentive period.
Choose a characteristic to measure that is amenable to change.
Choose a reward or penalty associated with the metric that is of sufficient value to induce the intended change.
Ensure that the entity being offered the incentive has sufficient control over itself and others to change in ways and magnitudes measureable by the metric.
Ensure that the entity has sufficient resources (e.g., staff, funding, influence, authority) to effect the change.
Determine when the incentive will be awarded (e.g., at the start of the effort to effect change, throughout the effort to produce change, or withheld pending final measurement).
Assure that the incentive associated with the metric will be awarded.
Plan to develop new metrics if present metrics prove inadequate.

From Pestronk RM: Using metrics to improve population health. Prev Chronic Dis 2010; 7(4): A70. Used with permission.

Table 22-2 ▼ Questions for Linking Performance Incentives to Population Health Metrics
Are the measures actionable?
Are the measures sensitive to interventions?
Are the measures affected by population migration?
Are the measures easily understood by collaborating organizations, policy makers, and the public?
Is the meaning of an increase or decrease in a measure unambiguous?
Do the measures stand alone or are they aggregated into an index or summary measure?
Are the measures uniform across communities?
To what extent do measures address disparities as well as overall burden?
Can unintended consequences be tracked?

From Bilheimer LT: Evaluating metrics to improve population health. 2010; 7(4): A69. Used with permission.

ACKNOWLEDGMENT

The authors wish to thank Steven Teutsch, M.D., M.P.H., for his review of this chapter.

REFERENCES

Sorenson C, Gusmano M, Oliver A. The politics of comparative effectiveness research: lessons from recent history. J Health Polit Policy Law 2014; 39(1): 139–170.

Center for Medicare and Medicaid Services. Accountable Care Organization 2012 Program Analysis: Quality Performance Standards Narrative Measure Specifications. Final Report. 2011. Available at: http://www.cms.gov/medicare/medicare-fee-for-service-payment/sharedsavingsprogram/downloads/aco_qualitymeasures.pdf

U.S. Department of Health and Human Services: Healthy People 2020. Leading health indicators: Progress update. Executive summary. 2014. Available at: http://www.healthypeople.gov./2020/LHI/LHI-ProgressReport-ExecSum.pdf.

Additional Resources

Centers for Disease Control and Prevention. Community Health Assessment for Population Health Improvement: Resource of Most Frequently Recommended Health Outcomes and Determinants, Atlanta, GA: Office of Surveillance, Epidemiology, and Laboratory Services, 2013. Available at: http://stacks.cdc.gov/view/cdc/20707. *This report provides a referenced list of the most frequently recommended health outcomes and determinants and, where possible, links each health outcome and determinant to valid and reliable indicators available at the metropolitan statistical area (MSA), county, or sub-county level.*

Jacobson DM, Teutsch S. An Environmental Scan of Integrated Approaches for Defining and Measuring Total Population Health by the Clinical Care System, the Government Public Health System and Stakeholder

Organizations. 2012. Available at: http://www.improvingpopulationhealth.org/ PopHealthPhaseIICommissionedPaper.pdf. Reviews definitions, conceptual frameworks, and lists considerations and sources for various metrics.

National Quality Forum. Available at: http://www.qualityforum.org/QPS. The National Quality Forum promotes measurement as means to improve health care quality and cost, and establishes health care metrics towards that end.

Results-Based Accountability Implementation Guide. Available at: (http://raguide. org/1-1-what-are-the-basic-ideas-behind-results-based-accountability-and-results-based-decision-making-and-budgeting/). *Provides an overview of results-based accountability.*

U.S. Department of Health and Human Services. National Prevention Strategy. 2011. Available at: http://www.surgeongeneral.gov/initiatives/prevention/strategy/ report.pdf. National Prevention Strategy aims to guide our nation in the most effective and achievable means for improving health and well-being. *The Strategy prioritizes prevention by integrating recommendations and actions across multiple settings to improve health and save lives.*

U.S. Department of Health and Human Services. 2011. National Quality Strategy. *National Quality Strategy provides a focus for addressing the abundance of clinical quality measures currently used in national programs.* The goal is to get to measures that matter and minimize provider burden. Available at: http://www. ahrq.gov/workingforquality/index.html

World Health Organization Indicator and Measurement Registry. Available at: http://www.who.int/gho/indicator_registry/en/. *This website provides an extensive list of indicators for measuring health and global data for these indicators.*

Chapter 23

Use of Electronic Health Records for Population Health

DENISE KOO, RAYMOND J. KING, AND SETH FOLDY

SUMMARY

The interaction between primary care and public health has historically been based largely on mandated communicable disease reporting from providers to public health for monitoring diseases and
detecting outbreaks. In return, public health intermittently provided primary care clinicians with guidance on the management of cases and alerts
regarding outbreaks of disease. Beginning in the 1990s, the establishment of
public health immunization information systems (IIS, known then as immunization registries) enabled clinicians to view patient immunization histories
across providers, facilitating better coverage for both individual patients and
communities. At present, the increasingly widespread use of electronic health
records (EHRs) in clinical settings is enabling near-real-time automation of
health information exchange, their extension to chronic disease, environmental health, maternal-child health and other areas of mutual interest, and
partnerships for preventive services, quality improvement, and community
health. Section IV provides a few examples of the ways primary care and
public health are sharing data electronically to improve the health of their
communities. Such data sharing is a key capability for population health,
one that was hardly imagined a few decades ago. Consistent with the theme
of *The Practical Playbook: Public Health and Primary Care Together*, public
health and primary care partners can build relationships, discuss goals and
data needs, and work through the data-sharing challenges together to achieve
mutual goals of improving health (Institute of Medicine, 2012).

BACKGROUND
What Is an Electronic Health Record?

An EHR is a record created by systematic collection of patient electronic
health information. Digital formatting enables the information to be used

and shared over secure networks. An EHR includes an electronic medical record combined with information exchange with other health systems (e.g., laboratories), providing users with access to longitudinal patient data across multiple providers and even health systems. The EHR information can be accessed by all authorized individuals involved in the patient's care, including the patients themselves. (For more information on EHR basics, see Additional Resources at the end of the chapter.)

What Can Electronic Health Records Do?

Electronic health records record and track selected information as standardized data elements to describe the health status of patients, including, for example, positive or negative trends in vital signs (e.g., blood pressure), behaviors (e.g., smoking), laboratory results, medications, and events like hospitalizations or seizures. Such information can be exchanged electronically, for services (like ePrescribing, laboratory test ordering and results, or public health reporting), with other providers (as when a patient is referred to an ambulatory clinic or discharged to skilled nursing), and also with patients to allow them to participate more fully in their own care. Electronic health records can use such digital information to trigger preventive warnings and reminders ("clinical decision support"), such as when a patient is due for immunization, requires adjustment of diabetic treatment, or is at risk of an adverse medication interaction. Electronic health record systems are now certified by the Office of the National Coordinator for HIT (http://www.healthit.gov/policy-researchers-implementers/certification-programs-policy) to ensure that data capture and exchange are standardized to enable sending and receiving orders, reports, results, and prescriptions. (For more information on getting started with EHRs and their uses, see Additional Resources at the end of the chapter.)

CHANGING LANDSCAPE OF ELECTRONIC HEALTH RECORDS

In 2013, 78% of office-based physicians used some type of EHR system, up from 18% in 2001 (Hsiao & Hing, 2014). However, just because data are stored in electronic format does not mean that they are available for secondary use by public health. Until recently there were few broadly implemented standards to help ensure that different brands of EHRs recorded and exchanged information in ways that could allow communication, also known as interoperability (http://www.healthit.gov/buzz-blog/electronic-health-and-medical-records/ehr-interoperability-structured-data-capture-initiative/) between systems. The Centers for Medicare and Medicaid Services (CMS) EHR Incentive Program, commonly called "Meaningful Use," provides economic incentives to health care providers to acquire EHR technology that does feature such standards. Those seeking incentives typically need to use EHR systems that exchange information with public health programs, which themselves are gradually adopting the same standards. The objectives for Meaningful Use are staged, and each stage includes some requirements that involve EHR capture of data relevant to prevention and sharing of information with public health. As of 2014, incentivized exchange with public health included electronic laboratory results reporting for reportable conditions, sharing immunization data with population immunization registries, sharing near-real-time complaints and diagnosis data from emergency departments and urgent care (a form of "syndromic surveillance"), and submissions to cancer and other population health registries. Once more providers and public health agencies are routinely exchanging such information, it will be easier to partner around using these systems for shared interests, like supporting Million Hearts blood pressure and smoking goals (Centers for Disease Control and Prevention, 2012). (For more information on Meaningful Use, see Additional Resources at the end of the chapter.)

PUBLIC HEALTH INFORMATION SYSTEMS

Like clinicians with their EHRs, public health agencies manage electronic information in disease surveillance systems, IIS, syndromic surveillance systems (for near-real-time tracking of symptoms appearing among patients presenting to emergency departments), and chronic disease registries. Immunization information systems are among the most sophisticated applications when it comes to bi-directional communication with health care providers, simultaneously tracking individuals' immunizations (to aid doctors, nurses, and schools); providing reminders to clinicians and patients of overdue immunization (a form of decision support); monitoring community-level vaccine coverage; supporting clinic quality measurement and improvement; and supporting clinic vaccine inventory management. Chronic disease registries are often used jointly by public health agencies and clinical providers to identify and fill gaps in care at the community level (for example, spurring the development of cancer screening programs when too many cancers are diagnosed at advanced stages). When such public health concepts cross with EHR systems, improvements in clinical preventive care can be driven dynamically in real-time (e.g., identifying individuals lacking preventive care while visiting the clinic, or those lacking vaccines during an outbreak). (For more information regarding public health surveillance and links to selected national information systems supporting this and other public health functions, please see http://www.cdc.gov/surveillancepractice/.)

OPPORTUNITIES FOR POPULATION HEALTH

Electronic health records facilitate the ability to improve and measure preventive care in clinical settings across entire communities (Klompas et al., 2011). In addition, public health agencies provide considerable information to clinicians (alerts, trends, recommendations). Providing such information when relevant in the context of care (e.g., through clinical decision support systems) can help make such information easier to use on a day-to-day clinical basis (CDC, 2014). In addition, because public health surveillance and information systems have previously provided information for individual diseases or conditions in separate systems, increasing standardization of EHRs and data exchange offer the promise of easier use, reuse, and analysis for population health. They can automate public health notifiable disease reporting, ensuring more complete and faster reporting of existing data, with less manual data entry (CDC, 2008). They can also enhance public health surveillance for chronic diseases, with access to clinical data not previously available to public health, and for populations not easily reached by surveys (Institute of Medicine, 2011; McVeigh et al., 2013; Nichols et al., 2012). Public health professionals have participated in development of national standards relevant to EHRs, such as Health Level 7 and clinical vocabulary standards, for many years to enhance the ability of EHR systems to share data in a more timely, comprehensive fashion with public health for surveillance, vital records, and disease registries. Consistently collected, standardized, and comprehensive EHRs shared with public health will provide a more complete picture of the health status of communities, and analysis of such will offer crucial data to help target population health interventions.

Here are some examples in which EHRs improve communication between public health and health providers in the context of care.

- Rhode Island Department of Health tracked use of dispensed antivirals during H1N1, and learned that 5% of Tamiflu prescriptions were being filled more than 5 days after being prescribed. They alerted patients and providers about the danger of these delays. They also let providers know how much non-H1N1 influenza-like illness was prevalent in the community, which led to a drop in Tamiflu prescriptions (described during CDC Public Health Grand Rounds in July 2011: http://www.cdc.gov/cdc-grandrounds/pdf/grehrallfinal21jul2011.pdf—Zimmerman).
- In many communities, medical assistants download each patient's vaccination history (along with indicators of missing immunizations) from their community IIS before the patient is seen, to help ensure better immunization coverage. They may also run statistics from within the IIS to identify gaps in vaccine coverage.
- The New York City Department of Health and Mental Hygiene Primary Care Information Project, which helped many primary care practices implement EHRs, also offers assistance to improve

preventive quality measures, and has documented the benefit of ongoing quality measurement and incentives (Wang et al., 2013). The New York City Macroscope project is validating the use of these ambulatory EHRs for public health surveillance by comparing such data to its own population-based surveys (http://www.nyc.gov/html/doh/html/data/nycmacroscope.shtml).

- The Springfield Center for Family Medicine and HealthBridge created an EHR linkage to Ohio's Prescription Narcotic Database Program systems, to alert clinicians to possible medical narcotic abuse and diversion. The Southeast Minnesota Beacon Project is linking school nurses, parents, and children's physicians in collaboration related to asthma action plans.

(For more information on the secondary use of EHR data for population health, see Additional Resources at the end of the chapter.)

BARRIERS FOR POPULATION HEALTH

Clinicians are often concerned about EHRs detracting from their ability to interact with patients, or that some EHRs are not designed optimally for patient care (DesRoches et al., 2008; Furukawa, 2011; Miller et al., 2005; Poissant et al., 2005). The introduction of EHR can temporarily reduce clinical productivity, and there are additional costs for creating exchange interfaces with other systems, for upgrading their EHRs to keep up with new Meaningful Use criteria, and for maintaining the technology. There will also be projects competing for the use of EHR data, such as internal quality measurement and improvement. Given that public health Meaningful Use objectives come with incentive payments attached, projects focused on these might be the most acceptable for clinical technology and financial officers. Another driver for physicians is the CMS Physician Quality Reporting System (PQRS), a reporting system that promotes reporting of quality information with a combination of incentive payment and payment adjustments (http://www.cms.gov/Medicare/Quality-Initiatives-Patient-Assessment-Instruments/PQRS/indcx.html). It can take time and effort to establish reliable data quality and interoperability across different information systems. Clinical and other EHR data can be incomplete or inconsistently collected, or even outright inaccurate (Botsis et al., 2010; Chan et al., 2010). The standardization of data elements in certified EHRs used for clinical quality measures and public health reports is beginning to address this. Section IV, Working with Data, offers additional guidance for interpreting data.

Many public health partners have limited resources to exchange data with many different EHRs. Health information exchange organizations can sometimes reduce the cost and complexity of such exchanges (Klompas et al., 2011).

GETTING STARTED

Start with a shared need. Focus on the task, not the technology. It is easy to spend large and get little by focusing primarily on technology. Instead, find a problem of mutual interest (ideally measurable) that might be solved by getting the right information to the right person at the right time, and ask if EHR technology might help. Consider the following:

- Do clinicians routinely overlook an opportunity for prevention?
- Do they lack information (about the patient, about resources, about how-to) to deliver a preventive intervention?
- Do patients lack information, confidence, or reinforcement to execute prevention prescriptions? Do referrals to community-based services fail often?
- Do professionals spend time re-entering data for sharing with public health, for example, for reporting notifiable diseases?
- Are there opportunities to integrate information or messages from public health (e.g., prevalence of drug-resistance for a given infectious disease, tobacco quit lines, clusters of persons with lead exposure or asthma in geographic areas) into the electronic record?
- Do you lack current information to know if your projects are working?

These questions are examples that *information* can help fix, and where information technology might be useful.

Build your relationships first. Clinical partners can be reluctant to share data outside their organization, but public health often has the mandate and authority to serve as a "neutral" aggregator of such data.

Align to incentives. Health care organizations are under intense financial and time pressure to accomplish the Meaningful Use EHR objectives, to produce and improve quality metrics (PQRS for physicians), to achieve and maintain primary care medical home certification, to reduce Medicare readmissions, to manage at-risk contracts, and much more. Consider seeking projects that will address such bottom-line issues.

Assemble people with the right skills. At minimum, this includes someone engaged in clinic medical management, someone who understands the public health science involved, someone who understands how to make information technology produce results (sometimes called an "informatician"), and a skilled project manager. If none of these persons is familiar with legal and ethical stewardship of electronic personal health information, you will need someone who can do this as well.

Start small. Work gets complicated fast when addressing multiple roles in clinics and health departments, multiple electronic systems, multiple users, and multiple agreements. Start with small pilots, and grow incrementally from there as you learn together. Seek to share only the information needed for each task; resistance increases with each demand for more information (because of

> ### Box 23-1 | New York Combats Diabetes with Primary Care Referral Programs
>
> New York City Department of Health and Mental Hygiene worked with a physician–community task force to automate EHR alerts to refer prediabetic and diabetic patients to free diabetes prevention and management programs in the community.
>
> Read the full success story in the *Practical Playbook*. https://practicalplaybook.org/success-story/new-york-city-promotes-primary-care-referral-programs-combat-diabetes-south-bronx

the work involved and security and privacy concerns). Establish metrics of improvement in advance so you can tell whether early efforts hit the mark.

Address security, privacy and data governance from the start. Unsafe practices will put a rapid end to any project. Stakeholders should ensure that all activities comply with the Health Insurance Portability and Accountability Act, which permits sharing protected health information with public health authorities for public health purposes (CDC, 2003) at the project outset and seek legal counsel and Institutional Review Board waivers as appropriate. Expect the process of establishing data use agreements between new partners to take a lot of time (http://privacyruleandresearch.nih.gov/irbandprivacyrule.asp).

Consider local capabilities and infrastructure. Consider starting at a level that matches the capability of both the practice and the public health partner as well as the local infrastructure for health information exchange (Box 23-1).

CONCLUSION

The emergence of increasingly standardized and sophisticated EHRs, public health systems, and patient-controlled information technology offers rich opportunities for primary care and public health integration around population health. Different practices and communities have different levels of capability, depending on how EHRs are currently being used, whether there are already easy-to-use connections to public health systems, and the degree of robustness of local health information exchange. A key is to focus on how problems can be solved by better information management, and not primarily on the deployment of technology for technology's sake.

In addition, it is worth remembering that although EHRs provide valuable data, such data will often need to be used in conjunction with other data to get a complete picture of the health of the community and of opportunities to improve health. One primary care doctor even linked park locations to his patients' EHRs, to encourage his patients to get into parks and exercise (http://www.npr.org/blogs/health/2014/07/14/327338918/to-make-children-healthier-a-doctor-prescribes-a-trip-to-the-park). Collaboration among primary care and public health partners to share data and information makes an important contribution toward a more comprehensive view of the community's health.

ACKNOWLEDGMENT

We thank Dr. Robin Helm for her thoughtful review of this chapter.

REFERENCES

Botsis T, Hartvigsen G, Chen F, Weng C. Secondary use of EHR: Data quality issues and informatics opportunities. AMIA Jt Summits Transl Sci Proc 2010; 2010: 1–5.

Centers for Disease Control and Prevention (CDC). Automated detection and reporting of notifiable diseases using electronic medical records versus passive surveillance. MMWR Morb Mortal Wkly Rep 2008; 57(14): 373–376. Available at: http://www.cdc.gov/mmwr/preview/mmwrhtml/mm5714a4.htm. Accessed October 19, 2014.

CDC. The Community Guide: Clinical Decision-Support Systems Improve Provider Practices for Cardiovascular Disease Prevention. Community Guide News. Available at: http://www.thecommunityguide.org/news/2013/CVD-CDSS.html. Accessed February 12, 2014.

CDC. CDC Grand Rounds: The million hearts initiative. MMWR Morb Mortal Wkly Rep 2012; 61(50): 1017–1021. Available at: http://www.cdc.gov/mmwr/preview/mmwrhtml/mm6150a1.htm. Accessed October 19, 2014.

CDC. HIPAA privacy rule and public health: Guidance from CDC and the U.S. Department of Health and Human Services. MMWR Morb Mortal Wkly Rep 2003; 52: 1–12. Available at: http://www.cdc.gov/mmwr/preview/mmwrhtml/m2e411a1.htm. Accessed October 19, 2014.

Chan KS, Fowles JB, Weiner JP. Review: Electronic health records and the reliability and validity of quality measures: A review of the literature. Med Care Res Rev 2010; 67: 503–527

DesRoches CM, Campbell EG, Rao SR, et al. Electronic health records in ambulatory care—a national survey of physicians. N Engl J Med 2008; 359(1): 50–60.

Furukawa M. Electronic medical records and efficiency and productivity during office visits. Am J Manag Care 2011; 17(4): 296–303.

Hsiao C, Hing E. Use and Characteristics of Electronic Health Record Systems Among Office-based Physician Practices: United States, 2001–2013. Centers for Disease Control and Prevention, January 2014. Available at: http://www.cdc.gov/nchs/data/databriefs/db143.pdf. Accessed February 12, 2014.

Institute of Medicine (IOM) (US) Committee on a National Surveillance System for Cardiovascular and Select Chronic Diseases. A Nationwide Framework for Surveillance of Cardiovascular and Chronic Lung Diseases. Washington (DC): National Academies Press, 2011. Available at: http://www.ncbi.nlm.nih.gov/books/NBK83155/. Accessed February 12, 2014.

IOM. Primary Care and Public Health: Exploring Integration to Improve Population Health. Washington, DC: The National Academies Press, 2012.

Klompas M., Murphy M., Lankiewicz J et al. Harnessing electronic health records for public health surveillance. Online J Public Health Inform 2011; 3(3): pii. doi:10.5210/ojphi.v3i3.3794

McVeigh K, Newton-Dame R., Chernov C., et. al. Electronic health record surveillance systems: A new approach to chronic disease surveillance. American Public Health Association annual meeting, November 2013, Boston. Available at: https://apha.confex.com/apha/141am/webprogram/Paper295185.html. Accessed February 12, 2014.

Miller RH, West C, Brown TM, Sim I, Ganchoff C. The value of electronic health records in solo or small group practices. Health Aff (Millwood) 2005; 24(5): 1127–1137.

Nichols GA, Desai J, Elston LJ, Lawrence JM, O'Connor PJ, Pathak RD, et al. Construction of a multisite datalink using electronic health records for the identification, surveillance, prevention, and management of diabetes mellitus: The SUPREME-DM Project. Prev Chron Dis 2012; 9: E110. doi:http://dx.doi.org/10.5888/pcd9.110311

Poissant L, Pereira J, Tamblyn R, Kawasumi Y. The impact of electronic health records on time efficiency of physicians and nurses: a systematic review. J Am Med Inform Assoc 2005; 12(5): 505–516.

Wang JJ, Sebek KM, McCullough CM, Amirfar SJ, Parsons AS, Singer J, et al. Sustained improvement in clinical preventive service delivery among independent primary care practices after implementing electronic health record systems. Prev Chronic Dis 2013; 10: 120341. doi:http://dx.doi.org/10.5888/pcd10.120341

Additional Resources

EHR Basics

Learn EHR Basics provides an overview of EHRs and links to other related topics, on the website of the National Coordinator for Health Information Technology (ONC), HealthIT.gov. (http://www.healthit.gov/providers-professionals/learn-ehr-basics)

See this ONC link for a discussion of the differences between an EHR and an EMR. (http://www.healthit.gov/buzz-blog/electronic-health-and-medical-records/emr-vs-ehr-difference/)

This page from an IOM report describes the Key Capabilities of an Electronic Health Record System. (http://www.nap.edu/openbook.php?record_id=10781&page=1)

HealthIT.gov further describes advantages of EHRs. (http://www.healthit.gov/providers-professionals/faqs/what-are-advantages-electronic-health-records)

The HealthIT.gov site supports users who haven't yet started to use an EHR. (http://www.healthit.gov/providers-professionals/ehr-implementation-steps)

HealthIT.gov provides an overview and support for Meaningful Use. (http://www.healthit.gov/providers-professionals/meaningful-use-definition-objectives)CDC also has a site describing Meaningful Use implications for public health. (http://www.cdc.gov/ehrmeaningfuluse/)

Vision for Integration

From the Office of the National Coordinator (ONC): Connecting Health and Care for the Nation: A 10-Year Vision to Achieve an Interoperable Health IT Infrastructure. Available at: (http://healthit.gov/sites/default/files/ONC10yearInteroperabilityConceptPaper.pdf)

Learn more about how electronic health records can improve population health on the HealthIT.gov site (http://www.healthit.gov/providers-professionals/faqs/how-can-electronic-health-records-improve-public-and-population-health.)

EHR Data Management, Data Exchange Basics

ONC also supports the Beacon Community Cooperative Agreement Program to improve health with EHRs. Available at: (http://healthit.gov/policy-researchers-implementers/beacon-community-program)

HealthIT.gov provides information on policies for privacy and security. Available at: (http://www.healthit.gov/policy-researchers-implementers/privacy-security-policy)

The National Committee on Vital and Health Statistics provided guidance on Health Data Stewardship: What, Why, Who, How. Available at: (http://www.ncvhs.hhs.gov/090930lt.pdf)

The State of Illinois made available some useful guidance and examples for Establishing Governance for Health and Human Services Interoperability Initiatives. Illinois Framework for Healthcare and Human Services. Available at: (http://illinoisframework.org/governance/handbook-for-states/)

ONC supported a State Health Information Exchange Program. Available at: (http://www.healthit.gov/policy-researchers-implementers/state-health-inf)

Learn more about Health Information Exchange (HIE) organizations, networks and initiatives. Available at: (http://www.himss.org/library/health-information-exchange)

Electronic Health Records: Forging Common Ground for Primary Care and Public Health

Essay I

DAVID A. ROSS

Patient data encoded in electronic health records (EHRs) are changing our nation's health care delivery sector and have reached the point where public health must understand if and how these data can inform population health interventions and policy. Passage of the 2009 Health Information Technology for Economic and Clinical Health (HITECH) Act served as a stimulus to EHR adoption throughout the medical care establishment and, in doing so, may open a new era in understanding population health dynamics. The HITECH Act introduced the concept of meaningful use of the EHR in ways that lead to improved care coordination, reduced health care disparities, engaged patients and families, and improved population health, while simultaneously protecting privacy and security of digital health data (U.S. Department of Health and Human Services, 2014). These ambitious goals support the national need to understand how to improve health promotion programs, how to intervene early to reduce preventable disease burden, and how to use knowledge of social determinants of health to improve overall health metrics while also driving down total cost of health care (Institute of Medicine, 2014).

In their landmark 1993 article, McGinnis and Foege showed that behaviors and socioeconomic factors provided a useful way of understanding actual causes of death. Their work explained that altering population health status to a significant degree hinges heavily upon understanding the contributions of smoking, diet and activity, and alcohol consumption, as well as socioeconomic-related factors. Understanding the influences of behavioral, psychological, and socioeconomic variables informs our thinking about health promotion and disease prevention in ways that merely looking at medically coded diagnoses, procedure codes, and summary health statistics cannot.

Twenty years ago, data relating behavior, psychological, and social determinants of health—a major focus of public health activity—came almost exclusively from surveys. Since the McGinnis and Foege article, the nation's health care delivery sector has steadily automated processes of care and

built clinical data repositories that we refer to as EHRs. Medical practices have also extended the meaning of e-health through patient web portals and e-pharmacy applications. Electronic health records have moved from hospital-based departmental support systems, like those found in pharmacies and laboratories, to systems that integrate the entire suite of care processes within systems of care to systems that support ambulatory care in office-based practices. Because of the potential residing in the clinical repository of patient data, we must ask if it is possible to use EHR data to inform and influence the health of individuals and of populations.

In 2013, 78% of office-based physicians used some form of EHR, up from 18% in 2001. Today, roughly a quarter of office-based practices have software that qualifies as fully functional as defined by Meaningful Use Criteria (e.g., able to send a prescription to a pharmacy electronically or remind clinicians of needed screening tests) (Hsiao & Hing, 2014). These data demonstrate that EHRs in physician practices have gone from a novelty to the norm.

Given the rapid pace of EHR adoption by office-based physicians, public health and primary care should address, in a formal collaborative manner, the promise and potential of using EHR data for population health purposes. We must acknowledge that data gathered to document personal health care services and assist reimbursement do not automatically become useful for population health purposes. The mere presence of these clinical data repositories raises questions about the utility of the data as instruments that inform population health status and progress in health status tied to new population-based interventions. Can these data aid our understanding of how to measure changes in population health status? Is it possible to relate medical encounter data

to interventions aimed at reducing preventable morbidity? Do these data enable an understanding of provider adherence to standards of practice and preventive service guidelines? Many questions can be raised, but none can be answered without the combined efforts of public health working in partnership with their health care partners.

Conceiving of the potential of EHRs to aid in attaining public health objectives requires that we first define EHR—the instrument creating the potential. An electronic health record is "a repository of electronically maintained information about an individual's health status and health care, stored such that it can serve the multiple legitimate uses and users of the record" (McDonald et al., 2013). The EHR system is the software tool or suite of tools that creates and accesses the record. These tools offer capabilities that the paper record lacks. The EHR makes the record available to all who need it when they need it while also offering comprehensive and structured data. At their best, these systems provide an integrated view of patient data, support clinician order entry, offer clinical decision support and access to knowledge resources, improve communication among the care team, and support more efficient and timely reporting. The utility of these systems has been enhanced over time by the use of standardized data definitions, code sets, and vocabularies (generally referred to as "semantic standards"), uniform envelopes for transmitting digital health data (e.g., HL7), and clarity around processes that generate the data.

Now that many physicians use EHRs, the benefits touted by early adopters have shifted to complaints about their utility as an aid to practice. New terms, such as "good health IT" and "bad health IT" have been injected into the fermenting discussion about the utility of these systems to aid individual care. The degree to which EHRs and health IT in general provide "a good

user experience, enhances cognitive function, puts essential information as effortlessly as possible into the physician's hands, can be easily, substantively, and cost-effectively customized to the needs of medical specialists and subspecialists, keeps eHealth information secure, protects patient privacy, and facilitates better practice of medicine and better outcomes" makes it good health IT (Silverstein, 2014). Public health needs to alter that definition to include population-based purposes of the data (i.e., facilitating better practice of medicine). Health IT and EHRs have been designed around supporting care and health care finance. We must ask, can EHR data be viewed as useful beyond serving the care of individuals, and can these data be used to promote population health?

Contributing to population health requires that the EHR data cover an entire population, definable subpopulations, or representative samples of populations (Friedman et al., 2013). In addition to these basic requirements, we would want EHR data to have standardized measures for disease, condition, and functional status.

Passage of the Patient Protection and Affordable Care Act incentivizes prevention and population-type thinking among health care provider organizations. Will they use their EHR data to understand the dynamics of their patient populations? Almost assuredly, the answer is yes. Will they join with public health to understand population-level health dynamics? That remains an open question in many jurisdictions. Will EHRs contribute to building comprehensive and accurate patient problem lists that can be linked over time, and even aggregated for populations and subpopulations? To realize the potential

for EHRs to inform incidence and prevalence of many diseases, and very importantly among them chronic diseases, public health and primary care practitioners must join forces to ask the questions that these data should inform. A new public health and health care partnership needs to form. Working together, we must succeed to the greatest degree possible in translating person-centered data into population-based information.

REFERENCES

Institute of Medicine. Capturing Social and Behavioral Domains in Electronic Health Records: Phase 1. pp. 136. Washington, DC: Institute of Medicine, 2014.

Friedman DJ, Parrish RG, Ross DA. Electronic health records and US public health: current realities and future promise. Am J Public Health 2013; 03(9): 1560–1567. doi:10.2105/AJPH.2013.301220

Hsiao CJ, Hing E. Use and characteristics of electronic health record systems among office-based physician practices: United States, 2001–2013. NCHS Data Brief 2014 Jan; (143): 1–8.

McDonald CJ, Tang PC, Hripcsak G. Electronic health records systems. In EH Shortliffe & JJ Cimino (Eds.), Biomedical Informatics: Computer Applications In Health Care And Biomedicine, 4th ed. New York: Springer, 2013.

McGinnis JM, Foege WH. Actual causes of death in the United States. JAMA 1993; 270(18): 2207–2212.

U.S. Department of Health and Human Services. Meaningful Use Criteria and How to Attain Meaningful Use of EHRs. (2014 Jul 16). Accessed Jul 16, 2014, from http://www.healthit.gov/providers-professionals/how-attain-meaningful-use

Silverstein S. Contemporary Issues in Medical Informatics: Good Health IT, Bad Health IT, and Common Examples of Healthcare IT Difficulties. 2014. Accessed April 14, 2014 from http://listserv/cci.drexel.edu/faculty/silverstein/cases/

Public and Population Health IT in the Age of EHRs and the ACA: Expert Perspectives on Current Trends

JOHN W. LOONSK

OVERVIEW

The rapid adoption of electronic health records (EHRs) (Charles et al., 2014) is making clinical care data more accessible for population health purposes (see definition of "population health" later). Regulatory changes and new provider payment methodologies are also expanding interest in managing populations of patients in clinical care organizations. Chronic disease management, "hot spotting" of high utilizers of care, risk segmentation, and predictive analytics are developing population health activities near the point of care at which there is ready access to data. At the same time, state and local health departments, which have historically supported many population health activities, are hard pressed to match the recent technology investment in clinical care and, at times, face challenges in accessing the data they need, even though access is frequently required by state laws.

In this environment, in December 2013 the de Beaumont Foundation convened more than 40 experts in public health, clinical care and informatics policy, and health information technology (HIT) to discuss these developing trends and make suggestions about strategies for moving forward. This essay describes the perspectives of the participants in this convening and expresses concepts for the future.

CONTEXT FOR TERMINOLOGY USED

In the context of the rapidly developing HIT and growth in population health areas and in the context of the sometimes different perspectives held by clinical care and health departments, it is critical to have a shared definition of commonly used terms. For the purpose of the convening, the participants agreed to use the following terms as described.

Electronic health records are software programs that principally focus on supporting providers in treating patients for episodes of care. They have a direct provider interface, record and communicate patient data, function as a medicolegal record, and support reimbursement.

"**Population health**" is a broad term that relates to "the health outcomes of a group of individuals, including the distribution of such outcomes within the group" (Kindig & Stoddart, 2008). The "populations" might be defined by jurisdictions, health care organizations, or a wide variety of other distinguishing attributes.

"**Population health management**" is a name for population health activities in and around clinical care that have been driven by the availability of EHR data, the Patient Protection and Affordable Care Act (ACA), and new payment methodologies. Emanating from clinical care, its emphasis has been on risk segmentation, efficiency, and quality of care for clinical populations. These populations are frequently defined by a patient list or a subpopulation of high resource utilizers.

"**Public health**" is, in the context of the convening described earlier, associated with population health programs and activities emanating from health departments. As such, public health is a funding orientation and a perspective that is frequently related to jurisdictional populations and data. Public health is advanced by health departments and some federal agencies, but may be carried out in clinical care environments or elsewhere. State law frequently provides a direct regulatory basis for public health activities.

"**HITECH**" is the Health Information Technology for Economic and Clinical Health Act of 2009, which provides the U.S. Department of Health and Human Services (DHHS) with the authority to establish programs to improve health care quality, safety, and efficiency through the promotion of health IT. It is the conduit for what is now more than $26 billion in public funds paid to hospitals and community health care providers to implement EHRs.

"**Meaningful Use**" is both a term and a process that originated in the HITECH legislation. The term stipulates that those who receive HITECH funds will need to "meaningfully use" the implemented EHRs. DHHS and its advisory committees have subsequently developed specific criteria to define several stages of a Meaningful Use process. The completion of Meaningful Use criteria is necessary to receive HITECH funds.

"**Health Information Exchange**" is used as a verb to describe the activity of exchanging health information between participant organizations and/or the software systems used by the organizations. "**Health Information Exchange Organizations**" are entities that were created, or principally function, to exchange health information.

"**Genomic data**" refers to DNA sequence and other related genetic information that are increasingly useful in understanding individual susceptibility to conditions and in tailoring precise treatment and care.

IDENTIFIED CHALLENGES AND TRENDS

Long-standing patient privacy concerns and reduced funding for government public health as well as changes in clinical care represent challenges to cohesive nationwide population health. Many of the challenges to the use of electronic health data by health departments relate to accessing comparable data by individuals who are pursuing public health activities. Sending or reporting data to health departments is one approach, but having health department personnel directly access data in clinical care settings is another. Some of the challenges and the trends identified in the convening can be categorized as follows:

Essay II

Accessing Electronic Clinical Care Data

Increasing amounts of electronic clinical care data could be available for direct access, but issues of privacy, scalability, data comparability, and query support are significant obstacles. Electronic health data are accumulating rapidly in health system data warehouses, in some EHR vendor organizations, and in some outsourced population health management services. Patient-linked health data and data query tools are currently getting the greatest attention in clinical care organizations in which data access is relatively straightforward. Direct clinical care data access by health department personnel is limited except in some ad hoc emergency investigations, disease-specific areas, and regulation-supported quarantine efforts. Clinical data organized in EHRs are not always well understood by health department personnel who do gain access. Accountable care organizations (ACOs) may provide easier direct access than EHRs alone, but public health needs to undertake the following to access and best use data: 1) Understand how ACOs are themselves leveraging patient-linked data, 2) get training in retrieval and data analytic tools, and 3) work though authorization and access roles for direct data access.

Genomic data to support personalized health care are also accumulating rapidly in clinical care. These data are appealing for public health purposes as well. Data about social determinants of health, however, that are important to public health are not routinely recorded in the process of care. Public health has had a limited ability to induce the recording of these non–care-specific public health data into EHRs. Vendors cite EHR structure, workflows, provider resistance, and the cost of changing their programs as reasons for not including more such data.

Reporting Data from Clinical Care to Health Departments

Challenges exist for health departments trying to gain access to operational data and systems inside of clinical care. Moreover the traditional alternative of "reporting" data to a health department also takes on new complexities when both sides are using electronic information systems. Public health is always under pressure to optimize the use of pre-existing clinical care data and to minimize the reporting burden on providers of care, but the advent of EHRs has made even basic public health reporting more complicated. Historically, EHRs have not used standards to facilitate interoperability and health information exchange. Electronic reporting that does exist must frequently be initiated when a provider recognizes the reportability of a condition and can navigate reporting variations in state and local health departments. Manually initiated reporting also tends to not be timely enough for some public health needs.

And, specifically, the core public health function of "case reporting" has not been automated, to date, through the HITECH Meaningful Use process. One reason is that there are usually more than 90 conditions that are required by state laws. Additionally, what is specifically required can differ in different jurisdictions. Different state reporting laws define differently when health departments will get data and what data they will get.

As another example, immunization reporting is a well-recognized and valued public health function. However, reporting immunization data to states though Meaningful Use demonstrated the excruciating specificity and consistency needed to report from the many different EHR systems to the many different jurisdictions. Meaningful Use criteria have advanced the domains of cancer,

lab results, and syndromic surveillance in addition to immunizations. However, Meaningful Use measures for any public health domain have consistently been the least chosen measures by providers seeking these incentive funds, according to reports from the Centers for Medicare and Medicaid Services (Center for Medicare and Medicaid Services, 2014). Questions remain about what would be the most effective incentives to advance data sharing for public health purposes.

Public health is being pushed to make reporting more consistent and to use standard terminologies, data exchange messages, and transactions. Defining standards (semantic, vocabulary, transport, etc.) that make data exchange possible is a labor intensive and slow process that is difficult for states to support. Little to no funding has been provided to public health agencies to support their involvement in these activities from a standards or infrastructure implementation perspective.

Shared, cloud-based, technology platforms may offer a new approach to managing and supporting technology for health departments. The Public Health Community Platform, which is run by the Association of State and Territorial Health Officers, is a developing example. It may offer opportunities for the sharing of public health applications while retaining jurisdictional data ownership. Nonetheless, significant work remains to implement shared infrastructure and to break down individual jurisdictional and program funding silos that sometimes preclude sharing of investment and infrastructure.

In some circumstances, HIEOs have facilitated information exchange with health departments and reporting is supported in this way. Ongoing concerns about sustainability of health information exchange organizations continue, however, and experts at the convening were evenly divided over whether this is a potential path forward.

"Private" health information exchanges inside of ACOs or health system boundaries are developing to foster clinical care data needs, but because they are not focused on extra-organizational exchange, they do not connect to health department infrastructure.

For clinical care purposes, it is anticipated that health reform and market-based incentives will advance health information exchange. However, these business of care–related incentives, while increasingly aligned for clinical care, are not aligned with public health exchange needs.

Providing Public Health Information in Clinical Care

Public health can affect clinical care outcomes by promoting prevention activities and guideline adherence to providers, patients, and the healthy well. Unfortunately, distributing such guidelines through many different EHRs is difficult because of a lack of standards. Such information delivery also must battle provider "alert fatigue" and other resistance to use. Currently, guideline tools used in clinical care are generally commercially produced adjunct systems rather than health department services, and the separation of many public health and clinical care prevention activities is likely to continue.

Public Health and Population Health Management: Rationalizing the Overlap

For some time, population health management will likely focus on the ~5% of the patients that use 50% to 80% of health care resources and on the patient populations defined by particular ACOs and health systems. Initially, much of the focus will continue to be on risk stratification and not on applications to manage identified populations

at risk. Almost by definition, these patient populations do not include people for whom health disparities identify challenges to ready access to care. Being care oriented, they have not historically stressed the social determinants of health or upstream factors that can be key to prevention.

For its part, public health will need to play an ongoing role in generating denominator data for measuring health progress. Public health itself will continue to have disparate surveillance systems as well as inadequate resources and expertise to develop robust interoperable data systems. What is more, some registries and surveillance systems will continue to develop differently in different locales. The term "registry" itself is so loosely defined that it includes systems in clinical care, health departments, specialty organizations, and, at times, federal agencies. Even if these systems have shared data and technology needs, it is difficult to identify commonalties across different functions and organizations. The lack of coordination will challenge the advancement of both chronic and infectious disease programs.

With all of these difficulties, public health agencies are interested in creating health department–clinical care partnerships that enable population health action. Public health can provide population health and prevention expertise, epidemiologic services, jurisdiction-wide insight, and governmental leverage. Clinical care and population health management can provide ready access to data and increasing support for population health goals that align with health care business needs. The technology infrastructures for clinical population health management and public health do seem to share many needs, even though they may be organizationally separated.

Opportunities exist for data access in developing all-payer and other regional or state-wide data stores, to which public health and population health management can have common access. Many of these data repositories started with claims data but are now adding discharge summaries and other clinical data. As data warehouses that frequently receive batches of irregular data, they are not useful for case management or active surveillance, but they may be a starting point for better accumulations of broader population, if not full jurisdictional, data.

STRATEGY AND APPROACHES

Many strategies were discussed at the convening to break though some of the existing issues. One thrust was for public health to demonstrate value to ACOs and other clinical organizations. Others suggested novel approaches to accessing clinical care data. Some sought to break through the "siloed" funding of public health programs to express a more coordinated interface with clinical care.

As an example, public health departments can work with hospitals in their communities to develop effective, integrated community health needs assessments, as is required for nonprofits in the ACA. This would benefit hospitals, as it would support them in developing their individual community health needs assessments. It would reduce duplication of effort and demonstrate the value of public health data and expertise. The support of these efforts might even become a viable source of funding. It was also thought that developing business proposals for the use of public health departments to promote collaboration between ACOs and public health would be helpful. The proposals could document the benefits and savings that the ACOs, Federally Qualified Health Centers and others could realize by leveraging public health expertise and resources.

The use of automated, standards-based methods for case reporting of reportable conditions is clearly needed. Public health case report data can be sent from clinical EHRs and consumed by state surveillance systems. Toward this goal, it would be useful to identify and document the experience of public health organizations that have direct access to EHRs. Access should include individual and aggregate approaches and access for a variety of different purposes, such as investigations, population health, and surveillance. Data are critical for many purposes, such as monitoring the progression of specific influenza strains and guiding prevention and antiviral treatment strategies.

Another innovative approach involves working with EHR vendors to demonstrate and document how role-based access can be used to allow entree to EHRs by public health. Access to EHRs has been granted in limited circumstances during outbreaks, but it would be possible to restrict access to patient names and other sensitive information on a routine basis, while still allowing health departments direct access to needed data.

Work still needs to be done with federal agencies and other funders to better incorporate requirements for IT infrastructure as part of the grants and cooperative agreements. Although there has been progress, obstacles still exist to supporting ongoing, cross-cutting, technical infrastructure through condition-specific funding and grants.

Public health departments have significant work to do to catch up to the major new investment in clinical care IT infrastructure. New and better integrated funding streams are needed for investment in health department health IT. The support and placement of high-level informatics leadership in health departments also needs to be considered.

This time of great change in clinical care and health IT presents a rare opportunity for public health to come together with clinicians and health care delivery organizations to collaborate and share data and resources for population health. Building relationships to foster this collaboration will be a critical factor for success. To do so, both public health and clinical care will need to put aside some old ways of doing business, broaden the perspective on their roles, and deepen their population health informatics focus, expertise, and resources.

REFERENCES

Centers for Medicare and Medicaid Services: 2014 Definition Stage 1 of Meaningful Use. 2014, Available at: http://www.cms.gov/ Regulations-and-Guidance/Legislation/ EHRIncentivePrograms/Meaningful_Use.html

Charles D, Gabriel M, Furukawa MF. Adoption of Electronic Health Record Systems among U.S. Non-federal Acute Care Hospitals: 2008–2013. Office of the Coordinator for Information Health and Technology, ONC Data Brief, No. 16, May 2014.

Kindig D, Stoddart G. What is population health? Am J Public Health 2003; 93(3): 380–383.

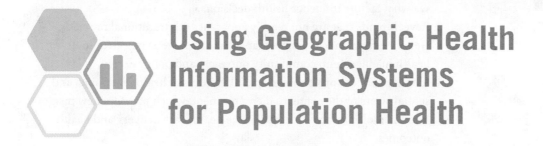

Using Geographic Health Information Systems for Population Health

JOSHUA L. TOOTOO, BRIAN C. CASTRUCCI, PAMELA MAXSON, MICHELE CASPER, AND MARIE LYNN MIRANDA

WHAT ARE GEOGRAPHIC HEALTH INFORMATION SYSTEMS?

GIS or GHIS?

Techniques based on geographic information systems (GIS) have been historically grounded in fields related to environmental sciences. Because these same techniques are widely adopted and applied in health-focused fields, it is useful to make the distinction between GIS (an abbreviation used elsewhere in this book) and GHIS, or geographic health information systems. A GHIS links health system and social and environmental data via shared geography to provide a multidimensional understanding of individual and community health status and vulnerabilities.

Geographic health information systems are computer-based systems that allow users to capture, store, analyze, and display/map geographically referenced data. Health data (e.g., disease registries, vital records, electronic health records [EHRs]) can be linked to social and environmental data via shared geography, which improves the understanding of community health strengths and vulnerabilities and allows for better design of health-promoting interventions (Miranda et al., 2013).

The use of GHIS elucidates complex relationships among different health information categories, connects individual patient records to social and environmental datasets (e.g., census, crime, business data), and addresses how the social and environmental context of each patient influences health outcomes. Using GIS software allows users to explore and overlay data by location, generating clear and accessible maps that can serve as powerful tools for understanding and improving community health.

GHIS helps us to:

1. Understand why health outcomes manifest in particular patterns and to see what factors influence health decisions.
2. Reveal trends that are not readily apparent with traditional methods.
3. Generate clear and accessible maps that can serve as powerful tools for health management, community outreach, and policy design.
4. Identify connections between spatial patterns of health endpoints and spatial layers of the contextual environment, which provides new insights into the multiple factors the influence health care delivery and health outcomes.

The principles for integration of public health and primary care medicine put forth by the Institute of Medicine are facilitated through GHIS. The underlying motivation of GHIS is to improve population health through community-clinical linkages. The visualization of health and contextual issues can engage the community in a way that tabular data typically cannot. Community, health, and social data are combined, leveraging and strengthening partnerships by explicitly incorporating a broad range of factors deemed important. Once the data architecture is built, GHIS is sustainable because data updates are incremental.

HOW CAN YOU USE GHIS MAPS?

Although maps can be visually appealing, a good map is much more than a pretty image. Employing GHIS allows users to overlay data of interest with geographic data. Good maps create opportunities to visualize patterns, relationships, and trends in data that would otherwise not be apparent. The following specific examples show how GHIS maps are being used in a variety of settings.

Using GHIS for Clinical–Community Linkages

Although data about community health needs have been available for many years, the format in which the data have been present has not always been easy to use. The data have typically been presented numerically, and a large volume of numerical data makes identification of trends difficult. With the ability to overlay numeric data onto a map, thereby combining a large amount of data into a succinct visual display, primary care providers can use maps to better understand the importance of social and environmental factors for health outcomes in the communities they serve. Maps created with GHIS also clarify gaps in access to care services and resources and make community risk factors explicit.

Carolinas HealthCare System has developed the Multiple Attribute Primary Care Targeting Strategy. The health care system has applied this model with some success to the planning of health services delivery and also to targeting and evaluating interventions designed to improve health access (Dunlin et al., 2010).

An example of GHIS mapping using the Multiple Attribute Primary Care Targeting Strategy, Figure 24-1 shows multiple neighborhood-level attributes used to assess primary care needs for Mecklenburg County, North Carolina. The attributes used in this analysis (socioeconomic status, population density, insurance status, and emergency department and primary care safety-net utilization) were identified by a collaborative partnership within a practice-based research network, and maps were created using these individual datasets as overlays.

Public Health and GHIS

Increasingly, local and state health departments are using GHIS maps for community outreach, for policy design, and for the planning, implementation, and evaluation of various interventions.

The Alameda County Department of Public Health in California has used maps as a starting point for understanding emergency department (ED) utilization for conditions that are treatable in primary care settings. Figure 24-2 shows the percentage of ED visits, grouped by census tract, that were either nonemergent or could have been treated in primary care clinics. The darker the color value, the higher the proportion of cases in that census tract that ideally should not have resulted in an ED visit. These maps may be used to plan the sites of new clinics, to improve accessibility to existing clinics, and to market the clinic sites to target populations (Williams et al., 2011). Figure 24-2 illustrates how individual-level data can be used to create maps that highlight needs of the community related to public health or health care services they receive.

The chronic disease service of the Oklahoma State Department of Health is using GHIS to determine how to prioritize the delivery and types of interventions across the state (Children's Environmental Health Initiative, 2014). The health department was interested in the proximity of Oklahomans to either a rural health clinic (RHC) or federally qualified health center (FQHC). Using network analysis, the health department identified all geographic areas that were within a 30-minute drive of one of these types of clinics. Figure 24-3 shows the 30-minute drive-time areas around RHCs (mapped as squares) and FQHCs (mapped as circles). Combining the network analysis with Census 2010 data revealed that approximately 70% and 42% of the state's population are within a 30-minute drive of an FQHC or RHC, respectively. However, there are populations that are not within a 30-minute drive, particularly in the western and northwestern parts of the state.

Using GHIS for Clinical and Public Health Integration Projects

When primary care clinicians and local/state health departments are able to partner and collaborate, improved community health outcomes often

Figure 24-1 ▶

Use of GIS by Carolinas HealthCare System for Multiple Attribute Primary Care Targeting Program, Mecklenburg County, North Carolina.

(From Dulin MF, Ludden TM, Tapp H, Blackwell J, de Hernandez BU, Smith HA, Furuseth OJ. Using Geographic Information Systems (GIS) to understand a community's primary care needs. J Am Board Fam Med 2010; 23: 13–21. http://intl.jabfm.org/content/23/1/13.short. Used with permission.)

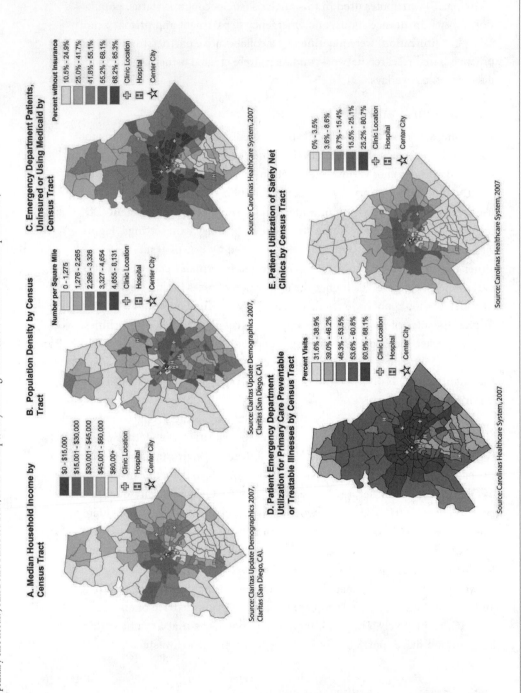

result, and GHIS can aid that collaboration. Primary care has access to large datasets of patient health data that could be a starting point for collaborating, including from clinics and acute care facilities; hospitalization information, and ambulance run data. Health departments can help local clinicians better understand the data they need. Relevant contextual data for understanding the health and behavioral choices of patient populations include the location of, for example, sidewalks, parks, community centers, liquor stores, schools, pharmacies, grocery stores, churches, fast-food outlets, dilapidated housing, housing code violations, or crime. Local health departments can work with primary care providers to feed that information back to EHR vendors, who

Figure 24-2 ▼

Alameda County, California, emergency department mapping project.

(From Williams M, Dubowitz, T, Jacobson, D. Mapping the Gaps: Ideas for Using GIS to Enhance Local Health Department Priority Setting and Program Planning. Santa Monica, CA: RAND, 2011. Used with permission.)

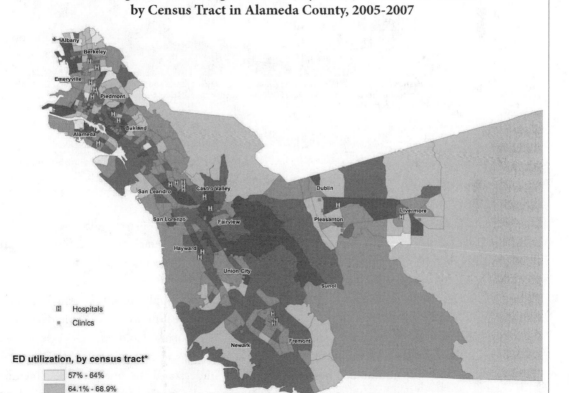

Percentage of Non-Emergent or Primary-Care-Treatable ED Visits, by Census Tract in Alameda County, 2005-2007

ED utilization, by census tract*

	57% - 64%
	64.1% - 68.9%
	69% - 71.8%
	71.9% - 74.7%
	74.8% - 79.4%

*Non-emergent or primary care treatable ED visits as a percentage of all ED visits.
RAND *TR1146-5.2*

Figure 24-3 ▼

Oklahoma State Department of Health project to identify locations for interventions.

(From Children's Environmental Health Initiative (CEHI). Mapping Heart Disease, Stroke and Other Chronic Diseases: A Program to Enhance GIS Capacity within State Health Departments. http://cehi.snre.umich.edu/sites/default/files/Phase5_HL_060914_web.pdf. Published May 01, 2014. Accessed May 22, 2014. Used with permission.)

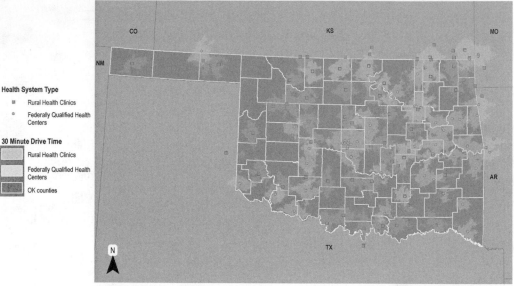

Geographic Accessibility of Primary Care Services for Oklahomans

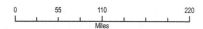

Data Source: Health Care Information (November 2013 Oklahoma FQHCs and 2013 Rural Health Clinics), Centers for Disease Control and Prevention (2012 FQHCs in bordering states), OSDH Geodatabase, ArcGIS Online, and the ESRI 9.1 Network Dataset.

Chronic Disease Service
Prevention and Preparedness Services
Oklahoma State Department of Health

would produce maps in an iterative loop that includes input from clinicians. Primary care and public health partners can work together to conduct focus groups and community surveys.

Kaiser Permanente (KP) has been applying GHIS and map-based visualizations to its EHRs in concert with publicly available datasets for seven KP regions in eight states (California, Colorado, Georgia, Hawaii, Maryland, Oregon, Virginia, and Washington) and the District of Columbia. These maps help KP understand the needs of their members within the social and environmental context of the communities where they live (Clift et al., 2014). Figure 24-4 shows the spatial relationship between child and adult obesity rates and educational attainment in the Los Angeles area.

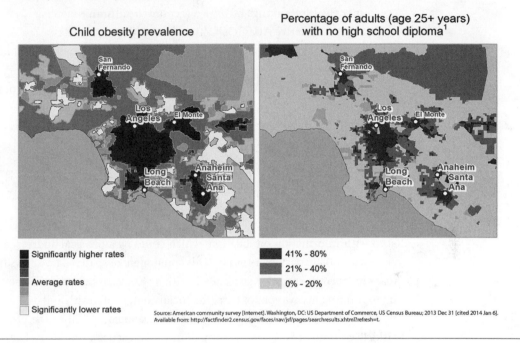

Figure 24-4 ▼

Comparison of education level for the overall population and health outcomes for Kaiser Permanente members across Los Angeles, CA.

(From Clift K, Scott L, Johnson M, Gonzalez C. Leveraging geographic information systems in an integrated health care delivery organization. Perm J 2014; 18(2): 71–75. http://www.thepermanentejournal.org/files/Spring2014/ACA-GIS-KP.pdf. Used with permission.)

CREATING GHIS MAPS

To make your own maps, you will need software tools, spatial data, and time. The initial investment for all of these components may seem daunting, but the rewards can be substantial. In addition, consider partnering with your city planners or public health departments, who may already have this expertise.

Tools

To create your own maps you will need GIS software. A number of proprietary and open-source options are available and are configured for both desktop and web-based use.

In selecting either proprietary or open-source desktop GIS software, look for products that are well-documented, have established user bases, and offer options for training and support.

A growing number of web-based interactive GHIS sites enable health professionals to create health-related maps at various geographic scales and to access related sociodemographic information for each community. A few sites that provide nationwide data include the following:

Interactive Atlas of Heart Disease and Stroke, CDC http://nccd.cdc.gov/dhdspatlas/

County Health Rankings http://www.countyhealthrankings.org/

Diabetes Interactive Atlas, CDC http://www.cdc.gov/diabetes/atlas/

Community Commons: Maps and Data http://www.communitycommons.org/maps-data/

National Center for HIV/AIDS, Viral Hepatitis, STD and TB Prevention Atlas, CDC http://www.cdc.gov/nchhstp/atlas/

Social Vulnerability Index, CDC http://svi.cdc.gov/

US Health Map http://www.healthdata.org/data-visualization/us-health-map

Data

A GHIS is driven by spatial data. This means that data used to create maps start with information on location, which could be a physical address, a ZIP code, a school district, or a county. This component of spatial data allows them to be mapped in space, or geo-coded, with a variety of reference datasets. By incorporating many types of data, the social context of health and disease can be addressed. Understanding the resources available as well as the potential risks (e.g., limited access to healthy food and presence of industrial sites) of a particular geographic locale can give a more robust picture of individual, community, and public health. Data sources that can be displayed geographically may include social, economic, crime, education, business, and green space data.

You may already have access to spatial data; here are some common data sources well suited for geo-referencing:

- Electronic health records
- Reports of individual case and epidemic investigations
- Mortality data, such as vital statistics
- Hospital discharge data
- Surveys of health and general populations
- Data on disease indicators, such as information on animal reservoirs and vectors, animal morbidity, environmental data, or drug/biologic utilization
- Student and employee data, such as absentee reports or workers' compensation claims

1. Getting started making maps can be challenging. Some initial training can be extremely helpful. Online training content is available at https://practicalplaybook.org/tool/cdc-gis-training. The National Center for Geospatial Medicine at the Rice University also offers a series of courses, funded by the Centers for Disease Control and Prevention. Contact: cehi.rice.edu.

2. Becoming part of a community of GHIS users will also be very helpful. Make a point of connecting with other GHIS users, as there are many opportunities to learn from the experience of others. You can find a series of individuals from across the United States at the CDC's Chronic Disease GIS Exchange website http://www.cdc.gov/dhdsp/maps/gisx/. The Chronic Disease GIS Exchange website also hosts a large number of GIS maps that may spur your own creativity in thinking about how to use GIS to advance the health mission of your own organization.

3. Enlist community buy-in for how you gather and use the data. Avoid sharing data without respecting the needs and wishes of the community itself. When mapping unhealthy outcomes in low-income or underserved neighborhoods, be sure to also map the good things that are happening in the community, such as churches and co-operative gardens. When analyzing and geomapping community data, enlist community members in helping to determine whether observed patterns are consistent with community members' lived experience.

4. You can drown in the available data, so it's important to identify the first-priority data needed to create a useful GHIS project and map. Be specific about the metrics you want to track. Claims datasets, for example, are truncated, and are therefore incomplete. It's better to use EHR datasets, which are much larger and more complete. However, do not make the mistake of assuming that EHR data represent community data. EHRs alone do not constitute a community.

5. The potential of GHIS can be fully realized only if local health providers and public health organizations are willing and technologically prepared to participate in the hard work of developing operational health information exchanges.

6. If your organization does not have the time or capacity to learn GIS, consider whether there are others with whom you might partner. Some state and local health departments have this capacity and may be able to help support your efforts. Almost every academic institution has some GIS capacity and thus could serve as an additional local resource/partner.

7. Remember that maps are visual representations of data and often can show associations. They do not, however, prove causality, and care should be taken in appropriately interpreting the information conveyed in GIS map products.

8. When presenting any maps or other visualizations from GHIS in public settings, care must be taken to ensure that no protected information is presented. Providers and researchers are accustomed to thinking about protecting medical record data, but specialized training in confidentiality considerations in map graphics is necessary.

REFERENCES

Children's Environmental Health Initiative. Mapping Heart Disease, Stroke and Other Chronic Diseases: A Program to Enhance GIS Capacity within State Health Departments. Published and approved May 01, 2014. Available at: http://cehi.snre.umich.edu/sites/default/files/Phase5_HL_060914_web.pdf. Accessed May 22, 2014.

Clift K, Scott L, Johnson M, Gonzalez C. Leveraging geographic information systems in an integrated health care delivery organization. Perm J 2014; 18(2): 71–75. Available at: http://www.thepermanentejournal.org/files/Spring2014/ACA-GIS-KP.pdf

Dulin MF, Ludden TM, Tapp H, Blackwell J, de Hernandez BU, Smith HA, Furuseth OJ. Using geographic information systems (GIS) to understand a community's primary care needs. J Am Board Fam Med 2010; 23: 13–21. Available at: http://intl.jabfm.org/content/23/1/13.short

Miranda ML, Casper M, Tootoo J, Schieb L. Putting chronic disease on the map: building gis capacity in state and local health departments. Prev Chronic Dis 2013; 10: E100. Available at: http://www.cdc.gov/pcd/issues/2013/12_0321.htm

Miranda ML, Ferranti J, Strauss B, Neelon B, Califf RM. Geographic health information systems: A platform for supporting the "triple aim." Health Aff (Millwood) 2013; 32(9): 1608–1615. PMID: 24019366. Available at: http://content.healthaffairs.org/content/32/9/1608

Williams M, Dubowitz, T, Jacobson, D. Mapping the Gaps: Ideas for Using GIS to Enhance Local Health Department Priority Setting and Program Planning. Santa Monica, CA: RAND Corporation, 2011. Available at: http://www.rand.org/pubs/technical_reports/TR1146.html

Shared Space: Using Geography to Identify Relationships and Increase Understanding in Primary Care and Public Health

ROBERT L. PHILLIPS, JR AND ANDREW BAZEMORE

Although Curtis Hames's Evans County Heart Study produced more than 560 publications, one of his most important innovations was the use of geography to study the population he served and to better understand the social and environmental milieu influencing their health (McDonough et al., 1963). Friends of Hames, who led the study, describe one such map made up of photographs taken from a hot air balloon. Such were the tools available nearly 60 years ago to primary care providers hoping to understand context in caring for their patients.

Forty years ago, one of the first family medicine departments in the country began organizing patient charts by family and by geography as a means of organizing practice data and assessing health risk (Farley, 1977). This data organization scheme allowed them to look at their practice population geographically and gave them a community vital sign with which to better treat their patients during clinical visits.

Today, geographic information systems (GIS) have advanced to a stage that allows public health and primary care providers to channel these innovative dreams of the past into powerful implements for nearly every clinic and community. These tools are capable of producing maps that reveal patterns and rivet attention by contextualizing statistics in place. But, they are capable of so much more than mapmaking. Geographic information systems tools connect data that would not otherwise be relatable, increasing the value of the data manyfold by enriching their ability to inform population-level analyses and even clinical care. These tools identify relationships and increase understanding through data connections. There is a real opportunity for public health, and specifically local health departments, to partner with primary care providers in using GIS to turn clinical data into population health tools. It could be a boon to both primary care and public health.

Georgia's initiative to improve infant mortality is a relevant and brilliant example of the use of geospatial tools and available data to target public and clinical health interventions and improve outcomes (Chapple-McGruder et al., 2012). In 2006, the infant mortality rate in Georgia was 8.4 deaths per 1,000 live births, nearly 20% higher than the national average. The Georgia Department of Public Health (DPH) used geospatial tools to identify geographical clusters of infant deaths that were stable over time in order to target interventions in those areas (Figure 24E-1). They identified six clusters with infant mortality rates as high as 17.5 deaths per 1,000 live births. By examining infant deaths in these areas in greater detail, the Georgia DPH determined the leading causes of infant death and implemented targeted interventions after developing strategies through partnership with communities, clinicians, public health, and specialty organizations. The partnership was greatly aided by sharing the clustering maps and data in information-sharing meetings in areas that had high infant mortality. During each meeting, participants assessed community needs and looked at interventions currently in place to determine which ones were working and which ones were not. The mapped data facilitated community engagement, galvanizing a need for action, getting community input on strategies that might work locally, and focusing resources. While it is unclear how much of a role this effort played in improvement, within 5 years, statewide infant mortality dropped nearly 20% (8.4 to 6.8 per 1,000 live births).

Georgia is just one brilliant example, and geospatial tools have many other roles to play in connecting, analyzing, and representing data to provide new information, guide action, and galvanize collaboration. We offer other ways that these tools can aid identification of relationships and improve understanding, especially for primary care and public health.

DEFINING AND CHARACTERIZING COMMUNITY

Another 60-year-old innovation, community-oriented primary care (COPC), is a systematic approach to identify and address factors that affect health in the community. It blends the fundamentals of public health and primary care, and begins with two difficult steps: community definition and characterization. Modern GIS enhances COPC, allowing providers to "retrofit" their clinical data to create a health care service area and then to draw on other data linked to that geography to characterize the population living there.(Mullan et al., 2004). Census data, for example, can be used to explore clusters of social determinants influencing patients' health within a clinic's service area (Comer et al., 2011). Clearing these two important hurdles can put clinics on the path to engaging their defined community in developing solutions. In fact, this 60-year-old innovation is very similar to how Georgia addressed infant mortality.

This process of geographic retrofitting patient data has been expanded to help identify holes in the nation's health care safety net writ large. The Uniform Data System (UDS) Mapper uses reporting data from more than 8,000 community health centers serving 20 million patients to define the service area for each federally funded community health center in the country (www.udsmapper. org). It also draws on population data to characterize the proportion of people eligible for their services who are using their services in order to estimate remaining need. It has also been used to identify pockets of uninsurance where Medicaid expansion and health insurance exchanges could

Figure 24E-1 ▼

Georgia's geographic clusters of high infant mortality rates.

(From Chapple-McGruder T, Zhou Y, Castrucci B. From Preconception to Infant Protection. Atlanta, Georgia Department of Public Health, 2012. Used with permission.)

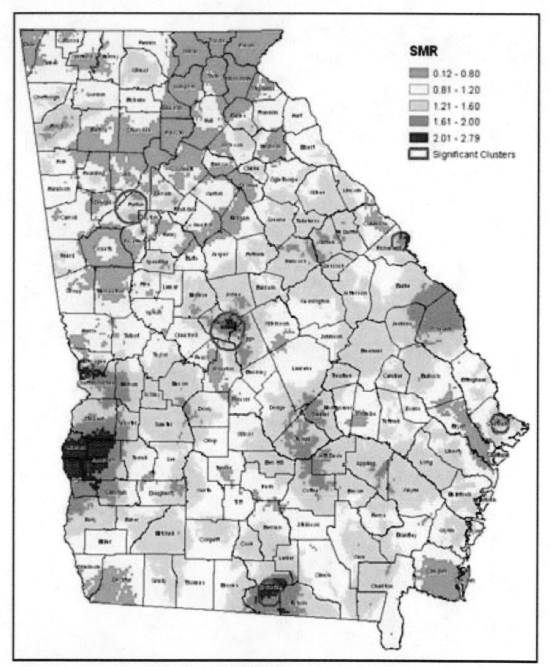

Reference: Chapple-McGruder T, Ammons K, Zhou Y, Freymann G, Weldon A, Csukas S, Castrucci B.*Using Data to Actualize Efforts to Reduce Infant Mortality Rates for Georgia.* Atlanta, GA: Georgia Department of Public Health. 2012.

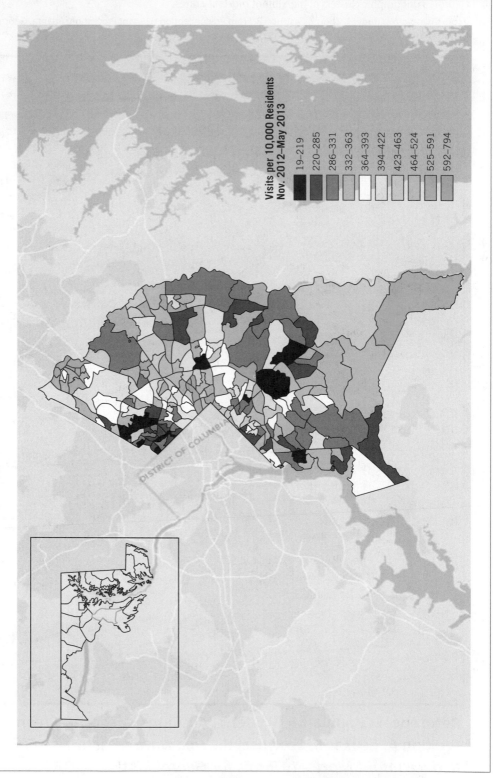

Figure 24E-2 ▼

Prince George County, Maryland, Inpatient Utilization, 2014.

(Map produced from the Maryland SHIP tool mentioned in the text of the chapter: State Health Improvement Process (SHIP) at http://dhmh.maryland.gov/ship/)

Visits per 10,000 Residents
Nov. 2012–May 2013

19–219
220–285
286–331
332–363
364–393
394–422
423–463
464–524
525–591
592–794

DISTRICT OF COLUMBIA

increase need for safety net services. The recent development of a curriculum for COPC around the UDS Mapper presents an opportunity to expand its use and utility by medical educators and students (The Robert Graham Center, 2013).

The community orientation of COPC can be paired with GIS to advance understanding and identify relationships for hospitals, too. Thanks to the Patient Protection and Affordable Care Act (ACA), tax-exempt hospitals are now required to conduct community health needs assessments (CHNA) every 3 years, specifically to characterize the health needs of their communities, to act on them, and to measure the effects. As a first step, hospitals could tap into their wealth of patient data to identify service areas for inpatient and emergency services. They could pinpoint hotspots for high utilization and for specific outcomes, such as avoidable hospitalizations, readmissions, or other undesirable events. Seeing where these intersect with "coldspots" in population and public health data (i.e., areas of social deprivation, poverty, and predictors of poor health), could serve as the foundation for community partnership and effective use of the mandated community investment under CHNA process required by the ACA. Beyond looking at their own data, hospitals could partner with community health centers and other primary care providers to look at overlaps of their service areas to identify patterns of health and health outcomes that none of their individual data could identify alone. Hospitals could be a powerful partner in defining shared areas of service and characterizing the populations and problems within them. A nationally scaled GIS enterprise, like the UDS Mapper, that included data from a variety of settings could begin to more effectively deploy national, state, and local resources.

ASSESSING COMMUNITY NEEDS

We alluded to the new requirement for tax-exempt hospitals to conduct CHNAs, but there is a broader need and opportunity. Hospitals are not the only ones with this requirement; community health centers and public health departments also have assessment requirements. In most communities, these three do their assessments in parallel play. Actually, most hospitals choose to do theirs alone. Most hospitals routinely report ZIP code level patient data to the Healthcare Cost and Utilization Project. These data could be used to define the geography of key emergency and outpatient utilization and outcomes. The geographic representation of these data can then be overlapped with social determinant data, public health data, and clinical data to identify hotspots of need as well as the potential partnerships to address them. This is what Georgia did to resolve infant mortality disparities, and the tools can also be used for CHNAs.

INTEGRATING PRIMARY CARE AND PUBLIC HEALTH

The Institute of Medicine (IOM) report, *Primary Care and Public Health: Exploring Integration to Improve Population Health*, calls for a geospatial platform for combining clinical and public health datasets (IOM, 2012). First, it says,

"... data from clinical settings can be combined with geographical data to create maps that would illustrate the burden of disease by neighborhood. These maps could be used by primary care providers as well as public health professionals. Thus, to take one example, patterns of diabetes and poor control of the disease could be displayed on maps that could direct shared primary care and public health resources. These maps could then be tracked over time, making visible the efficacy of integrated primary care and public health efforts."

The IOM points to an opportunity for clinical data to inform and evaluate public health interventions. The Centers for Disease Control and Prevention (CDC) could support this effort through creating a platform for safely using clinical data in this way, and by deploying its epidemiologic resources to help make sense of them nationally and locally. The CDC typically steers clear of clinical services, but it could be a powerful partner in realizing the vision laid out by the IOM. The CDC has already developed a basic site for mapping community and social determinant data, the value of which could be greatly enhanced by supporting inclusion of clinical data, and even further by supporting cross-analysis of clinical and community data (Center for Applied Research and Environmental Systems, 2014). By bringing together their respective data and expertise, geospatial tools, and analytic capacity, the CDC, local health departments, and health services providers could turn clinical data into public health gold. The IOM also suggested that federal agencies could turn their public health information into tools for primary care:

"Currently, HRSA [Health Resources and Services Administration] and CDC have separate databases that hold information on cardiovascular health at the local, state, and national levels. While each of these databases is accessible to the public, they need to be coordinated to provide a comprehensive picture of the population's health with respect to cardiovascular disease. HRSA and CDC could develop new and perhaps standardized databases for joint use. They also could jointly create and utilize maps and geographic data that reflect the health status of the population and highlight the areas of greatest need."

Geospatial tools can enhance the utility of mostly dormant public data for local consumption. Communities and their clinicians could use these to better characterize their population needs and frame community solutions. It is worth noting that all these data are available right now. These tools exist. The IOM's recommendation calls on HRSA and CDC to partner in bringing the data and tools together for their own use, as well as locally, and thus to empower communities.

Like Georgia, the Maryland Department of Health and Mental Hygiene appreciates the value of mapped data to inform local improvement. Maryland recently launched the State Health Improvement Process (SHIP) at http://dhmh.maryland.gov/ship/. The goal of this data and mapping platform is to provide a framework of 41 population health measures for accountability, local action, public engagement, and health integration. The overall goal is to improve health and reduce disparities. The Maryland Department of Health and Mental Hygiene is using it to encourage the development of Local Health Improvement Coalitions, which are led by local health officers and provide a forum for county health departments, nonprofit hospitals, primary care, and community-based organizations to analyze and prioritize community health needs. Simultaneously, the health information exchange Chesapeake Regional Information System for our Patients is providing hospital and clinic patient data via reporting and mapping capabilities to support the community integrated medical home model that is core to the Maryland approach. Figure 24E-2 offers an example of mapping of inpatient visits per 10,000 patients by community in Prince George County. These two tools bring community and clinical data into a shared space to inform community and clinical health decisions.

FROM "GEOMAPPING" TO ASSESSING PERSONAL RISK: COMMUNITY VITAL SIGNS

A GIS can produce maps, but it can also be used to personalize health risks. Social determinants of health, violence, drug abuse, and many other neighborhood factors are highly correlated with personal health outcomes (Butler et al., 2012). Clinical data can locate people in their neighborhood and GIS tools can attach neighborhood characteristics to them. These can be used to analytically assess a person's risk of poor health outcomes, of using drugs, of being a victim of violence, or of dying prematurely. This leads to the opportunity to create a new vital sign, a community vital sign, that can become a focus of clinical and public health intervention at the individual level. The American Board of Family Medicine (ABFM) aims to help its physician-diplomates use their data in this fashion. The ABFM will develop population health maintenance of certification tools that allow physicians to map their service area, look at population health measure clusters within that area, and translate these into Community Vital Signs.

BACK TO THE FUTURE

The use of GIS tools to create personalized measures of risk with clinical utility brings us full circle to the pioneering work of Hames as well as that of Farley (1977). But what a difference 60 years makes: Modern GIS tools, electronic clinical data, more available public health data, and robust analytic computing make their efforts easier and more accessible, and heralds the potential availability of these tools to providers of health care and public health nationwide. These tools and resources make COPC possible, and the process could be extended to hospitals and public health departments. These tools could align CHNA requirements and make them more complete. They could inform national, local, clinical, and personal understanding and interventions. The best opportunity is for HRSA and the CDC to partner to make the tools and data more available. The HRSA is already investing in the UDS Mapper with health centers, but it has additional services and data that could be brought into the effort. The CDC oversees public health, but it is also working with many clinical and public health partners to create a framework and technical toolbox to support the community health improvement process and to align various CHNA efforts for greater impact on community health (CDC, 2014). Finally, the IOM specifically advised HRSA and the CDC to create geospatial data platforms to support primary care integration with public health. This confluence identifies specific and unique opportunities for the public health and primary care communities to share geography, and advance our nation's health care agenda.

REFERENCES

Butler DC, Petterson S, Phillips RL, Bazemore AW. Measures of social deprivation that predict health care access and need within a rational area of primary care service delivery. Health Services Research 2013; 48(2 Pt 1): 539–559.

Center for Applied Research and Environmental Systems. Community Commons. 2014. Retrieved July 1, 2014, from http://assessment.communitycommons.org/footprint/.

Centers for Disease Control and Prevention). Resources for Implementing the Community Health Needs Assessment Process. 2014. Retrieved July 1, 2014, 2014, from http://www.cdc.gov/policy/chna/.

Chapple-McGruder T, Zhou Y, Castrucci B. From Preconception to Infant Protection. Atlanta: Georgia Department of Public Health, 2012.

Comer KF, Grannis S, Dixon BE, Bodenhamer DJ, Wiehe SE. Incorporating geospatial capacity within clinical data systems to address social determinants of health. Public Health Rep 2011; 126(Suppl 3): 54.

Farley ESJ. An integrated medical record and data system for primary care. Part 5: Iimplications of filing family folders by area of residence. J Fam Pract 1977; 5(3): 427–432.

Institute of Medicine. Primary Care and Public Health: Exploring Integration to Improve Population Health. Washington, DC, The National Academies Press, 2012.

McDonough JR, Hames CG, Stulb SC, Garrison GE. Cardiovascular disease field study in Evans County, Ga. Public Health Reports 1963; 78(12): 1051–1060.

Mullan F, Phillips R, Kinman E. Geographic retrofitting: A method of community definition in community-oriented primary care practices. Fam Med 2004; 36: 440–446.

The Robert Graham Center. Community Oriented Primary Care Curriculum. 2013. Retrieved May 19, 2014, 2014, from http://www.graham-center.org/online/graham/home/tools-resources/copc.html.

Chapter 25

Data and the Future of Public Health

JEFFREY ENGEL

I am imagining a future time not far from now, as the year is 2025. All clinical encounters between a provider or hospital and an individual patient are recorded in an electronic health record (EHR). There are still dozens of vendors in the EHR marketplace, but all EHRs are standardized and interoperable, using the same vocabulary and messaging guidelines. Local and state public health agencies have strategically invested in their informatics capacity with infrastructure, platform, and software that align with the clinical information systems. Further in this imaginary not-too-distant time, the clinical and public health workforce have job descriptions and career ladders for health informaticians as defined by the 2018 U.S. Department of Labor Bureau of Labor of Statistics Standard Occupational Classification (U.S. Department of Labor, 2014).

This data utopia was funded in 2016, after years of congressional wrangling, by enacting the 2012 recommendation of the Institute of Medicine (IOM) of a national tax on medical care transactions (IOM, 2012). This "dedicated, stable and long-term financing structure" was used to "deliver the *minimum package of public health services* (italics theirs) in every community." Recognizing that sharing information from clinical data sources (IOM, 2011) was the basis of true integration of public health and medical care (Fig. 25-1), communities built the governance and exchange infrastructure necessary for data, information, and knowledge transfer between the public and private health sectors needed to improve the public's health.

WORKING WITH DATA IN AN INTEGRATED WORLD

Being a former clinician, now an applied public health epidemiologist, I thought it would be instructive to discuss case studies that illustrate what working with data might be like in the model depicted in Figure 25-1B.

Public Health Reporting and the Case of Community-Acquired Pneumonia

A 58-year-old man presents to clinic with a 3-day history of a productive cough, fever, and worsening shortness of breath. He has smoked cigarettes, 1 to 2 packs per day, since he was in his early 20s. On exam he looks acutely ill; he has shortness of breath sitting at rest and has diminished breath sounds in the right lower lung zone. He is admitted to the hospital, where a chest radiograph shows an infiltrate on the right side. Many laboratory tests are obtained whose results are consistent with pneumonia, but no definitive microbial cause is identified. He is given supplemental oxygen and intravenous broad-spectrum antibiotics, but his condition deteriorates, requiring transfer to the intensive care unit (ICU), where he is placed on mechanical ventilation. A week later in the ICU, the patient develops diarrhea; *Clostridium difficile*-associated disease (CDAD) is diagnosed (Bartlett, 2006).

This is a fairly typical presentation, and an all-too-frequent hospital course, of an individual with community-acquired pneumonia with probable pre-existing lung disease from longtime smoking. Normally, the vast amounts of clinical data that would be generated from his outpatient and inpatient episodes of care would never be shared with public health. Working in isolation (see Fig. 25-1A), and given that community-acquired pneumonia with no definitive cause is not reportable to public health in 2014 (Fig. 25-1B) (CDC, 2014), this case would remain in the medical care sector. However, in 2025, something very different happens.

On the patient's presentation in the clinic, the provider enters all the clinical data in the EHR: name, address, gender, age, smoking history, vital signs,

Figure 25-1 ▼
A, Integration of public health and primary care: IOM model. **B,** Integration of public health and all medical care: the data-sharing model.

(From Institute of Medicine. Primary Care and Public Health: Exploring Integration to Improve Population Health. Washington, DC. The National Academies Press, 2012. Used with permission.)

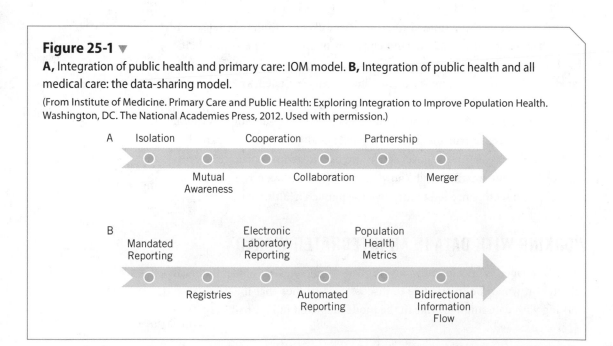

physical exam, assessment, and plan. Within seconds of data entry, an alert appears on the EHR screen:

"Public Health Alert! In cases of community-acquired pneumonia, please consider Legionnaires' disease. There are an increased number of sporadic cases occurring in the community, likely due to recent rain and flooding" (Hicks et al., 2007).

As the patient is being admitted to the hospital, the public health alert remains on the hospital EHR; the emergency room physician orders specific tests for Legionnaires' disease, which return positive results within 4 hours of admission; electronic laboratory reporting from the hospital laboratory to the public health electronic disease surveillance system automatically reports the case to public health. An appropriate antibiotic is prescribed, and the patient recovers well enough in 3 days to be discharged to home to complete a course of oral antibiotics. At discharge, the EHR reminds the providers that the patient is a candidate for the influenza and pneumococcal vaccines (the adult immunization registry shows that this patient is unimmunized), and provides community resources for evidence-based smoking cessation interventions. Public health environmental investigation reveals that the patient's basement flooded during the recent rains. Cultures of pooled water in the basement are positive for the Legionnaires' bacillus. The family has the sump pump repaired the next day, and the patient has enrolled in a smoking cessation counseling group offered by the local health department.

Community Health Assessments and the Case of the Well-Child Visit

An 11-year-old fifth grader appears for her annual well-child visit at her new pediatrician's office. The family moved across the state during the past summer. From the state immunization registry, the new office documents that her immunizations are up to date. She appears overweight, but is otherwise in good health. Her exam is normal except for a calculated body mass index (BMI) in the 90th percentile. The child's growth chart is not available at the new pediatric office; however, the mother reports that her daughter "has always been a little chubby." A point-of-care test for diabetes is negative. At the end of the visit, the pediatrician's EHR's clinical decision support module alerts the physician that the patient is overweight, and also that she, based on her age, should begin the human papillomavirus (HPV) vaccination series. In the remaining 10 minutes of the visit, the pediatrician counsels the mother and child on nutrition, physical activity, and the importance of beginning the HPV vaccine series. A vaccine information sheet is provided and a return appointment is scheduled in the next month to follow up on the BMI and to start HPV vaccinations.

In this family's community, the local health department is pursuing accreditation from the Public Health Accreditation Board. A community health assessment and community health improvement plan are prerequisites for accreditation (Public Health Accreditation Board, 2014). The health department has a general idea of the community health status based on statewide data, national reports, and anecdotes from community stakeholders but has no reliable local data sources, including from the single health care system that serves the entire community. The health director is struggling with an already thin workforce and little epidemiology capacity. A rising rate of childhood obesity is a concern, but the only data from the community on this metric is from episodic statewide random sampling of fifth graders. This survey provides a reasonable benchmark or median expected rate (indicator), but may not be representative of the community, and the published survey is always at least 2 years behind. An attempt at a school-based BMI survey of fifth grade classrooms was met by resistance from parents and school administrators.

How would this scenario unfold in the data utopia of 2025? First, in the clinic, because the parent signed an on-line release-of-information form, the new pediatrician had seamless access to the child's electronic medical record, including the growth chart. The doctor notes that over the past 3 years the child was crossing percentile lines for BMI and now, at the 90th percentile, is overweight for the first time. The clinical decision support module in the EHR displays available evidence-based interventions for the prevention and treatment of childhood obesity that is shared with the mother. Additionally, the mother watches a 5-minute on-line video describing the efficacy and safety of the HPV vaccine, including addressing the leading beliefs surrounding vaccine hesitancy. The performance management module of the EHR of the group practice informs the providers in this clinic that their rates of HPV vaccination and childhood obesity and overweight are steadily improving amongst the practice's population of children.

On the public health side, the local health department is due for re-accreditation (Public Health Accreditation Board, 2014), after becoming accredited in 2015, and is updating the community health assessment. In 2017, a regional health information exchange (HIE) was created with funding provided by the national tax on medical care transactions (IOM, 2012). The regional HIE governance board (Office of the National Coordinator for Health Information Technology, 2013) was established with representation from public health, health care, elected officials, community-based organizations, and consumers. The local health department was able to hire an epidemiologist with informatics training who accesses de-identified BMI data by date of birth and ZIP code from the HIE. Using geographic positioning system software, the epidemiologist also displays and analyzes childhood obesity and overweight rates by age and location in quarterly reviews. Although rates are improving, geographic hot spots persist that are associated with economic and racial disparities. The updated community health improvement plan seeks to target these hot spots by improving safe access to outdoor physical activity and healthful nutrition.

MERGER OR BIDIRECTIONAL INFORMATION FLOW?

In this essay, I have used two common clinical case scenarios to illustrate how a mature integrated health system might work, using a framework of data sharing rather than business models of integration (see Fig. 25-1). As an epidemiologist, I find the data-sharing model of integration better to address my daily reality of working with data to improve the public's health. In 2014, we are making great progress toward the data utopia of ongoing bidirectional flow of information between the public health and medical care sectors. As the cases show, today EHRs are nearly ubiquitous (and contain clinical decisional support modules), statewide immunization (and cancer) registries are on-line and working (at least for childhood vaccines), and electronic laboratory reporting between hospital laboratories and public health surveillance systems is present to some degree in the majority of states (Council of State and Territorial Epidemiologists, 2010).

In the case of community-acquired pneumonia, I show how bidirectional information flow (from data analysis at public health), assists the clinician at the point of care in the early diagnosis of the cause of the pneumonia. The patient has a much better outcome because the correct therapy was initiated promptly, avoiding a prolonged ICU stay, antibiotic-associated diarrhea (CDAD), and perhaps even death. The condition, Legionnaires' disease, is reported to public health on the day and hour of diagnosis by the electronic laboratory report, prompting a timely public health investigation and environmental remediation at the patient's home. I'm also happy to report that 6 months later, the patient has quit smoking and successfully weaned himself from nicotine replacement therapy!

In the second case, I describe how bidirectional information flow can transform a routine office visit to a better patient outcome and can provide efficient data collection and analysis for a community health assessment. The future patient-centered medical home, staffed by a team of primary care physicians, family nurse practitioners, and physician assistants, has access to community resources that use evidence-based strategies to prevent and treat childhood obesity. The girl, now 12 and in the sixth grade, completed her three-shot HPV vaccine series and is involved at an after-school program at her local YMCA (Schwartz et al., 2012). Her school and the local agriculture extension agency and health department have instituted a farm-to-school program, expanding access to fresh fruits and vegetables for lunch and snacks. She has adjusted well to her new community, has many friends, and her BMI is in the 65th percentile. The local health department was re-accredited with a high score and received special acclamation for their use of data to improve population health.

Both cases (one acute, one chronic; one reportable, one not; one emergent, one routine; one adult, one child) underscore the essential nature of working with data at the bedside and in the community. From the point of care to the public health agency, timely information flow can save lives, reduce costs, and improve population health. This is the Triple Aim (Institute for Healthcare Improvement, 2014), and it is achievable by timely collection and sharing of data, transformation of data to information and knowledge that inform both individual and community action.

REFERENCES

Bartlett JG. Narrative review: The new epidemic of Clostridium difficile–associated enteric disease. Annals Intern Med 2006; 145(10): 758–764.

Centers for Disease Control and Prevention. National Notifiable Diseases Surveillance System. Available at: http://wwwn.cdc.gov/nndss/, accessed May 7, 2014.

Council of State and Territorial Epidemiologists. 2010 National Electronic Disease Surveillance System Assessment. Available at: http://c.ymcdn.com/sites/www.cste.org/resource/resmgr/SurveillanceInformatics/2010NEDSSASSESSMENT.pdf, accessed May 2, 2014.

Hicks LA, Rose CE Jr., Fields BS, et al. Increased rainfall is associated with increased risk for legionellosis. Epidemiol Infect 2007; 135(5): 811–817.

IOM (Institute of Medicine). For the Public's Health: The Role of Measurement in Action and Accountability. Washington, DC: The National Academies Press, 2011.

IOM (Institute of Medicine). Primary Care and Public Health: Exploring Integration to Improve Population Health. Washington, DC: The National Academies Press, 2012.

IOM (Institute of Medicine). For the Public's Health: Investing in a Healthier Future. Washington, DC: The National Academies Press, 2012.

Public Health Accreditation Board. Standards and Measures. Available at: http://www.phaboard.org/, accessed May 8, 2014.

Schwartz RP, Vitolins MZ, Case LD, et al. The YMCA Healthy, Fit, and Strong Program: A community-based, family-centered, low-cost obesity prevention/treatment pilot study. Child Obesity. 2012; 8(6): 577–582.

The Institute for Healthcare Improvement. The IHI Triple Aim. Available at: http://www.ihi.org/Engage/Initiatives/TripleAim/Pages/default.aspx, accessed May 8, 2014.

The National Farm to School Network. Resources. Available at: www.farmtoschool.org, accessed June 17, 2014.

The Office of the National Coordinator for Health Information Technology: Governance Framework for Trusted Electronic Health Information Exchange. Available at: http://www.healthit.gov/sites/default/files/GovernanceFrameworkTrustedEHIE_Final.pdf, accessed May 8, 2014.

United States Depart of Labor, Bureau of Labor Statistics. Standard Occupational Classification. Available at: http://www.bls.gov/soc/home.htm, accessed May 5, 2014.

Success Stories

Chapter 26

San Diego, California, Promotes Healthy Weight to Improve Community Health

SHAILA SERPAS, CHRISTINA KHAOKHAM, SHARON HILLIDGE, AND VIRGINIA WATSON

At a Glance: The San Diego Healthy Weight Collaborative

- **Disease area**: Nutrition, physical activity, obesity
- **Target health outcomes:** Develop and test community level strategies based on the "Plan-Do-Study-Act" (PDSA) format of quality improvement project models
- **Primary strategies**: Health communication, surveillance, policy change
- **Key principles of integration:** Shared goal of population health; community engagement

Lesson Learned: ➜ Partners need to align work plans and donate resources for a common mission. ➜ Primary care providers need to act outside of their clinics to have the widest impact.

Doctors from the Scripps Family Medicine Residency program had growing concerns about children they saw in their family medicine clinic. The clinic, a Federally Qualified Health Center located 6 miles north of the United States-Mexico border in south San Diego, is visited annually by over 18,000 patients and attends to a predominantly Latino and underserved population. Medical residents were diagnosing a variety of health problems related to obesity in children as young as 10 years old—from hypertension to diabetes to liver disease. They were also delivering 9-lb babies to women who had excessive weight gain during pregnancy. Physicians were frustrated as they treated weight-related problems in children and at the same time watched families come into the clinic with bags of chips and soda, in part because the nearby convenience stores did not stock healthy snacks. How could medical residents engage in a conversation about healthy lifestyle choices when the environment did not support their advice?

"Obesity is just one of the issues that needs to be addressed with patients during brief office visits, and it can be overwhelming to physicians who want to have an impact on the health of their patients but realize there are many obstacles that patients face outside the clinic," says Shaila Serpas, MD, family physician and the Associate Director of the Scripps Residency program. "Rather than just teaching medical residents to manage chronic disease, we need to learn how to reach outside the clinic walls to help families prevent these conditions before they start."

THREE INITIATIVES MERGE TO MEET A COMMON GOAL

What eventually became known as the San Diego Healthy Weight Collaborative was created by reaching outside the walls of that clinic *and* a school *and* a local government office, because public health officials, educators, and primary care providers recognized that they were addressing similar problems in overlapping areas. By partnering to acheive their goals, they capitalized on a synergy generated through a shared vision of success and aligned work plans. Here's how they did it.

Primary Care Initiative

In 2009, the Scripps program partnered with the University of California, Los Angeles, to pilot a primary care residency curriculum aimed at improving doctors' ability to identify children with unhealthy weights and increasing their skills in counseling on healthy lifestyles (UCLA, 2014). Physicians visited community organizations to identify obesity prevention resources that were available and learned communication skills and strategies to support behavior change in families. As part of the year-long obesity prevention project, participants tracked body mass index (BMI) percentile, healthy lifestyle counseling, and community referrals.

During the project, patients reported difficulty accessing healthy foods, challenges being physically active each day, and concerns regarding children's school lunches. The physicians were not prepared to address these social and environmental factors impacting their patients' abilities to follow recommended lifestyle changes. Project leaders realized that the project's focus on individual and family behavior was limiting the impact of the intervention and that additional partners from outside the clinic were needed to have greater impact on obesity prevention.

School District Initiative

Around the same time, the Chula Vista Elementary School District, serving approximately 28,000 students between kindergarten and 6th grade, initiated

Figure 26-1 ▶

District demographic data and City of Chula Vista 2010 GIS data related to open space and fast food (serve and go) establishments.

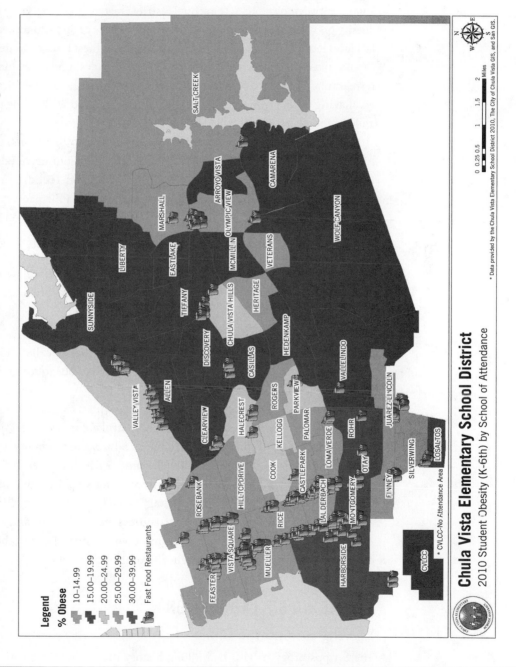

Chula Vista Elementary School District

2010 Student Obesity (K–6th) by School of Attendance

* Data provided by the Chula Vista Elementary School District 2010, The City of Chula Vista GIS, and San GIS.

a height and weight surveillance project to assess the health of its student population. With analytic support from the County of San Diego Health and Human Services Agency (the local public health authority), their surveillance data showed that nearly 40% of the 24,000 students measured had an unhealthy BMI percentile for their age. Using attendance information and community demographics, the school district created maps (Fig. 26-1) to show obesity prevalence by school and identify open space access and unhealthy or fast food locations. The maps illustrated that the highest rates of student obesity occurred in areas with limited parks and an overabundance of fast food restaurants. The data clearly revealed the impact that the built environment was having on the community's health, which mirrored what clinic patients and families had long described to their primary care providers.

"We presented our school and district-level data to principals, parents, health care professionals, the Chula Vista Chamber of Commerce Education Committee, and city and county officials," says Sharon Hillidge, MA, the Physical Education Resource Teacher for the Chula Vista Elementary School District. "The reaction from the community was the same reaction that we first had. It was startling. When we took our obesity maps and layered in environmental factors, such as a school's proximity to fast-food restaurants and access, or rather the lack of access, to parks and green space, we all realized that the problem and the solutions didn't stop at the schoolhouse doors."

Public Health Initiative

In 2010, county public health developed a 10-year initiative called "Live Well San Diego" with a messaging campaign known as "3-4-50" to reach the population of San Diego County. The campaign raised awareness about three behaviors (tobacco use, poor nutrition, and lack of physical activity) that contribute to four chronic diseases (heart disease/stroke, cancer, type-2 diabetes, and respiratory conditions) and result in over 50% of the morbidity and mortality in San Diego County (San Diego County, 2010). This message aligned well with local primary care providers' concerns for smoking, low consumption of fruits and vegetables, and sedentary behavior. However, public health and primary care did not share a plan to address these behaviors and diseases. Although they shared common concerns about chronic diseases, they were developing strategies to address the health of their populations in silos.

FOSTERING COLLABORATION

Looking Beyond the Clinic

The Scripps program also had a long history of collaborating with county public health. Past projects included physicians and public health staff developing and disseminating a healthy living toolkit to primary care offices, public health nurses, and schools throughout the county. Public health offices also provided orientation to new residency physicians with presentations and site visits to public health clinics.

As part of this tradition of forming community partnerships, the Scripps program developed several high school health clinics with the local school district. In an effort to reach a younger age group, the Scripps program decided to "adopt" an elementary school to improve the health of the entire campus, which included students, staff, and parents. This required a different approach from the high school clinic where the focus is on individual students accessing care through the clinic. The Scripps program reached out to Chula Vista's Lillian J. Rice Elementary School to address the obesity problem together in what would become the Scripps–Rice Wellness project. The school was chosen for several reasons; one was because of its proximity to the Family Medicine Clinic, with the assumption that families enrolled in the clinic would have children attending the school, and the other reason was because the district's BMI data indicated that 43% of Rice Elementary School students were classified as overweight or obese, one of the highest obesity rates in the district.

The goal of the partnership was twofold: to improve the school's health and wellness for students, staff, and parents as well as to expose medical residents to a population-based approach to implementing community-oriented primary care projects at a school site. Medical residents have a long history of providing classroom presentations, cooking classes, and mentoring at several schools in the area. However, the Scripps–Rice project offered an opportunity to have a focused relationship between primary care and one elementary school. The medical residents would participate in campus-wide wellness activities including pedometer projects, fitness testing preparation, cooking classes, nutrition sessions, and health fairs, and they would monitor the impact of these efforts. Medical residents were therefore learning how to measure the impact and how to adapt to the needs of the school community.

Adding Partners, Aligning Resources, and Taking Community-Level Action

Meanwhile, an opportunity to collaborate with additional stakeholders emerged through the National Initiative for Children's Healthcare Quality (NICHQ), which was searching for communities with teams ready to work on a national collaborative approach to address childhood obesity. Phil Nader, MD, a researcher and community leader at the University of California, San Diego (UCSD), recognized the history of collaborative efforts already in place in San Diego (Nader, 2012) and brought key partners together to launch a proposal for the Healthy Weight Collaborative. Several partners had recently completed a 4-year California Endowment–funded project together called Healthy Eating, Active Communities, and were well positioned to regroup and invite additional partners to participate. An initial meeting was held at

UCSD to discuss the opportunity and gauge interest from the group in forming a team and applying for the NICHQ initiative. Public health, community clinics, researchers, schools, and community organizations were all involved in this early commitment. The NICHQ initiative offered no funding to participate other than travel expenses for two national meetings. Despite this lack of financial incentive, most of the representatives at the initial meeting committed support for the application, starting with assistance in writing the proposal. The team was named The San Diego Healthy Weight Collaborative (a.k.a. The San Diego Collaborative or the Collaborative), and included members from primary care, public health, education, and the community. Over 200 applications were submitted to NICHQ and the San Diego Collaborative was chosen to be one of ten community teams from across the country to participate in Phase One of their national Healthy Weight Collaborative Project (Box 26-1).

The San Diego Collaborative was an opportunity for professionals in primary care roles, school districts, and public health offices to deepen their relationships through monthly meetings, specific strategies, and aligned work plans. The possibility of combining school health information, public health resources, and primary care narratives crossed traditional domains. All Collaborative partners shared several core beliefs as follows:

1. Change cannot be recognized unless it is measured.
2. The causes of obesity are complex and require a systems approach to achieve long-lived results.

Box 26-1 | Member Organizations of San Diego Healthy Weight Collaborative

San Diego Healthy Weight Collaborative members are representatives from public health, primary care, local government, schools, and neighborhood grass-roots organizations and include the following:

- American Academy of Pediatrics, California Chapter 3
- Chula Vista Community Collaborative
- Chula Vista Elementary School District
- Community Health Improvement Partners
- County of San Diego, Health & Human Services Agency
- San Diego County Childhood Obesity Initiative
- San Ysidro Health Center
- Scripps Family Medicine Residency Program
- Scripps Mercy Hospital San Diego Border Area Health Education Center
- University of California, San Diego Division of Child Development and Community Health
- University of California, San Diego, Network for a Healthy California
- YMCA Childcare Resource Services

3. All sectors and stakeholders must actively participate in learning and change to break the status quo.

Sustained participation in the Collaborative was encouraged by these key factors:

- Assessing collaborative strengths and weakness
- Aligning individual agencies' work plans with the collaborative effort
- Identifying a neutral, trusted leader
- Including a community representative
- Meeting regularly

YOU CAN DO THIS!

Important First Steps

The San Diego Healthy Weight Collaborative may seem like a best-case scenario, beyond your reach in typical circumstances. But its members took these important initial steps that you and your partners can match before you get started, regardless of the size and scope of your project:

- Take the time to agree on your core beliefs, from the philosophical to the practical.
- Craft a mission statement that will clearly define success for your group, and revisit it often to make sure you're on course.
- Determine the strengths of each member and let them focus their work in this direction in order to maximize your accomplishments . . . and then don't spread people too thin!
- Strategize about efforts already underway as well as upcoming activities and try to eliminate overlap by aligning your work plans.
- Commit to meet regularly and choose how you want to communicate in between face-to-face meetings.

The Collaborative designed a map to outline the specific commitments of each partnering agency (Serpas, 2013). This roadmap helped the Collaborative to share resources of the individual members and demonstrate how all were contributing resources to achieve the overall strategies. Specific shared activities that involved donation of resources included:

- Web designer services to upgrade the website with new resources the team developed for its healthy messaging campaign
- Translation services to be certain the translation of materials to Spanish were linguistically and culturally relevant for the community
- Printing costs for materials used at community events
- Staff time at community events
- Staff time to develop and administer surveys to community members
- Staff time to participate in focus groups in the community

Defining Success

The Collaborative members developed a collective mission statement: "The San Diego Healthy Weight Collaborative is dedicated to the development and implementation of sustainable community-based strategies to support healthy weight. The team efforts will improve and enhance the systems in South San Diego that promote healthy weight." In addition to this statement, the group defined its population, intentions, measurements, and strategies, which established a common language to begin their work (Serpas, 2013).

Some of the measurements defined at the beginning of the project included:

1. Measure team strengths and weaknesses with a Collaboration Factors Inventory tool.
2. Reach 50% of the target population with a healthy message campaign, comprised of simple behavioral strategies for healthy eating and exercise.
3. Reach 25% of the target population to assess weight status.
4. 10% of the target population will have been offered an evidence-based, standardized healthy weight plan.
5. Develop action plans to implement two policies: one to promote healthy eating and one to promote physical activity.

Defining the Target Population

The Collaborative members worked together to define the target population for the year-long initiative. For public health, population had traditionally been defined as all the residents of South San Diego. For primary care, population had meant the clinic patients and the Rice Elementary School students. The Collaborative's population definition was a West Chula Vista neighborhood of 8,810 people: 8,000 patients and staff of the Scripps residency clinic; 750 Rice Elementary School students, family, and staff; and 60 children and staff at a nearby childcare center. The decisions to identify the target population were made through consensus as a team building exercise. Because of the Scripps–Rice partnership that was already underway, targeting these two sites was logical to all team members. However, one team member wanted to include the younger child population, and test the Collaborative's work at a child care site in the same geographic region. Several members knew the local YMCA director and suggested she could be invited to join the team to help identify a childcare site to include in our target population. No one disagreed with this suggestion, even though it broadened the scope of work and increased the workload. Because of this networking of team members, a child care site was quickly identified within a few blocks from the clinic and elementary school and included in the target population.

YOU CAN DO THIS!

Is Your Group Ready For Success?

The San Diego Healthy Weight Collaborative used a free online tool called The Wilder Collaboration Factors Inventory (Mattessich et al., 2001) to strengthen their team. The tool, created by The Amherst H. Wilder Foundation, assesses members of a collaboration using 20 research-tested success factors. Members take about 15 minutes to individually answer 42 questions covering the context of the community (leaders, social/political climate) and opinions about the group's level of trust and respect for each other and their level of commitment. Examples of more specific multiple choice questions are:

- There is a lot of flexibility when decisions are made; people are open to discussing different options.
- People in this collaborative group have a clear sense of their roles and responsibilities.
- People in our collaborative group know and understand our goals.

Scores range from 1 to 5 and show areas of strength and areas that should be addressed.

Team lead Shaila Serpas, MD, said the assessment results led to positive changes in the Collaborative. "Feedback included the suggestion to share the credit of the group more visibly. This resulted in incorporating 17 logos in all materials to equally credit all collaborative participants."

Developing a Healthy Message Campaign in the Target Population

The team selected a healthy message that could easily be adapted in multiple settings and addressed the core behaviors (poor diet and inactivity) that had the greatest impact on obesity in our target population. They adopted "5-2-1-0 Every Day," a health message from the "Let's Go!" program developed by the Kids CO-OP at The Barbara Bush Children's Hospital at the Maine Medical Center in partnership with Maine Health. The message reminds children and families to eat 5 or more fruits and vegetables; to limit recreational screen time to 2 hours or fewer; to be physically active 1 hour or more; and to drink zero sugary beverages each day (Rogers, 2009). The 5-2-1-0 message overlapped with county public health's existing 3-4-50 message that described the countywide chronic disease trends. However, 5-2-1-0 was specific to behaviors that individuals could understand and adopt. The Collaborative developed and tested the message based on the "Plan-Do-Study-Act" (PDSA) format of Quality Improvement Project Models (Langley, 2009). Focus groups at the clinic included staff and medical residents to discuss the purpose of the message, how to implement 5-2-1-0 into the work flow, and how to adapt the electronic health record to support the message.

Scripps medical residents quickly incorporated the 5-2-1-0 message into their medical visits as an opportunity to discuss healthy lifestyle choices with their families and provide a 5-2-1-0 prescription summarizing the goals selected by the family. The medical residents also used the 5-2-1-0 message at school-based wellness events. Focus groups at the school and early child care site gave the team an opportunity to test the message, ensure it was culturally appropriate, and accurately translate the message to Spanish.

Policy Change

Another strategy of the Collaborative was to advocate for policies to support population wellness. The Collaborative tested wellness strategies in small incremental PDSA cycles at Rice Elementary School, where a wellness committee was developed with parents, staff, and community members. The committee met on campus regularly to implement new policy changes for healthy fundraising, nonfood birthday celebrations, and increasing student physical activity. Examples of programs developed by the committee include a running club, salad bar events, changing fundraising efforts from nacho sales to fun-runs, and making local produce available to staff. These projects translate wellness policy into sustainable models that could be replicated at other schools. Extensive media attention and interviews covering the wellness initiative at Rice helped them to receive recognition as a model for the district (Calvert, 2012).

Concurrent to the Collaborative's work, the district was undertaking a major revision to its wellness policy. Many collaborative members worked closely with the district to support and encourage strong wellness policy language to address nutrition and physical activity. The school board formally adopted the district-wide wellness policy, which includes these key guidelines (Chula Vista Elementary School District, 2011):

1. Delivering foods and beverages through federally mandated reimbursable school meal programs that meet or exceed federal regulations. For example, the District has chosen not to serve flavored milk at meals or snacks.
2. Prohibiting food items in celebration of a student's birthday on the school site during the school day. For example, instead of cupcakes, parents are encouraged to bring books, pencils or other non-food items to celebrate their child's birthday at school.
3. Permitting no more than two parties/celebrations with food for each class, per school year, to be scheduled after lunch whenever possible. All food items should be store-bought, prepackaged, and/or prewrapped for food safety and allergies.

4. Restricting school staff and other entities from using non-compliant food as a reward for academic performance, accomplishments, or classroom behavior. The district emphasizes nonfood incentives as alternatives to all school staff.

Funding and Sustainability

After piloting the work at a small child care site, the team recognized the need to implement more policy and environment changes in this age group. They gathered data and reached out to additional partners, such as WIC, to explore ways to leverage additional resources to expand their work for this age group. Several team members worked together to successfully apply for Centers for Disease Control and Prevention (CDC) funding to replicate some of the strategies from the original San Diego Healthy Weight collaborative efforts for this segment of the target population. Another application to the American Academy of Pediatrics was accepted, which will impact the older children in the target population and improve the wellness policies in a different school district. Additionally, the Collaborative received funding to join the Promise Neighborhood 5-year initiative (Promise Neighborhoods, 2013) to replicate the Scripps–Rice wellness program at another school in the district. Each of these grants would not have been possible without the Collaborative's initial year-long improvement efforts to test and demonstrate outcomes in the target population.

A clear marker of success and an example of how the initiative has become sustainable is the cultural shift that has occurred at Rice Elementary. The principal acknowledged he could no longer walk across campus carrying a fast food lunch because students would question him, and he wanted to be their role model for wellness. Physicians on campus supported the cultural shift with fitness projects, classroom curriculum to reinforce the 5-2-1-0 messaging, and parent wellness events. Parents took the 5-2-1-0 message home and implemented changes to meal preparation and shared physical activities with their children (Calvert, 2013). The 5-2-1-0 message has extended beyond the pilot school at Rice to other schools in the district and other districts throughout the county. The message is also used in several primary care offices beyond the pilot residency clinic, and it is displayed on County of San Diego websites and in public health clinics.

PUBLIC HEALTH SURVEILLANCE AND EVALUATION

Albert Einstein is credited with saying, "Not everything that counts can be counted, and not everything that can be counted counts." In developing programs designed to improve health, one defines everything that counts and can be counted (i.e., what really matters [evaluation] and can be counted [surveillance]). Weight-related issues are challenging to measure, especially at the community level, because they are multi-factorial and complex. The Collaborative is currently focusing its evaluation efforts on collecting and analyzing BMI surveillance data in an effort to track the impact of community level changes over time.

School-Based Evaluation

Christina Khaokham, RN, MSN/MPH, a CDC Health Systems Integration Program Epidemiologist, helped the school district analyze its BMI Surveillance Project data by school, gender, race and ethnicity, socioeconomic status, and academic achievement. The school district was also able to improve its 2012 data collection and reliability using repeat testing with public health evaluation support. "Implementing the surveillance project was an enormous effort, and the school district made policy and program decisions based on that data," says Khaokham. "We wanted to help them answer questions about their student population, and provide strategies to improve data quality so they could have confidence in their decisions." As the collaborative moves forward, the district and health department will continue to gather and analyze BMI prevalence data to monitor population health and the impact of interventions, just as primary care will continue to use BMI percentile to monitor individual health.

Clinic-Based Evaluation

Generally, BMI assessment and counseling to support healthy weight goals are not consistently implemented in primary care. To improve the process, the Scripps program implemented system changes to incorporate assessment and documentation of BMI or BMI percentile into practice through a PDSA quality improvement model. Staff training and input led to several changes in the workflow, new tools, and adoption of electronic heath record (EHR) templates to support the assessments and counseling. The changes were monitored with monthly chart reviews. Documentation of adult health assessments increased from 20% at baseline to 90% by the end of the year-long intervention. The pediatric charts with documented health assessments similarly increased from 40% to 90%. At baseline, 83% of pediatric charts had a BMI percentile and 90% of adult charts had a BMI documented within the prior 6 months. After the intervention and change to a new EHR system that automatically calculates BMI percentile, 99% of charts reviewed had a BMI and BMI percentile documented. Having such consistent and ongoing BMI information in each chart accomplishes several things: Not only does it help physicians tailor feedback and provide encouragement to individual patients, it also meets federal quality measure requirements (HEIDIS) and follows national medical guidelines from the American Academy of Pediatrics and the American Academy of Family Physicians.

Important Lessons

"Physicians can impact individuals and communities beyond simply suggesting that a family should pack a healthy lunch," Serpas explains. "Partnering with public health departments and schools to advocate for policies that create healthy environments can have a significant impact on the individuals we serve. By reaching beyond the clinic, our physicians can increase their ability to influence patient behavior by supporting the school district wellness policy and reinforcing consistent health messaging directly with their patients."

Building bridges between public health, primary care, the school district, and other community organizations began with recognizing a common problem, making a cooperative decision to merge expertise and resources, and determining shared interventions. The Collaborative's greatest achievement was improving how each discipline understood obesity at the individual, organizational, and population level, and finding ways to support each member's work. "Instead of agency or organizational silos, we've combined resources and talents," says Hillidge. "We had to learn about each other's systems and responsibilities. I've learned so much, and they've learned about the school system. Now we are working smarter, side-by-side, instead of parallel to each other."

Lessons Learned

1. Forming a sustainable team involves a commitment of each partner to align work plans and donate resources for a common mission.
2. Selecting and disseminating a healthy message campaign, "5-2-1-0 Every Day," was tested on a small scale in multiple settings before wider dissemination to ensure acceptability, cultural appropriateness, and inclusion of community input. Having public health, primary care, a school district, and community organizations involved helped to have a wide reach and share expenses.
3. Assigning dedicated staff to serve in the administrative role is necessary. For the Collaborative, this position required approximately 16 hours/week and was funded for the first year through the original NICHQ initiative. This important position is now funded with grant support.
4. Other communities were very interested in hearing and sharing success stories. Our team benefited from hearing what other teams were implementing in their communities, the barriers they faced, and how they overcame them.
5. Policy changes can be implemented with greater impact when a system-wide approach is taken with support from all sectors. For example, public health, primary care, and community members all participated to support community based wellness efforts and the school district wellness policy.

6. Primary care cannot combat obesity in the office. Physicians need to reach outside the walls of the clinic and learn skills during their careers to partner and support community-based efforts to improve wellness.

Contact:

Shaila Serpas, MD, Team leader

619-691-7587

serpas.shaila@scrippshealth.org

REFERENCES

Calvert K. Doctors Partner with Chula Vista School to Combat Obesity. April, 2012. KPBS News. Available at: http://www.kpbs.org/news/2012/apr/12/doctors-partner-chula-vista-school-combat-obesity/. Accessed July 9, 2014.

Calvert K. Family Brings Schools Health Message Home. June, 2013. KPBS. Available at: http://www.kpbs.org/news/2013/jun/19/family-brings-schools-health-message-home/ Accessed July 9, 2014.

Chula Vista Elementary School District, Wellness Policy. 2011. Available at: http://www.cvesd.org/COMMUNITY/Pages/wellness_policy.aspx. Accessed July 9, 2014.

County of San Diego Health and Human Services Agency. 3–4–50: Chronic disease in San Diego County. Available at: http://www.sdcounty.ca.gov/hhsa/programs/phs/documents/CHS-3-4-50SanDiegoCounty2010.pdf. Accessed July 9, 2014.

Langley G, Nolan K, Nolan T, et al. The Improvement Guide. San Francosco, CA. The Jossey-Bass Business and Management Series, 2009.

Mattessich P, Murray-Close M, Monsey B. Wilder Collaboration Factors Inventory. St. Paul, MN: Wilder Research, 2001.

Nader PR, Huang TT, Gahagan S, et al. Next steps in obesity prevention: Altering early life systems to support healthy parents, infants, and toddlers. Child Obes.2012; 8(3): 195–204.

Promise Neighborhoods, 2013. Available at: http://www2.ed.gov/programs/promiseneighborhoods/index.html. Accessed July 9, 2014.

Rogers VW, Motyka E. 5-2-1-0 goes to school: a pilot project testing the feasibility of schools adopting and delivering healthy messages during the school day. Pediatrics 2009; 123(Suppl 5): S272–276.

Serpas S, Brandstein K, McKennett M, et al. San Diego Healthy Weight Collaborative: A systems approach to address childhood obesity. J Health Care Poor Underserved 2013; 24(2 Suppl): 80–96.

UCLA. Fit for residency curriculum. Available at: http://fitprogram.ucla.edu/body.cfm?id=60 Accessed July 9, 2014.

Additional Resources

Contact team leader: Shaila Serpas, MD serpas.shaila@scrippshealth.org 619-691-7587

San Diego Healthy Weight Collaborative—The Collaboration Story. Available at: https://www.youtube.com/watch?v=OYJmn7_qF4g

The BMI Toolkit. http://www.sdcounty.ca.gov/hhsa/programs/sd/live_well_san_diego/BMI-toolkit.pdf

Chula Vista Elementary School District. Article summarizes team efforts to lower obesity rate. Available at: http://chulavistaesd.wordpress.com/2013/03/21/students-improved-health-lowered-obesity-rates/

The San Diego County Childhood Obesity Initiative. Available at: http://www.ourcommunityourkids.org/

Chapter 27

Indiana Reduces the Burden of Asthma

VIRGINIA WATSON

At a Glance

- Disease area: Asthma
- Critical process and/or health outcomes: reduction in the number of asthma-related ER visits
- Primary activities/strategies: Patient outreach
- Partners: Parkview Health System, Indiana State Department of Health Chronic Respiratory Disease Section, Allen County Health Department, Allen County Asthma Coalition
- Key principles of integration: Shared goal of population health; aligned leadership; shared data and analysis
- Tips:
    - Gather baseline information to assess complexities and severities in the community, and from there, form your hypothesis.
    - Align champions within your organization and bring them on board. Incorporate the views of these key stakeholders and get buy-in.
    - Follow organizational processes before starting new project. Assure that all departments (legal, compliance, HIPAA) understand and are aware of your project.
    - Communicate and keep people informed of your progress and celebrate little successes that happen every day.

Al suffered with asthma all his life, but had little understanding of the disease. As a young boy in an impoverished Alabama sharecropper family, he would be strapped to his mother's back and carried to the local doctor when he couldn't breathe; they would put him inside a refrigerator to cool him down, and then he would be carried back home. By his late 40s, Al was working as a janitor, a job that provided health insurance but no prescription coverage. He needed very expensive medication and couldn't afford to maintain a steady supply, so he continually went to the local hospital's emergency department (ED) for rescue inhalers. Several days after one such trip, Al got a call from a community health nurse in the ED. She was part of a new initiative designed to identify asthma patients like Al who could benefit from some additional resources to manage his condition. That call changed his life.

The nurse helped him fill out some forms to be part of the federal Pharmacy Assistance Program so he could afford his medication. She found a physician for him who he could see after hours when he was off from work. She also visited the house he shared with his sister, who was a smoker and an avid cat lover.

"She was going to get rid of Al before she got rid of the cats!" says Connie Kerrigan, RN, BSN, manager of Community Nursing at Parkview Health in northeast Indiana. After he got his own apartment, Al asked for another home visit. Kerrigan explains that during this environmental intervention, Al was told he should have blinds instead of curtains, and he was taught how to clean the blinds. The nurse was able to get him a free HEPA filter to remove allergens from the air, and she talked with him about the cleaning products he was using at work that were harmful to his health. He changed jobs and now works in a factory.

Whereas he was "barely surviving" before, and visiting the ED at least twice a month, he now has a regular health care provider and only visited the ED once when he had the flu, says Kerrigan. "That goes to show the power of education. We take for granted that people are being noncompliant, but this shows people don't always know what to do. When we peel back the layers, oftentimes I think it's our failure. We think, 'surely they know better,' but Al had such a knowledge deficit, he didn't know what to do—just that he was always short of breath. Once we connected with him, he was all in. He really wanted to change his life."

NEW INITIATIVE BUILDS ON EXISTING PARTNERSHIP

A 2007 community health survey conducted by Parkview Health, a not-for-profit regional health system consisting of seven hospitals and multiple specialty clinics and physicians' offices in northeast Indiana, identified asthma

Box 27-1 | Indiana Asthma Initiative

From 2000 to 2009, Indiana experienced an increase in the prevalence of asthma, from a low of 7.5% in 2001 to 9.1% in 2009 (Indiana State Health Department, 2011). In 2010, an estimated 457,700 (9.5%) Indiana adults and 136,200 (8.8%) children reported currently having asthma (Centers for Disease Control and Prevention, 2011). Estimated costs attributed to asthma-related hospitalization in Indiana were $122 million in 2009, and the estimated cost of asthma-related emergency department visits throughout Indiana was $46 million (ISDH, 2011).

as a major problem. The survey showed that asthma caused significant school and work absenteeism as well as unnecessary use of the emergency department (ED). Not long after the survey, staff at the system's Community Nursing Services program heard about funding from the Centers for Disease Control and Prevention (CDC) for asthma programs at the Indiana State Department of Health (ISDH). A partnership between Parkview Health, which serves a population of more than 820,000 in Fort Wayne and the surrounding areas, and the state health department had been in place for quite some time, as they already conducted education and outreach programs through the county's Healthy Homes Program.

YOU CAN DO IT!

Make the Most of Every Encounter

Initiating partnerships between primary care and public health doesn't have to be a painstaking process. The Asthma Emergency Department Callback Program went from an idea to reality due to a relationship fostered at a Joint Asthma Coalition meeting between a nurse and someone at the state department of health. If you are involved in overlapping projects with potential partners or casually come together in schools, at conferences, or at community health fairs, strike up a conversation! Share your thoughts on issues that impact both your groups and any ideas you have for possible collaborations. What do you have to lose?

"It's a big small town," says Connie Kerrigan, RN, BSN, manager of the Integrated Community Health Nursing Program at Parkview Health. "There are many opportunities to work together. It's a very casual, long-standing relationship."

So, when they discovered the possible CDC funding, one of the Parkview nurses placed a call to a colleague at the Chronic Respiratory Disease Section (CRDS) of the ISDH and asked about the CDC grant. Parkview was primed as an excellent candidate to receive subgrant funds from ISDH because of the prior work of Deb Lulling, RN, BSN, Asthma Educator and Registered Community Nurse, and Jan Moore, RRT-NPS, Asthma Educator and Registered Respiratory Therapist. The two Parkview nurses had researched best practices, attended an Environmental Protection Agency (EPA) conference, and received a small amount of initial funding from EPA for an asthma project at the hospital. It was very promising, so when asthma grant funds became available for subgrants, Parkview was one of the first to receive funding for what would later become known as the Emergency Department Asthma Call Back Program, explains Barbara Lucas, MS, former director of the health department's CRDS (she is currently the director of the West Central Indiana Area Health Education

The ISDH CRDS has many resources available online, including materials for patients, clinicians, and childcare providers. See the Resources section at the end of this chapter for URLs.

Center). "Through time, community nursing staff knew they were making a difference with their efforts related to asthma, but needed help collecting data in a format that could be analyzed. The CRDS offered its services and became a very close working partner in the project. Parkview continued providing all the patient-level work while ISDH developed data collection instruments and analyzed data." The partnership resulted in a report documenting the overwhelming success of the program with statistically significant decreases in asthma-related ED visits each year. (ISDH, 2011; Lucas et al, 2012)

"Having that partnership with the state health department was huge for us," Kerrigan says of the collaboration. "We are using the resources they've developed every day to help people. And their expertise and resources provided the evaluation that will help us keep improving the program. It allows us to continue to share our story across the state so others can accomplish similar programs."

> *"It's really becoming more about population health management. We're figuring out that it's not just about the patients who cross the doorway. We need to take care of entire community."*
>
> *Connie Kerrigan, RN, BSN, manager of the Integrated Community Health Nursing Program at Parkview Health*

YOU CAN DO IT!

What to Ask During the First Call

The Asthma Call Back Program is a simple but powerful intervention. If you are ready to try something similar, get a jumpstart by using Parkview's ED Asthma Telephone Call Back Initial Contact Form (Fig. 27-1). The first call is mostly about education and assessment: Did the patients get their prescriptions filled? Do they understand how they work? What barriers do they face? Do they know when to use a controller and when to use an emergency inhaler? Forms for use after 1 to 2 months and 6 months for follow-up are similar but highlight whether the patient has followed up with a physician and if they need more information about asthma.

Short on clinician time? Instead of calling all patients who visit the ED with asthma-related issues, consider a smaller target group. For example, you could focus on high-risk groups, such as people without access to needed resources. Or you could stratify by previous visits to the ED and call only those patients who've already been treated at least once in a given amount of time.

Figure 27-1 ▼

Initial contact form for Asthma Call Back Program, Indiana State Department of Public Health.
(Used with permission.)

❖ PARKVIEW _____ Emergency Department Asthma Telephone Call Back Form

Initial Contact

Patient Name: _____ Call Date/Time: _____

Medical Record Number: _____ Phone Number: _____

Emergency Department Visit Date: _____ Parent/Correspondent Name: _____

How is (patient name) doing today? ❑ Worse ❑ Same ❑ Better

Have you had any asthma symptoms since seen in the Emergency Room? ❑ Yes ❑ No Comments: _____

Symptoms of asthma include coughing, wheezing, shortness of breath, chest tightness and film production when you don't have a cold or respiratory infection. During the past 30 days:

How often did you have any symptoms of asthma? _____

How many nights did symptoms of asthma make it difficult for you to stay asleep? _____

What medications are you currently taking? _____

Do you understand how and when to use your (name of medication) and do you understand what their role is in the control of

your asthma? ❑ Yes ❑ No If no, went over the following medications with patient: _____

_____

How many times per day are you using your quick relief medication? _____

Have you returned to work or school? ❑ Yes ❑ No If yes, when were you able to return to work/school? _____

What school does your child attend? _____

Did you inform your child's school nurse of their ER visit for asthma? ❑ Yes ❑ No

During the past 12 months:

Have you had an episode of asthma or asthma attack? ❑ Yes ❑ No Comments: _____

How many times did you see a healthcare professional for urgent treatment of worsening asthma symptoms? _____

How many times did you see a healthcare professional for a routine checkup for your asthma? _____

How many days were you unable to work or carryout your usual activities because of asthma? _____

How many times did you visit an emergency room or urgent care because of asthma? _____

How many times have you been hospitalized for asthma? _____

How old were you when you were first told by a doctor, nurse or other healthcare professional that you have asthma? _____

Do you live in a smoke free environment? ❑ Yes ❑ No If no, may we send you smoking cessation materials? ❑ Yes ❑ No

What questions do you have about your visit? _____

_____

Did (patient name) understand their asthma discharge instructions? ❑ Yes ❑ No If no, what questions do you have? _____

_____

Did (patient name) receive their prescriptions and get them filled? ❑ Yes ❑ No If no, why did they not get them filled? _____

_____

Do you have a physician to follow up with? ❑ Yes ❑ No

Physician's Name: _____ Follow up appointment is scheduled on: _____

If no, was the physician referral number (260-373-3395) given to them? ❑ Yes ❑ No

What other questions, comments, or concerns do you have about your asthma? _____

_____

Would it be all right if I send some information about asthma? ❑ Yes ❑ No

Would it be okay if I contact you in another month to make sure you are continuing to get better and see if you have any further needs we can help you with related to your asthma? ❑ Yes ❑ No

Asthma Educator Signature: __ **DRAFT 6-7-10** __ Date: _____ Time: _____

3979 (6-09)

Targeted Intervention as a Better Rescue for Asthma Sufferers

Because Parkview Health's Community Nursing Program has a strong focus on community engagement, it was the obvious choice to manage the new, expanded Asthma Call Back initiative. The Community Nursing Program, initially a partnership with local school districts to improve nurse-to-student ratio in low income schools, has evolved into a multi-faceted system with multiple community partners. It was recognized by the American Hospital Association as one of five recipients of its prestigious NOVA award in 2011 and one of three national recipients of the EPA's National Environmental Leadership Award in Asthma Management in 2013.

Here's how Parkview's ED Asthma Call Back Program works: At each of the system's hospitals, a community health nurse and a respiratory therapist staff the program and operate with a specific intervention process (Fig 27-2). They contact all asthma patients seen in the ED, via phone or email, within 7 days of their visit. During the first telephone conversation, they ask the patient general questions, offer assistance, and record responses on an initial contact form. They review discharge instructions, assess whether the patient can afford medications, offer to send educational materials, and offer a home visit. Follow-up calls are made at 3 and 6 months post discharge, again to offer various types of assistance, including a home visit. Additionally, they offer encouragement, try to discern the patient's health status, and ask whether there have been any additional ED visits. They often refer patients to Parkview physicians, encourage them to develop an ongoing relationship with their physician in order to establish a medical home, and encourage patients to make and keep regular follow-up appointments in order to improve control over their asthma.

The Healthy Homes Program

Another component of the program involves a partnership with the Allen County Asthma Coalition and the Allen County Health Department through the Healthy Homes Program. When the health department visits a home, they do a quick asthma screening and share the results with the asthma nurse educators from Parkview by faxing a completed form. The nurses then contact the home occupant to see if they can provide educational materials and/or a home visit.

A New Neighborhood Health Care Center

A recent development involves a partnership with a clinic called the Neighborhood Health Care Center. Kerrigan explains that many of the asthma visits to Parkview Health were coming from the district served by this clinic, so the hospital and the clinic found a location and built a new building together. The clinic, a satellite Federally Qualified Health Center, provides health care to the community and pays rent, while Parkview Health provides asthma education for children and parents and hosts a summer camp.

Figure 27-2 ▼

Intervention process flow chart for Asthma Call Back Program, Indiana State Department of Public Health. (Used with permission.)

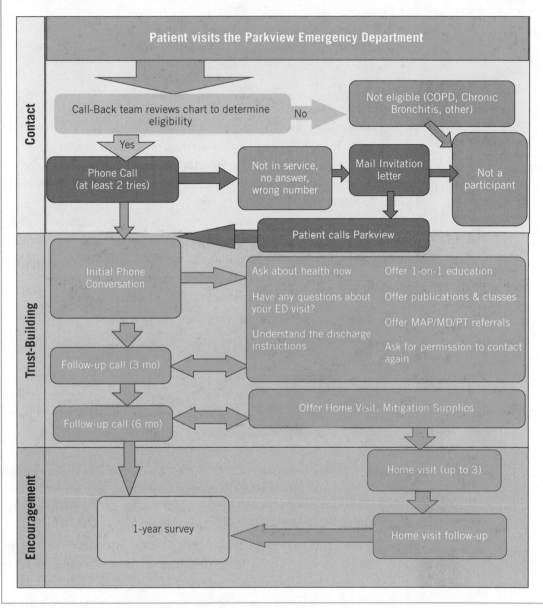

"Their hospital administration has supported and encouraged the innovations they have made, so the entire team is a 'perfect storm' that developed from having all the right people in the right places at the right time, all putting forth concerted efforts. Working with them and supporting their efforts has been an honor."

—*Barbara Lucas, MS, former director of the Indiana State Health Department, Chronic Respiratory Disease Section*

DEFINING SUCCESS

The official goals of the ISDH Asthma Program are as follows:

- Help patients manage and control their asthma.
- Reduce ED visits related to asthma.
- Establish a medical home for (asthma) patients.
- Assist with access to financial assistance programs for medications.
- Provide resources for trigger management.
- Improve quality of life.

But to Kerrigan, success in a nutshell meant establishing effective practices, getting feedback and using it to improve the program, and seeing changes in patients' lives. Providing education, connecting people to a medical home, and helping them with insurance or transportation if needed turned out to be key elements that made the program meaningful to patients. "Our wins were in the day-to-day operations," Kerrigan says.

Lucas adds that partners at ISDH knew this project could add essential knowledge to the evidence behind practice improvement, and ISDH continues to encourage other hospitals to follow the example established by Parkview. The big win for the agency was the ability to make such a huge contribution to the literature that is relied on to improve public health, she says.

FUNDING AND SUSTAINABILITY

As stated earlier, a grant from the ISDH provided funding for the Integrated Community Health Nursing Program at Parkview Health to start the Asthma Call Back Program. To cover salary and benefits for the pilot year, $53,000 was needed. About $14,000 in additional support covered printing, mileage, postage, and home environment mitigation supplies, some of which came from another ISDH CRDS grant. A St. Joseph Community Health Foundation grant supplied translation services for non-English speakers.

For the future, the hospital system will continue to allocate money to sustain the program; Parkview Hospital contributes on average $3.5 million a year for the Parkview Health Community Health Improvement Program, which includes the Asthma Call Back Program. These funds support/defray most of the costs because the Community Nursing Program provides documented community benefit, as described in section 501(c)(3) of the Internal Revenue Code (see chapter 15). Additional grant funding will continue to be necessary to enhance innovation, though, especially to carry out some of the next steps. These steps include providing technical assistance to other hospitals and hospital systems as they implement similar programs, implementation of a Best Practice Advisory in the electronic medical record (EMR) that will provide guidelines for asthma treatment, and the development of an Asthma Registry.

Also, some basic changes to the Asthma Call Back Program model itself may be necessary to sustain it. Kerrigan says as the program gets bigger, it may need to get more specific and targeted. "We may have to do more risk stratification of patients admitted for asthma," she explains. "We may develop something like risk scores for patients who have no insurance, no provider, or are at most at risk for repeat. That way, if we come up with criteria for those most in need, we may not have to follow up with *everyone* who comes to the emergency room for asthma." However, Kerrigan notes that data clearly demonstrate any intervention, whether it's a phone call or a letter, had a statistically significant impact on repeat visits to the ED for *all* groups, not just high-risk groups.

MONITORING AND EVALUATION

After patients have been enrolled in the Asthma Call Back Program for 1 year, they are sent a survey, the results of which are analyzed by the Asthma Program at the ISDH. The Asthma Call Back Program was recently evaluated in order to understand what interventions can reduce the burden of asthma in Indiana. Analysis included qualitative data from the surveys as well as quantitative data from program records based on ED visits and on hospital financial data for patients who were treated (Lucas et al., 2012). Not only do the evaluation results add to the evidence base for public health, they will be used in planning potential replication of the program in other hospitals.

The evaluation was designed to answer the following questions:

1. Does the intervention reduce the number of ED and hospital visits for patients in the program?
2. Do patients seen in the ED establish a medical home as a result of the intervention?
3. Does the intervention help patients reduce their exposure to environmental triggers?
4. How are patients and their families benefiting from the implementation of the ED Asthma Call Back Program?
5. What, if any, financial benefits for the Parkview Health System derive from this intervention?
6. What challenges exist in the program implementation?

Reduction in Visits

The program record analysis involved a review of patient encounter data from the year before the program began (July 1, 2008, to June 30, 2009). This allowed for a baseline period that could be compared to the following 3-year intervention period (July 1, 2009, to June 30, 2012). Among the baseline group, the prevalence of repeat ED visits within 1 year of discharge date was 22%. In the first year of the intervention, only 20% returned to the ED because of their asthma, and by the third year, the total number was down to 15%.

New Medical Home

The data indicate that 11.2% of participants reported having acted on the referrals to a Parkview physician group office, another physician, or local free clinics. Eighty-two percent of the participants who completed the 1-year survey reported having a physician they visited regularly, thus making it their medical home. As part of their efforts to move the patients toward more frequent contact with a doctor, the nurse/asthma educators provided a variety of educational literature, distributing more than 1,700 pieces. They were not able to track what actions the literature inspired, but end-of-the-year comments indicated that it was appreciated. "The majority of patients perceive our program as beneficial to them, and numbers of ED visits have decreased in comparison to the previous year," says Kerrigan. "One change is that we have followed some patients longer than the year, because they requested further contact and guidance." The evaluation demonstrated that asthma care is a longer, more sustained process, she explains, and the Asthma Call Back Program is a way for the physicians and the hospital to provide care and support for patients and "fold them into the family."

Environmental Triggers

At the time of the evaluation, the Asthma Call Back Program team had conducted 34 home visits. Survey responses show that many patients found these interventions helpful and made changes in their home. A home visit is key to helping families identify and remove environmental triggers that contribute to asthma exacerbations, says Kerrigan. "It takes a pretty strong belief that we are on their side and not going to judge them, for people to invite us into their homes to look for bugs, dust, pet dander, and molds," says Kerrigan. "We are careful in the phone calls with them to help them understand that we can help and there are things they can do to feel better. Having things we can give them, like pillow encasements, smoking cessation programs, referrals to free clinics, and even a few HEPA-filtration vacuum sweepers, warms the relationship and builds trust for other changes, too." Since the evaluation survey, the team has conducted 20 more home visits.

Benefits of the Program

Since their involvement in the Asthma Call Back Program, 59% of the participants said they didn't miss any days of work or school, and never had trouble carrying out normal activities because of their asthma, according to their responses on the 1-year survey. Another 13% reported only missing 1 or 2 days and being unable to carry out normal activities during those absences. "The impact [this program] has at a personal level is a big deal," says Kerrigan. "Numbers are great, but a lot of this is about life change, being at school and work and [being] healthier while they are there."

Financial Benefits to the Hospital

The cost to Parkview Health for asthma-related Medicaid and self-pay encounters decreased substantially from 2009 to 2012. This savings "didn't happen overnight" Kerrigan notes. "The first year we had a moderate savings, then the next year it was more substantial." Compared to the baseline year, Parkview Hospital saved nearly $1.9 million just in ED costs during 2011—2012. The program's return on investment (ROI) is 24:1, she adds (Box 27-2). In addition to fewer ED visits from asthma patients, Kerrigan believes their improved management processes could be impacting the numbers.

Challenges: Based on the evaluation results, it appears that the biggest challenges in implementing the program are the transience of the population and the ability to establish trust with the patient to be invited for a home visit. Transience makes it difficult to follow up with patients, and with no follow up, there is no opportunity for a home visit. Patients in general are often wary of agreeing to let strangers into their house, an issue that Kerrigan was surprised by at first, but realized in retrospect makes perfect sense. One successful work-around to this problem was to engage primary care providers. When their doctors recommend a home visit to root out potential environmental triggers, patients are much more likely to agree to this invasion of their private lives. How do you get busy doctors on board? Kerrigan explains that their plan is currently being piloted with one practice, and here are the steps they have taken:

- The president of the hospital system's provider group became a champion for the initiative and laid the groundwork by describing the need for the physicians' help.
- Each provider in the practice received a letter asking if someone from the Asthma Call Back Program could come visit them to answer any of their questions.
- After in-person visits to get the entire office staff on board, the Asthma Call Back Program wrote another letter asking for a point of contact in their office. This could be a site supervisor, a nurse, or anyone who was willing to be a bridge between the provider, the asthma patients, and the Asthma Call Back Program by providing contact information and educational materials to the patients.

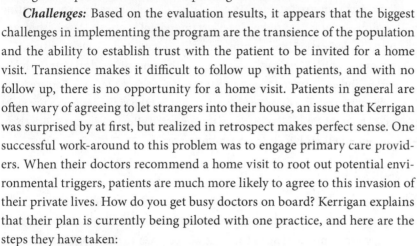

Box 27-2 | Return on Investment

Return On Investment (ROI) is a financial analysis from the perspective of the investor to assess financial return. A 24:1 ROI for the Asthma Call Back Program means that for every dollar invested, $24 was saved.

For additional perspectives on ROI, including a discussion of using cost-benefit analysis or cost effectiveness analysis instead, see chapter 19.

Another challenge has been the rapid growth of the Parkview Health infrastructure. Many provider practices have recently been brought under one umbrella, she explains. The multiple EMR systems had to be merged, and there was a learning curve associated with utilizing all the tools that were part of it.

"We've become so large we're struggling to meet all the needs," Kerrigan laments. "But things will look different in the future than they look today. It's really becoming more about population health management. We're figuring out that it's not just about the patients who cross the doorway; we need to take care of entire community."

Parkview is preparing for this population-based future by experimenting with promising practices today. "The key ingredient to the success of this program is the dedication and commitment demonstrated by Deb Lulling, Jan Moore, and Connie Kerrigan" says Lucas. "Their hospital administration has supported and encouraged the innovations they have made, so the entire team is a 'perfect storm' that developed from having all the right people in the right places at the right time, all putting forth concerted efforts. Working with them and supporting their efforts has been an honor."

Lessons Learned

1. Challenges invariably come down to communication issues. Don't make assumptions. Most things can be resolved by simply talking them through.
2. Bring your own expertise to the table but be open to the possibility that you may actually have more to offer, sometimes just showing up and being part of the process is what is needed. The evolving synergy of a partnership will result in a better product than any one person or group working alone.
3. Keep your eye on the ball—the patient is the ball!—and don't get lost in layers of complexity associated with the medical system. Your work can be exhausting but it's meaningful; you get to improve people's lives every day.

Contact

Carmen Moore, RN, BSN, CLS, Manager of Community Nursing, Parkview
 Integrated Community Nursing and Care Navigation,

(260) 266–2464

Carmen.Moore@parkview.com

REFERENCES

Centers for Disease Control and Prevention. Behavioral Risk Factor Surveillance System Prevalence Data. Atlanta, Geogia, 2011. Available at: http://www.cdc.gov/brfss/data_tools.htm

Indiana State Department of Health. Burden of Asthma in Indiana, 2011. Indianapolis: ISDH, 2011. Available at: http://www.in.gov/isdh/files/BR_Asthma_5-11-11gw.pdf.

Lucas B, Brandt A, Lulling D, Moore J, Kerrigan C, Cunningham C. Parkview Health Systems Asthma Call Back Program Evaluation Report. Indianapolis: Indiana State Department of Health and Parkview Health Systems, 2012.

Additional Resources

The Indiana State Department of Health (ISDH) Chronic Respiratory Disease
 Section (CRDS) has many resources available online:

For consumers: http://www.in.gov/isdh/25776.htm

For providers: http://www.in.gov/isdh/17272.htm

For schools and childcare centers: http://www.in.gov/isdh/25321.htm

"Top-Down" and "Bottom-Up" Initiatives Create a Comprehensive Prescription Drug Overdose Prevention Program in North Carolina

VIRGINIA WATSON

At a Glance

- **Cross-cutting topics**: Community resources; State health models for population health
- **Disease area**: Injury prevention; prescription drug use
- **Target health outcomes:** Reduce deaths attributable to prescription drug overdoses
- **Primary strategies**: Public awareness, coalition action, prescriber education, policy change
- **Key Principles of Integration:** Shared goal of population health; community engagement; sharing and collaborative use of data and analysis

Lessons Learned: ➔ Communities are ultimately responsible for their own health, but they have to have intervention strategies and an infrastructure to keep them going, ➔ Have a long-term plan and keep stakeholders informed along the way. ➔ Be prepared to make changes to your plan when you recognize areas for improvement.

Project Lazarus is a nonprofit drug overdose prevention program developed and successfully pilot-tested in Wilkes County, NC, a rural region in the foothills of the Appalachians. It is now serving as a model that incorporates both bottom-up (i.e., community-based) and top-down (i.e., medically based) public health approaches for the rest of the state to use as it confronts its epidemic of the misuse and abuse of prescription drugs and other illicit substances. The partnerships formed by Project Lazarus among community stakeholders, primary care providers, and state-level epidemiologists, convened by the county health department, has been vital to the effectiveness of the program in Wilkes County, which had the third highest county-level mortality rate in the nation from overdoses of narcotics and hallucinogens in 2005. It took 3 years, but accidental deaths from drug overdoses in Wilkes decreased by 72%, from 46.0 to 14.4 deaths per 100,000 residents per year. Their hope is that the scale-up to the rest of the state will be as successful.

Fred Wells Brason was familiar with people helping themselves to others' medications. As the director and chaplain of hospice for the Regional Medical Center in Wilkes County, NC, it didn't surprise him that family members would occasionally take or sell pain medications belonging to patients. But by 2005, the misuse had become "astronomical," he says. "Physicians were calling me and saying they couldn't prescribe to certain patients anymore, which results in an access to care issue. I've never seen it to that magnitude."

Those who know Brason will tell you he is an extroverted, let's-get-things-done kind of guy. So when the prescription drug problem came to his attention, he started looking for answers. He talked to people at the local health department, with the local sheriff, and with some emergency department doctors, who were all familiar with the problem. He started attending community meetings of all kinds where he would use the public question and answer time to ask, "what are you doing about the prescription drug problem in our county?" He says they had no response; "it wasn't even on their radar."

But it was on the radar at the county health department. A community health assessment indicated deaths from poisonings were on the rise. "My first thought was, 'We need to get the Drano out from under the sinks!'" recalls Beth Lovette, RN, BSN, MPH, who was the Health Director of the Wilkes County Health Department at the time. "I didn't make the connection that prescription drug overdose is considered a poisoning."

Wilkes is a large, rural county nestled in the foothills of the Blue Ridge mountains, with rich traditions found in generations of close-knit communities based on industries such as logging, manufacturing, and farming (Box 28-1). Lovette says no one quite understands why, but poverty and physically demanding labor might have played a role in Wilkes' designation by 2005 as the county with the third highest death rate from drug overdose *in the nation* (Centers for Disease Control and Prevention, 2008). The mortality rate of unintentional poisoning in Wilkes County several years later (2009)—primarily from prescription opioid drug overdoses—was four times as high as that in the rest of the North Carolina (46.6 vs. 11.0 per 100,000 population) (North Carolina State Center for Health Statistics, 2010).

The state's injury epidemiologist, Kay Sanford, MSPH, had noticed the alarming numbers several years before Lovette and Brason. Her early research

Box 28-1 | From Moonshine to Prescription Drugs

Wilkes County, NC, was once the "Moonshine Capital of the World," where young men rallied against poverty by distilling and selling bootleg liquor, and chased thrills by outrunning the police with their illegal bounty in souped up cars. They eventually started trying to outrun each other, and stock car racing was born. In fact, Wilkes became the home of the first National Association of Stock Car Auto Racing (NASCAR) track. Stock car racing is "a sport with an explicit history intertwined with moonshine, suggesting generations of substance misuse and abuse at the margins of the law" (Albert et al., 2011).

on fatal poisonings in conjunction with officers of the Epidemic Intelligence Service from the Centers for Disease Control and Prevention in 2002 revealed several intriguing findings. First, the rise in poisoning deaths in North Carolina was real and not a statistical fluke due to changes in vital statistics coding. Second, all of the increases in poisoning-related deaths were classified as unintentional, and the decedents who fell into this category were primarily white, middle-aged males. Third, although one-third of these deaths involved heroin and cocaine, the other two-thirds were caused by taking too much pain medication, such as hydrocodone, methadone, morphine, and oxycodone. Finally, when she stratified the numbers by county, Sanford could see that Wilkes was in trouble. She reached out to Lovette and began attending meetings of the Wilkes County Health Department's Substance Abuse Task Force (SATF), a loose collaboration of people who cared about prevention of substance abuse and services that should be offered in the community.

By 2003, Sanford was the facilitator of the statewide Task Force to Reduce Deaths from Unintentional Drug Overdoses. A year later, this group made recommendations in several categories, one of which was to create a prescription drug monitoring program (Box 28-2), known in North Carolina as the Controlled Substances Reporting System (CSRS). Other "top-down" recommendations—standardized, accepted practices—involved law enforcement, legislative initiatives, educational interventions for the public and for professionals, and clinical interventions. So, by the time Lovette and Brason were looking for data and resources to support Wilkes county's "bottom-up" efforts—community-recognized, -selected, and -supported practices—Sanford had plenty of it and even more to offer.

FOSTERING COLLABORATION

Whereas Brason's early efforts to stir up interest in the overdose problem were not exactly fruitful, people started listening when he cited Sanford's state and county statistics about the people who died of drug overdoses. In addition to this use of local data, the key to Brason's success in rallying the Wilkes community was the wide net he cast for stakeholders. He listed all possible stakeholders on a spreadsheet and set out to learn "what they do and how they do it," in order to find the intersection point with prescription medication misuse and abuse. For those on his list—school superintendents and principals, the United Way, the faith community, hospital CEOs, as well as groups focused on child abuse, domestic violence, and HIV, just to name a few—he helped answer the following questions, which he says "kept them in their own sphere of influence:"

1. Why am I needed?
2. What do I need to know?
3. What needs to be done?

When Brason was able to describe the statistics of the people who had died from prescription medication overdoses in the local community, the stakeholders started seeing common ground. Eventually he was asked to become the chair of the SATF, and he, the current SATF members, and the stakeholders

> **Box 28-3 | Be Careful of Your Terminology**
>
> Start researching the topic of drug overdose and you'll quickly find that people who are passionate about it are very careful with their words. For example, they resist using the word "drugs" and instead will say "medications" when they talk about prescriptions that ease pain. And they'd like people to understand the continuum of use, misuse, and abuse. "Use," of course, is following the prescribing physician's directions correctly. "Misuse" is using the medication above and beyond the levels prescribed, or the misguided generosity that leads to sharing with others who are in pain who can't or won't go to the doctor. "Abuse" is selling the medication or using it recreationally.

he had brought onboard agreed on a shared goal of reducing the number of deaths from prescription misuse and abuse in the county (Box 28-3). Despite the 2-hour drive from her home in Durham, Sanford was a visiting speaker at SATF meetings, as was Nabarun Dasgupta, PhD, MPH, an epidemiologist at the University of North Carolina, Chapel Hill, who at that time already had years of practical experience in drug overdose prevention across the country. Another key partner was Su Albert, MD, MPH, the Wilkes County health department's Medical Director, who worked tirelessly with local physicians to convince them to change their practice behaviors so that opioids would be more carefully prescribed for those in need of optimal pain management. Often this peer-to-peer education was conducted in the physicians' offices, requiring extensive travel across the county's 760 square miles. All the efforts paid off: as early as 2006, not only was the community mobilized to combat the overdose problem, but new and safer emergency department prescribing guidelines had also been initiated.

Other counties, noticing via community health assessments their own growing death and emergency department visit rates from the misuse or abuse of prescription pain medication, requested information about how Wilkes managed to organize the community and educate prescribers and patients. By 2007, the Northwest Community Care Network (NWCCN) took notice as well. The NWCCN is the local network of health professionals that provide primary care for Medicaid enrollees. A year later, NWCCN initiated and funded the Chronic Pain Initiative (CPI) for Wilkes County, and Brason became the project director.

THE BEGINNINGS OF PROJECT LAZARUS

That same year, Sanford retired as the state's injury epidemiologist and dedicated more time to the work being done in Wilkes County. She and Brason, along with Albert and Dasgupta, became co-founders of a community-based overdose prevention program called "Project Lazarus." They felt they needed an official name because they were receiving so many requests for help from other communities facing similar drug overdose problems. This name was chosen in honor of the opioid antidote called naloxone, which has the ability to "bring back to life"—like the biblical man raised from the dead—those who have over-dosed on opioids. The group's grass-roots efforts resulted in a model that incor-porates both bottom-up (i.e., community-based) and top-down (i.e., medically based) public health approaches that engage and empower local communities to choose from an array of evidence-based overdose prevention strategies that they believe will ultimately decrease the number of accidental deaths in the commu-nity from misuse and abuse of opioid prescription pain medications.

The Project Lazarus model (Fig. 28-1) can be seen as a wheel, the axle of which is the community. The co-founders believed in this so strongly that they put it front and center in the mission statement of the project: *The Project Lazarus public health model is based on the premise that drug overdose deaths are preventable and that all communities are ultimately responsible for their own health*. Three components, which must always be present, form the hub of the wheel—public awareness, coalition action, and data and evaluation—and they operate in a cyclical manner, with community advisory boards playing the central role in developing or selecting and sustaining each intervention. These advisory boards are composed of clinicians, parents, health officials, faith

Figure 28-1 ▼
The Project Lazarus Model can be conceptualized as a wheel, with three core components (The Hub) that must always be present, and seven components (The Spokes) which can be initiated based on the specific needs of a community.

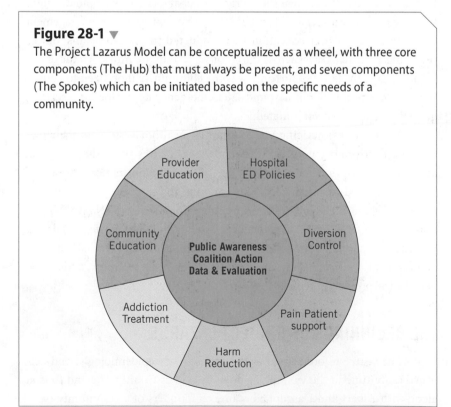

community representatives, school and college officials, law enforcement, and others. Finally, the spokes of the wheel, which can be initiated based on the specific needs of a community, are elements such as community and provider education, changes in hospital emergency department policies, diversion control, support for patients with chronic pain, harm reduction, and access to addiction treatment. The main public health message of Project Lazarus is that prescription pain medications must be: "taken correctly, stored securely, disposed of properly, and never shared."

YOU CAN DO THIS!

Components of a Successful Overdose Prevention Strategy

Is your prescription drug overdose program as effective as it could be? Whether you'd like to tweak your program or start from the ground up, use some of the interventions that proved successful in Wilkes County (see the Resources section at the end of this chapter for free, downloadable guides and other tools).

The following prevention efforts were proposed by Project Lazarus coalition members and developed and implemented by professionals and volunteers:

- Community organization and activation (e.g., town hall meetings, coalition building, "Managing Chronic Pain" toolkit)
- Prescriber education and behavior (e.g., one-on-one and continuing medical education and training about pain management)
- Supply reduction and diversion control (e.g., modification to hospital ED opioid dispensing policy, unused medication take-back events by sheriff and police departments)

  ○ Pain patient services and drug safety (e.g., Medicaid policy change: mandatory use of patient-prescriber agreement and pharmacy home, support groups for patients)
  ○ Drug treatment and demand reduction (e.g., drug detox programs)
  ○ Harm reduction (naloxone prescription)
  ○ Community-based prevention education (e.g., school-based education, Red Ribbon campaign, billboards, radio and newspaper features)
  ○ For addition details, see Albert et al. (2011)

MONITORING AND EVALUATION: CAN A HUGE LOCAL SUCCESS SCALE UP TO STATE LEVEL?

In North Carolina, four data sources are used to describe and characterize drug overdoses. One is the CSRS, the prescription monitoring program put into place as a result of Sanford's Task Force recommendations. Another is the state's mandatory syndromic surveillance infrastructure, which is called

North Carolina Disease Event Tracking and Epidemiologic Collection Tool (NC DETECT). These data show the number of ED visits for poisonings by intent (all, unintentional, intentional, and intent undetermined) for all poisonings, medication or drug poisonings, opiates, prescription opioids, heroin, and methadone. The third is field reports, postmortem autopsies, and toxicology data for fatal poisonings from the state's Office of the Chief Medical Examiner; and the fourth is vital statistics recorded on death certificates from the North Carolina State Center for Health Statistics.

Data from the above sources show that the initiative put into place through the Project Lazarus model in Wilkes County had major impact within 2 years. By the third year, the results were extraordinary (Fig. 28-2). Accidental deaths from drug overdoses decreased by 72%, from 46.0 deaths per 100,000 residents per year in 2009 to 29.0 in 2010 (Albert et al., 2011) and to 14.4 in 2011, even though the number of filled prescriptions for opioids was higher than the state average (Brason et al., 2013). According to Brason, in 2008 (before the interventions began), of the 75% who had filled a prescription for an opioid pain medication within 30 days of their accidental death from an overdose, 82%

Figure 28-2 ▼

Number of deaths per 100,000 population from unintentional drug poisoning in Wilkes County, the state of North Carolina, and the United States, 2004–2011.

(From Brason FW, Roe C, Dasgupta N. Project Lazarus: An innovative community response to prescription drug overdose. N C Med J 2013; 74(3): 259–261. Used with permission.) http://www.ncmedicaljournal.com/archives/?74323)

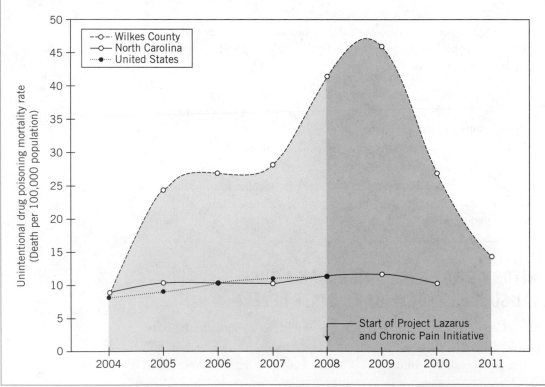

of the decedents had obtained an opioid prescription from a Wilkes-based clinician; by 2011, not a single resident of Wilkes County who died from an overdose had filled a prescription for an opioid from a Wilkes-based clinician immediately prior to death, he says.

"When I heard the astounding results of this intervention for our population in Wilkes, I thought, there's no way we can't take this to scale and do it for all 100 counties of the state," says Michael Lancaster, MD, medical director of Behavioral Health Integration for Community Care of North Carolina (CCNC). CCNC is the not-for-profit primary care organization that administers all of Medicaid's programs in 14 networks made up of physicians, nurses, pharmacists, hospitals, health departments, social service agencies, and other community organizations (NWCCN is its local subsidiary in Wilkes).

FUNDING AND SUSTAINABILITY

Community Care of North Carolina sets up practicing principles for delivering cooperative, coordinated care to all Medicaid patients in North Carolina through the medical home model. When CCNC looked at the numbers of Medicaid patients who had filled more than 12 opioid prescriptions and had at least 10 ED visits in the past year, they found 2,256 patients with an average per-visit cost of $2,610, totaling $5,881,160. They also looked at the cost of inpatient hospitalizations for unintentional poisonings. Based on data from the Agency for Healthcare Research and Quality and the North Carolina State Center for Health Statistics, Lancaster says estimated costs for North Carolinians (not just Medicaid recipients) in 2008 were nearly $1 billion. Armed with these cost data and with feedback from Medicaid doctors about their concerns regarding depression and pain management in their patients, Lancaster applied to the Kate B. Reynolds Foundation (KBR) and received $1.3 million to take the Project Lazarus model to scale. Then the federal Office of Rural Health matched these funds dollar for dollar, for a total of $2.6 million for the project, which officially became known as the Chronic Pain Initiative (CPI).

The CPI is a different entity from the not-for-profit initiative set up and run by Brason, although there is significant collaboration. CCNC also partners with all 14 of its local networks, as well as the North Carolina Hospital Association, local hospitals, local health departments, primary care doctors, faith-based programs, and law enforcement. The KBR grant funded three regional consultants to help kick things off, but Lancaster says the goal is to have local leadership take over. The initiative is grounded in local coalitions, convened by public health, which is why the involvement of the 85 local health departments in the state is such a key element in its future success and sustainability, he adds. Counties with coalitions had a 6.2% lower rate of ED visits for substance abuse than other counties, but counties with coalitions that had health department as the lead agency had a statistically significant 23% lower rate of ED visits (CSRS, 2008-2010; NC DETECT, 2010).

The statewide CPI has the following components, with accompanying resources, available for free download on the CCNC website (see Additional Resources at the end of this chapter):

1. **Community-based coalitions** help spread the message to people in their area about the extent and seriousness of unintentional drug poisonings, and the consequences of the misuse and abuse of prescription pain medication—the traditional "bottom-up" public health approach. Coalition members support community involvement in prevention and early intervention. To facilitate the creation, management, and sustainability of these groups, CCNC implemented a 180-page Community Toolkit developed by Project Lazarus, which contains a leader manual and training related to leadership, coalition structure, capacity building, strategic planning, and assessment/data/evaluation. Fact sheets that focus on the distribution and control of medications are included for a variety of community sectors, including business and industry, the courts, EDs, faith communities, the media, the military, pharmacies, schools, seniors, and youth. Lastly, the toolkit has information about the rescue drug, naloxone, and lists of other resources. In addition to the toolkit, community training is offered on a regular basis.

2. **The clinical process** focuses on the medical assessment and treatment of chronic pain—a component of a top-down approach. CCNC developed toolkits to help guide provider treatment decisions, based on patients' individual care needs. Separate toolkits are available for care managers (nurses and social workers), primary care providers, and ED physicians. Each toolkit addresses specific issues, such as identifying patients at increased risk of an overdose, supporting the use of pain treatment agreements and encouraging physicians to amend office or ED policy to address evaluation and prescribing practices. An example of a policy change is the number of pills for opioids prescribed to a patient visiting the emergency room for pain. Understandably, ED doctors don't want those patients coming back every few days, but giving them a 30-day supply is problematic, says Lancaster. Instead, the doctors can give Medicaid patients a prescription to last a few days and then connect them to one of 600 care managers in the CCNC network, who will provide follow-up by visiting the patients at home or at the hospital. In addition, CCNC worked with the Governor's Institute on Substance Abuse to create a clinical teaching program delivered throughout the state by a cadre of physicians trained in "Safer Opioid Prescribing" (Finch & McEwen, 2013).

MONITORING AND EVALUATION AT THE STATE LEVEL

The CPI has the following outcome goals:

- Decrease mortality due to unintentional poisonings
- Decrease inappropriate utilization of ED for pain management

- Decrease inappropriate utilization of imaging with diagnosis of chronic pain
- Increase use of CCNC's Provider Portal and the CSRS

Assessment and evaluation of the initiative, assimilation of feedback, and dissemination of outcomes to stakeholders are ongoing, says Lancaster, and are critical to its success. Each participating community-based coalition will receive periodic data relating to the particular objectives on which it is focused, as well as benchmark data that can be used to measure progress (Lancaster et al., 2013).

The Injury Prevention Research Center (IPRC) at UNC Chapel Hill is tracking the various activities sponsored by the CPI, as well as key outcomes of interest, to evaluate whether the program goals are being met. The evaluation design was created and submitted along with the grant application to KBR. "It would have been impossible to do after the initiative got started," says Chris Ringwalt, DrPH, Senior Research Scientist for Evaluation at the Center. "It all had to be carefully planned in advance."

Ringwalt and his team use the four data sources mentioned for outcome measures. For process measures, the Center conducts surveys that include the annual Health Directors' Survey on Community Readiness to Implement Drug Overdose Prevention Programs, which has been administered every year since 2011. The IPRC also administers a quarterly survey for CCNC's chronic pain coordinators, and a bi-annual survey of leaders of community coalitions that target substance abuse prevention. The IPRC also gets data from non-Project Lazarus partners, such as law enforcement training and Operation Medicine Drop prescription take back event logs. They also communicate frequently with the North Carolina Harm Reduction Coalition (NCHRC), a non-profit group that advocates for policy changes related to overdose prevention and the reduction of adverse consequences associated with the use of controlled substances, and distributes free naloxone rescue kits on the street and through clinics and treatment facilities.

"We have established a tracking system for attempted rescues," Ringwalt explains. "On every kit there is a label and instructions to visit naloxonesaves. org to fill out a brief survey. This, as far as we know, is the first national effort to track reversals." Between August 2013 and November 2014, there have been reports of over 200 documented overdose reversals in the state, but most of these have been conveyed directly to NCHRC, not through the site for the web-based survey. Ringwalt says a smart phone-based app or even a way to text the information may result in more data from people who have actually attempted to reverse an overdose using naloxone.

He describes the CPI as a top-down and bottom-up program that is changing behaviors due to the training of medical care providers and empowerment of community-based coalitions. However, he notes "there are many actors doing many things," about the prescription drug problem in the state, not just CCNC, and it will be challenging to attribute outcomes to their program. For example, some communities have initiated Pill Take-Back programs unrelated to CPI or Project Lazarus. "We're trying to keep tabs on who is doing what, where, and when, but there are many confounders—that is, alternate explanations of any effects found—that we will need to disentangle," Ringwalt says. Even more unfortunate, he adds, is that mortality data—deaths from overdose—take a long time to show up, and he's worried the project will run out of funding and time before IPRC can get all the data they need to produce an evaluation that yields meaningful results.

CHALLENGES

One of the CPI's challenges is that available data suggest statewide deaths from opioid overdoses have plateaued but have not really started to decrease. A closer inspection reveals that deaths from prescription pain medications *are* decreasing. So why haven't the mortality data followed suit? It turns out the answer is a simple. The number of people dying in North Carolina from heroin overdoses has more than doubled since 2011 (North Carolina State Center for Health Statistics, 2014). Increases in heroin deaths are cancelling out the decreases in fatal overdoses from pain medication.

Initiatives like Project Lazarus and the CPI confront prescription misuse and abuse from both a demand and a supply perspective. By making patients aware of the potential dangers of using opioids, they may request ("demand") them less often and use them for fewer days. By teaching physicians to make conservative prescribing decisions to the specific needs or requests of each patient and by encouraging pill take-back events, the amount of pain medications in circulation is reduced ("supply"). But if the overall demand for opioids is resilient while the supply is restricted, people who use opioids outside of the recommendations of medical care providers may gravitate away from prescription opioids toward alternatives. The substitute for prescription opioids today is heroin, which has recently become more available and less expensive. Both are opioids, but the overdose prevention strategies needed to deal with illicit heroin fall outside the purview of the Project Lazarus model because it is a community-based medical model that was developed to primarily address the misuse, abuse, and diversion of prescription opioids, not street heroin. However, to combat this additional challenge, Project Lazarus and CCNC teamed up with the NCHRC, which devotes many of its resources to address the adverse consequences of the use of heroin and advocates for the preservation of the lives of injection drug users. These partners are working together to actively promote the community-based distribution of naloxone, the safe and non-narcotic antidote that reverses the life-threatening respiratory depression that can result from opioid overdose, whether from prescription medication or from heroin.

POLICY AND LEGISLATION

States that have only tried to suppress the use of prescription opioids have all seen increases in deaths from heroin, says Scott Proescholdbell, MPH, who took over as the state's injury epidemiologist after Sanford retired. With this foreknowledge, he took the initiative to work with others to get legislation in place that could help prevent fatal overdoses, whether from prescribed medication or from heroin. Fear of prosecution can impede requests for help during an overdose, either from the victim or from witnesses. Therefore, the resulting policy package involved civil and criminal immunity for overdose victims, those people seeking to assist the victims, and prescribers of naloxone (often referred to as 911 or Good Samaritan laws).

"Legislation is always difficult," Proescholdbell says. "There were plenty of people who didn't want to see this happen, but eventually the supporters won out." Senate Bill (SB) 20 was passed in April of 2013 after 3 years of having no momentum, with NCHRC playing a key role in driving the legislation (Box 28-4). Proescholdbell says the success of Project Lazarus in Wilkes was very helpful in finally making it happen. Also helpful was that his injury branch at the state health department was seen as the source of technical expertise on the subject, so Proescholdbell was able to stay involved and even convene influential groups to discuss evidence-based practices, such as the state's medical society, pharmacy board, various coalitions, CCNC, and other state agencies. He was even able to work with a public health lawyer to draft recommended language for a complementary bill, SB 222, which delineated improvements for the

---

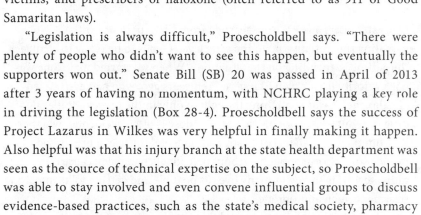

Box 28-4 | Overdose Prevention Law in NC

SB20, the 911 Good Samaritan/Naloxone Access law, states that "individuals who experience a drug overdose or persons who witness an overdose and seek help for the victim can no longer be prosecuted for possession of small amounts of drugs, paraphernalia, or underage drinking. The purpose of the law is to remove the fear of criminal repercussions for calling 911 to report an overdose, and to instead focus efforts on getting help to the victim."

As for the opioid antidote naloxone, SB20 "removes civil liabilities from doctors who prescribe and bystanders who administer naloxone, or Narcan, an opiate antidote which reverses drug overdose from opiates, thereby saving the life of the victim. SB20 also allows community based organizations to dispense Narcan under the guidance of a medical provider."

The full text of SB20 is available here:

http://openstates.org/nc/bills/2013/SB20/document s/NCD00022391/

states' CSRS. The language "got torqued and compromised, but the intent was the same," he says.

Lessons Learned

1. Regarding policy change, Proescholdbell advises having a long-term plan about what you want to accomplish, and continually keeping people informed and updated, especially those groups not excited about it or that aren't directly involved. Groups that don't know about your plan can cause it to get sidetracked or even squashed during legislative session. He also suggests avoiding approaching decision-makers with only the problem; rather, come up with your version of a solution and present it to them.

2. Lancaster offers a few lessons learned from his experience with CCNC in scaling the initiative up to the state level. One is to be ready to change "on a dime" depending on the situation. "When we started, naloxone was not a priority in our plan," he says. "Ten years ago, who had even heard of naloxone? It was something thought of only in the context of illegal drug use. But we know now that an overdose is often accidental, whether it's from the use of illegal drugs or an accidental misuse of prescribed medications. So our thoughts [about naloxone] changed because our ultimate goal is saving as many lives as possible and getting folks into treatment when appropriate."

3. Which leads to another lesson, and that is to be aware of the continuum of drug use—from a first-time user to someone caught in the cycle of addiction—and not to stigmatize people, Lancaster says. Everyone needs to know there is treatment available, whatever their situation.

4. He also stresses that responsibility for this type of issue lies with everyone. "It's not a provider issue, it's not a police issue, it's not a school issue," Lancaster says. "Everyone has to be engaged in the entire initiative."

5. Brason agrees and adds that having everyone involved helps you to strike a balance when addressing opioid overdoses. "If you are too heavy on the law enforcement side of things, it makes the doctors less likely to prescribe pain medications and this is not good for patients" he says. "They just won't make that drug available. People will go somewhere else to get it. They'll go outside the county and bring it back."

6. Project Lazarus model as designed has become very successful and is now being implemented in various states, tribal groups, and the military. But Brason has also learned that addiction support services are paramount. He is currently launching a corollary to Project Lazarus called Lazarus Recovery Services. It will be a peer navigator service whereby drug users who have experienced an overdose reversal are trained to offer assistance to people with drug addiction, which he says is ideal for rural areas. "In a small community, if you've burned enough bridges, it's hard, for example,

just to get a job. And if you've overdosed, it's intimidating to wake up to someone in a white coat standing over you. It's better to have someone who has already walked that road."

7. Sanford says the stakeholders of the Project Lazarus model believe in its potential to save lives because of its deliberate integration of top-down and bottom-up initiatives. Communities are ultimately responsible for their own health, but they have to have a cadre of viable intervention strategies from which to choose, and they have to have the infrastructure to keep them going. Last, but most importantly, Sanford encourages communities who tackle this problem to plan for the long term and to resist getting discouraged. "I am convinced public health succeeds with passion and perseverance," she says. "Those two are hard to marry, but they lead to an enduring relationship."

Contacts:

Fred Wells Brason II, President/CEO, Project Lazarus

336-667-8100 (Office); 336-262-6768 (Cell)

http://www.projectlazarus.org

Kay Sanford, MPH, Injury Epidemiologist/Consultant

kay.sanford@gmail.com

919-937-9357

Scott K. Proescholdbell, MPH, Head, Injury Epidemiology and Surveillance Unit Injury and Violence Prevention Branch, Chronic Disease and Injury Section, Division of Public Health, N.C. Department of Health and Human Services

Phone: 919-707-5442; Fax: 919-870-4803

Scott.Proescholdbell@dhhs.nc.gov

www.injuryfreenc.ncdhhs.gov

REFERENCES

North Carolina State Center for Health Statistics. Substances Identified From T-codes Involved in Poisoning Deaths or Undetermined Intent North Carolina Residents: 200-2009. Annually generated report. Raleigh, NC: NC Department of Health and Human Services, State Center for Health Statistics, 2010.

NC DETECT (2010) and CSRS (2008-2010). In Project Lazarus: A community-wide response to managing pain (Powerpoint slides). Available at: https://www.communitycarenc.org/media/related-downloads/pl-training-overview.pptx

Albert S, Brason FW, Sanford CK, et al. Project Lazarus: Community-based overdose prevention in rural North Carolina. Pain Med 2011; 12: S77–S85.

Brason FW, Roe C, Dasgupta N. Project Lazarus: An innovative community response to prescription drug overdose. N C Med J 2013; 74(3): 259–261. http://www.ncmedicaljournal.com/archives/?74323

Finch JW, McEwen S. Educating medical practitioners about safe opioid prescribing: Training from the Governor's Institute on Substance Abuse. N C Med J 2013; 74(3): 233–234. http://www.ncmedicaljournal.com/archives/?74313

Lancaster M, McKee J, Mahan A. The chronic pain initiative and community care of North Carolina. N C Med J 2013; 74(3): 237–241. http://www.ncmedicaljournal.com/archives/?74314

North Carolina State Center for Health Statistics Death Files. Substances Identified From T-codes Involved in Poisoning Deaths or Undetermined Intent North Carolina Residents: 1999–2013. Annually generated data tables by the NC Injury Epidemiology and Surveillance Unit, Division of Public Health, Department of Health and Human Services, Raleigh, NC, 2014.

Additional Resources

- Free downloads from Community Care of North Carolina (CCNC), as well as links to media coverage videos. Available at: https://www.communitycarenc.org/population-management/chronic-pain-project/:

  - Project Lazarus Community Toolkit: Provides guidance for communities to start their own Project Lazarus coalition

  - Project Lazarus Toolkit—PCPs: Toolkit designed for Primary Care Physicians

  - Project Lazarus Toolkit—EDs: Toolkit designed for Emergency Department physicians.

  - Project Lazarus Training Overview: PowerPoint presentation

  - Naloxone Information for Community Pharmacies: Dispensing, patient counseling, contact information, etc.

- *CDC Vital Signs* is a monthly report that includes an MMWR Early Release, a graphic fact sheet and website, a media release, and social media tools. Most of the materials are available in English and Spanish. Some recent reports on Opioid Painkiller Prescribing include the following:

  - "Where You Live Makes a Difference," July 2014. Available at: http://www.cdc.gov/vitalsigns/opioid-prescribing/index.html

  - "A growing epidemic, especially among women," July 2013. Available at: http://www.cdc.gov/vitalsigns/prescriptionpainkilleroverdoses/index.html

  - "Use and Abuse of Methadone as a Painkiller," July 2012. Available at: http://www.cdc.gov/vitalsigns/methadoneoverdoses/index.html

- North Carolina Harm Reduction Coalition (NCHRC) is North Carolina's only comprehensive harm reduction program. NCHRC engages in grassroots advocacy, resource development, coalition building and direct services for law enforcement and those made vulnerable by drug use, sex work, overdose, immigration status, gender, STIs, HIV and hepatitis. The group maintains a multimedia presence, offering podcasts, videos, and Twitter feed. robert@nchrc.net Available at: http://www.nchrc.org/

- The Governor's Institute on Substance Abuse connects researchers with health care professionals to promote evidence-based practices through educational conferences, technical support, and workforce development programs. Available at: http://www.governorsinstitute.org/

Videos

Project Lazarus Overview: Available at: https://www.youtube.com/watch?v=a2FQQutz02g

Project Lazarus Patient Education Video: Featuring Wilkes County pain medication patients, as well as the families of overdose victims. Available at: http://www.projectlazarus.org/patients-families/videos

Feature Film

"Find a Way" is based on the tragic story of Harry Cohen, a high school senior and star football player from Burlington, North Carolina. Seeking relief from pain after the first football game of the season in 2011, he took methadone from his grandmother's medicine cabinet, went to sleep and never woke up. Available at: http://www.corneliusmullerproductions.com/find-a-way.html

ACRONYM LIST

AAFP American Academy of Family Physicians

AAMC Association of American Medical Colleges

ABFM American Board of Family Medicine

ACA Patient Protection and Affordable Care Act

ACGME Accreditation Council for Graduate Medical Education

ACIP Advisory Committee on Immunization Practices

ACO accountable care organization

AHRQ Agency for Health care Research and Quality

ASTHO Association of State and Territorial Health Officials

BRFSS Behavioral Risk Factor Surveillance System

CBO community-based organization

CDC Centers for Disease Control and Prevention

CEHI Children's Environmental Health Initiative

CHCs community health centers

CHIP Children's Health Insurance Program; Community Health Improvement Plan

CHNA community health needs assessment

CHWs community health workers

CLER Clinical Learning Environmental Review

CMMI Center for Medicare and Medicaid Innovation

CMS Centers for Medicare and Medicaid Services

CNA community needs assessment

CON certificate of need

COPC community-oriented primary care

CSBG Community Services Block Grant

CTG Community Transformation Grants

DHHS U.S. Department of Health and Human Services

EHRs electronic health records

EMRs electronic medical records

EPA Environmental Protection Agency

FDA US Food and Drug Administration

FQHC Federally Qualified Health Center

GIS geographic information system

HCUP Healthcare Cost and Utilization Project

HIA health impact assessment

HIE health information exchange

HIOs health information exchange organizations

HIT health information technology

HITECH Act Health Information Technology for Economic and Clinical Health Act

HL7 Health Level 7

HMO health maintenance organization

HPSAs Health Professions Shortage Areas

HRSA Health Resources and Services Administration
IHI Institute for Healthcare Improvement
IIS immunization information systems
LHIC Local Health Improvement Coalition
MCH maternal and child health
MSSP Medicare Shared Savings Program
MUAs medically underserved areas
NAACOS National Association of ACOs
NHANES National Health and Nutrition Examination Survey
OECD Organization for Economic Cooperation and Development
PCEP Primary Care Extension Program
PCMH patient-centered medical home
PCORI Patient Centered Outcomes Research Institute
PCIP Primary Care Information Project
PCPs primary care provider
PHAB Public Health Accreditation Board
PHI protected health information
PHM population health management
QALY quality-adjusted life year
QI quality improvement
RBA Results-Based Accountability
RECs regional extension centers
RHC rural health clinic
SAMHSA Substance Abuse and Mental Health Services Administration
SAUP Specialty Access for the Uninsured Program
SHAs state health agencies
SHIP State Health Improvement Process
SNAP Supplemental Nutrition Assistance Program
USDA US Department of Agriculture
USPSTF US Preventive Services Task Force
WHO World Health Organization
WIC Special Supplemental Nutrition Program for Women, Infants, and Children

GLOSSARY

TERM	DEFINITION	REFERENCE/SOURCE
Accountable Care Organization	ACOs are groups of doctors, hospitals, and other health care providers, who come together voluntarily with the goal of providing coordinated high quality care to the Medicare patients they serve. Coordinated care helps ensure that patients, especially the chronically ill, get the right care at the right time, with the goal of avoiding unnecessary duplication of services and preventing medical errors. When an ACO succeeds in both delivering high-quality care and spending health care dollars more wisely, it will share in the savings it achieves for the Medicare program.	Accountable Care Organizations (ACOs): General Information. Centers for Medicare & Medicaid Services. 2014. http://innovation.cms.gov/initiatives/aco/.
Ambulatory Care Sensitive Conditions	Age-standardized acute care hospitalization rate for conditions in which appropriate ambulatory care prevents or reduces the need for admission to the hospital, per 100,000 population younger than age 75 years. Hospitalization for an ambulatory care sensitive condition is considered to be a measure of access to appropriate primary health care. Although not all admissions for these conditions are avoidable, it is assumed that appropriate ambulatory care could prevent the onset of this type of illness or condition, control an acute episodic illness or condition, or manage a chronic disease or condition. A disproportionately high rate is presumed to reflect problems in obtaining access to appropriate primary care.	National Quality Measures Clearinghouse Agency for Healthcare Research and Quality Published. Updated. 2008. http://www.qualitymeasures.ahrq.gov/content.aspx?id=35186.
Behavioral determinant	A proposed or established causal factor based on individual personal choices of lifestyle or habits (either spontaneously or in response to incentives), such as diet, exercise, and substance abuse.	Kindig DA. Understanding population health terminology. Milbank Q 2007; 85(1): 139–161.
Biological determinant	Often, a biological mediator variable between a determinant and an outcome, such as the role of endocrine and immunologic processes in stress. In any case, all determinants must have biological mediator variables in order to affect the organism to produce the health outcomes.	Kindig DA. Understanding population health terminology. Milbank Q 2007; 85(1): 139–161.
Collective Impact	Collective impact is the commitment of a group of actors from different sectors to a common agenda for solving a complex social problem.	FSG: Collective Impact. 2014. http://www.fsg.org/OurApproach/WhatIsCollectiveImpact.aspx
Community	A group of people who have common characteristics; communities can be defined by location, race, ethnicity, age, occupation, interest in particular problems or outcomes, or other common bonds.	Turnock, B.J. 2004. *Public Health: What It Is and How It Works*. Boston:Jones and Bartlett.
	Individuals with a shared affinity, and perhaps geography, who organize around an issue, with collective discussion, decision making, and action.	Labonte, R. 1988. Health Promotion: From Concepts to Strategies. *Healthcare Management Forum* 1(3):24–30.
Community Action Agency	Community Action Agencies are private or public nonprofit organizations that were created by the federal government in 1964 to combat poverty in geographically designated areas. Status as a Community Action Agency is the result of an explicit designation by local or state government. A Community Action Agency has a tripartite board structure that is designated to promote the participation of the entire community in the reduction or elimination of poverty. Community Action Agencies seek to involve the community, including elected public officials, private sector representatives, and especially low-income residents, in assessing local needs and attacking the causes and conditions of poverty.	Community Services Consortium: What is a community action agency? 2015. http://communityservices.us/about/detail/category/community-action-agency/
Community Engagement	The process of working collaboratively with and through groups of people affiliated by geographic proximity, special interest, or similar situations to address issues affecting the well-being of those people. In general, the goals of community engagement are to build trust, enlist new resources and allies, create better communication, and improve overall health outcomes as successful projects evolve into lasting collaborations.	Principles of Community Engagement. 2nd ed. Centers for Disease Control and Prevention. http://www.atsdr.cdc.gov/communityengagement/pdf/PCE_Report_508_FINAL.pdf. 2014.
Community Guide	The Community Preventive Services Task Force (Task Force) was established in 1996 by the U.S. Department of Health and Human Services to identify population health interventions that are scientifically proven to save lives, increase lifespans, and improve quality of life. The Task Force produces recommendations (and identifies evidence gaps) to help inform the decision making of federal, state, and local health departments, other government agencies, communities, health care providers, employers, schools, and research organizations	The Guide to Community Preventive Services: The Community Guide. 2014. http://www.thecommunityguide.org/about/aboutTF.html

TERM	DEFINITION	REFERENCE/SOURCE
Community Health	A perspective on public health that assumes community to be an essential determinant of health and the indispensable ingredient for effective public health practice. It takes into account the tangible and intangible characteristics of the community—its formal and informal networks and support systems, its norms and cultural nuances, and its institutions, politics, and belief systems.	Kindig DA. Understanding population health terminology. Milbank Q 2007; 85 (1): 139–161.
	The state of wellness or well-being in a defined community; affected by forces in addition to health care services, including adequate housing, quality of schools, safe streets, economic stability, and the environment.	Prevention Institute: A Prepared Glossary of Terms. 2014. http://www.eatbettermovemore.org/thrive/documents/Toolkitglossary.pdf
Community Health Assessment	A community health assessment is a process that uses quantitative and qualitative methods to systematically collect and analyze data to understand health within a specific community. An ideal assessment includes information on risk factors, quality of life, mortality, morbidity, community assets, forces of change, social determinants of health and health inequity, and information on how well the public health system provides essential services. Community health assessment data are intended to inform community decision making, the prioritization of health problems, and the development, implementation, and evaluation of community health improvement plans.	Definitions of Community Health Assessments (CHA) and Community Health Improvement Plans (CHIPs). NACCHO. http://www.naccho.org/topics/infrastructure/community-health-assessment....
Community Health Center	Facilities that administer the delivery of health care services to people living in a community or neighborhood	National Library of Medicine - MeSH. 1979.
Community Health Improvement Plan	A long-term, systematic effort to address health problems on the basis of the results of assessment activities and the community health improvement process. This plan is used by health and other governmental education and human service agencies, in collaboration with community partners, to set priorities and coordinate and target resources. An HIP is critical for developing policies and defining actions to target efforts that promote health. It should define the vision for the health of the community inclusively and should be done in a timely way. (See also Community health improvement process.) This definition of community health improvement plan also refers to a Tribal, state or territorial community health improvement plan.	HP2010 via CDC (Adapted from: United States Department of Health and Human Services. Healthy People 2010. Washington, DC: US Department of Health and Human Services; 2000.)
Community Health Needs Assessment-IRS	A community health needs assessment (CHNA) is required under the Internal Revenue Code (IRS) by the Patient Protection and Affordable Care Act (ACA). The IRS requires hospital organizations to document compliance with CHNA requirements for each of their facilities in a written report that includes: · A description of the community served · A description of the process and methods used to conduct the assessment · A description of methods used to include input from people representing the broad interests of the community served · A prioritized description of all community health needs identified in the CHNA, as well as a description of the process and criteria used in prioritizing such needs · A description of existing health care facilities and other resources in the community available to meet the needs identified in the CHNA. (www.irs.gov/pub/irs-drop/n-10–39.pdf).	Public Health Accreditation Board. 2011. http://www.phaboard.org/accreditation-overview/getting-started/
Community Health Workers	Community health workers should be members of the communities where they work, should be selected by the communities, should be answerable to the communities for their activities, should be supported by the health system but not necessarily a part of its organization, and have shorter training than professional workers.	WHO: Lehman U: Mid-level health workers. The state of the evidence on programmes, activities, costs and impact on health outcomes A literature review. 2008. http://www.who.int/workforcealliance/knowledge/resources/mlp_review/en/.
Community-Centered Health Homes	Community health centers (CHCs) are one ideal venue for developing an integrated approach that builds on the strengths of each approach. The community-centered health home provides high-quality health care services while also applying diagnostic and critical thinking skills to the underlying factors that shape patterns of injury and illness. By strategically engaging in efforts to improve community environments, CCHHs can improve the health and safety of their patient population, improve health equity, and reduce the need for medical treatment. The CCHH model advances a number of existing health care delivery models and practices, including the patient-centered medical home, as defined by the Patient-Centered Primary Care Collaborative, and the health home, as defined in the ACA. The community-centered health home concept takes previous models a transformative step further by not only acknowledging that factors outside the health care system affect patient health outcomes, but also actively participating in improving them.	Prevention Institute: Community - Centered Health Homes: Bridging the Gap Between Health Services and Community Prevention. 2011. http://www.preventioninstitute.org/component/jlibrary/article/id-298/127.html

TERM	DEFINITION	REFERENCE/SOURCE
Cost—Benefit Analysis	A method of comparing the cost of a program with its expected benefits in dollars (or other currency). The benefit-to-cost ratio is a measure of total return expected per unit of money spent. This analysis generally excludes consideration of factors that are not measured ultimately in economic terms. Cost effectiveness compares alternative ways to achieve a specific set of results	National Library of Medicine - Medical Subject Headings
Cost-Effective Analysis	This form of analysis seeks to determine the costs and effectiveness of an activity or to compare similar alternative activities to determine the relative degree to which they will obtain the desired objectives or outcomes. The preferred action or alternative is one that requires the least cost to produce a given level of effectiveness or that provides the greatest effectiveness for a given level of cost. In the health care field, outcomes are measured in terms of health status.	(2014-05-23). A Dictionary of Epidemiology (Kindle Locations 3551–3557). Oxford University Press. Kindle Edition.
	An analytic tool in which the costs and effects of at least one alternative are calculated and presented as in a ratio of incremental cost to incremental effect. Effects are health outcomes, such as cases of disease prevented, years of life gained, or qualityadjusted life years, rather than monetary measures, as in cost-benefit analysis.	Kindig DA. Understanding population health terminology. Milbank Q 2007; 85(1): 139—161.
Disability-Adjusted Life Year	A DALY lost is a measure of the burden of disease on a defined population. it is hence an indicator of population health. DALYs are advocated as an alternative to quality-adjusted life years (QALYs). They are based on adjustment of life expectancy to allow for long-term disability as estimated from official statistics; the necessary data to do so may not be available in some areas. The concept postulates a continuum from disease to disability to death that is not universally accepted, particularly by the community of persons with disabilities. DALYs are calculated using a "disability weight" (a proportion less than 1) multiplied by chronological age to reflect the burden of the disability. DALYs can thus produce estimates that accord greater value to fit than to disabled persons and to the middle years of life rather than to youth or old age.	(2014-05-23). A Dictionary of Epidemiology (Kindle Locations 4251–4259). Oxford University Press. Kindle Edition.
Essential Public Health Functions/Services	The ten services identified in Public Health in America: monitoring health status; diagnosing and investigating health problems; informing, educating, and empowering people; mobilizing community partnerships; developing policies and plans; enforcing laws and regulations; linking people to needed services; assuring a competent workforce; conducting evaluations; and conducting research. (United States Department of Health and Human Services. Healthy People 2010. Washington, DC: US Department of Health and Human Services; 2000.) Representatives from federal agencies and national organizations developed the statement made in Public Health in America. This statement includes two lists, one that describes what public health seeks to accomplish and the second that describes how it will carry out its basic responsibilities. The second list, the Essential Services, provides a list of 10 public health services that define the practice of public health.	CDC National Public Health Performance Standards Program, Acronyms, Glossary, and Reference Terms. CDC, 2007.
Evaluation	Evaluation is the systematic investigation of a project or program by assigning value to its efforts by addressing these three inter-related domains: Merit (or quality), worth (or value, i.e., cost-effectiveness), and significance (or importance)	CDC: A framework for program evaluation. 2012. http://www.cdc.gov/eval/framework/
Federally Qualified Health Center	Health centers are community-based and patient directed organizations that serve populations with limited access to health care. These include low income populations, the uninsured, those with limited English proficiency, migrant and seasonal farm workers, individuals and families experiencing homelessness, and those living in public housing. A sliding fee scale provides accessibility to individuals who are living at or below 200% of the federal poverty level.	FAQs about Federally Qualified Health Centers and their Oral Health Programs. American Dental Association. 2011.
Genetic Determinant	A proposed or established causal factor from the genetic composition of individuals or populations that affects health outcomes.	Kindig DA. Understanding population health terminology. Milbank Q 2007; 85(1): 139—161.
Geographic Information System	An information system that incorporates digitally constructed maps and uses sophisticated modeling techniques to analyze and display information patterns. Satellite imaging and remote sensing have greatly expanded the scope of GISs (e.g., trendS in specific diseases are suggested after analyzing the composition of vegetation and the amounts of precipitation in tropical regions, which relate to changes in the distribution and abundance of predators and insect vectors). Another application is digitally prepared spot maps of disease clusters using postal codes and notified cases. An important application is in Geomatics. See also Disease Mapping; Medical Geography; Satellite Epidemiology.	(2014-05-23). A Dictionary of Epidemiology (Kindle Locations 6381–6384). Oxford University Press. Kindle Edition.

TERM	DEFINITION	REFERENCE/SOURCE
Health	The state of complete physical, mental, and social well-being and not merely the absence of disease or infirmity.	WHO: Constitution of the World Health Organization, ed 45. 2006. http://www.who.int/governance/eb/who_constitution_en.pdf.
	The extent to which an individual or group is able to realize aspirations and satisfy needs, and to change or cope with the environment. Health is a resource for everyday life, not the objective of living; it is a positive concept, emphasizing social and personal resources as well as physical capabilities.	WHO: Glossary of humanitarian terms. 2015. http://www.who.int/hac/about/definitions/en/
	A state characterized by anatomic, physiologic, and psychological integrity; an ability to perform personally valued family, work, and community roles; an ability to deal with physical, biological, and psychological stress; a feeling of well-being; and freedom from the risk of disease and untimely death.	AFMC: AFMC Primer on population health. 2011. http://phprimer.afmc.ca/Part1-TheoryThinkingAboutHealth/ConceptsOfHealthAndIllness/DefinitionsofHealth
	A state of equilibrium between humans and the physical, biological, and social environment, compatible with full functional activity.	Last JM. Public Health and Human Ecology. Stamford, Conn.: Appleton and Lange; 1997.
Health Care Determinant	A proposed or established causal factor in health care that affects health outcomes (e.g., access, quantity, and quality of health care services).	Kindig DA. Understanding population health terminology. Milbank Q 2007; 85(1): 139–161.
Health Care Reform	Innovation and improvement of the health care system by reappraisal, amendment of services, and removal of faults and abuses in providing and distributing health services to patients. It includes a re-alignment of health services and health insurance to maximum demographic elements (the unemployed, indigent, uninsured, elderly, inner cities, rural areas) with reference to coverage, hospitalization, pricing and cost containment, insurers' and employers' costs, pre-existing medical conditions, prescribed drugs, equipment, and services	National Library of Medicine - MeSH. 1993.
Health Equity [Equity]	Equity in health is the absence of systematic disparities in health (or in the major social determinants of health) between groups with different levels of underlying social advantage/disadvantage—that is, wealth, power, or prestige. Equity is an ethical principle; it also is consonant with and closely related to human rights principles.	Prevention Institute: Health Equity and Prevention Primer. 2015. http://www.preventioninstitute.org/tools/focus-area-tools/health-equity-toolkit.html
Health Information Exchange	Electronic health information exchange (HIE) allows doctors, nurses, pharmacists, other health care providers and patients to appropriately access and securely share a patient's vital medical information electronically—improving the speed, quality, safety, and cost of patient care.	Health Information Exchange: What Is HIE? 2014. http://www.healthit.gov/providers-professionals/health-information-exchange/what-hie
Health Insurance Portability and Accountability Act (HIPAA)	Public Law 104–91 enacted in 1996, was designed to improve the efficiency and effectiveness of the healthcare system, protect health insurance coverage for workers and their families, and to protect individual personal health information.	National Library of Medicine - MeSH. 1998.
Meaningful Use	Using certified electronic health records (HER) technology to improve quality, safety, efficiency, and reduce healthcare disparities; engage patients and families in their health care; improve care coordination; improve population and public health; while maintaining privacy and security.	National Library of Medicine - MeSH. 2014.
	Meaningful use (MU) refers to the Medicare and Medicaid EHR incentive programs that provide economic incentives to hospitals and physicians to demonstrate meaningful use of certified EHR technology. The incentives help offset the hard work of implementing EHRs and initiating information exchange. The objectives for MU are staged, and each stage includes some requirements that involve EHR capture of data points relevant to prevention (e.g., body mass index, BMI), and sharing of information with public health.	CDC: Meaningful use. 2014. http://www.cdc.gov/ehrmeaningfuluse/.
Medicaid	Federal program, created by Public Law 89–97, Title XIX, a 1965 amendment to the Social Security Act, administered by the states, that provides health care benefits to indigent and medically indigent persons	National Library of Medicine - MeSH. 1999.
Medicare	US only; federal program, created by Public Law 89–97, Title XVIII-Health Insurance for the Aged, a 1965 amendment to the Social Security Act, that provides health insurance benefits to persons over the age of 65 and others eligible for Social Security benefits. It consists of two separate but coordinated programs: hospital insurance (MEDICARE PART A) and supplementary medical insurance (MEDICARE PART B). (Hospital Administration Terminology, AHA, 2d ed and A Discursive Dictionary of Health Care, US House of Representatives, 1976)	National Library of Medicine - MeSH. 1999.

TERM	DEFINITION	REFERENCE/SOURCE
Morbidity	The proportion of patients with a particular disease during a given year per given unit of population	National Library of Medicine - MeSH. 1999.
Mortality rate	The number of deaths in a population within a prescribed time, expressed as either crude death rates or death rates specific to diseases and sometimes to age, sex, and other attributes.	Kindig DA. Understanding population health terminology. Milbank Q 2007; 85(1): 139–161.
Patient-Centered Medical Home	The medical home model is a potential way to improve health care in America by transforming how primary care is organized and delivered. Building on the work of a large and growing community, the Agency for Healthcare Research and Quality (AHRQ) defines a medical home not simply as a place but as a model of the organization of primary care that delivers the core functions of primary health care. The medical home encompasses five functions and attributes: · Comprehensive Care · Patient Centered · Coordinated Care · Accessible Services · Quality and Safety	Patient Centered Medical Home Resource Center. Agency for Healthcare Research and Quality. http://pcmh.ahrq.gov/.
Patient Protection and Affordable Care Act	On March 23, 2010, President Obama signed the health care reform bill, or Affordable Care Act (ACA), into law. ACA makes sweeping changes to the U.S. health care system. ACA's health care reforms, which are primarily focused on reducing the uninsured population and decreasing health care costs, will be implemented over the next several years.	Patient Protection and Affordable Care Act (PPACA). Marrs Maddocks + Associates. 2013.
Population Health	1. A conceptual framework for thinking about why some populations are healthier than others, as well as the policy development, research agenda, and resource allocation that flow from it. 2. The health outcomes of a group of individuals, including the distribution of such outcomes within the group. 3. The health of a population as measured by health status indicators and as influenced by social, economic, and physical environments; personal health practices; individual capacity and coping skills; human biology; early childhood development; and health services.	Kindig DA. Understanding population health terminology. Milbank Q 2007; 85(1): 139–161.
Primary Care	The provision of integrated, accessible health care services by clinicians who are accountable for addressing a large majority of personal health care needs, developing a sustained partnership with patients, and practicing in the context of family and community.	Institute of Medicine. Defining Primary Care: An Interim Report. 1994. The National Academies Press, Washington, DC.
Primary Prevention	Primary prevention aims to prevent the disease from occurring. Primary prevention reduces both the incidence and prevalence of a disease.	Levels of Disease Prevention. CDC EXCITE. Updated April 24, 2007. Accessed February 19, 2014.
Public Health	Activities that a society undertakes to assure the conditions in which people can be healthy. These include organized community efforts to prevent, identify, and counter threats to the health of the public.	Kindig DA. Understanding population health terminology. Milbank Q 2007; 85(1): 139–161.
	What we do as a society collectively to assure conditions in which people can be healthy.	IOM: The future of public health. 1988. Washington, DC.
	The science and art of preventing disease, prolonging life and promoting health through the organized efforts and informed choices of society, organizations, public and private, communities and individuals.	Winslow C-E A. The untilled fields of public health. Science 1920; 51(1306): 23–33. doi:10.1126/science.51.1306.23. PMID 17838891.
Public Health Surveillance	Public health surveillance is officially defined as "the ongoing, systematic collection, analysis, and interpretation of health-related data essential to the planning, implementation, and evaluation of public health practice, closely integrated with the timely dissemination of these data to those responsible for prevention and control."	WHO: Public health surveillance. 2015. http://www.who.int/topics/public_health_surveillance/en/
Public Health System	Activities undertaken within the formal structure of government and the associated efforts of private and voluntary organizations and individuals.	Kindig DA. Understanding population health terminology. Milbank Q 2007; 85(1): 139–161.
Quality Improvement	The attainment or process of attaining a new level of performance or quality.	National Library of Medicine - MeSH. 2014.

TERM	DEFINITION	REFERENCE/SOURCE
Quality-Adjusted Life Years	A measurement index derived from a modification of standard life-table procedures and designed to take account of the quality as well as the duration of survival. This index can be used in assessing the outcome of health care procedures or services. (Bioethics Thesaurus, 1994)	National Library of Medicine - MeSH. 2014.
Return on Investment	Return on investment (ROI) is a useful tool for understanding a project's costs and benefits from the perspective of an investor. ROI analysis originally was developed in a commercial, business context to assess the performance of a financial investment. Its focus is the return that a specific investor receives from his/her own financial investment. By application of a standard ROI equation, an investor who purchases goods for $1 and resells them for $3 has received a 200% return on the cost of the initial investment: (Proceeds of investment [$3] — Cost of Investment [$1]) / Cost of Investment [$1] × 100% = ROI [200%]	Rochester Institute of Technology (RIT). Outreach and Education, S&H Management Systems - Module 5, Measurement of Performance — Supplementary Materials: Cost Benefit Analysis. RIT website. https://www.rit.edu/~w-outrea/training/Module5/M5_CostBenefitAnalysis.pdf.
Safey Net Provider	Providers that by mandate or mission organize and deliver a significant level of health care and other health-related services to the uninsured, Medicaid recipients, and other vulnerable patients	National Library of Medicine - MeSH (safety-net providers - mesh). 2013.
Secondary Prevention	The prevention of recurrences or exacerbations of a disease or complications of its therapy.	National Library of Medicine - MeSH. 2014.
Shared Savings	An initiative established by the Affordable Care Act and operated by the Centers for Medicare and Medicaid Services (CMS) to incentivize coordination and cooperation among health care providers. Providers who increase quality while controlling costs are allowed to keep some of the savings.	CMS: Shared savings program. 2015. https://www.cms.gov/Medicare/Medicare-Fee-for-Service-Payment/sharedsavingsprogram/index.html?redirect=/sharedsavingsprogram.
Social Determinants of Health	Social determinants of health are conditions in the environments in which people are born, live, learn, work, play, worship, and age that affect a wide range of health, functioning, and quality-of-life outcomes and risks.	Social Determinants of Health. HealthyPeople.gov. Updated November 13, 2013.
Teaching Hospital	Hospitals engaged in educational and research programs, as well as providing medical care to the patients.	National Library of Medicine - MeSH. 1999.
Tertiary Prevention	Measures aimed at providing appropriate supportive and rehabilitative services to minimize morbidity and maximize quality of life after a long-term disease or injury is present	National Library of Medicine - MeSH. 2014.
Vulnerable Populations	Groups of persons whose range of options is severely limited, who are frequently subjected to coercion in their decision making, or who may be compromised in their ability to give informed consent	National Library of Medicine - MeSH. 2002.

Index

Page numbers followed by *f* and *t* indicate figures and tables, respectively. Numbers followed by *b* indicate boxes.

Program Sustainability
Assessment Tool
(Center for Public
Health Systems
Science), 94
project
evaluation, 56–59
Project Lazarus, 175*b*,
343–359, 348*f*
Community Toolkit,
352, 358
Overview, 359
Patient Education
Video, 359
Toolkits, 358
Training Overview, 358
projects, 106–107
Promise
Neighborhoods, 323
proposals, 77
provider-patient
relationship, 15–16
public health, 4–5, 7–8,
132–133, 289
core functions of,
131–132, 132*f*
current challenges,
133–138
definition of, 7, 129,
281, 380
future directions,
305–310
governmental,
129–131, 138
integration with
primary care, 83–84,
217–219, 301–302,
306, 306*f*
partnerships with,
1–61, 30f, 46b, 96,
148–149, 195–205
Project Lazarus model,
348–349, 348f
role in accountable
care, 211
role in addressing
social determinants,
154, 155
role in clinical care,
136–138
role in population
health management,
283–284
as safety net provider,
136–137

strategies and
approaches for,
284–285
tips for, 189, 191, 192
public health
accreditation, 381
Public Health
Accreditation Board,
169, 308
public health agencies,
169–170
public health care
spending, 144–145
Public Health
Community
Platform, 283
public health data, 237
local, 248
statewide, 248
public health
information, 283
public health information
systems, 269
Public Health Leadership
Institute, 219–220
public health practice,
129–141
public health practice
improvement, 18–19
public health
practitioners, 132
public health reporting,
306–307
Public Health Service
Act, 29, 171
public health services,
222–224, 305
public health
surveillance,
135–136,
324–326, 368
public health system, 129,
130*f*, 368, 372
public health
workforce, 136
public relations, 321–322
public sector
agencies, 173

quality, 260, 265
quality-adjusted life years
(QALYs), 228, 262,
368, 381
quality
improvement, 368

quality of care, 192
quality of life, 381

racial differences, 71–72
RBA. *see* Results-Based
Accountability
readmissions, 182
reflection, 107–108
regression analysis, 381
reliability, 261
reporting clinical care
data, 282–283
research, 181–182, 190
resources, 94, 358–359
for addressing social
determinants, 161
aligning, 318–319
community, 381
for community health
assessments (CHAs),
178–179
community
resources, 29
data, 39, 294
for economic
evaluation, 232
for electronic health
records (EHRs),
275–276
financial, 39
for finding
partners, 46*b*
GIS software, 293–294
human, 39
identification of, 49–50
for return on
investment
(ROI), 231
for social media, 124
for spatial data, 294
for success stories, 340
respect, mutual, 101–102
responsibilities, 106
responsibility bias, 67
Results-Based
Accountability
(RBA), 259
Results-Based
Accountability
Implementation
Guide, 265
return on investment
(ROI), 225–232,
227*t*, 229*t*, 339*b*,
369, 381

Rhode Island Department
of Health, 270
Lillian J. Rice Elementary
School (Chula Vista,
CA), 317–318, 322
risk assessment, 303
risk factors, 381
Robert Wood Johnson
Foundation, 90,
158, 249
Rochester Institute of
Technology, 232

safety net, 216–221
safety-net providers, 369
San Diego, California
Chula Vista
Elementary School
District (San Diego,
CA), 314, 315*f*
County of San Diego
Health and Human
Services Agency, 316
"Live Well San Diego"
initiative, 316
San Diego County
Childhood Obesity
Initiative, 327
San Diego Healthy
Weight
Collaborative,
73, 258–259, 313,
314–317, 314*b*,
317–326
Sanford, Kay, 344–345,
347, 357
San Francisco
Community Benefit
Partnership, 170
San Francisco
Department of
Public Health
(SFDPH), 170
savings, shared, 369
scheduling visits, 78–79
school-based
evaluation, 324
screening, preventive, 189
Scripps Family Medicine
Residency, 313–314,
317–318, 324–325
secondary
prevention, 369
self-assessments, 172
service centers, 224